Praise for the work of George A. Mason

A great city needs great leaders. Leaders who will stand for what is right when it is unpopular. Leaders with the courage to make themselves bridges between people who are divided. Leaders who think, speak and act with humility, kindness and love for all people. Leaders who can guide us to be better today than we were yesterday.

In a time when such leaders seem few and far between, Dallas has been fortunate to have one in George Mason. He has seen the city endure many trials in his three decades of service as senior pastor of Wilshire Baptist Church. ... Then, of course, there are the countless private struggles Mason has shepherded his church members through while standing on the pulpit each Sunday to spread the Gospel of Jesus Christ with a message of forgiveness, honesty and, most of all, the fundamental importance of our love for one another. ...

The demonstration of real moral courage is no easy thing. ... Yet Mason always called on us to listen to those who have been marginalized, left out, cast aside, pushed away, not fully embraced in the arms and love of our society. He asked for more from us as individuals, as people called to love one another.

That isn't politics. It's Gospel. And that was how George Mason led, as a preacher of the Gospel. And even if we did not attend his church, or listen to his sermons, or even know his name, he was leading us.

He was showing us a better way.

Excerpt from the Opinion page of The Dallas Morning News, *January 9, 2022, published the Sunday after the announcement of George Mason's retirement.*

The Word Made Fresh

Preaching God's Love for Every Body

George A. Mason

Edited by:
Ann Bell Worley
Gail S. Brookshire
Jake Hall
Julie Merritt Lee

For additional audio and video resources, please visit:

GeorgeAMason.com

Cover design by Rick Nease
RickNeaseArt.com

Published by
Front Edge Publishing
42807 Ford Road, No. 234
Canton, MI, 48187

Front Edge Publishing books are available for discount bulk purchases for events, corporate use and small groups. Special editions, including books with corporate logos, personalized covers and customized interiors are available for purchase. For more information, contact Front Edge Publishing at info@FrontEdgePublishing.com.

Dedicated to
Wilshire Baptist Church
Dallas, Texas

Building a community of faith shaped by the Spirit of Jesus Christ.

"Who I am today has a lot to do with the family of faith I have been
part of for the past thirty years. You continue to make me who I am.
And I have no regrets and only gratitude for who you have made
me to be. But even deeper than that, I believe the Christ we have
committed to follow together has been at work
remaking us both into his image."

~ **George A. Mason, September 8, 2019**

Contents

Acknowledgments

This is a book I would not have created on my own initiative, partly because of the work involved in producing it, partly because of the presumption it would entail of whether my preaching is worthy of reproduction. As my retirement loomed and the personnel committee of the church that I preached to for thirty-three years, Wilshire Baptist Church in Dallas, Texas, considered how to mark my tenure, the idea of publishing a book of my sermons was floated.

My longtime colleague, Doug Haney, gets credit and blame for the idea. Doug and I have served two churches together totaling more than two decades. As minister of music, he has listened to more than half of these sermons. He has great regard for good preaching and an ear for quality. He pushed me to publish my sermons in hopes that they would not be lost to history and might be useful to others beyond the time and place of their original proclamation. I demurred. His end-around suggestion was received by the committee, and now you see the result.

The final shape of the book is owed to the skilled team at Front Edge Publishing. David Crumm, editor and co-founder, Dmitri Barvinok, director of production, and Susan Stitt, director of marketing, re-envisioned its form and function. They conjured their creative wizardry to turn a compilation of church sermons into a compendium of Church resources. And then they spun out touches of beauty to wrap the words in compelling fashion.

Special thanks go to the editors of this volume, Ann Bell Worley, Gail Brookshire, Julie Merritt Lee, and Jake Hall. Doug approached Ann about spearheading the project, as she is an accomplished writer and has published several children's books. Ann enlisted the other three to help. Ann, Julie, and Jake are all former pastoral residents at Wilshire. The four of them divvied up and poured through more than 1,400 sermons, selecting the ones included here by some mysterious criteria protected by high security clearance. Which is to say, whatever objective metrics can be employed to evaluate preaching, subjectivity prevails. Judging their judgments, I am most grateful for the educated intuition evident in their choices. Beyond that part of the process, Gail especially shepherded the project through the search for a publisher and final contract. The only layperson in the group, she proves that a spiritually keen parishioner is what makes the preaching task worthwhile. The countless hours these friends devoted to this work reveals the deeper friendship that motivated them. I am sure the hours they gave to this effort far exceeded their expectations. I cannot thank them enough.

My longtime assistant, Debby Burton, was the source for recovering all these sermons. The treasure hunt required more than mere data transfer. Over the course of my ministry career, sermons were written in longhand and then typed, after which they were placed in paper files. Later they were created on word processors and filed on floppy disks. Later still they were stored in the virtual cloud. Debby had to dive into the chaos of my physical and online filing systems to find and forward all these sermons. I cherish the many years we shared in this loving partnership.

I am grateful to Allan Akins, David Clanton, David Hammons, Susan Kimball, and Mark McKenzie—all Wilshire members—for lending their time and expertise to this project, as well as to Christen Kinard for giving shape and life to the website.

For more than twenty years, Wilshire has hosted a pastoral residency program for young ministers. The three former residents who participated in this project are part of a larger community of residents to whom I owe a debt of gratitude. The proverb is right that "iron sharpens iron." There's no telling how much better my preaching has been through the years because of the weekly conversations about the craft that have shaped me as much as them.

My thanks also go to those who wrote prefaces for each section of this book. They are all longtime colleagues and friends who have encouraged me in the ministry journey, and I am honored by their contributions to this volume. They have analyzed the sermons and eloquently expressed their appreciation for my preaching and their affection for our relationship. When you receive such a generous gift of words from those who are themselves extraordinary wordsmiths, practitioners and theologians, the blessing is doubled.

All preaching is contextual. I have been privileged to preach to a courageous congregation across three decades that received my priestly offerings and prophetic challenges with enormous grace. Unlike many churches, the Wilshire church understands that the preacher often must bear the word for the sake of both the care and cure of souls. I pray they are better for it. I know I am better because of them.

Finally, my beloved wife, Kim, has been a source of love and encouragement every step of the way. She has been front and center in the pew for every one of these sermons, always cheering me on. Long ago, she began to offer me a ritual reminder when I left the house each Sunday morning for church: "Give them heaven," she would say. In the end, that's the only proper aim of Christian preaching.

George A. Mason, Spring 2023

Preface

At its best, preaching delivers a prophetic word to a congregation at a specific place and time, taking into account not only the scriptural passage at hand but also current events in the local community, the nation, and the world. George A. Mason was faithful to this fine art throughout his career of preaching at Wilshire Baptist Church for thirty-three years.

The book you are holding in your hands began as a gift, a surprise to honor George on the occasion of his retirement in August 2022. Our team of four was tasked with the formidable challenge of reading all of the sermons we could locate and determining a selection process, being mindful of both the breadth of George's time at Wilshire and what we felt was most representative of his theology, craft, and capacity to shape the faith of his listeners. In a few short months, the collection emerged with twelve parts of sermons and a vision to include contributions from George's colleagues. These remarks of friends and diverse faith leaders now make up the prefaces to each part, lending further weight to the impact of George's life and ministry.

In this collection of sermons, readers have the privilege of observing the relationship between God, minister, and people develop over an extended period of time to a point of mature faith. With the long lens of hindsight, we have the benefit of witnessing some of George's own progression, as well. It is a rare and unique gift and one that unfolds here—in the middle of America's "Bible Belt"—to reveal God's love for every body, no exceptions.

Early in our process, it was clear to us that this book was more than a keepsake for a singular congregation. These sermons merit a wider audience. Not only do they present the hearer/reader with solid theology, thoughtfully presented; they also provide ministers (and aspiring ministers) a much-needed model for engaging faithfully with the world around us. In short, they show why preaching still matters and how to do it effectively.

As former residents and front-row witnesses for two years not only to George's preaching, but also his preparation (Ann, Jake, and Julie), and as a congregant and friend whose membership at Wilshire precedes and spans the full length of George's tenure (Gail), we feel compelled to remark upon a few observations:

1. The saying goes, when you truly understand something, you can teach it to a child. The beauty of George's sermons is that he is able to communicate complex theological concepts and address controversial current events in common language and simple syntax. His preaching is so accessible that the depth of intelligence and artistry he brings to it might not be apparent to the unsuspecting hearer/reader. But over and again, from beginning to end, the hearer/reader finds herself with greater understanding and new perspective, often challenging previously-held beliefs or assumptions.

2. George typically preaches from a pre-appointed list of scriptures known as the Revised Common Lectionary, which is notable, if not entirely novel, among Baptists. George will tell you that he uses the lectionary more as a guide than a master and that some of his sermons—especially those that are part of a series—do veer from the appointed readings. That said, this practice is one of many ways his preaching takes on ecumenical character, as the lectionary ties churches together across denominations with readings from the same passages of the Bible each Sunday during worship, covering the entirety of the Bible in a three-year cycle. The lectionary also guides churches through the six traditional holy days and seasons of the church year: Advent, Christmas, Epiphany, Lent, Easter, and Pentecost, which you will see noted along with the dates for each sermon.

3. George's preaching is playful in a way that can only develop in a long, intimate relationship of mutual trust shared between pastor and congregation. In his penultimate sermon at Wilshire, he tells the origin story of a hidden catchphrase which appears in every sermon he preached in his thirty-three-year tenure at Wilshire. What began as a way to keep a child's attention became something of a weekly game. When a pastor has a relationship with a congregation for as long as George has, she/he can introduce a level of playfulness that is indicative of a familial relationship. Can you find all of the "don't you knows?!"

4. George has a passion for "calling the called." One of his great legacies is Wilshire's Pathways to Ministry program, which recognizes, names, and nurtures candidates for vocational ministry. Pathways to Ministry is a three-tiered program: "YourCall" for high school students, "Summer Internships" for college and seminary students, and the flagship "Pastoral Residency Program" for recent seminary or divinity school graduates. The program was initially funded by a grant from the Lilly Endowment; more recently, however, Wilshire established the George A. Mason Pathways Endowment to fund the residency and make it sustainable in perpetuity. Calling is a theme in many of George's sermons, and his mentoring of young ministers is a gift to the Church for generations to come.

5. Finally, it's important to note that a good pastor preaches both to and for a congregation. So while this is a collection of George's sermons, it is also, in a very real sense, a collection of Wilshire's sermons, giving voice to the church's mission to build "a community of faith shaped by the Spirit of Jesus Christ."

George tells the story of when he was first called to Wilshire as Senior Pastor in 1989. While some members expressed concern that he was too young for the post, an elderly deacon countered, saying, "I'm not worried about whether he is up to the challenge, because I know we are. Great pastors do not make great churches; great churches make great pastors."

Whether the greatness started with the church or the pastor, who knows? Either way, the greatness grew. Clearly God has done something amazing in this relationship between pastor and congregation, pulpit and pew, and we are all richer because of it.

May this tremendous gift of stewardship continue to bear fruit in your retirement, George, in the life of Wilshire, and in all who hear and read these words.

Thanks be to God,
Ann Bell Worley, Gail S. Brookshire, Jake Hall, and Julie Merritt Lee
Spring 2023

Introduction

There is no such thing as timeless preaching. Every moment of proclamation is timely. The hope for reproduced sermons like these is that they can be timely again and relevant in your life today as they were in the original preaching event. Since sermons are normally based upon biblical texts, they are already engaged in a process of re-presenting something from the past into the present. So, I am inviting you to revisit scripture as you read these sermons. Whether they speak to you will depend in part on whether they spoke to the original listeners, in part on your sanctified imagination of putting yourself in their place, and in part on the Spirit putting me in your place as if the sermon is intended for you in your new moment of encountering it.

This is how the Word is made fresh, as the title of this book suggests. Christians claim that the Word became flesh in Jesus of Nazareth once upon a time. But we also believe that his Resurrection (Easter) and the gift of the Spirit (Pentecost) allow that same Word to become fresh in any and every time.

The sermons are organized thematically. If you cared to do so, you could read them chronologically to see how my preaching changed over the course of thirty-three years as the senior pastor of Wilshire Baptist Church in Dallas, Texas. I could tell you how I think my preaching changed, but that isn't the point of this book. There are certain throughlines of the sermons across all those years that are more important to attend to. I will mention three.

The gospel itself is the main one. Can you find the good news in each sermon? The gospel is God's redemption narrative from creation to consummation: beginning and continuing through the people of God—Israel, revealed most clearly in Jesus, and including now the Church. It's a story like any good story that includes movement from order to disorder to new order, from promising beginnings to up-and-down middles to hopeful endings. That's true of the Bible generally, when read and preached rightly. I tell young preachers whom I mentor that we don't preach the Bible; we preach the gospel from the Bible. What I mean by that is that you can lose the Story in the stories, if you aren't careful, mistaking a middling episode for the fulsome drama. The gospel invites us to live abundantly in the meantime, joining the adventure of faith that never settles down or settles for less than "the life that really is life" (1 Timothy 6:19).

The congregation is another constant. Sermons should shape the soul of a people as well as that of a person. Faith is personal but never private. Disciples need disciples to be disciples. We are never a church of one. The transformation wrought in any of our lives over time is a product of those we are spiritually connected to in the dynamic community of the church. Preaching, therefore, addresses one and all—if not at the same time, at least at some time.

Third, these sermons draw from sources beyond the biblical text. These are not mere illustrations of some biblical principle laid alongside it for amplification. Art, literature, music, film, poetry, business, politics, sports, entertainment, nature, and science are sacramental fields where truth, goodness, and beauty may be unearthed. (Of course, they can be a wasteland, too, but even then, we can glean something important.) Switching metaphors, the gospel is not an island in a sea of surrounding culture; it is itself saturated in culture. The preacher is not just an exegete of texts but an exegete of contexts. The Spirit is not confined to the church; like the wind, Jesus tells us, she blows where she wills. Which means that the preacher is something like (another metaphor shift) a museum docent, pointing here and there to signs of God's presence everywhere.

You are holding in your hands a specially designed multimedia book with links sprinkled throughout the text to click to see and hear the original sermon. Preaching is an oral art, so the text on the pages of this book should be fit for the ear as well as for the eye. If you want more of the original experience, simply point your smartphone or tablet at the QR codes throughout the book for a video recording.

One last note about these sermons: each betrays "a bias toward the last," as the title of one of them puts it. This is true in two ways: the last who shall be first in the New Creation that God is bringing to pass, and the last that is that New Creation itself. Thus, there are many more who will find themselves welcome in the future realm of God, and the end is greater than the beginning. In the first case of the last, the gospel takes sides with the marginalized and excluded, not to marginalize the marginalizers or exclude the excluders but precisely so that all may be welcomed and included on the same terms of grace and mercy. The oppressor is saved through the oppressed, not the other way round, as the Crucified Savior makes plain. In the second case of the last, the preacher is a like a town crier who goes out early before the people wake to see what is coming on the horizon of world events and returns to yell about it. "Prepare the way of the Lord," John the Baptist cried out in the spirit of Isaiah. And every faithful preacher since has been crying out loud just the same.

George A. Mason, Spring 2023

The Wilshire Tapestry

The tapestry that adorns the baptistery of Wilshire Baptist Church is a mosaic-like fabric work of art created for that space. A Jewish tapestry artist, Liora Manne, from Jerusalem, produced the work through her New York City firm, LaMontage, under the creative direction of a subcommittee of the church's Building and Grounds Committee. It was installed on February 27, 1994.

The piece was commissioned as part of a renovation and redesign of the baptistery. The tile in the baptistery suggests an ancient Roman tomb. Baptizands know they are moving by faith into an experience of surrender to God in solidarity with Christ. St. Paul wrote in Romans 6:3-4: *Do you not know that all of us who have been baptized into Christ Jesus were baptized into his death? Therefore, we have been buried with him by baptism into death, so that, just as Christ was raised from the dead by the glory of the Father, so we too might walk in newness of life.*

The Symbols of the Tapestry

The Three Circles. The Triune God—Father, Son and Holy Spirit—is depicted by the three circles of burning bush, chalice, and dove, respectively. The circles are not arranged hierarchically; rather, they are meant to convey the dynamic movement of love among the persons of the one God. There is a sequence, however, moving from left to right with the priority of origin and initiative coming from God the Father to the Son and the Spirit.

The circle of the Father reminds us of the call of Moses, the call to lead in the liberation of God's people who were enslaved and oppressed in Egypt. The circle of the

Son is closest to the water, as the Son is the incarnate one who came to live among us. The circle of the Spirit hovers highest and reminds the one being baptized of the descent of the dove of peace at Jesus' baptism, which was accompanied by the voice from heaven saying, "This is my beloved Son, in whom I am well pleased." Baptizands are called to share in the liberating work of God through Jesus Christ in the power of the Holy Spirit. The same promise of peace and new life that was given to Jesus is ours as well.

The Three Greek Crosses. There are three crosses in the tapestry that connect the three circles. These crosses have equal arms, according to the pattern of Greek (rather than Latin) crosses. The connecting crosses suggest the full involvement of God in the redemptive death of Christ. The Son suffers death, the Father suffers the death of the Son as the one who grieves, and the Spirit suffers the death of the Son and the grief of the Father while holding them together in eternal love and opening the grave to resurrection life.

The three circles also gesture toward the three crosses at the time of Jesus' death, thus inviting us to participate in his suffering by our response to his sacrifice of love. The path of salvation for us involves the same suffering love for the world that Jesus demonstrated by giving his life as a ransom for all.

The Bordering Waves. The tapestry border suggests flowing water, which is the historic tradition of baptism in living water. We enter the fellowship of God and the church through our baptism. While it is a border per se, it is not a wall. The threshold of baptism may be crossed by any and all who willingly put their faith in God and confess Jesus as Lord.

Lifting High the Cross

"Lifting High the Cross" marks the fifty-year anniversary of Wilshire Baptist Church on June 10, 2001, and offers a window into the history and character of the church as well as its pastor, George A. Mason. Wilshire met at the Meyerson Symphony Center to celebrate the occasion.

June 10, 2001
Trinity Sunday
Mark 8:34-37

We began worshipping in a movie theater and we've ended up in a symphony hall. Not bad. You've come a long way, Wilshire! A long way from popcorn butter sticking to your soles. A long way from a nursery in the women's restroom. A long way from men's Bible classes in a carpet store, the men sitting on rolls of rugs for chairs. A long way from worship in Cabell's Ice Cream Parlor.

When our first pastor, Huber Drumwright, got up to preach at the ice creamery, there was a Cabell's sign lifted high over the makeshift pulpit that read, *Frozen Divinity 10¢*. Having listened to Huber preach on tape, I suspect the frozen divinity melted quickly under his hot-blooded preaching. I'll try not to make your blood run cold today.

Our theme for this Golden Jubilee celebration is "Lifting High the Cross." It may seem an odd pairing—celebration and the cross. But I'm thinking it's like *Beauty and the Beast*: There's hidden beauty lurking in the beast waiting to be revealed, and there is reason in the cross to celebrate. For fifty years Wilshire has tried to carry its cross in a winsome enough way that the world might see in this symbol of death the throbbing pulse of life. God knows people don't always get it.

A few days ago our staff met for lunch in Lakewood at Angelo's Italian restaurant. It's not the food or service that made us go, God knows. We went to pay homage to the aforementioned spot Wilshire gathered on Sunday nights years ago. So, after we put away a few plates of warmed-over pizza from the buffet, our young tongue-studded waitress came by the table to ask, *How many for bread pudding?* Feeling nostalgic, I asked her, *Do you want to know why we are here today?* Blank stare. Undaunted, I continued, as I do Sunday by Sunday when confronted with the same. *We are the staff of Wilshire Baptist Church*, I said. Rolling eyes. Undaunted, I continued, as I do day by day as the father of three teenagers. *Well, fifty years ago our church worshipped right here in this place when it was an ice cream parlor.* Polite smirk. Undaunted, she continued, *So, how many for bread pudding?*

Figure she's known some not-so-winsome Baptists? Figure she's known some cross-wielding Baptists instead of cross-yielding Baptists? Jesus says if we are to be his followers, we must take up our cross, not as a weapon of war but as a promise of peace. There's more to choosing this "Lifting High the Cross" theme than simply liking the hymn. It epitomizes who we have been and who we want to be. We are a church that wants to take up its cross in a way that gives cause to others to follow Christ too.

I suspect the waitress at Angelo's was afraid we were going to lift high the cross and clobber her over the head with it. Lifting high the cross is an excuse for some Christians to coerce people into faith the way Conquistadors and Inquisitors once forced conversions on native peoples and Jews. There's an old tendency in Christianity to use the cross as a symbol that should strike terror in all who do not confess him.

A few years ago, we joined with Temple Emanu-El for an interfaith Shabbat service. As we were dressing in the clergy robing room, Rabbi Klein looked at the stole I had brought to dress up my plain black robe. It was white, with gold embroidered crosses on each end. A little gold fringe, too. Quite lovely really, as Baptist vestments go! He suggested I might go without the stole. You know why, don't you? Because Christians have for so long accused Jews of killing our Christ, they have come to see the cross itself as a symbol of secret hate instead of love. It wasn't only Blacks in the South who were terrorized by burning crosses.

Even in our own church we have been ambivalent about crosses as symbols, although, if you look at the magnificent blooming flower cross behind me, you'd think we are getting over it nicely. The program cover today pictures the St. Andrew's Cross that adorns our church steeple. When we lifted that up thirty-some years ago, some objected because it didn't quite fit the Georgian Colonial architecture. And through the years, as we've become increasingly bold about putting crosses in the sanctuary and the garden, some have feared we were moving a little too close to Rome. *Oh, Lord, we've left the Southern Baptists and we're becoming Catholics! Before you know it, we'll have crucifixes instead of crosses, and we'll be genuflecting before the altar.*

No, we prefer our crosses empty, thank you. We say it's to show that we believe in the resurrection, but maybe it's also because they make for lighter jewelry that way and aren't quite so aesthetically offensive. Who wants to think about suffering and death after all, especially on a day like this? *Bad form, George.* But I tell you, when the cross becomes more decoration than declaration, it's spiritual defamation. When we prefer to wear crosses around our necks instead of carrying them on our backs, we have turned from following the Jesus whose cross alone saves.

So, what does it mean to take up our cross? The first thing to realize is that this phrase is a modifier of Jesus' command to follow him. If you want to be a disciple of Jesus, you take his terms. And his terms are cross terms. You can't make up your own. If we want to follow Jesus as a church, we must take up our cross. Period.

But the way we take up our cross and follow Jesus is qualified by what Jesus says before that—*deny self, take up your cross, and follow me*. To take up our cross means voluntarily to enter into a life of humble service that will involve suffering and ultimately even death. It means standing with those who cannot stand by themselves, lifting up the fallen, and finding when we do that God is the one who is lifting us all up. This is what it means to deny ourselves and take up our cross. We take up our cross the way Jesus did: not to conquer the world with force but to serve the world with sacrificial love. We do not live for ourselves. We do not live by the world's standards of success. We live by Christ's standards of faithfulness, and we find when we do—and only when we do—that the joy of resurrection life is known. Carry the cross, find life.

Here then is the paradox of faith, the oddity of joining celebration and cross: Jesus offers us abundant life, yet he bids us come and die. Why? Because we don't know what life is until he gives it to us. And we can't receive it until we empty ourselves of all our notions of what it is. We have to die to earthly ambitions if we are to live by heavenly provisions.

The cross is an eternal judgment on the world of success. If the one and only sinless man should be condemned to die on the cross by a world of religious and political powers that should have rewarded him rather than killed him, then we must be wary of all systems and strategies, all powers and programs that seek to build the kingdom of God by our own wit and wisdom.

A church as much as an individual can gain the whole world and lose its own soul. And what can a church, any more than a person, trade for its soul? It doesn't take God to build a big church; it takes only God to build a great church. The temptation churches face is to leave no room for God to work because they design their plans first and then pray for God to bless them. They take their cues from everyone but God. That's getting it backwards. If a church first learns to deny itself, it will ask what God wants rather than what members or prospective members want. That will lead us again and again to the cross: to sacrificial service over superficial success.

The shape of obedience, Wilshire, must always be cruciform—cross-shaped. We love God (vertical arm of the cross) and we love our neighbor as ourselves (horizontal arm). We are not here to occupy America, conquering culture in order to rule the country on behalf of Jesus. We are here to serve it for Jesus' sake. This is the way we serve Christ and the gospel rather than our own designs.

We have not, and we must not, worry about the future of our church as an institution. If Jesus had worried about his future, he never would have taken up his cross for the sake of the world. No matter what you think about his closeness to God, in the hour of his death Jesus had to trust himself by faith to the power of God. And so must we. We face the future as a faith-based rather than a fear-based people.

If anything has rightly marked the first fifty years of Wilshire's life, it is a passion for missions. Mission-minded members have traveled at their own expense to all continents except Antarctica. (All penguins go to heaven, don't you know?!) We have dropped everything and gone to help in disaster relief. We adopted the Albanian peoples and have worked for their welfare spiritually and materially. We have given millions in missions support. We are learning nowadays to add working for justice to evangelism and charity missions.

Some from among us have even found a call to missions or ministry as a career. They have found their lives by losing them for Christ's sake and the gospel's. They have learned that in their weakness they are made strong, and in their brokenness they are blessed.

The late Henri Nouwen was a remarkable soul, a quiet voice for the Spirit that speaks still. In his book *The Life of the Beloved*, written to a Jewish friend about what it means to him to be a Christian, he says: "As I write you now about our brokenness, I recall a scene from Leonard Bernstein's Mass (a musical work written in memory of John F. Kennedy) that embodied for me the thought of brokenness put under the blessing. Toward the end of this work, the priest, richly dressed in splendid liturgical vestments, is lifted up by his people. He towers high above the adoring crowd, carrying in his hands a glass chalice. Suddenly, the human pyramid collapses, and the priest comes tumbling down. His vestments are ripped off, and his glass chalice falls to the ground and is shattered. As he walks slowly through the debris of his former glory—barefoot, wearing only blue jeans and a T-shirt—children's voices are heard singing, *Laude, laude, laude—Praise, praise, praise.* Suddenly, the priest notices the broken chalice. He looks at it for a long time and then, haltingly, he says, *I never realized that broken glass could shine so brightly.*"[1]

You've shone brightly for fifty years, Wilshire, not because you have kept it all together all the time, not because your pastors have been high and lifted up, not because they any more than you have been an example of spiritual perfection, but because you have allowed Christ to shine through your brokenness. You have found your life because time and again you have lost yourself in service to Christ and his gospel. This is the way forward, too.

We celebrate the cross of Christ today. We marvel at what God has done in us and among us. And now "lifting high the cross" for the next fifty years, we offer ourselves anew to God through Jesus Christ our Lord.

---

1 *Life of the Beloved: Spiritual Living in a Secular World,* (New York: Crossroad Publishing, 1992), pp. 82-83.

PART I

For the Love of God

Theology

"Our hearts are restless until they find their rest in Thee."

- St. Augustine

Preface by Curtis Freeman

Pastors serve in many roles: *priests* who lead in worship, *prophets* who declare the word, *shepherds* who care for souls, *evangelists* who proclaim the good news, and *teachers* who instruct the faithful.[2]

God calls leaders to be *pastors-and-teachers*, to equip the saints for the work of ministry, to build up the body of Christ (Eph 4:11-12). The teaching vocation is essential to the church's disciple-making mission that begins with baptism in the triune name of God followed by instruction in the basic teaching of Christ (Matt 28:19-20, Heb 6:1-2). The pastor as teacher is a *servant* of Christ and a *steward* of God's mysteries (1 Cor 4:1). The teaching vocation is necessary for the church to be the church because the Christian faith is not innate or intuitive. It is a gift to be passed on. For this reason, the apostle Paul urged Timothy to entrust his teaching to faithful people who would be able to teach others the teaching he received from the apostles (2 Tim 2:2).[3]

George Mason is widely known as a gifted preacher, but these ten sermons demonstrate that he is also a creative theologian and an effective teacher. Anyone who reads these selections will quickly recognize them, not simply as interesting homiletical transcripts, but as important theological texts. Sermons, to be sure, are meant to be heard, but as long as I have known George, he has made his sermon manuscripts available for study and reflection by his congregation and the wider church. They display his skills as a pastoral theologian.

---

2 William H. Willimon, *Pastor: The Theology and Practice of Ordained Ministry*, revised ed. (Nashville: Abingdon Press, 2016).

3 Curtis W. Freeman, *Pilgrim Letters: Instruction in the Basic Teaching of Christ* (Minneapolis: Fortress Press, 2021); and Freeman, *Pilgrim Journey: Instruction in the Mystery of the Gospel* (Minneapolis: Fortress Press, 2023).

Being a pastoral theologian in the Baptistic Free Church tradition is not an easy matter. There is neither a specified liturgy nor are there prescribed creeds to perform and profess the faith. Nevertheless, Mason utilizes the tools available in his theological toolbox—Scripture and hymnody, poetry and literature, culture and history, and more—all of which he uses to speak about God more coherently so that we might learn to love God more completely.

Even in a secular age, where the overwhelming majority of people in the United States still say they believe in God, these sermons contend that the meaning of the word "G-o-d" is not at all transparent. We must learn what it means to believe in God by learning to speak as Christians. These sermons challenge us to examine our conceptions and convictions, by considering faith not as a way of thinking, but more as a way of loving. We are invited to consider the confessional approach of Augustine and Anselm who propose that we not seek to understand so that we may believe but believe so that we may understand.[4]

These sermons remind us that the Christian faith trusts in the God who is *God alone*, but who is not *a lone God*. God exists in relation as a Trinity of persons: Father, Son, and Spirit. To the extent that the Trinity is a problem for Christians, it is a love problem, not a math problem. We find God in loving God, and love God by finding God. These sermons guide us in learning the grammar of faith by showing us how to speak about our love for the God in whom we trust that we might understand the love of the God that we trust. The theological movement is clear and cogent, alluring but liberative, simple yet profound.

Love draws us in freedom to the God who freely loves us, not by the convincing power of the angels of truth, but by the attractive influence of the angels of beauty. The intelligent design of nature does not reveal the God who made all things, but rather the God who made all things reveals the divine self to us in nature. This sort of faith, we are warned, is not simply a matter of belief or disbelief, but of holding out for the possibility that something real and deep is going on that challenges all of our categories and invites our trust in a God who is always more than enough for whatever our hunger is at any given time. The God we freely love who loves in freedom is always doing something new, not as a spectacle of sovereign power, but as a sign to guide us into the way of flourishing.

Christians today need preaching like this to help us begin to understand the faith that has sustained believers from generation to generation, a faith we have received by transmission from the apostolic community down to the contemporary church. Teaching like this distinguishes the world of difference between the triune God and the other alleged deities being worshipped and served in God's world. Instruction like this explores the distinctive identity and activity of the God we seek in love and find by loving. Theology like this provides us not only with a grammar to offer an account for the hope that is in us (1 Pet 3:15). It calls us to arm ourselves

---

4 Augustine, *On the Trinity*, 15.2.2, trans. Arthur West Haddan and William G. T. Shedd, in *The Nicene and Post-Nicene Fathers* (Grand Rapids: Eerdmans, 1978), 3:200; and Anselm, *Proslogion*, 1, in *The Prayers and Meditations of Saint Anselm*, trans., Benedicta Ward (New York: Penguin, 1973), pp. 243-44.

for spiritual battle (Eph 6:11-12) with the basic teaching of Christian resistance.[5] It commends us to love God (Matt 22:37). Such love, to borrow a line from Isaac Watts, demands our soul, our life, our all.[6]

Curtis W. Freeman is Research Professor of Theology and Director of the Baptist House of Studies at Duke University Divinity School. He is the editor of the American Baptist Quarterly *and is a member of the Doctrine and Christian Unity Commission of the Baptist World Alliance. He is the author of many books and articles, most recently* Pilgrim Letters *and* Pilgrim Journey.

---

5 K. H. Miskotte, *Biblical ABCs: The Basics of Christian Resistance*, trans. Elenora Hof and Collin Cornell (Lanham, MD: Lexington Books/Fortress Academic, 2022).

6 Isaac Watts, *Psalms, Hymns, and Spiritual Songs*, Book III, Hymn 7 (Boston: Crocker and Brewster, 1840), p. 478.

I

Glimpses of Truth

February 6, 2005
Fifth Sunday after Epiphany
Matthew 17:1-9

Once upon a time, when angels still walked the earth, there was a man who resisted God Almighty. But the Lord took mercy on him and sent to him the Angel of Truth, that he might be enlightened. The angel descended to earth and knocked at the window of the defiant man, craving entrance.

"Who are you, and what is it you wish?" demanded the man impatiently, opening the window slightly. The Angel of Truth told of his request, but the man slammed the window, and the angel stood outside, not knowing what to do. He waited a long time, walking up and down in front of the house, knocking again and again at the door, but nobody opened it. So he flew back to heaven and was very sad indeed, because his visit had been a failure.

Presently his sister, the Angel of Beauty, saw him and asked the reason for his distress. The Angel of Truth told of his grievance. "Take courage, brother," she said. "What you could not achieve alone, we will accomplish together." And so they both glided down to earth through the hanging garden of beautiful stars. When they came in sight of the man's house, the Angel of Beauty turned to the Angel of Truth and said, "Wait awhile," and she went to the window and knocked. But the man thought it was again someone come to disturb his peace, and he grumbled angrily.

Then the Angel of Beauty knocked again. This time she made the knocking sound like the sweet tones of a harp, and the window shone in many-colored radiance like the stained-glass windows of a cathedral. The man listened and looked up in astonishment from his work, and when he saw the Angel of Beauty standing before his window, the frown disappeared from his face, and his heart was warm and glad. He quickly opened the window, asking, "Who are you, my beautiful child?" "I am Beauty," said the angel. "Oh, come in and be welcome," said the man, opening the door wide.

"I should like to enter," said Beauty reluctantly. "I think I should enjoy being with you. But—"

"There is no but," said the man. Whatever you wish you shall have. Come in."

"Very well," said the Angel of Beauty, "But I have a brother outside. Do you see him? Have you room for both of us?"

"Room for a dozen children as charming as you," the man answered gleefully.

So the Angel of Beauty flew to the Angel of Truth and said, "Come," and so Truth and Beauty took possession of the heart of the defiant man.[7]

How are we to understand what happens on the Mount of Transfiguration in our Gospel lesson today? In the first three Gospel accounts, this event, this epiphany, this glimpse of truth about Jesus, is the turning point in his ministry. He's been on an upswing, so to speak, to this mount, and now it will be all downhill until he mounts the cross. His popularity with the crowds has wound up right up to this moment, but after this, things will begin to unravel. His closest friends need to see the light before things get darker. They must recognize him for who he is, not for what they want him to be.

And just so they see him—all lit up. His face shines like those old paintings with halos round the heads of the saints to show their godlikeness. Moses appears there with Jesus, and Elijah, too. The two key figures in the history of Israel. Symbolizing the unity of the Law and the Prophets, these two undisputed men of God summarize the history and hopes of God's people in the world. They don't have the same shine about them, Moses and Elijah; they simply add weight to the truth that beauty already bears in the dazzling whiteness of the Lord Jesus. They confirm the unique divinity of this one who is called the Son of God.

And we wonder why this happened at all. Was it for Jesus' sake or for the sake of the disciples? If it were for Jesus' sake, we can imagine that at this moment in his life when his ministry was about to become all the more cruciform, God would want to assure him of who he truly is and what he must do. The same voice that spoke at his baptism commencing his ministry repeats itself now at the turning point of his ministry: *This is my Son, the Beloved; with him I am well pleased.* The first part of these words is from Psalm 2. These words were a crowd chant at the coronation ceremony of a new king. The people would declare that the new king bore a special relationship to God, and they would obey him. The second part comes from the Prophet Isaiah. It is part of the Suffering Servant passages that speak of the mission of Israel to the world as a messianic mission—to suffer and die for the sins of the world. Jesus is reminded at this important stage of his life who he is and what he must do.

The popular film trilogy *The Matrix* is filled with biblical imagery. The story line is somewhat complicated—at least for a middle-aged man, don't you know?! But the abiding conflict that is being waged in the films is between a world on the one hand that is programmed and closed, a world ruled by fate that eliminates the frailties of human beings along with all emotion, chance, and choice; and, on the other hand, an open world of human beings where love and passion defy fixed destiny.

7 *Context*, (Jan. 2005), Part A, 37.1.

The Christ figure, Neo, is also called The One. At one point in the second film, he enters a door that leads him from one world to the next. It is a door of pure light that takes him to one called The Source. The Source turns out to be the maker of the machine world that is trying to eliminate the "anomalies," the remnant of resistant human beings whom Neo represents. Neo is given the choice between two doors. One will allow him to save Zion, the city of resistance, in which case he would have to lose the woman he loves, called Trinity. (I told you there's a lot of theological language, hard to follow.) If he chooses Trinity, the city of Zion is destroyed. His head tells him he must accept her death for the sake of the rest, but his heart will not allow the cold logic of evil to dictate his decision. He chooses love and the story continues ...

Jesus learns in the midst of this bright shining moment, standing with his head in the clouds and God's servants of old beside him, that love has logic of its own, and that only love will defeat the enemies of God. He is sustained to the cross by the power of this experience.

But while Western Christianity has long thought that the miracle of transfiguration was mainly to be focused on Jesus, Eastern Christians have attended to the experience of the disciples. They believe Jesus always bore a shining radiance as the Son of God, but that the miracle was in the seeing. The eyes of the disciples were opened to see what was always there. They had an epiphany. The veil between the visible and the invisible worlds became so thin in that moment that they could see what was always true. Beauty, in other words, led them to Truth, not the other way round.

We are reminded of John Keats' wondrous poem, *Ode on a Grecian Urn*. It concludes with the urn addressing the viewer. "Beauty is truth, truth beauty—that is all / Ye know on earth, and all ye need to know." Beauty and Truth may be one, or they may be sibling angels in the service of God, but, like the story at the first, we are all more charmed into faith than reasoned into it. The heart draws us more than the head drives us to it.

Think of it: How many of you put your trust in Christ because someone answered all your questions? I know I have never talked anyone into becoming a Christian. The most I can do is to lower the bar of objections. But I was not converted that way. I was just like most children who grew up in the church. We are drawn to faith by the smells and bells (you would understand that better if you grew up Catholic); by the stitching and color and symbols in the tapestry that you stare at when the preacher is boring; by the mystery of the waters of baptism; by the taste of Wonder Bread and wine at the Table; by the sound of voices singing and organ pipes piping and shafts of light that break in through the windows on Easter Sunday; by the gentle touch of a Sunday school teacher; and by a youth minister who was just the right blend of reverent and irreverent enough to make you want to be like him.

Jake Whitten is six. He was with his parents at a little Mexican restaurant last week. He noticed the elements on the table and said to his father, "Dad, open your mouth." Jon asked his son what he was doing, and the boy persisted. Next thing you know, Jake had spilled the saltshaker, wetted his finger, and touched some salt to his father's tongue, saying, "You are the salt of the earth." Then he grabbed the candle on the table and gave it him and said, "You are the light of the world."

That's it, see. We come to faith in ways we cannot fully grasp, by a movement of the heart before the head. Now we want to get the mind into the act sooner rather than later, we want to leave our encounter with more than a powerful feeling of God upon us, we want to come away declaring that Jesus is indeed the Son of God and that we will listen to him. Faith is touchy-feely; and yet it is also bright and brainy. But beauty leads. It's art before science. The heart first thirsts. The eyes must open to see. Which is what we mean when we say that seeing is believing. We don't mean that you have to see something with your everyday eyes before you can believe; we mean that you have to SEE, really SEE. Do you see?

Some of us are so busy with important things in our lives that we believe we must do that we miss the wonder of life and the wondrous shining presence of Christ in the everydayness of life. This gift of seeing was not a one-time break-through intended only for Jesus' closest three friends. It's for any and every friend of God who is willing to attend to the heart and look upon Christ.

The minister and writer Robert Fulghum tells about a woman who was so stressed out that she went to see a psychiatrist. After listening for a long time, he wrote out a prescription and handed it to her. She expected some kind of mood-altering drug, but what she got were these words: "Spend one hour a week watching the sunrise while walking in a cemetery." Not wanting to waste her money for the visit and desperate enough to try anything, she entered a cemetery one morning just before sunrise. She watched the sun come up. She listened to nature awake. She wanted to sing along with the birds. She came alive again with the world that morning because she attended to it.[8]

Jesus is still shining in the world. Remember the Christmas carol of just more than a month ago: "Joy to the world the Lord IS come, let heaven and nature sing." Well, they are singing if we will attend to them. But the thing to attend to is not just heaven and nature but that the Lord of whom they sing is come. We are to look upon the world to find those thin places that draw us as if by Beauty into Truth. We are to look for those glimpses of truth in the moments of each day that lead us deeper into the knowledge of the one who is the Beloved Son in whom God is well pleased. And when we look upon his shining face long enough, we may hear that voice from heaven and wonder if it isn't speaking to us, too: "You are my beloved child; in you I am well pleased."

Now do you see?

8 *Pulpit Resource* (Jan.-Mar. 2005): 27.

Intelligible Design

October 2, 2011
Sixteenth Sunday after Pentecost
Psalm 19

In 1802, a Cambridge University philosopher and Christian apologist named William Paley wrote a book called *Natural Theology*. Even the renowned father of the theory of evolution, Charles Darwin, was taken with Paley's thoughts about nature having a sense of purpose, although Darwin would later take that idea in a different direction. The book included an analogy called "the watchmaker," which became a so-called proof for the existence of God. Paley suggests that if he were to stumble upon a stone one day in a heath, he might think it had simply been there forever; but if he stumbled upon a pocket watch there, he would think someone had dropped it there. The watch's complexity and order, the way the parts fit together, make it clear that there was a purpose behind its making. As Paley put it: *The marks of design are too strong to be got over. Design must have had a designer. That designer must have been a person. That person is GOD.*

Nowadays, followers of Darwin employ the idea of random selection to explain nature's adaptive progress. Nonetheless, the scientifically minded stare at the design of nature with awe and wonder. And we Christians ought to admit that those who do not believe in God are not all dullards who simply prefer data to deity. They marvel at the creation, too; they just do so without reference to a Creator. When Christians react to people like these, we often wrongly suppose we have to oppose the idea of evolution itself, as if the choice is either faith in a Creator who made the world in all its marvelous complexity in six twenty-four-hour days and rested on the seventh, or faith in a cold and godless process that leaves us on our own in the darkness.

Paley's argument has been renewed today by some as an alternative called Intelligent Design. Many see it as a better explanation of the origin and ends of nature than Darwin's theory. They want it taught in public schools in order to balance or replace evolution. I am not one of them because I don't think it's really science. Christians are too often on the wrong side of science. We like it as long as it comes to the same conclusions we've come to without it; but when it doesn't, we'd rather be accused of being unintelligent believers than intelligent unbelievers.

There is another way, though, that is more biblical and faithful. It recognizes the wonders of creation and sees in them and through them a loving hand at work in all things. It sees faith walking alongside science without pretending to be science. It looks at nature and can even see the process of evolution, and then it can go to church and sing to God without its brains falling out.

Listen again to the psalmist: *The heavens are telling the glory of God; ... Day to day pours forth speech, and night to night declares knowledge. There is no speech, nor are there words; their voice is not heard; yet their voice goes out through all the earth, and their words to the end of the world.*

Steve Holley was telling me once about how he experienced this while hunting turkeys. (Being a city kid, I have no experience hunting anything but birdies and eagles on a golf course, don't you know?!) He told me about sitting in the dark before the dawn on his Central Texas ranch, in the stillness and blackness and quietness of things, where he feels that nothing is alive but the beat of his own heart. Then, all of a sudden, as the first rays of the sun begin to change the color of the sky at daybreak, the world wakes up. It begins to speak. Birds sing and crickets chirp and insects buzz and coyotes howl and roosters crow, and all he can do is think of the psalmist, the speech of creation, and the voice of nature declaring the glory of God.

The poet Mary Oliver says, *The leaf has a song in it. / Stone is the face of patience. / Inside the river there is an unfinished story / and you are somewhere in it / and it will never end until all ends.*[9]

This is the poetry of faith; it's not the prose of science. There's nothing inherently unfaithful about the prose of science, but neither is there anything inherently untruthful about the poetry of faith. They are beautiful together so long as one does not pretend to be the other or deny the possibility of the other.

Sometimes science presumes to know more than it does, ignoring some of the most powerful realms of human experience, such as art and beauty, compassion and conscience, guilt and pleasure.[10] But faith can do the same to science. In truth, if you want to say that the Bible is literally true in the way some do, then Psalm 19 is simply wrong about the sun and the sky. When the psalmist looks up and sees the sun running its course in the heavens as a bridegroom emerging from his tent after a night of rest and romance, he wrongly thinks the sun is doing the moving. We know today that the sun is just one star that is composed of about three parts hydrogen and one part helium, that its mass is 109 times that of Earth, that it orbits the center of the Milky Way counterclockwise and completes its journey every 200 to 250 million years, and that the light it emits takes 8 minutes and 19 seconds to arrive at our blue planet.

9 What Can I Say?" in *Swan: Poems and Prose Poems* (Beacon Press, 2010).

10 A point made by Marilynne Robinson about what she calls "parascience," in *Absence of Mind* (Yale Press, 2010).

All of that, however, only makes a better and more interesting point, I think: Instead of arguing intelligent design, we would do better to speak of *intelligible design*. The fact that nature reveals itself to us and that we can understand it is a gift that keeps on giving. Christians believe it isn't nature that reveals itself to us but the Maker who reveals nature to us.

Just this week we learned about the possibility that Einstein might have been wrong about the speed limit of the universe. He had established the speed of light at about 186,000 miles per second as a constant that could not be exceeded. But researchers at Switzerland's CERN laboratory report clocking subatomic ghostlike particles, called neutrinos, at a speed that should have been ticketed. Who knows where this will lead, but the very fact that we believe it might lead to more knowledge is the point of intelligible design.

If people of the Book are right about God being the Creator, what should cause us to break out in song and not in war is that by means of science we can understand something more to add to our wonderment while still sitting at dawn in the bushes waiting to shoot turkeys and hearing nature sing to the glory of God. Any advance in understanding creation is, for people of faith, the result of the Creator's desire to be known in and through and by God's own handiwork and is cause for praise.

But nature is only one part of this psalm, torah is the other. If wordless nature speaks to us of God's glory, the word of God speaks all the more clearly. God doesn't want us to know just that God exists; God wants us to know God. Said another way, God reveals a sure way for us to live in the world God has made. God hasn't just made a wilderness; God has made a trail through it for us to follow.

The law of the Lord is perfect, ... the decrees of the Lord are sure, ... the precepts of the Lord are right, ... the commandment of the Lord is clear, ... the ordinances of the Lord are true and righteous altogether.

At the heart of biblical faith is the conviction that God made the world out of love and loves the world enough to give it direction. God has not left us on our own, but instead has been from the first day of creation revealing to us how all things are made, how things are meant to work together for good, and how we might be good in the midst of all things made.

Children, think of it this way: What if your parents never showed you how to do anything? Imagine they gave you life and left you alone. Well, sometimes you probably wish they would, right? But what if your mother never taught you how to tie your shoelaces or your father how to throw a ball? Would you know how to ride a bicycle by picking it up yourself?

Some ways of living are better than others because we live in a moral universe that makes sense. Even when senseless things happen, we call them senseless because we believe they're not supposed to be that way. So instead of dreading that obeying commandments means that we have to do this or can't do that, the more we understand them, the more grateful we can be that God loves us and cares for us enough to share with us the design secrets of the world.

God's instruction to us is sweeter than honey and more desirable than gold, the psalmist says. By God's laws we are warned, and in keeping them is great reward.

Now this is the point at which I could easily—too easily—simply say that the law of God warns us for our own good and that, if we heed it, we will be rewarded. But while that might often be true, it's no sure thing. And it would turn our religion into something we hang around our necks like an amulet for good luck. Which it isn't. Sometimes you do what's right and wrong happens anyway—sometimes to you. But that isn't the end of the story.

My granddaughter, Finley, has recently discovered her shadow. She loves to see it on the staircase in our house. She has figured out that she can make it move as she moves, and she loves the power she has over it. But shadows are also symbolic of something deep within us that has power over us unless we become conscious of it by light being shed on it. The psychotherapist Carl Jung said that it is part of our repressed weaknesses, our animal instincts, that we have to get under control lest they control us. *Everyone carries a shadow*, he said, *and the less it is embodied in the individual's conscious life, the blacker and denser it is.*

Well, the psalmist says that the commandments of the Lord enlighten the eyes. And even where it says that by them we are warned, the word translated *warned* there is again the word for *enlightened*. In other words, the law that the Lord discloses to us is meant to shine light on us so as to remove our darkness and reveal our hidden faults. This frees us to see the way clearly between right and wrong and to follow the path that leads to a good, not an easy life. Science and Scripture both shed light.

Dietrich Bonhoeffer should have had a good and easy life. But he was hanged in 1945 in the Flossenburg Prison as a conspirator to assassinate Adolf Hitler. Bonhoeffer was a German Lutheran scholar and pastor who could have joined most of his peers in supporting the racial and national ideology of the Nazis that co-opted the state church. But early in his life, Bonhoeffer had learned to question things from a father who was a medical doctor and a man of science more than faith, and from a mother who came from two generations of theologians who did the same. His mind was formed by the hard truths of science and Scripture; both were a lamp to his feet and a light to his path.

When he was only sixteen, he and his classmates heard the sound of gunfire only three hundred meters from their classroom. A gang of thugs had killed Walther Rathenau, a politically moderate Jew who had advocated that Germany pay off all its war debts as agreed upon in the Treaty of Versailles. Hitler later made the thugs heroes, but Bonhoeffer's classmate remembered Dietrich's anger about the killing. Said his friend: *I remember it because I was surprised at the time that someone could know so exactly where he stood.*[11]

And even as he stood in a hangman's noose twenty-three years later, he knew that he stood squarely within the intelligible design of a loving God.

---

11 Eric Metaxas, *Bonhoeffer: Pastor, Martyr, Prophet, Spy* (Thomas Nelson, 2010), p. 40.

3

The Magnificent Word

December 24, 2006
Fourth Sunday of Advent
Luke 1:39-55

My soul magnifies the Lord—Magnificat in the Latin.

The magnificent tenor <u>Andrea Bocelli</u> sings his own *Magnificat* of sorts, called *When a Child Is Born. A ray of hope flickers in the sky. / A tiny star lights up way up high. / All across the land dawns a brand new morn. / This comes to pass when a child is born. / A silent wish sails the seven seas. / The winds of change whisper in the trees. / And the walls of doubt tumble tossed and turn. / This comes to pass when a child is born.*

When *a* child is born, he sings. On this day we think about when *the* child is born. And we use the present tense, don't you know?!, when speaking about the birth of the child Jesus. It's the same as when we sing "Joy to the World, the Lord Is Come." Of course, it happened in the past, not once upon a time as in a fairy tale as if it never really happened in history. It happened in history once upon a time, but <u>its effects</u>—<u>the birth of this Child</u>—are of such a nature that they light up our imaginations still. They are like a dream too good not to be true. They are like a fairy tale that hits the earth running and never looks back. <u>Everything changes</u>. <u>Nothing is the same</u>.

That's the way it is any time a child is born, of course. I remember being there in the delivery room when a child was born to Kim and me, three times. Each time it was the same: amazement, wonder, joy. And each time I would leave the hospital thinking how sad it was that all these people I was passing looked like nothing much had happened that day. They walked on with their same numbing resolve, stuck in routines like ruts leading nowhere. I just wanted them to know that it would be all right now, things would be different now; a ray of hope was flickering in the sky, a tiny star lighting up way up high. I wanted them to feel the change the way I did, to know that things would be different now because a child is born.

How much more Mary must have felt that night in the stable! It didn't even take the nativity event itself to do the trick, just a kick from the child in Elizabeth's womb and the blessing of her dear cousin. They give her assurance that it was indeed true and that everything would change because of this child.

The lovely new movie *The Nativity* pictures this scene beautifully. Mary has gone from her home village in Nazareth to visit her much older cousin, who was considered barren. She goes to be with her and to help her with the birth of her child, John the would-be Baptist. And immediately upon Mary's greeting Elizabeth, the child in her cousin's womb leaps for joy, and we get the Hail Mary blessing in return that has been expanded in Catholic devotion to recognize the important role of this young woman who said yes to the angel. The movie has a sweet take on how this very greeting from Elizabeth helps to confirm Mary's belief that she is indeed with child, and that that child is indeed the Son of God.

The seventeenth-century divine poet John Donne wrote Holy Sonnets in praise of the key moments of the incarnation, in which the Word became flesh and dwelt among us. In the second sonnet, he sees the astonishing significance of what the Greeks called *theotokos*, mother of God; how the one who was the agent of all creation should allow himself to be the child of one of his creations. Listen to Donne's words to Mary: ... *Ere by the spheares time was created, thou / Wast in his minde, who is thy Sonne, and Brother; / Whom thou conceiv'st, conceiv'd; yea thou art now / Thy Maker's maker, and thy Father's mother; / Thou' hast light in darke; and shutst in little roome, immensity cloystered in thy deare wombe.*

Immensity, indeed. Songs, carols, films, poems: These are just a few of the fields in which the womb of the human heart has been opened and the mind stretched to conceive the inconceivable and to wonder at the wonderful.

Madeleine L'Engle, the author of the ever-popular fable, *A Wrinkle in Time*, wrote also these immortal lines about this time of year: *This is the irrational season / When love blooms bright and wild. / Had Mary been filled with reason / There'd have been no room for the child.*[12]

We think about that phrase "no room for the child," and where do our minds go? To the "no room in the inn" line of Luke's nativity story, right? We know Jesus was born in a stable because there was no room in the inn. But we also know that no one but that innkeeper was willing to make room for them, either. The shunning of this poor traveling couple, the woman great with child, has seared our consciences with the ethic of hospitality. We know that Jesus would grow up to say that *inasmuch as you have done unto the least of these, my brothers and sisters, you have done it unto me.* When we welcome strangers, when we clothe the naked and feed the hungry and give drink to the thirsty and visit the widows and orphans and imprisoned, we are making room in our lives for Christ himself. In other words, the story of Bethlehem's hospitality, or the lack of it, has affected our sense of neighborliness forever. Love makes room for our neighbor, where reason only hangs out "No Vacancy" signs.

---

12 "After Annunciation," in *The Weather of the Heart* (Shaw, 2000).

But even that must be seen in light of the first act of hospitality Mary showed us. Imagine you are a humble young girl of no more than maybe fourteen. You live in a poor part of Palestine, in the country, in a village that cannot sustain itself without traveling miles to trade. Your Jewish family struggles to survive under the cruel rule of the narcissistic Romans, who seem to take delight in your suffering because it makes them feel powerful. You have simple hopes harbored in your heart: a good husband, strong children, a life among your neighbors in Nazareth that would be pleasing to God and praiseworthy to others.

It is a conservative family and community you grow up in. Although in some other places Jews considered betrothal enough like marriage that you could safely have intimate relations before the wedding, not so in Galilee. To be with child before the wedding would lead to scandal at best, stoning at worst. It would certainly destroy every dream you held so dear. But then an angel appears to you and declares God's intention that you should be the vessel for the enfleshing of the Word that would redeem all things just as it had made all things. You might be flattered by the offer, but would you really be eager to receive this gift? Mary had to make room in her heart for God's will in order to make room in her womb for God's Son. She welcomed him in a way that humbles us still, because it meant she would be giving up her lesser dreams for herself for God's greater ones for the world. She had to let God's love have its way with her before Joseph's love could have its way with her; and thereby she risked everything anyone might ever again believe about her.

The Florentine monk nicknamed Fra Angelico depicted this scene with utmost purity in his giant fresco that adorns the wall at the top of the steps that lead to the small monastic cells in the convent of San Marco. Mary bends low in humility, and we can imagine her saying to the angel, *Let it be unto me according to your word.* And when we look at the angel, we are not certain whether he is jealous that Mary should have such an honor or nervous that the future of the world should hang on the obedience of one so young and human. As the writer Frederick Buechner puts it, *The angel, the whole creation, even God himself, all hold their breath as they wait upon the answer of a girl.*[13] But before we are done looking, we might wonder whether Gabriel himself is in awe at the faith of this blessed woman who would be the mother of the Lord.

The world itself has learned to value children in a way it had not before the Word became flesh and dwelt among us. Before we imagined that God would deign to come in the form of a child, children were conceived only to be potential adults. They were cheap labor. But people of Christmas faith have come to see each of them through the light of the Christ child as reflections of divinity, as symbols of innocence, as signs of God's presence.

A four-year-old girl, soon after her brother was born, asked her parents to leave her alone for a little while with the baby. They worried that she was jealous of the little boy and might want to pinch him or shake him. So they told her she needed to be with Mommy and Daddy when she was with the baby. They started watching her for signs of jealousy, but such signs never appeared. Instead, everything pointed

13 *Listening to Your Life* (Harper Collins, 1992), p. 77.

to a sincere love for her baby brother. Again, the little girl asked to be left alone with the infant so finally the parents allowed it. They let her go into the nursery by herself, leaving the door open enough to keep an eye on her. The girl walked up to her baby brother, put her face close to his, and quietly said, *Baby, tell me what God feels like, because I'm starting to forget.*[14]

Lest we forget what God feels like, God keeps giving us children. And lest we think that only children conceived and born in the most respectable way bear the marks of God's presence, we remember the story of Jesus, Mary, and Joseph. This child was born out of wedlock, strictly speaking. The whole community raised an eyebrow, the family was no doubt shamed, and the husband of Mary had to swallow his pride to stand beside his wife and her child. Shepherds and wise men, sheep and goats and cows would worship him outside proper places.

Michael Lindval tells how the spirit struck the little Presbyterian church in Northhaven, Minnesota, in his novel, *The Good News from Northhaven.* One Sunday after a typical service of worship that included the baptism of an infant, a woman waited for the pastor. She was a nondescript back-row worshipper, *dressed in Salvation Army style, clutching a black plastic purse.* She informed the pastor that Tina had had a baby and thought it ought to be baptized. Tina had grown up in the church's youth group, but at eighteen she had gotten pregnant out of wedlock. On the Fourth Sunday in Advent—this day for us today—Tina brought her two-month-old baby, James, to the font at the front of the church. It was the pastor's custom to ask, *Who stands with this child?* Ordinarily, the parents and grandparents and godparents would stand. The pastor was too nervous to peek, lest no one stood. But he began to hear rustling through the sanctuary and finally looked up to find that a couple of the elders had stood, followed by the sixth-grade Sunday school teacher. Then a new young couple stood. And finally, much to the pastor's astonished eyes, the rest of the congregation joined them. The whole congregation joined Tina and her Salvation Army-dressed mother. They were all his family, his holy family.

My friends, I have given you one vignette after another, impressionistic in sermon style, this morning, to illustrate the impact of the incarnation. We have a limitless supply of impressions that emanate as light from the manger cradle and wrap themselves in our hearts. The world is changed by the Magnificent Word that has come to us all through Mary. Her song, her *Magnificat*, has become ours. Let us sing for joy!

---

14 Thanks to Carl Reeves for passing this on to me. From Ken Blanchard, *We Are the Beloved* (Zondervan, 1994.), p. 7.

4

More Than Enough

July 29, 2012
Ninth Sunday after Pentecost
John 6:1-15

I had a fascinating conversation recently with a man who confessed that he had lost whatever faith he had years ago. He didn't grow up in the church, but he had a vague sense of God as someone who was there to help him if only he cooperated with a positive attitude. He was driving through the Badlands of South Dakota and stopped into the museum of geology. He wandered about taking it all in. He saw the timeline of earth and life: the stratifications of the rock formations, organic growth, the age of the dinosaurs, and finally human beings. Along the vast timeline that stretched out billions of years, the history of humans was but a tiny sliver. It shook whatever faith he had. He saw in that exhibit a purely naturalist view of reality. There was no place for God in a world that had evolved. From that moment he continued to try to be a good person but without a sense of a living and active God in the world or in his life.

We were able to talk frankly about these things. I was able to tell him that the conflict he felt in his bones that day was not really between whether God was the creator or the world evolved on its own. The conflict was between who he believed God to be and what the world seemed to be. I was able to share with him my view that the world is open to God, not closed. It doesn't operate on its own. Evolution is one means by which God has been creating the world and engaging with it since the first moment.

This sermon today is not about creation and evolution. It's about whether we believe that God is at work in the world and how. It's about the Christian claim that miracles are not fairy tales; they are rather faith-evoked events and faith-evoking ones.

So, to the work. The miracle of the feeding of the five thousand was beloved in the early church. It's the only miracle story told in all four Gospels. Something clearly happened that the early church told and retold. We could discount it all today as tales of prescientific minds, but the story is told as if we were there ourselves, protesting with the disciples that there isn't anything to be done in the face of all that hunger, because they simply didn't have enough.

So where does that leave us? Three options: We can simply believe it by saying that God can do anything and that's that; we can disbelieve it by saying that even God wouldn't act to contradict the laws of nature that God set up, and therefore the most we can do is to turn it into a story that has a moral about the power of sharing; or we can consider whether something real and deep is going on in this event that challenges all of our categories and invites our faith in a God who wants to show us that there is always more than enough for whatever our hunger is at any given time. You can imagine that I'm going to hope you'll join me in the third view. Like so many sermons, three points and maybe a poem, don't you know?!

First, then, you may be of the mind that if it's in the Bible, that's that. You believe it because it's God's word. *God said it, I believe it, and that settles it.* Fine and good. But God's word intends to open your mind to new possibilities about the world that you might otherwise not imagine, not close your mind just when you are getting started. Setting the Bible against reason or science is no long-term strategy for persuading anyone of the trust of Christ. A miracle can't be proved or disproved, but it should at least be plausible to believe. Faith is about what's true. We don't need proof to believe, but we should at least join skeptical minds in asking if something might be so. If you take this first point of view, then you are open to belief. Keep going. Belief is a start; it just shouldn't be an end.

The second view can be as doctrinaire as the first, but in the opposite way. The world is as it is. If you've got five loaves and two small fish, you're going to have five loaves and two small fish. Period. Divide it up to make it go farther, break it up into smaller pieces; in any case you're going to have the same amount in the end that you had in the beginning. This is common sense. The world operates on certain laws that even God can't violate without everything falling apart. In fact, the only way we can be confident that we know anything for sure is that those rules aren't changed by the occasional whim of a God who dips in now and then to heal someone or quiet a storm or turn the wheel or make a bad investment good or multiply loaves and fish.

If you have this point of view, you have problems with stories like these in the Bible. You may have problems with any faith that comes from the Bible. But all who take this view don't become unbelieving atheists. Some still find a place for faith by saying that science is about facts and religion is about meaning. Bible stories like these are not to be taken literally. Jesus multiplying the loaves and fish is a story about what can happen when we all follow the boy's example and give what we have instead of hoarding. It's about the difference between selfishness and sharing. If we all give what little we have, we will find there is more than enough for everyone.

This isn't bad, given the truths of world hunger today. The problem of a hungry world is not food production; it's food distribution. There's more than enough food for everyone. It's a question of balance, justice, and access. If those of us who have so much would limit ourselves and share what we have with those who have little or nothing, all would be better if not all well. Religion teaches us to love our neighbor as ourselves. You don't need miracles to do that. You need keen insight, a compassionate heart, and a committed will. If all you get were those things, that itself would be miraculous.

To be honest, I think most of us in the church operate with this view without thinking about it. Faith is a matter of the heart more than the head. No one ever says that she has become a Christian by inviting Jesus into her head. We might admit that miracles are possible, and we might even pray for people to be healed. Most of the time, though, we expect that if people will get well, it will be through medicine, not in spite of it. And when we pray, we are really asking for peace and courage to accept whatever is going to happen. So, we may believe, but we accept a scientific worldview at the same time and limit how God can act. God can act inside us. God can change the way we feel about others and ourselves. God can forgive our sins and teach us to forgive those who sin against us. God can redeem our souls for heaven. But that's that.

I want to offer a third view for you this morning that takes both of these into account but goes beyond them. Jesus did indeed multiply the loaves and fish. It was a miracle. But what is a miracle?

A miracle is a breakthrough. It reveals the possibilities of nature that we have not yet known. It is contrary to what we have yet known but not contrary to what is yet to be known. God's proper mode of being is future. When we think of God, we should be thinking about how God wants the world to be, not just how the world is. A miracle reveals God drawing the world into God's own abundance instead of God being drawn into the world's scarcity. The world is open to God. A miracle shows us something about God's future and ours.

The feeding of the five thousand is a glimpse of the new heaven and new earth, in which there is always more than enough of everything for everyone. No hunger will be unmet—whether for food or meaning or love.

Evolutionists themselves talk about breakthrough moments when the slow adaptive processes of change seem to take leaps into startling new expressions of life. The birth of human consciousness is one of those. To be human is to be strikingly different from animals in one way: We can go beyond inherited instinct to think. What's more, we can think about thinking. We can contemplate the universe and understand it. We can consider our lives and ponder who we are, how we are made, and why.

Something new happened in the history of the world when a bush burned but was not consumed and God called to Moses from it, binding God and Israel in an adventure of freedom. Something new happened when God became flesh and dwelt among us in Jesus of Nazareth, uniting God to human destiny once and for all. Something new happened the day God raised Jesus from the dead, uniting human beings to divine destiny once and for all.

A miracle is not for the sake of God showing off, though. It's for showing us a path to new life. In this way, we agree that the boy with the loaves and fish is important, too, but not just in that he inspired others to act. The boy cooperated with God in making a miracle possible. Our faith matters. Our gift matters. God doesn't work alone. And if we want to see more miracles in our lives, we might pray for them more, live toward them, and give toward them.

Our nation held its breath in October 1942, when word came that Capt. Eddie Rickenbacker's B-17 Flying Fortress had run out of gas and gone down at sea. For three awful weeks Rickenbacker and his nine-member crew barely survived on three small rafts in the far Pacific. They battled storms. They ran out of food. Sharks up to ten feet long rammed their nine-foot boats. When asked how they were able to endure that experience, Rickenbacker said, "We prayed."

For days they drifted helplessly under the scorching tropical sun. The heat, the hunger, the exhaustion brought Rickenbacker and his young, inexperienced crew to the breaking point. They continued to pray. Were their prayers answered? You have to decide.

When he and his crew were almost at the end of their rope, a seagull flew in from out of nowhere and landed right on Eddie Rickenbacker's head. He caught the bird, and that day he and his crew had food. Not only did they have food for that day; they cut the intestines of the bird into strips of flesh so that they had bait for several more days for the two fishhooks they had. Then came their first rainstorm, and suddenly they had fresh water. The survivors were sustained, and their hopes renewed by that lone seagull, hundreds of miles from land. Two weeks later they were spotted and rescued.

It's said that one member of Rickenbacker's crew, James Whittaker, was an unbeliever. The plane crash didn't change that. Facing death didn't cause him to reconsider his destiny. In fact, Mrs. Whittaker, his wife, said her husband grew irritated with John Bartak, a crewmember who continually read his Bible out loud. But it was one morning after a Bible reading that the seagull landed on Captain Rickenbacker's head. At that moment, Whittaker believed.[15]

Indeed, you have to decide, too. John tells us that those who experienced the miracle of the loaves and fish took it as a sign and believed that Jesus was the prophet of God who is to come into the world. In other words, faith makes the miracle possible, but the miracle makes faith possible, too. In you, too?

---

15 *Dynamic Preaching Sermons*, Third Quarter 2012, King Duncan (ChristianGlobe Networks, Inc., 2012).

5

Dying to See the Light

March 17, 1996
Fourth Sunday in Lent
John 9:1-41

Going about his Father's business, Jesus sees a *man* blind from birth. His disciples see a *blind from birth* man. The difference is seen in the disciples' question. *Rabbi, who sinned to make this man blind, this man or his parents?* They want to turn the man into a theological case study, just as we do when we say: *Why does this "apartment" kid act up in school? Is it her fault or is the family to blame? Why is this family poor, because of their own sin or society's sin? Why does this man have AIDS, because of his sin or someone else's? Why did that child have a birth defect, was the genetic flaw his mother's fault or was there some environmental factor?* The farther you chase down that path, the less likely you ever get round to helping the person. You depersonalize the person and make the person an issue. By asking only why, you deny your opportunity to share in the person's life. Jesus first sees a *who*; the disciples see a *what*. Jesus sees a *who* and asks *what* is to be done; the disciples see a *what* and ask *who* is to blame.

Jesus dodges the question because he thinks it's wrongheaded. *Neither this man nor his parents sinned*, he says. *This man was born blind so that God's works might be revealed in him.* Now of course both the man and his parents had sinned, else their blood was alien green. But the point is that the man's blindness was not a result of anyone's sin in particular. The mystery of illness eludes our categories of explanation, whether those categories be genetic, social, moral, or religious. Jesus does not say that the *cause* is theological. He does not say that God did this to him to make a point. He points to the *purpose* of the blindness. Jesus looks to future possibilities of what is instead of past possibilities of why what is, is. The disciples ask *whence*; Jesus asks *whither*. He says, *There's no time for senseless conversation. We have to work the works of God while it is day, for night is coming. I am the light of the world and my job is to give light, which includes giving sight.*

• So, Jesus spits on the ground and makes mud. And somewhere in the back of our Sunday school memories we ought to call up the file marked "Creation of the World" and recall that God formed humankind out of the dust of the ground. Nothing less is about to happen here. This is no folk medicine; this is new creation by the One through whom all things were created in the beginning. He rubs the mud on the man's eyes and sends him to wash his eyes out with water.

We expect something other from Jesus than this. Don't you want him to do this miracle with a little more class? I mean, couldn't he just close his eyes and think real hard, maybe say a few magic words, do a little David Copperfield, touch him with one finger, sending an electrical charge to his optic nerve? If healing is a spiritual thing, why get down in the mud? Why be so earthy if the power is heavenly? Why water? It's the same question we Baptists get all the time. *If faith is a matter of the heart, why do you have to get into the water? Why baptism? If it's the idea that counts, then a change of mind is what really matters anyway. Why is churchgoing such a big deal? Hard pews, hardheaded sinners in them. Let's have our faith pure, just straight simple ideas.* But that's where we know more than God. God has never been ashamed of creation. The perversion of creation, yes; but not creation. God is Spirit, yes; but God is not opposed to stuff. God made it and called it good.

For heaven's sake (and ours), God became one of us in Jesus. And even if Joan Osborne might have chosen better grammar and a nicer word in her song, she is right in asking, *What if God was one of us, just a slob like one of us?* The Grammy nominated song makes the point that if God had a face and we could see it, we would have to change. We would have to be different. As long as God stays an idea, we can hide. But God is one of us in Jesus. We live in a material world. Any changes inside will have to be matched by changes outside. Just this is what mud and spittle, what water baptism, is about. Faith is other-worldly only in that it doesn't come from this world, but it is this-worldly in that it lives nowhere else.

Well, the man is healed. Can I hear an *amen*? Good, 'cause I can't find one in the text. The man is healed and immediately Jesus disappears until the end of the story, leaving the man to explain to his neighbors, religious leaders, and even his parents, what happened. And not only does he have to tell them what happened, he has to defend the fact that something actually did happen.

The neighbors don't come up to the man and slap him on the back and say, *Man, what's it like to see after all these years? Does the sun hurt your eyes? What's the most beautiful thing you see? What are you going to do now? Let's go have a cold drink and talk it over.* No, they ask if this can be the same guy they were used to seeing begging and bugging them every time they came to his intersection. They cannot imagine that people can change. They've figured him for a lifer loser. Always a blind beggar. He says, *No really, I am the man. This man called Jesus gave me sight, helped me see the light.* So they ask where he is. The man says, *I don't know.*

And isn't this the way it is with all of us to some degree or another? We've had a life-changing, miraculous encounter with Jesus. We are the same and not the same. We no longer fit the categories our buddies had us pegged in. We are different, and our neighbors, people who have known us otherwise, can't celebrate with us. And all we have to offer is to say that Jesus has made the difference. But we can't produce Jesus to prove our point. He's off somewhere. We live between his first coming and second coming. People have to encounter him without seeing him. He is present in spirit, absent in body. He is visibly absent, invisibly present. Only if you have eyes to see him, only if you are willing to believe, can you see him. All we can do is say what has happened to us and who is responsible.

But notice the man was not healed because he had enough faith. Sometimes, for reasons we do not understand, Jesus asked people if they had faith before they were healed. Sometimes he just heals them and then they develop faith. There's no formula in Scripture. So, watch out for those who make you think that if you just have enough faith, God will heal your sick mother. If you just believe hard enough, then God will be freed to work for you. Well, that sure won't hurt, but there's no guarantee.

God's salvation and healing are a mystery. Grace is God's work, not ours. Faith even is God's work, not ours. And, in this case, we see that the healing and the inquisition of the man over time leads the man to greater faith. He starts out calling Jesus a man, moves to calling him a man from God, then a prophet, and by the end of the story he affirms him to be the Son of Man—the final judge of the world.

Well, the neighbors bring the man to the Pharisees to judge the case. The Pharisees ask what has happened, and some of them say that since the man was healed on the Sabbath, Jesus cannot be from God. God would never make a man break the Sabbath, even to do good. Jesus is a sinner and a criminal. To their credit, some of them argue otherwise. They claim a sinner could not have done such a good thing. As always, whenever Jesus is involved, people are divided. The presence of God always creates a crisis. Some are open, others closed. Some see and believe or believe and see, others think they already see and do not believe or already believe and do not see. The man just simply says, *Look, all I know is "I once was lost but now am found, was blind but now I see."*

But the religious leaders could not accept that. Imagine! The man gets his sight and they try to prove he was never really blind at all, just faking it. How resistant we are to change! But see, if the man really was blind and now sees, then they have to accept Jesus themselves. And that means they have to change, too. This is a threat.

So, they call in the man's parents. But they don't stand up for him or for Jesus. They see that this has become a trial, and it is not just Jesus on trial but also any witnesses for the defense. So out of fear they refer the prosecution back to their son. And we see that even family is not always as supportive as we would hope when we are changed by Jesus. You'd think they would be doing back flips, making college plans, take the boy shopping, at least a little sightseeing. But no, they leave him to defend himself. They are more concerned with their own social standing than with celebrating their son's new life.

Recall the man to the stand. *Give God the glory!* they say. *This man who healed you is a sinner.* And, again, the man says, *Look, I don't know what you want from me or him. You're supposed to be the wise ones. You tell me how this could be if it is not from*

God. And they tell him that he is himself such an obvious sinner since he was born blind that he cannot teach them anything about God.

All through this story John uses the word *know* referring to the religious leaders who know so much that they cannot see. The word he uses is not the most common word for "know," though, don't you know?! Instead of *ginosko,* he uses *oida* every time. This word also means *see,* as in "I see what you mean." John's irony: the ones who claim to know don't see at all, they are blind. The one who claims not to know, the man born blind, sees. See?

And John means this to be a warning to us as well as a report on the Jews who refused to believe in him. This story was written down long after the controversy of Christians being expelled from the synagogue. The religious leaders of the church then and now must also be on guard against the same blindness to God's work, John is saying.

I was disgusted this week to read statements made by a Southern Baptist seminary president (Mark Coppenger, Midwestern), a religious leader who will shape the thinking of young ministers. He claimed that Baptists are tragically losing the important idea that all people who do not know Jesus are "bad." I quote: *Lost people are bad people. I hear it again and again: "Listen, he's a good man, he's a good husband, he just doesn't know Jesus." There's no such thing as a good man who doesn't know Jesus. The person who is not saved is in fact the son of the devil, a rebel, hating the light. Now they can mask it and bad men do some good things, but at the core they are bad people ... Now if that sounds mean to you, I don't think it's any meaner than the Bible. I don't want to build my ministry on being nicer than Jesus.*[16]

No danger there! Now who in the story does that voice most sound like? Who in the story was busy hating the light? Who in the story was preoccupied with asserting how bad and sinful the man was? Who in the story missed the sin and blindness in their own life, even though they were supposed to be spiritual guides to the blind?

On the other hand, four men were recently flying through an airport, running late for their plane. In their haste, with bags flailing, they knocked over a table on which some local girl had some things for sale. Being late for their flight, they hurried on, cleared security, and just made the gate before the door closed. But as they walked across the tarmac to the waiting plane, one of them said goodbye to the others and returned to the airport terminal, missing his flight home. He went back to the table they had overturned and was glad he did. He discovered that the girl was blind, and that some of the jars she was selling were broken. He helped as best he could, then said, *Here's fifty dollars to cover the cost of whatever is broken.* As he walked away, the blind girl called after him, *Mister, are you Jesus?*[17]

God grant that the blind see Jesus because of us.

---

16 *Associated Baptist Press* report, 13 March 1996.
17 Paul Wilson, "Imagination and Easter," in *Journal for Preachers,* 19.3:19.

6

God Alone, Not a Lone God

September 14, 1997
Seventeenth Sunday after Pentecost
Deuteronomy 6:4-5; Mark 15:24-39; 1 John 4:7-16

My eighth-grade daughter Cameron asked me to help her with math homework. Atomic numbers. Stuff like, if a period at the end of a sentence contains a trillion atoms, and if the volume of the dot is about 0.00000006 cubic centimeters, what is the approximate size in cubic centimeters of one atom? Child's play, right? Jack Dodgen gave me a book called *Innumeracy: Mathematical Illiteracy and Its Consequences.*[18] Wonder why he gave it to me? The author despairs of the widespread failure of the population to understand basic concepts of numbers and apply them to everyday life. People say things like, *Math was always my worst subject,* as if they're proud of it. You hear someone brag about being *a people person, not a numbers person.* Well, when it comes to trying to make sense of God being one in three and three in one, you've got to be both a people person and a numbers person to get anywhere. But even religion professionals feel incompetent in this one. The numbers make the mind go numb. The divine math defies our numerical logic.

Let's take a different tack and have a go at it biblically. Listen to the passage from Deuteronomy. Actually the passage is about listening. It begins, *Shema, Israel*—Hear, O Israel. Pay attention, is the point. *The Lord is our God, the Lord alone.* Now this is a starting point. Israel's confession of faith is that there is one God, the God of Israel. First commandment, don't you know?! Since there are no other gods, since the God of Israel is the only God there is, don't go making any up yourself to worship. And forget about those Egyptian and Canaanite deities; they're impostors, too. God alone is God.

So far so good. We've got the oneness down pat, right? Not so fast. We've got the oneness down insofar as there is one God over against other gods. But the *Shema* is richer than that. The word translated *alone* in the *Shema* is the Hebrew *echad.* It

18 John Allen Paulos (New York: Hill and Wang, 1988).

means *one*. The phrase is sometimes interpreted *The Lord is our God, the Lord is one.* Now clearly, Judaism has generally seen the word *echad* in the *Shema* as a way of saying "No" to the Christian notion of the Trinity. But even Judaism has said that God's uniqueness, God's being God alone, does not mean that God is closed off from the world. God is open in love to us. In fact, one rabbi has said that God goes out of himself in love to dwell with Israel in exile. God's *Shekinah* presence is with the people in love. So, to say the *Shema* is to pray for God's oneness, to pray that God may be unified, that God will one day be fully together, and this time with us.

Notice right after words about God's unity in the *Shema* is the command to love God in return. They are related: The only way to understand fully the oneness, the unity of God, is to share in it by sharing in God's love. If God's very nature is love, then experience of God's being is tied to the practice of God's love.

Just that is what 1 John says, too. If you want to know God, you must love. Then God's love abides in you and you in God. This love is what moved the Father to send the Son to die for us. And the Spirit is the one who teaches this to us. We sense the distinction of persons in the Godhead when we see the movement of God's love. The Trinity is not so much a math problem; it is a love problem. To understand the Trinity better we don't need most to be better at figuring numbers, we need most to be better at loving people.

This is the very thing I have struggled with this week as Mother Teresa has lain in state. I admire her love for the poor. But I have thought about the poor I meet here in Dallas. Those who stand on street corners begging, those who come to the church with a story you know is all scripted, tried and true, playing the compassion trump card. I want to love the poor, too, but only if they tell the truth and have good character. I want to love them if I don't get taken. I want to love them if they fit my categories of worthiness. I want to love them if they are more like the poor in Calcutta that Mother Teresa loved—the real poor, the worthy poor. But then it dawned on me that maybe the difference is not that the poor in Dallas are not more like the poor in Calcutta, but that I am not more like Mother Teresa. I look for excuses not to help the poor so that my love will not suffer loss; she looked for excuses to love the poor by her willingness to suffer loss as Christ did. I want to understand the poor in theory; she showed you can only love the poor as they are, and only if you are poor as they are. As long as we are unwilling to suffer with them, we will always suffer a lack of understanding of them.

Love goes out of itself, it does not stay closed in on itself. You can't love in theory, you can only love in practice. I don't understand the Trinity better because I would rather be a lone ranger than a sacrificial lover of the world like God. My preference is to be myself by myself, rather than to find myself in relation to others. I hesitate to show you myself, to let you know me deeply, because then you will have a part of my life, and I will have to deal with you more intimately. I would rather model myself after Howard Hughes, the recluse who needed no one. By this view, God's oneness would make God the Hermit of Heaven. But look what happened to the loveless Howard Hughes. He shriveled up and died a lonely and bizarre figure. God on the other hand, refuses to turn in upon himself and separate himself from others.

God's love is shown in God's willingness to die for us in order that we might live. God is not the lonely monarch in the sky we want to be ourselves. And if we are to understand God better, we will have to live ourselves more like God. Which leads to abundant life, not mere existence.

Christians affirm the doctrine of the Trinity because this is the way God reveals himself to us. We overhear Jesus praying to his Father. He is not meditating, he is praying. We watch him driven by the Spirit into the desert to be tempted and fed there by the Spirit, too. We see God with us in our suffering and death through Jesus. The one who claimed to be the Son of God, who said he was "one" with the Father—not identical but one in unity of life and purpose, this one is on the cross crying out to heaven. From this we perceive that God is both in Christ on the cross and not absent from heaven. God is both at the same time. God can be God and human at once, without being a divided self. This is a oneness of being with a distinction of persons.

Look more closely at the Gospel passage. Jesus is hanging on the cross, and he is mocked for saying he is God's Son. The people only think of God in terms of power. If he is God's Son, he should come down from the cross, show that he is incapable of suffering, act like a Son of God ought to act. Instead, he cries out, *My God, my God, why have you forsaken me?* One of the most profound moments in all of salvation history. Jesus speaks our words. He offers our cry. Where is God when we hurt?

Elie Wiesel is a Jewish survivor of the German death camps. In his chilling account of Auschwitz, called *Night*, he draws the picture for us: *The SS hanged two Jewish men and a youth in front of the whole camp. The men died quickly, but the death throes of the youth lasted for half an hour. Where is God? Where is he? someone asked behind me. As the youth still hung in torment in the noose after a long time, I heard the man call again, Where is God now? And I heard a voice in myself answer: Where is he? He is here. He is hanging there on the gallows … .*[19]

Wiesel saw God there in the midst of his suffering. He did so because as hard as it was to conceive how a good God could allow such suffering to take place to those he loved, harder still was the possibility of a loving God remaining aloof from those who suffered. Wiesel knew all the times when God's heart had heard the cries of the children of Israel in Egypt and came running, when God could not tolerate the oppression and wandering lostness of God's people. God had to go to them, be with them in loving power. When those whom God loved suffered, God suffered too, right there along with them.

And just this is what we see on the cross of Christ. God's identification with the world's sin and suffering is so complete, God's willingness to share our pain so profound, that God feels separated from God in that moment. God's love is stretched to the limit of death and beyond. When Jesus dies crying out to God, it is not only the world that cries out to a God it cannot feel, abandoned as it feels; it is the eternal Son of God who cries out to the eternal Father in the common Spirit of love between them. Here is the trinitarian point: God suffers in love for the world. God suffers as a Father who loves the Son but feels his loss in the world's rejection

---

19 Elie Wiesel, *Night* (Farrar, Straus and Giroux, 1969), pp. 75-76.

of love. God suffers as a Son who loves the world so fully that he takes upon himself the weight of its rejection and feels the loss of his Father's eternal joy. God suffers as the Spirit who from all eternity has carried the joy of love from Father to Son and from Son to Father, but now must hold them together only in the suffering love of grief. God suffers with us—God suffers from us—God suffers for us.

When the Roman centurion looked upon the dead Jesus on the cross and said, *Truly this man was God's Son*, he may not have known how right he was. But like Wiesel, he sensed in Jesus' sacrificial death a truth about God that we often miss in all our number games: God's love will go to any length to bring love in return. God is in the cross of Christ as a suffering God because God is love. God is the lover. God is the beloved. God is the love itself. Father, Son, and Holy Spirit.

The great North African St. Augustine saw this truth about the Trinity. If God is love, as 1 John says, then love needs an object to love. God is love, as the Father loves the Son and the Son the Father. If it sounds like the Spirit, as the love they share, is just an "it" and not the third person of the Trinity, keep in mind that the problem again may be more in us than in God. C. S. Lewis answers that God is such a living and throbbing love, such a pulsating activity, such a life, in other words, that love has often been called a divine dance. Love is such a dynamic spirit between two persons, it can be talked of as something real in itself. What grows out of the union of God, the joint life of Father and Son is so real, so profound, so alive, it cannot be thought of as a thing at all. It can only be described in personal terms.[20]

The Holy Spirit is a living, acting personality in God along with the Father and Son. Together, only together and always together, they have been, are, and will be the one God. *Echad*, one. The one God alone, but not a lone God. God is God as a divine community of love.

And we can perceive this by various analogies in our world. When a man and woman take their vows and become, as the Bible says, one flesh, they do not cease to be two persons. But their unity is a something much greater and richer than their separateness. The more they love each other, *for better for worse*, the more they understand the oneness that is theirs together. In them this oneness is imperfect, but in God it is so perfected that the three are truly one in unity. When the Chicago Bulls work together well, they are one unit on the floor though five in personalities. They are in unity, close harmony. When a choir sings with their many voices, each has a part to sing, each a voice to raise. But as they blend together in one song, they are harmoniously one group. They are one choir, not many. When the church acts like the church, we are many people with various gifts but one in life and mission, one in Spirit.

In each case the math is not pure numbers work. Same thing with God. To think of God as triune requires that you be a people person as well as a numbers person. For with God, the math works like this: Father, Son, and Holy Spirit are together God. Three persons, one God. God alone, but not a lone God. 1 + 1 + 1 = 1!

---

20 *Mere Christianity* (Macmillan, 1952) pp. 152-53.

7

Christlikeness

November 25, 2007
Christ the King Sunday
Colossians 1:11-29

Today we crown the church's year of worship by crowning again the Christ that rules our lives as King of kings and Lord of lords. The whole cycle of our worship across the year tracks the key markers in the life of Jesus the Christ. Advent looks forward to his coming—his first coming by remembrance and his second coming by hope. Christmas is the shortest season of all—twelve days of Christmas, right? Epiphany celebrates Christ being made known to all the world. Lent invites us to follow Jesus on his way to the cross to learn again how and why love led him to suffering and death. Easter opens not only Christ's grave, but also our grave hearts. The weight of sin and death is lifted and we can laugh again, even breathe again. And speaking of breath, Pentecost tells us that Christ has put the life back into us by the gift of the Holy Spirit. The Spirit is the wind of God that renews all things, including those of us who have had the wind knocked out of us by all the blows of the world. Then through the dog days of summer and cool nights of fall we find Christ reigning in the church and ordering our lives during what we call Ordinary Time, when nothing much special is happening—except of course the very miracles of life right under our noses every day.

In his opening lines of greeting to the church at Colossae, St. Paul prays that they (and we) will joyfully give thanks to God the Father for the beloved Son, who is the agent of our salvation and hope of eternal life. And then he proceeds to compose or to quote a lovely poem to Christ, which may even have been an early Christian hymn. I want us to consider the beauty of those words about Christ today as a way of offering gratitude to God on this weekend of Thanksgiving. Preaching always has to do with the head, the heart, and the hands—with thinking, feeling, and doing; with the True, the Beautiful, and the Good—sometimes one more than the others. Most times in church we focus on the True and the Good, on what is right and what should be done about it. Today, I want us simply to enjoy and meditate upon the beauty of Christ by turning our thoughts of him like a diamond in the sun.

Christ is the image of the invisible God, Paul says. Whatever God is like, Christ is like. In Christ the fullness of God was pleased to dwell. The word for image in the Greek is *eikon*, which we translate into English as icon. Now, Baptists aren't big on icons, although we've made a preacher or two into icons from time to time. We've done that in Dallas more than once, don't you know?! We have always been afraid of turning icons into idols, worshipping the thing itself instead of the thing signified. But the Orthodox Church—whether Greek or Russian or some other national version of it—has a rich history of seeing through the surface of an icon to a deeper realm. If you meditate upon the face of Christ in a painting, for instance, you are being drawn not to the visible oil and canvas, but through it to the invisible experience of the living Christ.

We have a powerful modern example of icons now with the advent of computers. If you go to your computer desktop, you will find an array of icons. Each one invites you to click on it and enter a whole new world that you would not have been able to access if you did not go through the icon. Click on the icon and an extraordinary program opens up before you that has been organized for you—databases and photo shops and word processors that will help you make sense of numbers or pictures or words.

To say that Christ is the image of the invisible God is to say that by entering into relationship with him, you are going beyond him to God. You enter into the wondrous world of God's creative life. You become part of what God is doing behind the scenes in what we call the kingdom of God.[21]

We are fond of saying as Paul does later that God was in Christ, that the fullness of God was pleased to dwell in Christ. But the converse is also true: If Christ is the perfect image of God, then Christ is not only like God; God is like Christ. The late Bishop of Durham, England, Michael Ramsay, put it this way: *God is Christlike and in [God] there is no unChristlikeness at all.* Nice. Big thought there. And the reason it's so big is that each of us to some degree or another fears that Jesus is one thing and God another.

Like the little boy who came home from Sunday school. His mother asked what he learned. He learned about God and Jesus, he said. And when his mother asked what he thought of God and Jesus, he replied: *I think I like Jesus a lot, but I'm not so sure about his Father.* Well, if you worry at all about that, St. Paul and Bishop Ramsay (not to mention St. John and the others) want to assure you that if you have seen one, you have seen the other. If Jesus is love personified, if Jesus is forgiving and gracious, if Jesus is patient and merciful, then God is nothing else. God is not angry and vengeful and demanding, as if Jesus and God play good cop, bad cop. They have the selfsame character. So whatever beauty you see in Christ, you can celebrate the beauty of God at the same time.

---

21 Thanks for this analogy to Fred Anderson in his sermon, *Image of the Invisible,* Day 1, https://day1.org/weekly-broadcast/5d9b820ef71918cdf200267a/image_of_the_invisible.

But why should it be so that in this one man, Jesus, all of the beauty of God should show forth? Many people in the world object to the idea that one human being should be elevated above all others. The whole idea of Paul's is objectionable—that the whole created world was made in and through Christ and that even now it holds together only by his powerful presence. But let's look a little deeper.

When the Hebrews thought about how the world was put together, they believed it had to be God's doing, which meant there must have been personal agency. But, in order to protect against God being trapped in the creation with us, they personified the Word of God and the Wisdom of God as if they were God's two hands making the world. God spoke and God shaped the world through God's Word and God's Wisdom. Similarly, when the Greeks came to see how orderly and rational the world appears to be, they spoke of the *logos*, the logic or reason of the natural world that can be observed. This *logos* is also in every person, making it possible to comprehend the world.

And when physicists today contemplate the remarkable dependability of the universe, they use words like the LAW of gravity or the LAW of thermodynamics. Although many scientists want to say that things simply are as they are without going into why they are as they are, many admit that the odds of having such a beautiful universe in which human beings would be able to evolve enough not only to exist but also to grasp the world as it is—well, that's just too unlikely to conceive if it were not supposed to be this way. This is called the Anthropic Principle: the idea that the world has developed in a certain way for the purpose of being fit for human beings.

Now, whether you are talking about the Hebrews or the Greeks or modern science, can you see that if one human being came along that embodied fully the order and beauty of creation, if one human being were to have come on the scene of history that by his life and death seemed to bring order out of chaos, peace out of conflict, and meaning out of meaninglessness, wouldn't that suggest that perhaps the whole of the purpose of creation is met in this one man? If the world is made in such a way that human beings might develop, why not one man who perfectly embodies what is possible? This is what Paul is saying, I think. God's idea of creation in the beginning finds perfection in Christ. He is the true image of God and the firstborn of creation.

It's too weak to say, as we often do, that beauty is in the eye of the beholder. Something is beautiful because it matches up closely with the deep structure of reality. A sculpture is beautiful not because a critic says it is, but rather a critic says it is because it is beautiful—that is, because its proportions are somehow right. Its line and symmetry and perspective are accurate. It matches the way the world really is. A film is beautiful, or a novel, because the story makes sense and the characters are lifelike. Likewise, Christ is beautiful because we see in his words and deeds that he matches the way God intended the world and made it. He fulfills it all.

The poet Gerard Manley Hopkins captures why such truth means that we can go back beyond the way a person acts to who the person is. In his poem *As Kingfishers Catch Fire*, he says that all living things act according to their nature. They cry out

What I do is me: for that I came. And he gives the example of a righteous person. Listen. *The just man justices; / Keeps grace: that keeps all his goings graces; / Acts in God's eye what in God's eye he is— / Christ. For Christ plays in ten thousand places, / Lovely in limbs, and lovely in eyes not his / To the Father through the features of men's faces.*

The first place he played in our understanding was through his own face in his earthly life. And because Hopkins is right that we can know who he is through what he does, it drives us backward all the way to God and the beginning of creation, so that we can say that he stands at the head of creation even before he showed up in Bethlehem two millennia ago. This is like celebrating the Queen's birthday: She wasn't the queen when she was born, but because she was destined to become queen, we count her so from the beginning. We can go forward, too, and see that he is in charge of the future because he is the firstborn of the dead. He is the head of the new creation also. He is living among us still. So now in every person that acts according to the manner of Christ, he may be seen. And he may be seen because the beauty of creation shines through the face of that person. Thus, Christ plays in ten thousand places.

The sweet, almost fable-like new movie *August Rush* gives us a picture of this. An orphan boy is the product of the union of two musical parents. Neither parent knows he is alive for the first twelve years of his life, since the mother's father secretly forged her signature without her consent after his birth in order to protect her career. She thought the baby had died. The father never knew he had a son. The boy always felt like he heard the music of the spheres in his head, as if the world was alive in song through every sound. He believed that if he could someday, somehow learn to play and compose music so that others could hear what he heard, somehow, they would hear, too, and would find him. He succeeds in ways beyond his imagining, and, in the process, he brings people joy and brings people together at the same time—his parents included. At one point in the film, August is asked what he wants to be when he grows up. *Found,* he says.

And I wonder if that isn't what Christ wants more than anything else—to be found. And not just in the church, but everywhere and in everything and by everyone.

Jesus heard the music of creation to the point where those who knew him could not help but say that he himself is the music, the music was made by him and continues through him even now. All that is beautiful, then, is beautiful because of its Christlikeness. Christ is beautiful. Christ is Beauty. And that is the greatest thing to be thankful for.

8

The Secret Joy of Angels

Watch and listen to "The Secret Joy of Angels" by following this link or scanning the QR code with your phone: youtu.be/djNogOb4MUg.

September 15, 2013
Seventeenth Sunday after Pentecost
Luke 15:1-10

I think I may finally be getting the hang of this titling thing: The Secret Joy of Angels. Now if I could only turn the sermon into a book, you could pick it up on the table at Sam's Club, and I could make enough money to endow our pastoral residency program. I mean seriously, this is the kind of thing American book buyers can't resist. Everyone loves to be in on a secret, don't you know?! And especially on secrets that give you an edge on the people who live next door. But I'm afraid the ones who are laughing the most are the angels who are snickering up their wings at this. Some of them may be sitting right out here in the pew this morning because you know they're known to do that sort of thing. If any of you angels are here today, be warned: I've got my eye out for your sly smiles.

All right then, before I get to the secret joy of angels part, let's look at what Luke has to say that Jesus had to say. Luke 15 is the heart of Luke's Gospel. There's a lot of Luke that you'll also find in Mark and Matthew, and some in John, but this is uniquely Luke, and vintage Luke. It starts out with Jesus being criticized by the religious leaders for eating and drinking with sinners. All the time with the criticizing! Luke's Jesus is always pushing boundaries, living close to the edge of respectability, hanging around morally questionable people. But the real rub is this: Luke says Jesus welcomes sinners and eats with them. It's one thing to call sinners to repentance from afar, keeping yourself clean in the process. It's another thing altogether to welcome sinners and eat with them. To do that, you run the risk of becoming one of them.

If you stop to think about it, Christians claim that God has done that very thing—risked becoming one of us. God could have remained distant and removed from a sinful creation. God could have protected God's holiness by steering clear of those who would contaminate the purity of God's divinity. Instead, God held nothing back.

While we were yet sinners, Christ died for the ungodly. The righteous for the unrighteous.

There is wisdom to God's ways that often eludes us. Behind these parables in Luke 15 are two ways to look at holiness that compete in any religious community. The first is represented by the Pharisees and scribes who criticize Jesus for welcoming sinners and eating with them. They have plenty of Scripture on their side, and in my experience, Christian Pharisees and scribes are quick to quote Scripture to back up their accusations about my worldly behavior or liberal ideas. Be ye holy as the Lord your God is holy, says Leviticus. 1 Peter quotes the same verse in calling for Christian discipline. Paul goes to the root of the Hebrew word for holiness, *qodesh*, which means to cut or separate. He tells the Corinthians as much by loosely quoting the Old Testament: *Come out from them, and be separate from them, says the Lord, and touch nothing unclean; then I will welcome you.*

Those of us who have grown up in earnest Evangelical Christian families and churches have been breastfed on this understanding of holiness. We have heard the argument of the Pharisees and scribes adopted by our mothers and preachers in order to protect our holiness. We have heard Paul's words that bad company corrupts good character, and we've been told that we need to stay away from certain people because of negative peer pressure.

But think of what that makes us over time. I have counseled with more people than I can tell you across the years who have gotten it into their heads that they are not welcome in church because they are sinners. And that's not just true of other churches. We also pride ourselves on being an open and welcoming church, but I can tell you about people who have come among us and gone from us because they have felt the stares, heard the whispers, and sensed that they would never be good enough in the eyes of some of us to be fully and openly themselves as followers of Jesus.

I was once told some years ago by a member who is no longer here that a couple whose sin happened too publicly in our community meant that we should not welcome them more than to just sit in a pew, because our church's reputation was at stake. What would people think of us if we made it seem that we not only welcomed sinners but also ate with them? That's what eating with them means, you understand—enjoying them and accepting them. And then I was told that it would be different if they moved away from these parts and a church accepted them there. Well, yes, that would be different, wouldn't it?

That's a kind of holiness that keeps its distance. And that's the very thing Jesus challenges here.

So, to the parables. There are three of them in a row in Luke 15: the so-called parable of the lost sheep, the lost coin, and the lost son—better known as the prodigal son. We read only the first two today, but I will bring in the third to round things out. But remember they are all about Jesus answering his critics for being too chummy with sinners.

Let's look first at this idea of lostness. Again, it's going to take some adjustment to our assumptions. Many of us grew up with the idea that everyone is lost without Jesus, that our natural state of being is sinful and we are all of us therefore bound for hell unless we repent and become children of God. Oddly, that's not really a Baptist way of looking at things. We believe that babies are born from sinful parents, but that doesn't make them guilty sinners themselves until they join the rest of us—as they always do—by their own free will and choice. Babies are safe with God before they need to be saved by God. So, we dedicate our babies; we don't baptize them. But somewhere along the way we got to thinking of everyone who has not made a profession of faith in Christ as being an outsider and in an excluded state in relationship to God. Yet the very word *lost* suggests that they were first in relationship to God and have only lost their way and need to be brought back.

Our parables say as much. A sheep is already a part of the fold but wanders off. The wandering off does not make the sheep anything but still a part of the shepherd's fold. The coin is lost, and, my goodness, there's the one that really makes the point: The coin has no wandering will of its own. When it's hiding under the bed or wherever it was misplaced, it didn't switch owners by being lost. In fact, the owner is the one who should be faulted, not the coin! The prodigal son chooses to leave his father and take his inheritance, and then he comes to believe that the relationship is forever changed. He thinks that the only way he can go home again is as a slave, not a son. But he never stops being his father's son, even if his holier-than-thou elder brother would like his father to believe that.

Here we see something about the kind of holiness that is at the center of God's heart. God's love is unconditional. God's purity is God's untainted and unmixed love. We may try to exclude ourselves, but in the eyes of God we each of us and all of us belong to God. Christ didn't come to change our status with God; Christ came to redeem us from our sense of lostness about our true identity. He came to bring us to our senses, to take us home to our true selves, to reunite us with our Father in heaven, who never turned his back on us.

Whether we nibbled our way away from the pasture of God unthinkingly like the lost sheep, or we never knew we were lost at all because it never occurred to us or we didn't have the capacity to know it (like the lost coin), or we willfully went into the foreign country and wasted our life like the prodigal—lost is lost. And yet lost does not mean being left. Even if you run from God, you cannot hide. God is coming after you. That's the gospel truth. We see the character of God in the characters of the shepherd, the woman, and the father. Each of them acts shamelessly and recklessly in pursuit of the lost.

Take the shepherd. Does it make any business sense to leave behind ninety-nine sheep that are hanging together to search for one that is lost? By the time he gets back, what are the odds all ninety-nine are all still there? What are the odds that wolves have gotten to some? But God is pictured here as being relentless in pursuit of every last one of us who strays. And the woman: Aren't you glad we have God pictured as a woman? She tosses her whole house in search of the coin. She could be content with nine silver coins, but she can't sleep until every last one is accounted for.

As for the father in the prodigal story, this is trickier in the way that human beings are trickier than sheep and coins. It seems at first that the father doesn't go searching for the lost son, that he keeps his dignity and waits for the boy to repent. But oddly, Jesus talks about a sheep and a coin that are found as sinners who repent. But when it comes to the lost son, there is no flourish at the end about the joy of sinners who repent. Instead, the boy is said to have been dead and to have come to life—lost and found.

What's happening here is interesting. The prodigal comes to his senses in the pigsty and goes home. We don't know that he was sorry for his sin; he may well have been doing his same old looking-out-for-number-one con on the old man. But the father will have none of it. Though he honors his son's wishes to be on his own, he never disowns him. And when the boy tries to make his speech about being an unworthy slave, the father slays the fatted calf and throws a party. At which point the elder brother is angry with the father. And for what? For welcoming a sinner and eating with him. Full circle.

Listen, the great fourth-century doctor of the church, Athanasius of Alexandria, said of God's decision to come to us in Jesus: *He became what we are that we might become what he is. And if we are to become what he is, then we need his definition of holiness, not ours.*

Holiness ultimately means usefulness. It means fitness for a purpose. An athlete is not fit for fitness' sake but for the sake of playing the game well. I can keep my golf clubs really clean by leaving them in the garage, but they are supposed to be clean so that they are useful when they hit the ball and slice up sod. Too often the church thinks of keeping itself holy by what it doesn't do—and that usually means not getting closely involved with people who behave the way we think is unseemly. But we should be defining holiness by what we do, by getting involved in the world of sinners and calling them to join us in our common vocation of glorifying God in the world.

This is the secret joy of angels. Every time a sinner repents, heaven rejoices. And every time religious people who don't think they need to repent understand that a life of repentance is the vocation to rescue the perishing, angels rejoice. Angels don't rejoice when human beings act like angels. Angels rejoice when human beings act like human beings made in the image of God. Angels rejoice when they see the people of God embrace people of God who don't yet know they are people of God. In fact, I think I see a few smiles out there right now, because some of you are getting it. There may be a few angels here after all.

9

Meant to Be

Watch and listen to "Meant to Be" by following this link or scanning the QR code with your phone: youtu.be/ZjVe_JXNhro. Sermon begins at 26:20.

July 15, 2018
Eighth Sunday after Pentecost
Ephesians 1:3-14

The world held its collective breath this week as we all followed the harrowing rescue of the twelve young teenage soccer players and their assistant coach who were trapped deep inside a cave in Thailand. They were all saved. They are all alive and doing well. But that outcome did not seem foreordained.

The boys left their soccer practice on their bicycles and convinced their coach to go on a cave adventure. This is the wrong time of year to do such a thing. It's monsoon season in Southeast Asia, don't you know?! And there were warning signs posted that they ignored, the way young people do with their intrepid sense that they are immortal. Once they found themselves deep in the cave, the rains drove the waters into the cave, flooding the treacherous pathways and blocking their exit. They could not save themselves.

For days their frantic parents worried, while professional rescue groups failed to find where they were trapped. Finally, a British expert convinced authorities they were looking in the wrong places. At long last, they located the cold and hungry trapped explorers. Things only got worse as their oxygen was running out and every possible rescue plan seemed impossible.

One Thai Navy SEAL died in the process. (By the way, who knew the Thai military had Navy SEALs?) The man had been transporting oxygen tanks to the cave hostages and tragically his own tank ran out. Hundreds of pumping machines lowered the waters to no avail and all other ideas such as drilling escape holes into the cave had been ruled out; time was running out. They finally came to the moment of truth when they had to try, as they said, "to save some or lose them all."

The creativity and courage required to get these boys and their coach to safety is something we will all learn more about in documentaries and made-for-TV movies. But thanks be to God, they were all saved in the end. The world exhaled and praised the rescuers. We saw photographs of the boys together in the hospital, signaling their gratitude.

Those boys clearly violated the rules. They trespassed and transgressed. They could have been left for dead in their sins, so to speak. The world could have viewed them as foolish youths and let the wages of sin be death, teaching others by their folly what happens when you sin. But no one was willing to treat them as expendable. They were and are precious human beings who crossed a boundary they shouldn't have crossed. But getting them reunited with their parents and giving them a future with hope was everything.

I wonder what they will say and do in the years ahead as they reflect upon being saved? I can't wait to hear.

The whole thing made me think afresh about salvation and what it cost God to redeem us. It made me think about whether we Christians have lost our sense of having been lost and saved. How do we talk about it? Do we even understand how precarious our predicament was that led to God moving heaven and earth by moving from heaven to earth to save us? Do we realize what love must have motivated God to act in such a dramatic way, giving his only begotten Son to die that we might be saved?

When we start to read the first chapter of Ephesians, we hear the writer expressing gratitude in extraordinary words for those early Christians who hadn't forgotten what the only begotten had done for them. You heard it read a few minutes ago, but if you could read it in the original Greek language, the difference would be striking to your ear. You see, these eleven verses are really one long run-on breathless sentence. It is a great eulogy, a blessing of God for what God has done for them.

These Ephesian Christians understood that they had been lost and were found, they had been rescued by the God who had loved them in a way that truly astonished them. How could it be that God had loved them so much that Christ would die for them? How could it be that they should enjoy the spiritual blessings of being adopted into the family of God and knowing that their future would also include the inheritance of the saints?

None of this could have been expected. The way the Roman world was organized in that time didn't make any of these Christians in the churches around Ephesus in Asia Minor assume they were special to anyone or deserving of being redeemed. For one thing, the church that was all Jewish at first had welcomed these Gentiles as brothers and sisters in Christ. That was certainly not a foregone conclusion.

The Jews as a people had once been rescued from slavery in Egypt. They had been considered less than human by their Egyptian oppressors. They were mistreated and used as manual laborers. They were considered bodies to be exploited in a foreign land, not souls to be cherished. God had delivered them unexpectedly and adopted them as a beloved people of God's own choosing.

So, it wouldn't be a surprise to Jews that God would remember them again in their suffering under Roman occupation and send a deliverer out of love. And it shouldn't have surprised them that God would extend that deliverance to the Gentiles and open the membership of Israel to these people whom they once thought of as dirty pagans unfit for inclusion among God's holy people. Jews, among all the peoples on earth, had been commanded by God to treat outsiders with kindness and dignity, no matter how unclean they considered them to be. But full inclusion without demanding them first to change and become like them in ways like circumcision and keeping kosher, that was a bridge too far.

But we all tend to do that, don't we? Instead of remembering that our own salvation was a surprising gift in the first place that we didn't deserve, we take it for granted now and focus on how underserving others are of the very love and grace that was shown to us.

The other surprise for these Gentiles in and around Ephesus was in how they should be adopted into God's holy family with all the rights and privileges of legitimate children of God. They had two fields of understanding for all this. First, Judaism; but then also Roman society. Roman citizenship was coveted status. You were entitled to legal and commercial privileges not accorded to aliens. But Roman society was based upon a system of blessing that derived from your class status. To receive maximum blessing and favors, you had to be a full citizen as a free male. But even then, everything depended upon your cooperating with the benefactor structure of things. People above you would grant you blessings or privileges in direct proportion to your gratitude and praise of them. If you withheld your praise of them and gratitude to them, you could be denied blessings, because the benefactor had the power to give or withhold.

St. Augustine illustrated his frustration with this system when he bemoaned the fact that when he was a professor of rhetoric at the University of Milan, he was expected from time to time to deliver speeches of praise for the emperor. *In a speech to the emperor,* he said, *I had to tell many lies and be approved by people who knew I was telling them.* This was just considered normal behavior, to have people telling the benefactor how wonderful he was and what an honor it was to be in his service.

Well, these Gentile Christians, Roman citizens all, did not waste their breath praising the emperor; they went over his head. They understood that Caesar was not really Lord and could not save. The whole system had been upended. They praised the God and Father of Jesus Christ who had given them all things out of love, rather than out of a need for their worship. All this was astonishing to them. All things were theirs, and they did nothing for it.

Paul even says that this is the way God had always intended it. They—we, all of us, you too, and every living being past, present, and future—had been chosen by God in Christ from before the foundation of the world. There's that sneaky interesting phrase—"before the foundation of the world." And along with it, in the same breathless blessing, he uses other words like "God's will," "God's plan," and "destined." This is important.

We were all of us meant to be included all along. God didn't start out choosing some and not others until having a change of heart and finally letting some of the rest of us get in on the blessings of heaven. Neither did God choose some for salvation and others for damnation, although that's been an unfortunate claim of the religious righteous for ages.

The Jewish Essenes thought that way about things, as did the Protestant reformer John Calvin. Each believed that God had decided before all creation to save some and not others. They were among the saved, of course, and those not of their tribe were the lost.

Ephesians talk about the church as an inclusive community in Christ. Christ is the head of the church, and the one in whom all the saved are saved. The more the church consists of different kinds of people who previously felt excluded, the more we bear witness to God's amazing grace.

But this "meant to be" doesn't just extend backwards; it stretches forward, too. We were all meant to be included in the family of God from the beginning of time and we are all "meant to be" mature and honorable members of God's family to the end of time. Privilege and responsibility go hand in hand in the Christian life.

We are meant to be a people who praise God for our being included and who join God's mission to the world of including others. This is our holy task.

My father-in-law, Bill O'Brien, reminded me of the words of W. O. Carver this week. Carver was a missiologist who liked to remind his Baptist kin that the church doesn't have a mission for God; God has a mission for the world and we just join it.

Which means that if God has chosen the whole world in Christ—no exceptions—then we are not permitted to get into the business of sorting who's in and who's out, who's deserving and who's undeserving, who gets forgiven and who doesn't, who gets to join our church and who doesn't. The church's job is to proclaim this good news in word and deed. We are to sing God's praises and invite others to feel the astonishing grace of being chosen and saved and blessed alongside those who already know it.

If you are here today (or reading this sermon any time) and wonder what God thinks of you, quit wondering. God loves you—Every|Body, as our church sign says out front. God has saved you in Jesus Christ. If you feel unworthy, all the better. It should make you grateful and want to live up to it and into it.

I've been thinking about what those boys went through for twenty-one days in that dark cave. I've wondered what it might have been like if only some were saved, and some were left. Thank God they were all saved. Thank God those rescuers cared so much for every single one of them that they stopped at nothing—even one giving his life—until they were all saved. Thank God. It's almost as if it were meant to be. Amen.

10

Until We Find Our Place

August 5, 2007
Tenth Sunday after Pentecost
John 14:1-6

Where are you from? It's one of our questions, the kind that we ask when getting to know someone. We figure it tells a lot about the person. Like when you hear my father talk and it clicks for you that I'm from New York. *Oh, well, that explains a lot,* you say. Same as it explains a lot when Bruce McIver used to drop his g's, as in singin' or preachin', and you knew he was from a small town in North Carolina. Regionalism is real. Where you are from doesn't mean everything but suggests certain things. We are not complete products of where we grew up, but place does shape us.

God put the first people in a place. Eden. Center of the world. When God cast them from their place, the world was off-center. They were displaced. Not just homeless, but eccentric, literally. Sent off to search forever for what they lost— home, Eden, their Place.

And that is our lot, too. Some of you remember Foy Valentine. Foy was a Baptist statesman. He died just a couple of years ago in Dallas, but he grew up in Van Zandt County. He once wrote: *As Greenwich in London is the bearing point from which all modern latitudinal and longitudinal measurements and orientations are reckoned the wide world over, so our Place was the only Greenwich I knew anything about from my Exodus from Edgewood ... Place is very special in helping you know who you are!*

It's harder for some people. Like when I ask that 'where are you from' question of, say, a couple engaged to be married, I sometimes get sort of a vacant stare from one of them. I usually know why. Military brat. Moved around a bunch. No sense of place. Could have been the kid of a Methodist minister, too. But even for the rest of us, our society has become so mobile that we are losing our sense of place, our particular piece of dirt that is the intersection of our worlds.

When she was thirteen, I took my now married daughter Cameron to New York, where I grew up. It was just a dad and daughter trip. (I did the same with son Rhett and daughter Jillian, too, when they got to that age. I recommend the experience.) We took the ferry to Staten Island and drove up Todt Hill to where I grew up. Strange feeling. It had been a few years for me. Twenty-some years since I had lived there. It was all grown up; like me, I guess. Which may account for why it seemed smaller. It was really big when I was a kid—the street, the neighborhood, the house. The house was strangest of all. Two owners, maybe three, removed from when it was our place. Now it's hardly recognizable. They cut the roof off and raised it one story. Pushed the sides out. Pulled down the post and rail fence with the rose bushes. They changed everything. I recognized a spruce tree. That was it, pretty much. That was my place. My father and grandfathers had built it together when I was three. I mowed the grass there. I played all over that place. Somebody gets the mail now at 76 Copperleaf Terrace, but it's not my Place anymore.

Almost eighteen years into our relationship together here, I realize my world has shifted again. After seventeen of those years in one house, we are now in a new one. I used to turn right out of the parking lot; now I turn left. I am still in transition.

Of course, transition is just what being displaced is all about. And we experience it in all kinds and ever-increasing ways. Used to be you could count on working for a good firm for your whole career, get the gold watch and the pension plan and read the stock market returns. Nowadays you might not only change companies several times, you might even change careers.

I was talking to Allen Walworth on the day he resigned as pastor of Park Cities Baptist Church ten years ago. I told him I never thought he would only be a transitional pastor. To which he replied, *Is there any other kind? No matter how long you are someplace, that place will go on without you at some point.* And he's right. Bruce was a thirty-year transitional pastor and I have been the same for nearly eighteen. Neither of us can claim pride of place. It will all change.

Some of you know this transitional feeling, this constant out-of-place-ness. You knew your place in grade school and now you will have to find your place all over again in junior high. Junior high to high school, high school to college, college to the workforce. And it doesn't stop there. Singleness to marriage, parenting children to parenting your parents, maybe marriage to singleness again, work to retirement, from your house to assisted living, life to death. Giving up your sense of place or especially having it taken from you against your will, as in a divorce or layoff, is an unwelcome grief. You feel like you are being kicked out of Eden even if you are not the one who grabbed for the forbidden fruit.

I remember being with Norma Lee, visiting her father in a health care facility. His physical distress was spiritual, too. He knew how out-of-place he was in that bed. As we said the 23rd Psalm together, he said how he longed for that to be true for him. To be with God, in the house of the Lord forever. He knew he couldn't go back, he could only go forward. He was looking for his place with God. It reminded me of Frederick Buechner's words in his book *Longing for Home*: "We carry inside us a vision of wholeness that we sense is our true home that beckons us."

And that is just what Jesus is trying to teach his disciples in John 14. Jesus has learned to think of his place not in Nazareth, or with his earthly family, or even with his closest friends. He understands that his place is not here. He is going to his place. But the disciples have left everything to follow him. They have left their family places and slept under the stars with him who said, *Foxes have holes and birds of the air have nests, but the Son of man has no place to lay his head.* They are feeling disoriented, dislocated, unsure. So Jesus assures them.

He tells them to trust him. He is going to prepare a place for them and will come again and take them to himself. Back of this is the Jewish wedding custom of a bridegroom who goes off to his father's house to add a room on or build another place altogether. The work is not finished until the groom's father says so. And not even the groom, let alone the bride, knows when that will be. The bride has to wait and trust the groom that he is really preparing a place for them and not just going off forever. This transition time is agony in the waiting, but necessary. She has to trust his love. There is no other way.

In the magical movie *Contact*, based upon the novel by the late astronomer Carl Sagan, the hardboiled scientist played by Jody Foster is contacted by a world beyond the senses. She has to learn that some things cannot be proven and tested and measured. Like belief in God, like her father's love, like whether she is believable when she tries to tell a disbelieving world that there is both a world beyond our space-time horizons and a way to get there and back. No conclusive proof, only trust.

When you are feeling out of place in your life, you ought as a Christian to see this as a necessary and spiritual state of affairs, rather than as a sign of doom. It is an opportunity for you to get unhooked from the dangerous ways we get attached to this world. Jesus spent much of his ministry telling us not to allow ourselves to become too settled. *Unless you are willing to leave father and mother, jobs, and place* (I paraphrase), *unless you are able to put your hand to the plowshare and not look back, you cannot be my disciple.* And what he means by that is that you cannot find your place in the future with him, the only place that is lasting and worth settling down to, unless you let go of the death grip that other places have on you in this world.

Life is a great journey from beginning to end. That is the very nature of life. We can try to deny it, we can fight it, we can try to sink concrete piers deep into the ground to keep us moored to one place or one time of life, but sooner or later, the earth will move under our feet. The tidal wave of change is the nature of the day, and only if we get on the surfboard and ride it out will we know the true thrill of it all.

My friend and Croatian native Miroslav Volf is one of the brightest lights in theology today. He took the pledge of allegiance to become a citizen of these United States on Good Friday ten years ago. The irony was not lost upon him. But his in-laws sent him a card of congratulations that reminded him of his rightful homelessness. The quotation was from the early second-century church, *Epistle of Mathetus to Diognetus: "As citizens, Christians share all things with others, and yet endure all things as foreigners. Every foreign land is to them as their native country, and every land of their birth as a land of strangers ... They pass their days on earth, but they are citizens of heaven."*

Ultimately our deep need for a place of our own is met in heaven. Heaven is our place. *This world is not my own, I'm just a passin' through. If heaven's not my home, O, Lord, what will I do?* You know the song. Now some people can be so heavenly minded they are no earthly good. I grant you that. And some people can live so much for later that they miss the now. No question. But Mother Teresa had it right when she said: *All the way to heaven is heaven.* Jesus said as much. *I am the way. You know the way because you know me.*

The most unusual thing happened as our family was driving to Louisville for the CBF meeting some years ago. Along the road from Little Rock to Memphis to Nashville, I realized someone was following us. Every time I changed lanes, this car would stay with me. The more I thought of it, the more I figured, well, this guy just likes following me because I like to go so slow, don't you know?! He figures he'll be safe trailing me. Well, after a few hours of this, we had to get gas and make a potty stop. So, I put on my blinker and waved at him good-bye, but sure enough, he followed us off the exit and right into the gas station. We got out of our cars and I said "Hello, sure good to have a traveling mate." He smiled and asked where we were going. Turns out he was going to D.C., where he worked at Walter Reed hospital. I asked him if he wanted to join us for dinner in Nashville. He did. So, there we were, the grubby-looking, travel weary Masons, and a thirty-something African American stranger piling into a booth at Outback Steakhouse. We had a good visit, found out he was an orphan, adopted by a couple in Arkadelphia. His adoptive parents were now dead and he only had two sisters. No other family. No sense of place. He latched on to us and we to him. We looked together for a place to stay that night, and when we parted, we exchanged addresses and all that. We stayed in touch for a while but have lost touch now.

Go figure. All the way to heaven. We are all looking for experiences of home on our way to Home. We find our place not so much in real estate, but in the people we travel with from place to place. Which is what I felt as I was showing my daughter the place I grew up. It wasn't my place anymore. But then I looked at her and realized, she is. My place, that is. The relationships with those we travel with through life are our place, until we find our final resting place.

One of the powerful names for God in Rabbinic tradition is, curiously enough, The Place. God is our place. God is our destination and our destiny. Our Place in the end is really a relationship. When we say the 23rd Psalm, we are not so much longing to be in the house of the Lord forever as to be at home with the Lord forever. There alone is our rest. Until then, we pray with St. Augustine, *Our hearts are restless until they find their rest in Thee.*

In the meantime, whom are you traveling with? And does the one you are following know the way to the place that is God? Jesus knows the way. Jesus is the Way. Follow him. To your Place, which he is even now preparing for you.

PART II

The Life That Really Is Life

Christian Faith and Formation

"Baptism is a once-and-for-all experience, requiring only a few minutes to initiate but taking our whole lives to finish."

~ **Will Willimon**

"The Christian ideal has not been tried and found wanting. It has been found difficult; and left untried."

~ **G.K. Chesterton**

"All human nature vigorously resists grace because grace changes us and the change is painful."

~ **Flannery O'Connor**

"We shall not cease from exploration, and the end of all our exploring will be to arrive where we started and know the place for the first time."

~ **T. S. Eliot**

Preface by Allen Walworth

My connection with George Mason is one of my longest and most cherished friend-ships, spanning over thirty years, during which we have been neighbors, fellow pastors, exercise companions, and theological sparring partners. At times he was my pastor, at others he was my ministry colleague, and at others he was my favorite person to share a long conversation at a café or a walk down a fairway. Here is what I know; George is a pastor, a preacher, a prophet, a poet, and a wordsmith *par excellence*. But as the sermons in this chapter make plain, and perhaps to the surprise of some who know him only from a distance, George is also an evangelist. He invites the hearer to experience the life-changing, world-changing Good News of life in Jesus Christ.

George carefully selects words like jewels, and then polishes and sets them in sentences designed to reflect light into the secret places of the heart. Sometimes his words of invitation to faith are a warm embrace, and at other times they are a poke in the ribs. But always George weaves together the strands of the Biblical story with the threads of the hearer's story, creating a tapestry unique and relevant, especially for those who usually feel far off from—or repelled by—the traditional language and practice of the Church. These sermons are a basket of flashlights, each of them pointing a beam of light at a different trajectory that might lead someone on the dark path back to their true home in relationship with God through Christ. His metaphors for faith are as varied as they are refreshing—a captivating freedom, being born of God, becoming an eighth-day person, walking toward the Light, losing a wrestling match with God, or falling into the arms of a God whose over-whelming character is joy.

As with all of George's sermons (or for that matter, all of his casual conversations as well), his words are winsome without being flippant, elegant without being elitist, wise without being arrogant. When George preaches, he stands beside us instead of over us. He is an evangelist who is on the journey of faith himself, sharing what he has learned thus far along the way, and making it sound so intriguing and so important you want to pick up your step and go with him.

These sermons reflect a broad and eclectic mind, drawing insights from William James to William Shakespeare, from Buechner to Kazantzakis, from songs and movies to personal anecdotes drawn from his own family experience. He is not captive to the small world of one denomination, or the blind spots of one social-economic class. Clearly George is well read, constantly curious, and always on the prowl for some gospel treasure hidden in plain sight, but this diversity is designed to remind the hearer that God is present in abundant and wide-flung places and voices, and that the path toward faith is accessible from any starting point.

And this collection of sermons illustrates that Christian faith is not a simple, nor single, transaction. It is not just a private matter of the heart. It is not just stamping a ticket to heaven by "walking an aisle" or "saying 'the prayer' while every head is bowed and every eye closed." Instead, George invites the hearer to a lifelong adventure with God, a relationship that is risky enough to demand courage, and mysterious enough to depend on hope. Like the Apostle Paul, who often described the Christian as "those of us who are *being* saved," George clearly speaks of Christian faith as a journey that transforms the worldview of the believer, but also sends her out into the world to join God in the work of transforming people and systems who are still tilted away from God's redeeming purpose for all creation. Grace comes to us, to be sure, but it also passes through us to the next person. And so, salvation is not just a one-time decision, but a process that is ongoing, growing, dynamic.

George calls the hearer to a Christian faith that engages the mind and the heart, but it also engages the hands and feet as we seek to live out that phrase of the Lord's Prayer, that "God's will be done on earth, as it is in heaven." And in this regard, one can understand why many of the people who have come to faith, and grown in faith, under George's pastoral ministry have been people who at one time wondered if the Church had any real purpose, or any relevant word, to make any real difference in the world. George's sermons "land the plane," that is, they lead the hearer to a new paradigm of faith that sees themselves differently as cherished children of God, and then sees God already at work in the world bidding us to join the Divine work of reconciliation and redemption.

I invite you to read these sermons knowing they were written for the ear, not the eye, "don't you know?!" So, listen to the words, pay attention to the cadence, notice the movements from the world of Scripture to the world of the latest headlines, hear the voice of a pastor who preached these sermons to a congregation he knew and loved—a pastor who trusted them enough to be vulnerable with his own struggles and shadows, and who loved them enough to challenge them beyond the safety and inertia of the spectator's pew.

Allen Walworth is Executive Vice President of Generis (church generosity consulting) and Teaching Pastor of First Presbyterian Church in Bonita Springs, Florida. He served as a senior pastor for seventeen years and resides in Dallas, Texas.

II

Captivating Freedom

May 24, 1998
Seventh Sunday of Easter
Acts 16:16-34

Bob Dylan got it. Shortly after his conversion to Christianity, after Pat Boone had baptized him in a swimming pool, the mumbling warbler came out with a song called, *You've Got to Serve Somebody.* Everybody's gotta serve somebody—either the devil or the Lord, either yourself or the world, either money or people. An old prayer of the Church refers to God as the one "in whose service is perfect freedom."

Luke tells us about a remarkable visit he made to the Greek city of Philippi with Paul and Silas on a missionary journey. As the story begins, an unnamed young woman is hounding Paul and the group as they were on their way to a *minyan,* a group of at least ten men gathered for prayer. She is a slave in two ways: She is owned by a spirit of divination which allows her to tell people's fortunes, and she must do it for her human owners who make a lot of money off her illness that her handlers call a gift. Isn't it just like some people to see a mentally unstable girl with no control of her own life, no doubt cut off from her own family and friends, and call her a precious commodity? They exploit sickness and vulnerability. Like a pimp who views a runaway as a cash cow for what she can do for him as a prostitute, these men have no interest in her except in how she can make money for them. Never mind she is not in her right mind and needs help to be freed of this possession, her slavery is their financial freedom.

The possessed fortune teller starts yelling in the streets as Paul's entourage makes its way. *These men are slaves of the Most High God, who proclaim a way of salvation.* Note the oddities here, the paradoxes. The slave girl calls free men slaves. She sees what most so-called free people miss, that all freedom involves obedience to a master of some kind. As Frederick Buechner has said, you do well to choose a master in terms of how much freedom you get back in return for your obedience.[22] Paul

---

22 *Wishful Thinking,* (Harper & Row, 1973), p. 29.

and his cohort had chosen the Most High God as their master, and through their obedience they knew true freedom.

The slave girl was obedient to her masters, too, but they gave her little freedom in return. And yet she could tell where freedom is to be found. During Jesus' ministry, when he would come upon the sick, they could see in him healing hope. When he came upon a demon possessed person, the possessive spirits would cry out in strange voice that this was God's son. It's odd, isn't it, how people who are supposed to be free cannot spot the source of true freedom, and those who are slaves can see it right off?

The girl says Paul and the others are slaves of God who proclaim freedom. The word *soteria* in the Greek means salvation theologically, but at its root, rescue, deliverance, freedom. All freedom involves slavery.

I was playing golf with a friend the other day. We were walking and carrying our bags, as I almost always do. He was too, but he was telling me how when he was younger—he's in his mid-fifties, I'd say—he would always ride in a cart. Figured he'd worked all week, deserved the treat. And over time, the money and privilege that bought him ease turned against him. He gained lots of weight and his health was betraying him. He found himself more a slave to his body and his appetites than a free man. He took to walking, working out, eating better, and now he's freer in his body. The paradox!

But we need more than willpower when the enslavement is great; we need a liberator to break the chains. We need a Higher Power, as the Big Book of AA puts it. We need the one who, whether we know his name or not, is the only one who can set anyone free of the things that enslave us—Jesus Christ. So, Paul turns to the girl and in the name of Jesus calls to the enslaving power within her to come out. And it does. Immediately.

I like the little note Luke puts in here that Paul took note of her and helped her because she was so annoying to him. We all feel like Paul at times, even if we are caregivers. We wish we were always acting out of deep compassion but sometimes we are just trying to give ourselves some peace by giving it to others, too. Maybe this is here just so we won't miss the point that Jesus is the one who heals.

Some of you are wondering this morning to yourself if Jesus can still give that kind of victory over the powers that enslave. You know how to hide your addictions and possessions, your insecurities and fears from the eyes of people. But you don't want to hide anymore, you want to be free of them. And what I want to tell you is yes, Jesus can still do that. But please note, Jesus is not a magic pill you take every morning with food. He will give you freedom from unholy chains only to fit you for service to God. Slavery to God is true freedom. And without a willingness to call God your master, to serve Christ fully, you will not have power in yourself to fight off the ungodly masters who seek to own you. If you want to be free, you must give yourself wholly to Christ.

So, the girl is freed by Jesus. She probably gets to go back to her family now. Maybe she gets her name back. No telling what her owners called her. Maybe *Toulouse La Cash*. Who knows? But she'll be no good to them now, whatever her name. And they don't take that lying down. No party for her wellness. They throw a fit. They are good, upstanding citizens, businessmen who don't mind a little religion, or even charity work. They give donations to the Mental Health Association and the Salvation Army. Their wives volunteer at the soup kitchen and the hospital. But religion that actually works is another thing. It's bad for business, don't you know?!

Same thing when a person with schizophrenia starts getting well in a hospital. Bring mother around and watch things fall apart again. An addict comes out of treatment after thirty days and the whole family, well-meaning as can be, can't make the adjustment. They knew how to manage the anxiety of the family by pinning it on the identified patient. But if the child or the father or whoever is not taking the blame anymore, the sabotage begins. Everything was fine as long as dad was drinking. Odd, isn't it?

Well, somebody's got to pay for this loss of business, and Paul and his pals are the problem. So they throw them into jail. And once again they don't seem to act like prisoners. They sit round singing hymns, dumbfounding fellow prisoners who are all grinding their teeth in hatred against their jailers. Reminds me of Richard Lovelace's wonderful poem *To Althea, from Prison*, in which the seventeenth-century poet, a political captive for views unpopular with powers to be, wrote: *Stone walls do not a prison make, / Nor iron bars a cage; / Minds innocent and quiet take / That for an hermitage. If I have freedom in my love, / And in my soul am free, / Angels alone, that soar above, / Enjoy such liberty.*

Freedom is not primarily about external circumstances, though those are important, too. Clearly, Chinese students in Tiananmen Square lying down in front of tanks, singing songs of peace, and going off to jail if they weren't catching bullets in the breast were freer than their captors. There is nothing admirable about doing nothing in the face of evil and injustice, all the while claiming that freedom is an internal quality. Ask any veteran in this room. No, the freedom that Christ gives within us drives us out of ourselves to break the chains that bind people. But that freedom can be found wherever you are.

I got a delightful surprise at the box office recently when I took the kids to see *Dancer, Texas, Pop. 81*. It's about four friends in a graduating class of five, who have vowed to get on a bus the Monday after commencement and seek their fortunes in the big city of Los Angeles. No more small town. No more nothing to do, nowhere to go. The whole story takes place over the weekend after graduation. The vistas are breathtaking in this little town, close to nowhere but sagebrush and heaven. All their lives the boys have thought that they were captives of the smallness that is Dancer. But they learn throughout the weekend that freedom doesn't have anything to do with where you are. It has to do with who you are no matter where you are.

Paul, Silas, and the boys are singing in prison, knowing they are freer than their captors. Then an earthquake hits and the chains fall off. Tragedy reveals character more than it makes it. The earthquake simply shows who are really free and who are not. The prisoners don't run away. They don't need to escape to find freedom. The jailer on the other hand is so enslaved, he almost takes his own life. He knows he'd be in big trouble if prisoners got away, and he has no internal strength to handle failure.

When the stock market crashed in 1929 and then again plunged on Black Monday in 1987, people were jumping out of windows in despair. They had built their lives on the lie of economic freedom. They were actually slaves to their money. When the Titanic went down, it took rich and poor alike. Some were ready to die with dignity because they were already free in their faith. Others showed their slavery by their fear and desperation. No one knows what is inside until an earthquake of some sort hits. It's easy to claim strength when you don't need it. But like a waiter who spills the soup when bumped on the way to the table, you don't know what is inside the bowl until the bump reveals it.

The jailer calls out to Paul, *What must I do to be saved?* He no doubt wasn't thinking much about heaven, as we do when we talk about being saved. He probably meant, what must I do to be like you people? How do you get that free? Freedom not only always involves some captivity, it is also captivating. It draws people to it. Free people fascinate the world. They undermine all systems of enslavement. Paul says how that is: *Believe on the Lord Jesus Christ and you will be saved.* He does, and he is, and he and his family are baptized.

Immediately he becomes a different kind of jailer. He washes the wounds of the prisoners, takes them into his house and feeds them as welcome guests. When Christ delivers you from slavery, he frees you to serve. Christ transforms everyday work into meaningful service. Relationships are renewed, priorities reordered.

Freedom in Christ is captivating freedom. Are you a captive of the liberating Christ?

12

Light Cometh

January 4, 2009
Epiphany Sunday
Isaiah 60:1-6; Matthew 2:1-12

Whenever you drive Northwest Highway between Central Expressway and the toll-way, you eventually pass a big and beautiful Baptist church on the south side. If you look up, and if you don't crash as you do, you may see the clock in the steeple. And if you squint just right, you may see the words on the face of the clock that read, *Night Cometh.*

These words come from the Gospel of John, chapter 9, at a point where Jesus and his disciples come upon a blind man. His followers ask the Savior why the man is blind—since things like that matter, don't you know?!—to everyone except the man who can't see. Jesus says, *We must work the works of him who sent me while it is day; night is coming when no one can work. As long as I am in the world, I am the light of the world.*

Even Jesus understood that a word of warning is sometimes called for. *Night cometh*, as the King James puts it more eloquently, reminds us that the two hands on the clock tower do not reckon the time of our lives—they track only the span of it. In Jesus' day, before the invention of electricity, night meant virtual inactivity. You couldn't produce anything at night. You couldn't fix what you had done wrong or what had gone wrong. It was a daylight society.

But he meant more than that by his saying that night cometh: He meant that, spiritually, there would come a time when you were in the ultimate sleep, underground, unable to rouse yourself or raise yourself. And, so, the saying on the church clock tower makes it a watchtower. Do something right today in the time you have. Get your act together. Set things in order with God and others. You don't have all the time in the world.

Left by itself, however, that word could come from anyone with wits, Christian or not. I have often wished that Herbert Howard, the pastor, who, I am told, saw to that inscription (he loved the Gospel of John, by the way, and all the inscriptions on the beams of the sanctuary come from that Gospel) would have included another inscription on the face of the clock opposite it that read, *Light Cometh.* Night Cometh—Light Cometh. For Jesus in that same Gospel of John is called the light that is coming into the world, and he calls himself the light of the world. What I wish the church—and by that I mean all churches, ours included—would proclaim is this most important truth. Jesus is the light that comes. If you are telling time by the clock or a watch, or by the sun and the moon, or by the seasons that come and go, you still aren't sufficiently aware of the time. Time is best told by the One the Bible calls the Bright and Morning Star. Dawn, not dusk, ought to be our guide—the coming light rather than the coming night.

And that is just what happens this time of year in the church as we move from Advent to Christmas, and now to Epiphany, which we observe today. We light candles each Sunday in Advent, increasing the light as the night grows longer each day. We light the Christ Candle at last when the child is born. And now we remember that the light that emanates from the manger in Bethlehem is matched by the light in the night sky that moves wise men from the East to find the one born King of the Jews.

You might say the whole of the story of salvation is the story of light overcoming darkness once and for all. At creation in the beginning, darkness was driven back by the first word of God: *Let there be light.* When the children of Israel suffered withering oppression in Pharaoh's land of darkness, God burned brightly in a bush to summon Moses to the task of deliverance. And when Israel had again fallen into the darkness of captivity in Babylon, God sent the prophet Isaiah to proclaim, *Arise, shine, for your light has come. … Nations shall come to your light, and kings to the brightness of your dawn.*

This passage helped make sense of what was happening when those three kings of Orient came bearing gifts of gold, frankincense, and myrrh, saying that they were simply following the light.

And when the Bible wraps up its vision of the new heaven and the new earth that God is bringing to pass at the end of time when all the clocks stop, Revelation records these words: *And there will be no more night; [the servants of God will] need no light of lamp or sun, for the Lord God will be their light, and they will reign forever and ever.*

In the meantime, Christians are called to live in the light of Christ, to bask in its warmth, to let it judge all that is yet dark within them, to see the world by the light and through the light, and to share the light with those who continue to love darkness rather than light. *You are the light of the world,* Jesus tells his followers then and now—something we repeat to everyone being baptized. *So let your light shine before others that they may see your good works and give glory to your Father in heaven.*

The light that comes brings judgment or hope, depending on where you are when it shines on you. Those who prefer night are set to flight or moved to fight when the light comes. This is one of the sad but honest truths to the gospel.

When Herod heard that the star of Bethlehem had led the wise men to his land and that they interpreted it to mean that someone had been born King of the Jews, Herod ordered the slaughter of all Jewish-born baby boys under the age of two. He had assigned himself the title King of the Jews, so Jesus became a threat to him right away. You know how this works: When you turn the light on in the kitchen at 3:00 a.m. because you can't sleep, you train yourself not to look down. You are afraid of seeing roaches scurry for cover when the light comes on.

Any time light comes, those who are living in darkness are challenged by it. There was a priest in a Midwestern city who wanted to help inner-city children. He wanted them to see something more than their own situations. He put them on a bus and took them to see some things of great beauty. They went to an art museum and saw paintings by the masters. They went to a symphony matinee and heard beautiful music. They went for a walk through a row of homes that had been refurbished by a creative team of architects. That young priest showed those children the best and brightest things he knew. Then they climbed back on the bus and went home.

That night, one of those same boys set his apartment complex on fire. They rescued the neighbors and family, but the place burned down. The priest was in tears when he visited the boy in a detention cell. "Why did you do it?" he asked. *I saw all those beautiful things*, said the boy, *and then I came home and saw how ugly my world was, and I hated the ugliness, so I wanted to burn it down.* Shine some light in a dark place, and there's no telling what will happen. When all you have ever seen is darkness, that's all you know. And when light comes, the contrast forces a choice. It's possible for light to come into the world and for somebody to say, "Turn out the lights!" It's possible for the Light of the world to shine on people, and those very people not accept it.[23]

Listen, the light of the world is Jesus the Christ. He has broken forth among us and painted this monochrome world with a palette of color. You can recede into the darkness and try to find solace there, but there is another choice: You can come out from your hiding, let go of the ugliness within you and around you, and live in the light. Neither flight from the light nor fight against the light is a strategy that wins in the end. Light is always more powerful than darkness, and the light of the world that is Jesus Christ has overcome the darkness once and for all. If you want to know life and live more abundantly, you must open yourself up to the light. Receive it by receiving him, and then begin to walk in the light of the Lord.

This is the second and preferable response to the light that comes. While some reject it, others accept it. Those who do find their hearts strangely warmed, as John Wesley put it. And they begin to see the world as God's creation to be cherished and nurtured rather than exploited.

When Maxie Dunnam was the pastor of Christ United Methodist Church in Memphis, Tennessee, he told of a trip he made to the Czech Republic, the former Yugoslavia, and Hungary. For forty-five years the huge red star of the Soviet Union had dominated the landscape from the pinnacle of the highest tower of the

23 William G. Carter, *Light of the World*, https://sermons.com/sermon/light-of-the-world/1345901.

Parliament building in one of those countries. With great joy one of the guides wanted the group to know that the red star was gone. He didn't know where it was, but it had been taken down after the Freedom Revolution.

That night, the group went to the church to preach and share fellowship. The sanctuary of the Methodist Church is in the headquarters building of the old Communist Party. It's a dilapidated building, five stories high, built around an inner court. Shell marks from the war are everywhere, and the deterioration of the building is so sad. It is shored up on the inside by large timbers. But when the group entered the little sanctuary, they felt like they were in another world. There was an atmosphere completely different from the exterior appearance of the building. The dominant Christian symbol in the sanctuary was a huge multi-pointed Advent star that comes out of the Moravian tradition. It's a central symbol of worship during the Advent season. The red star of the Soviet Union was gone from the Parliament building, but there in that place among those people, another star—the Star of Bethlehem—shone brightly.

The Star of Bethlehem is shining still. And wise men and women receive it with joy and follow it wherever it leads. Politics can take you only so far. Don't hang your hopes on that star. Work and money can take you only so far. Don't hang your hopes on that star. Even relationships can take you only so far. Don't hang your hopes on that star. Follow any star but the Star of Bethlehem and you end up in darkness. But set your sights on the coming light of Christ, and you will move from darkness to dawning and from dawning to noonday bright.

If you are looking for a change in your life this year, I urge you to begin this spiritual journey toward the light. And as you go, let the light of Christ shine in you so that others may see your good works and give glory to your Father in heaven.

13

Who Are You?

Watch and listen to "Who Are You?" by following this link or scanning the QR code with your phone: youtu.be/Va-bfBrwC2U. Sermon begins at 26:15.

August 6, 2017
Ninth Sunday after Pentecost
Genesis 32:22-31

Midway through the journey of our life, I woke to find myself in a dark wood, having lost my way.

That's the way Dante Alighieri begins the fantastical tale of his *Divine Comedy*, arguably the most important poetic work in Western civilization. If you aren't familiar with it, Dante's poem is an allegory and saga in three parts—Inferno, Purgatorio, and Paradiso; that is, hell, purgatory, and heaven. He sees the spiritual journey of life as a movement of transformation that takes you through hell in order to deliver you at last to heaven. There's no going up without going down and going through.

But notice again how it begins: "midway through the journey of *our* life." Not just his midlife, but all of ours. In other words, there's something of a pattern to all our lives that involves this descent into a dark wood, this getting lost along the way, before we can truly figure out who we are and where our hope lies.

That isn't to say that the first half of life doesn't matter, or the last. Midlife is more a metaphor of meaning than a chronological midpoint. It's a way of talking about our human identity crisis that runs all our life long but tends to be most intense at midlife. There are hints before and echoes after. The girl or guy who breaks up with you. The team you don't make. The debilitating illness. The spouse who dies first. There may be one defining moment at the midway point or thereabouts, but there are many moments before and after that that moment defines. We all come at last to a camp at the River Jabbok and wrestle all night long with ... well, I'm getting ahead of myself.

The story of Jacob in the Old Testament is filled with intrigue. Jacob will become Israel in the episode we look at today, but not before he has lived a life of deception and cunning where he keeps succeeding at the expense of others. Remember, the name Jacob stems from his grasping at the heel of his minutes-older brother Esau.

Being the younger brother didn't suit him. He was always reaching for first place in the family and everywhere else.

By the time we arrive at this story, Jacob has swindled his brother out of his inheritance and deceived his father, Isaac, by pretending to be Esau to gain his father's blessing that was meant for the older son. After the hunter Esau promised to hunt down his younger brother and kill him, Jacob heads for the hills. He goes to his mother's home country and there spends seven years in his uncle Laban's household working for the hand of his cousin Rachel. He first has to take her older sister Leah, and then works seven more years for the one he wants. He works six more years caring for Laban's flocks, and when he is ready to leave and go home, hoping Esau's had enough time to cool off, his wife, Rachel, steals her father's household goods. His life is one long con, a big act of grand larceny. But now the jig is up.

Jacob sends messengers ahead to see if Esau is ready to make peace with him. Word comes back that Esau has four hundred men with him, and he's heading toward him still bearing the grudge. So, Jacob sends everyone across the river and stays behind alone for the night. And it's a dark night of the soul.

In the middle of his sleep, a man jumps him and wrestles with him all night long. Who is the man? We don't know. We don't know that Jacob knows. And the truth is, that's often the nature of nightmares, isn't it? They seem so real. And they are. We wake up and try to answer the question of whom we wrestled with in the dream. It isn't always clear at first.

At early stages in our spiritual development, we tend to focus on how others are affecting our lives. We blame our father for not being more involved with us or being so involved that we felt like we could never please him. We look at our wife and wonder if she would just be more of this or less of that, everything would be great. We think the reason we haven't done better in our career is that we have always had someone holding us back—immigrants took our jobs, the boss promoted his son, our teacher didn't understand our true brilliance. Whatever.

Jacob may feel like he's on the cusp of getting everything he had hoped for, but one person is standing in his way and it could all fall apart right here. Esau. Is Esau the man he's wrestling with?

Pastors aren't immune from this. We don't like opposition. We like to be liked. Sometimes too much. Maybe we get into this work partly to feel the blessing of heaven through the people of earth. What group is better able to do that for us than the people we call the people of God? Then we come to a time when we feel like some are against us instead of for us. And we don't sleep well. We wrestle with them in the night.

But the truth is, they—you—are not the problem. Never are. Our struggle is not with Esau, however conceived. Our struggle is with ourselves. And who wants to struggle with the self? Not I. If I struggle with myself, I have to take responsibility for my actions. I have to deal with my regret and mistakes. And I may not be sure I have it in me to prevail if the problem I have is me. Anyone else, or am I the only one confessing today?

But in the midst of that long night of wrestling, we may find out that, being created in the image and likeness of God, we never struggle only with ourselves. Our struggle is not just with flesh and blood. And yet, we are flesh and blood, so when we struggle spiritually, it affects us physically. Which is why at the last, the man Jacob wrestles with, realizing Jacob is never going to give up, finally wounds him. He touches him in a place that sets his hip out of joint, causing a wound Jacob will limp with from that day forward.

Our spiritual struggles take a toll on us. We want them to be easy. We want to grow without being hurt, but there's no growth without pain. When we have tried our best and divorce leaves us wounded, it's not the end of our lives by any means, but we walk away with a limp. When we have felt betrayed by a friend or child or parent or employer, we are never the same again. But never being the same again can either lead to our spiraling downward or "falling upward," to use a lovely phrase by Richard Rohr.

Jacob is wounded, but he won't give up. He is not willing for this night to end unresolved. He will not waste a crisis. The man asks Jacob to let him go. Jacob holds on for dear life, literally. The man asks his name. *Jacob*, he answers. And that's true, of course. He's been a Jacob, a deceiver and trickster, all his life. It's served him well in the first half of his life, but he knows living without integrity like that won't work forever. He admits it. *I am a heel*, he says. *I am a sinner*. That's what we all need to be able to say if we are ever to know life as grace.

The man tells him he's getting a new name now. *You will be called Israel*. Israel. Meaning something like the one who has striven with God and prevailed. Or maybe it means God has striven with you and will fight for you. It's hard to say what it means exactly from the Hebrew.

What we do know is that somehow God is now in the picture. Jacob understands it's God he has been wrestling with after all. And it's a blessed standoff. God hasn't killed him, and Jacob hasn't defeated God either. They've been engaged in a contest of wills and they both come out of it changed.

The novelist Nikos Kazantzakis, who wrote *Zorba the Greek* and *The Last Temptation of Christ*, tells a story of a young man who visited a monk at one of the Orthodox monasteries on the Aegean Sea. The monks had built their cells on the face of the rock and lived there alone. The young man climbed up to the cell of the monk and asked, "Father, do you still wrestle with the devil?"

The monk answered, "Not anymore. I have grown old, and the devil has grown old with me. He no longer has the strength. Now I wrestle with God."

"With God?" the man asked. "You wrestle with God? Do you hope to win?"

"No," he said, "I hope to lose."[24]

Frederick Buechner calls this Jacob story "the magnificent defeat." But losing to God is really winning. It is a blessing in disguise.

Tell me your name, Jacob asks the man. *Who are you?* But God doesn't give away God's power like that. Instead, God blesses Jacob. God blesses him precisely because

---

24 Cited by Mark Trotter, https://sermons.com/sermon/night-moves/1352577.

he hung on and wouldn't give up, because he wouldn't let God go no matter how painful the struggle. This is the kind of man God can use, wounded but woke.

Richard Rohr again: "Mature spirituality will always teach us to enter willingly, trustingly into the dark periods of life, which is why we speak so much of 'faith' or trust. Transformative power is discovered in the dark, in questions and doubts, seldom in the answers. Yet this goes against our cultural instincts. We usually try to fix or change events in order to avoid changing ourselves. Wise people tell us we must learn to stay with the pain of life, without answers, without conclusions, and some days without meaning."

Who are you? The man Jacob wrestled with asks him that question. Jacob asks the man that question, too.

It's a question of identity, where we derive it. We find out that we only find out who we are through the struggle.

The song *Who Are You?* is by the British rock band *The Who*. Seems apt, don't you know?! We hear it at the beginning of the reruns of CSI. *Who are you? Who, who; who, who?* But the last lines are seldom heard. They culminate a song where a man is waking up from a drunken night in SoHo only to find he isn't dead, but that maybe grace has found him. It sounds like a prayer:

> *I know there's a place you walked / Where love falls from the trees. / My heart is like a broken cup, / I only feel right on my knees. / I spit out like a sewer hole, / Yet still receive your kiss. / How can I measure up to anyone now / After such a love as this?*

Well, that's really the point, isn't it? We don't have to measure up to anyone else after such a love as this.

Once we are loved as we are, we are never the same again. We know who we are; or better, whose we are.

I don't know all your stories in this room today, but here's what I believe. While each of our stories is different, all our stories are the same. If you haven't wrestled all night with God yet, you will. There will come a time in the struggle when you will think your life is over; but you will find it's only the life you have known that is over. There's another life waiting to be lived. Another you waiting to emerge by the grace of God.

You can tell people who've been through it already, I think, if you pay close attention. They've all got the slightest hint of a limp ... .

14

The Pregnant Possibility

March 11, 1990
Second Sunday in Lent
Genesis 12:1-4a; John 3:1-17

When peace, like a river, attendeth my way / When sorrows like sea billows roll /
Whatever my lot, thou hast taught me to say / It is well, it is well with my soul.[25] Maybe
the words, maybe the music had a part. But we had sung it before, this hymn. That
Sunday morning, though, Kim and I sat in a near-the-back pew together with tears
streaming down our faces as we sang those words. Earlier that morning we had
experienced our twenty-third month of disappointment.

In the days of Abraham and Sarah they called our state of being "barrenness."
We felt it to be more like a state of "non-being." "Infertility" is our modern word for
it. And in a modern world which values productivity most and hence producers, we
were as it seems at the deepest level, non-productive. We felt powerless in our effort
to produce life. Especially Kim, I guess, who has always believed that her first calling
was to be a mother. She could not understand this fate.

But in the singing of that hymn a "light surprised," a word was spoken, a call
was issued. It was almost as if God in that moment called upon us to let go of our
striving for a possible pregnancy and to grasp instead the pregnant possibilities God
would have for us, which may or may not have included a baby. We had to understand that the power to produce life does not belong to us. To realize that as long
as we allowed our whole lives to be determined by this issue from a flesh and blood
perspective, our lives would be barren in more ways than one. Our only possibility
was a pregnant possibility—to be born again ourselves, or better to be born from
above. The phrase Jesus used with Nicodemus is intentionally ambiguous. To be
born again or born from above means essentially to be born of God. By God's Spirit
to come to a new way of looking at life, a new way of experiencing life. A way which

---

25 Horatio Spafford, "It Is Well with My Soul," 1873.

has more to do with simply obeying God and trusting God for life and the future than trying to bring it to pass ourselves.

Not until Abraham and Sarah did as God had commanded did they see God's pregnant possibility become reality, and only then after another quarter of a century! Kim and I, too, did have children, though not right away. But having children is not the point.

Barrenness is more than infertility, and God's pregnant possibilities for us are far more rich than our minds can comprehend. Look at Nicodemus, for instance. When Jesus tells him that he must be born *anothen*, the Greek says, born "anew" or born "from above," he can see only one possibility: starting life over again by turning back the clock, crawling back into his mother's womb.

Oh, how many of us believe that that is our only real option! If we could just do it all over again, we'd get it right the next time. Poppycock. But even if we would, we all know how impossible it is to go back. And so we remain with only barren possibilities, possibilities formed by what could have been but cannot be.

Many of you here today are experiencing barrenness in a wide variety of ways, but it is barrenness nonetheless. You are holding on to an existence that leaves you with a deep void within you and without the power to do anything about it in yourself, let alone pass life on to others.

Our two texts give us models of barrenness. Barrenness of soul is the result of people who are too much stuck to the things of this world that claim them. Things of this world, no matter how good they are, do not in themselves have power to give life. They can only in the end render you lifeless and barren if you depend upon them and hope in them.

God told Abraham to let go of his country, the land he called his own. Before Abraham could receive life, he had to get unstuck from that which had a grip upon him. Abraham's country, his land, can be construed in more ways than one. Some people think that America is the last hope for the world, and they would do anything for her. America has no basic life-giving power. The last hope for the world and the only one with power to give life is God. If you hope ultimately in America this morning, truly, truly, you must be born again.

I know of seminary graduates who have answered God's call to the ministry but who do not find a church to serve because they say they will only serve in Texas. They wonder why God is not faithful to them, while churches all over the country clamor for pastors. There are people in this church, I'm sure, who in their heart of hearts believe that God has called them to mission service, but they are scared to let go of their homeland for fear God might send them to live in unseemly places. God might, but then the majority of the world today is clustered in cities not unlike Dallas. Of course, that's not the point, is it? To anyone who has not let go of this slavery to place, truly, truly you must be born from above.

This week I spent a few days with Christian and businessman Fred Smith. He shared an important truth he had learned from saint Oswald Chambers: "Sit loose to things." What a wonderful phrase. "Sit loose to things." Some people are sitting so tight to things, they cannot see a way to get free. They cannot imagine who they would be without their house on such-and-such street, their cars, their clothes, their bank accounts, and their pension funds. They are tied by them and stuck to them. When the economy hit bottom a few years ago, so did they. (Any of you?) Suddenly, it left people wondering who they were. It left many with great barrenness of soul. Even successful people, though, people who are on top today, are sometimes the loneliest, most barren people of all. Everybody wants to be like them, but they know inside that nobody should. Like "Nic at Night" who came to Jesus, they are searching for more. To all of you like that this morning, I say, truly, truly, you must be born of God.

Leave behind your kindred and your father's house, the Lord told Abraham. Now this may be hardest of all. Of all things we figure God loves and blesses, the family is on top of the list. But God is saying let go of your "stuckness" to family, because your stuckness to family brings you only barrenness of soul.

I know a man whose father once—whether flippantly or not, I don't know—called him and his twin baby sister a couple of ugly little "squirrels." He has believed that about himself all his life and has spent much of his life trying to prove himself a success to his father. Even now after his father's death, it haunts him. He is stuck to his "father's house." He has not gone from it with Abraham.

Others of you are dogged by marital failure, by the divorce of your parents, by your felt mistakes in raising your kids. You are stuck to your history and find yourself barren to new possibilities, new beginnings.

Some of you saw that astonishing movie *Dead Poets Society*. The young man who wanted to answer his unique calling to the theater was thwarted by his well-meaning father who had planned his life for him. His plans did not include anything so "frivolous" as the dramatic arts. Unable to stand up to his father, to get unstuck from him, the young man acted out the barrenness of his soul to its fatal end.

To all of you who are stuck to your families in ways that bind you and sap life from you, I say with Jesus, truly, truly you must be born anew.

Even sometimes our good attention to family that produces families that do not appear dysfunctional, families that spend time together, that love each other, that go to church each Sunday, even they can become subtle substitutes for God. The role of flesh and blood families is not eternal! In light of that, then, should not we as parents love our children enough to let them go, to be risked to the world, as Wendell Berry has put it? Isn't that what John 3:16 says God did with his Son, risked him to the world, let him go, sent him even? Is it not really our job to nurture them to hear the call of God for themselves so that they themselves can answer and be born of God not just born of us? Is that not the greatest blessing we can give them, not to allow them to become unduly stuck to us? If you are a parent holding the reins too tightly on your kids because you mistakenly believe they are your kids, then truly, truly you must be born of God.

Abraham and Sarah were older adults, upwards of seventy-five. Nicodemus was an upstanding elder statesman and religious leader. He had social status, an image to uphold. These people had a lot to lose by the world's standards in answering God's call. Too old to change, some of you may think. Too embarrassing to say publicly that no matter what other people think about you on the outside, you are really not alive to God on the inside. You know about Jesus, but you really do not know Jesus. Down deep you are barren and you know it. Truly, truly you must be born again.

God promised Abraham and Sarah that they would become a great nation. God promised Nicodemus that he could come alive to God in ways he could not imagine. God's pregnant possibilities for us turn into new births and new life for us when we but let go of our stuckness and embrace the God who alone can give us life. This is a word not only for non-Christians; it is even for Christians who continually get stuck where they should not.

The great eighteenth-century revivalist George Whitefield would preach this text John 3:3 over and over and over again. He was asked one time why he continually preached that "You must be born again." "Because," he replied, "you must be born again."

One fashionable London congregation challenged him on the matter. That kind of preaching might be all right for the Salvation Army but not for a church such as ours, they said. So that evening, Whitefield preached instead on John 3:7 which reads: "Marvel not that I say unto thee, Ye must be born again."[26]

How about in this church? Any room for that kind of preaching? Anyone here need to be born again?

Anyone stuck in their circumstances who needs the pregnant possibility of new life that only God can give?

What changes can you expect? David Redding tells the story about Orville Kelly—a man who learned years ago that he was suffering from terminal cancer. He and his wife went home to cry, and to die. What should they do now? They prayed about it. The answer was that they should not only pray but also play. So they decided to put on a big party. They invited all their friends. During the festivities, Orville held up his hand to make an announcement: "You may have wondered why I called you all together," he said. "This is a cancer party. I have been told that I have terminal cancer. Then my wife and I realized we are all terminal. We decided to start a new organization. It is called M.T.C.—'Make Today Count.' You are all charter members." Since that time his organization has spread wide and near, and spread hope with it.[27]

The power to get unstuck from the grip of any worldly circumstance and live each day to the fullest comes only from the God who can birth in you new life, a new perspective for living. How about you: You must be born of God. Will you let God birth you into new life today?

---

26 *Treasury of Anecdotes*, ed. A. Naismitz, (Baker Books, 1976).
27 "His Passion: A New Beginning," in *Dynamic Preaching*, Second Sunday in Lent, p. 2.

15

Breaking Through

February 23, 2003
Seventh Sunday after Epiphany
Mark 2:1-12

It's hard to say who wanted it more, my friends or me. They had been carrying me around for almost three years when you read about me in Mark's Gospel. It was embarrassing, to say the least, but they were good friends. I could hear people asking them about it sometimes. You'd be amazed at how stupid people can be around people with disabilities. You can't walk and they think you can't hear either. People would say how good it was of my friends to take care of me like they did, what a burden it must have been for them lugging me all over town on a stretcher. My friends would shrug, as if to say, *He ain't heavy, he's my brother.* I always thought that would make a good song, don't you know?! Of course, one of them was my brother—my older brother. I think he always felt responsible for what happened. They all did, really. We were all like brothers, growing up in a small town. Capernaum had maybe a thousand people, tops.

It was a lazy Friday, kind of like your Saturdays, day before the Sabbath. The five of us had nothing to do, so we went fishing on the Sea of Galilee—which is really more like a big lake than a sea. It was hot, but there was a good breeze in the morning that kept us cool. By midday, the fish weren't biting and we were all snoozing. One of us, I don't know who, woke up and said he was going for a swim. I was the youngest, and I guess I was trying to impress or something. I don't know what was going on in my mind, but I was thirteen, after all. You can guess what happened. I had to be first in the water. I dove in headfirst, like everything else I did. Why didn't I just jump in? What none of us realized is that during our nap we had drifted into the shoals. I had no sooner broken through the water than I hit bottom. I could feel a shock go right through my body. Then I couldn't feel anything—from my waist down.

By the time Jesus came back to town, he had already been doing amazing things. One guy from the neighborhood, who everybody always thought was just a little off, if you know what I mean, turned out to have a demon messing with his head. Jesus healed him right in the synagogue, put him back in his right mind, and the guy has been different ever since. I wasn't there myself, because back in those days, synagogues weren't handicap accessible. Not because they didn't have ramps or elevators, it was because they thought misfortune was caused by misbehavior. The scribes taught that bad things, like me getting paralyzed, were God's punishment for sin. Nice, huh? Well, some of you still think that, don't you?

Anyway, then Jesus went for dinner to Simon Peter's house and Peter's mother-in-law had a bad fever. He took her hand as she lay in bed and the fever lifted as he lifted her up. Then he went all over the countryside preaching and healing. They say he even healed a leper, which never happens. So, by the time he got back home to Capernaum, everyone was really excited. So many people crowded into Jesus' house, the fire marshal would have had a fit if he'd known. It could have been a tragedy like those nightclubs in Chicago or Rhode Island this week. But this time a miracle happened instead. I was the miracle.

My buddies came to get me. I was at home lying on my couch, as usual. Now try to imagine this. I'm a teenager. No TV. No ESPN SportsCenter to watch over and over all day long. There's no radio, no stereo, no CDs. And no computer or internet. I couldn't read much or write. What would have been the point of that? I wasn't going to be a priest, and we didn't have many books other than the Torah at the synagogue. My accident happened a few months before I was to study for my bar mitzvah. So, there was pretty much nothing to do all day long except lie around and listen to other people talk about having a life. We didn't even have wheelchairs back then, so forget about getting around by myself. I had pretty much slipped into depression and thought about how much easier it would be on everyone, including me, if I weren't around.

When my friends came to get me and told me about Jesus being back, I couldn't tell if they were really hopeful for me or desperate for themselves. I didn't want them feeling guilty for the rest of their lives. They had to get on with things. Two had already married; one had a child on the way. Things were changing for everyone … but me.

When we got to Jesus' house, whatever hope I had sank again. No way could we get to him. He was inside and the people were so crowded in the house you couldn't break though. My friends wouldn't give up. They carried me up the back steps that led to the roof. The house Jesus rented was kind of like the kind you see in New Mexico. Adobe. Dried mud. The roof was dried mud and thatch. My friends set me down on the edge of the roof and started clawing their way through between the wooden beams. By the time they broke through, all eyes below were looking up at us. People were yelling stuff about damaging other people's property. My friends didn't care what they said; they tied some ropes to the poles of the stretcher and let me down in the middle of the crowd.

For a few moments as I lay on the dirt floor, Jesus just kept looking up at the hole in his roof. He started shaking his head and smiling. If it were my roof, I'd have been thinking, the nerve of these people! Jesus was thinking, the faith of these people! He was actually moved by how much my friends wanted to get me to him.

He still is, you know? It's one of those things about Jesus you come to find out the better you know him. No matter how busy he is, he always finds time not only for people who know they need him but for people who have friends who need him, too. He never makes you feel like you're bugging him, imposing, bothering him, when you call on him. Praying to Jesus for your friends to be made whole or to be saved—it impresses him. He stops what he's doing and pays attention. Now, I'm not saying it always turns out the way things did with me, but the mystery of intercession—whether prayer or stretcher-carrying—is like love, I guess. When you love someone, you can't just flip a switch and turn it off and on. It's a given. And sometimes it makes miracles happen between people, things that never would have in a world of oughts and shoulds. There's no "supposed to" in love. On the other hand, sometimes even love doesn't change things the way you hope. Maybe in the long run. God has ways of doing things over time that we can't imagine in the moment. The thing to do is to stay open and keep hoping and longing.

Which is what faith is, at least to begin with. And it's what my friends had more of than I at that point. But sometimes that's enough—to believe for someone else when it seems hard for that person to believe.

When Jesus looked down at me, I could tell something was going to happen, but what came out of his mouth was not it. *Son, your sins are forgiven.* To be honest with you, I was a little mad about that. I mean, it seemed like Jesus was on the side of those bearded holier-than-thou types from the synagogue that were always trying to find ways to keep people out instead of get them in. I was thirteen at the time, for God's sake. How much sinning could I have done to make God mad enough to paralyze me? I'm not saying I was perfect, but that seemed kind of random to me that he would take it upon himself to forgive my sins, when it was obvious that what I needed was to be able to walk again. I thought he was missing the point. Turns out, I was missing the point.

We come to Jesus thinking we need one thing and finding out that he knows more about what we need than we do. Jesus had broken through my defensiveness by the time I realized what he was up to. He was talking to the scribes as much as he was to me. He wanted them to know that I was a "forgiven" sinner and they shouldn't keep me out of the life of the community. He was really on my side and I didn't see it right away.

Jesus wants the church to be on the side of people who need forgiveness, whether they know it or not. He wants the church to remember what the scribes needed to learn—that he has power from God to forgive sins, and he doesn't wait around for people like me to realize I need it before he forgives. In fact, when you forgive someone, everyone is off the hook: those who need forgiving, and those who do the forgiving. Jesus wants everyone to be spiritually free.

People can get so bound up by bitterness that it affects them physically. I don't know that that had anything much to do with my paralysis, but I have seen lots of people unable to get on with their lives because of a lack of forgiveness. Sometimes it's because they can't forgive themselves, and sometimes it's because they can't forgive others. What Jesus taught me is that forgiveness is a gift that gives life to everyone.

If there's anything in your life that needs forgiveness, let it go, let God release you. I am here to tell you that Jesus is here today in his house as much as he was there with me in his house in Capernaum. And he is saying to you, *Son, your sins are forgiven. Daughter, your sins are forgiven.* And if you are holding out on forgiving someone because you think you represent a God who wants to make sure everyone straightens up before they are forgiven, then get it through your head right now that Jesus is the one who represents God, and people don't straighten up in order to be forgiven, they straighten up when they are forgiven.

Which leads to the last thing that happened, which I thought at the time was the best thing. Jesus told the scribes that forgiving sins was the easy part of being the Son of Man with God's authority. But just to prove it, he looked at me again and said, *On your feet, boy. Stand up, straighten up, take your stretcher, and walk on home.* He didn't have to say it twice. I rolled onto my side, pushed myself onto my knees and felt the strength surging all the way to my feet. I stood up and walked back into life. I went from paralytic to peripatetic.

Some of you need to get on with it, too. You are forgiven, and now you need to get moving. Get beyond the paralysis that keeps you lying around, stuck, out of it, feeling sorry for yourself, and maybe even blaming God. God has broken through all barriers to your salvation. Now, stand up, I tell you. Go on, stand up. And when you go back to your home, glorify God, and live in a way that amazes people because of the difference Jesus has made in you.

16

Redeeming Life

April 12, 2009
Easter Sunday
John 20:1-18

My favorite moment in the Maundy Thursday service is the one that makes us all jump. If you were here or in another church on Thursday night, you would know what I am talking about. After we remember the night of Jesus' betrayal, the night he observed the Last Supper with his disciples, the lights dim as the darkness falls inside and outside our souls. And then, before the single flickering candle is walked out of the sanctuary, not to return until the light of Easter morn, the Bible—the Big Bible—is slammed shut. Case closed. No more words. Only a rumbling silence.

The word for that moment is *strepitus*. It would be Latin, don't you know?! It simply means "loud noise." It symbolizes the earth quaking and the rocks breaking at the moment of Jesus' death. It foreshadows the grave opening at the moment of Jesus' resurrection. Jesus' death and resurrection are seismic events that shake the world.

Jesus has thrown everything off balance, the Misfit says in Flannery O'Connor's short story, *A Good Man Is Hard to Find*. And indeed he has. He has thrown everything off balance in order to bring new balance. If even the grave can't hold a good man down, maybe we don't really have to fear death anymore, and if the powerful can't use intimidation and murder to control the world the way they tried to do with Jesus, maybe we don't have to fear them anymore either. Maybe our lives are truly being redeemed in Christ's resurrection—both the lives we live inside our own skin and the lives we live as we bump up against other people.

Not maybe. It is, if we would just believe this self-changing, world-changing thing God has done in the resurrection of the Son of God. But even if we don't believe it, the resurrection of the Son of God has shaken things for good and for good, has thrown everything off balance, and has changed the known world by bringing before us an unknown world in which we are invited to live.

So, in one sense Easter is by itself a big deal, the biggest deal that has nothing at all to do with eggs, bunnies, and chocolate. It's the most important moment in human and natural history, and the biggest circle on the Christian calendar. But in a more important sense, Easter is no big deal at all.

George Gagliardi made this point this week in his annual Easter letter to friends. Many of you know George as Wilshire's treasured bearded bard. He can play almost any instrument in classical or jazzy fashion. He's also a thoughtful ruminator on the Christian story. George writes Christmas and Easter letters to his friends, many of whom are suspicious of Christianity at best. In this year's offering, he poses a fictional conversation between a Christian and a skeptic. *Two men walk into a bar ...* That's how it begins, of course. In the course of the conversation, the skeptic mentions that Easter is almost here and he doesn't see what the big deal is. The Christian agrees, which puzzles the guy. The Christian explains: ... *if you consider Easter as a "deal" between God and humanity then you're right in saying it's no big deal because it isn't. It isn't any kind of deal at all. It's much more than that—more than an "I did this and now you have to do that" sort of thing. In the truest sense of the Word* (capital W), *Easter is no big "deal" at all.*

Exactly. Have you ever wondered why God didn't let anyone see what happened when Jesus was raised? I mean, it happened inside the dark of the tomb. All Mary or the disciples get to see at first is the stone rolled away and the body gone. The empty tomb is the first indication that something has happened. But there's no eyewitness to the resurrection; there are only eyewitnesses to the post-resurrection.

God does this without anyone's help or validation. It's a pure act of God, an act of grace that no one else has anything to do with—including Jesus. Jesus didn't rise from the dead; *he was raised.* He was as dead as any of us will be. There was no timing device inside him that kicked in after he had been in the tomb long enough to come back to life. God had to raise him. God had to do something without him or us contributing at all. It was a gift, just as all of life is—whether this mortal life we live now or the immortal one we receive by faith in Jesus Christ.

So the first thing about Easter to celebrate is that the *strepitus* is (apologies to Shakespeare) *full of sound and fury, signifying ... something.* It signifies a change to the world and for the world as the first day of the new world commences. It follows the whole creation story: On the seventh day God rested, and Jesus rested in the tomb on that Sabbath day. Resurrection morning was the eighth day of the old creation and the first day of the new creation. Which is why we worship on Sunday instead of Saturday now. We are children of the New Creation that began with the Resurrection of Jesus. He is the new Adam, the second Adam, the first man of the new creation. And he aims to have many children.

Which leads to two aspects of Easter for you and me. The first is our personal experience of it. Because Jesus was raised from the dead, he is now in the business of raising the dead himself. He's on the hunt for people like you and me.

When Mary comes to the tomb, she is dead inside herself and she is walking in the land of the dead and dying. She takes Jesus for the gardener. It isn't until Jesus speaks her name—*Mary*, he says—that she comes alive herself because he had come alive. Her grief turns to joy. She sees and believes. Her life is different now because she has seen him alive. She must have tried to hug him because Jesus tells her not to hold him or cling to him that way any longer. *Don't treat me according to the old form of existence,* he is saying. He is yet to ascend to his Father in heaven. *Don't look for me the way you used to. Go tell the others. And tell them I am going to my Father and your Father, to my God and your God.*

The construction of this saying personalizes Easter. Jesus tells them that they have the same Father, the same God. Which means that the God who did this miraculous thing for him is the same God who will raise them up. It also means that each of us may have an Easter experience now that anticipates our future resurrection.

When we preachers invite you to profess your faith in Jesus Christ, to become his followers, we are announcing to you that you can be changed into a new creation now. You can begin to live as eighth-day men and women, which is at the same time first-day men and women. The kingdom of God has dawned at dawn on Easter Day, and the new world has begun. You can be born again.

We know that the disciples were different people from that moment on. Those fearful, doubting, and bumbling followers of Jesus became brave, faithful, and able apostles of this good news. The resurrection of Jesus transformed them from self-centered to Christ-centered. He was with them. They would never be alone. So they didn't have to look out for themselves, and neither do we. We can put an end to all this talk about how we have to take care of ourselves first, how we shouldn't let the responsibilities of marriage or children or friendship or neighborliness get before our primary need to do what we need to do to care for ourselves. No, all that changes when you see the risen Christ and realize that he takes care of you so that you can take care of others.

And this leads to the second thing. We ask you, "Do you accept Jesus Christ as your personal Lord and Savior?" So good so far, but there's an equally important aspect of the Christian confession that goes along with the rest of the story about what happened on Easter Sunday, and why. Here's the way some theologians have posed it that gets to the point (get ready, because it's going to make you squirm): "Do you accept Jesus Christ as your political Lord and Savior?"[28]

Secular politicians who were egged on by political religious leaders crucified Jesus. He didn't die in his sleep. He wasn't hit by a runaway chariot. He was crucified because he preached the kingdom of God that would put every political kingdom in its place. Easter was God's vindication of Jesus' being Lord over every human ruler. Easter turned the tables and showed that those who think they are on top and can do whatever they want to people are under the judgment of God.

So, Easter is about God and about being born anew by placing your trust in the living Christ, but it is also about the kingdom of God and placing yourself in its service. Your loyalty is now to the politics of the kingdom of God.

---

28 Marcus J. Borg and John Dominic Crosson, *The Last Week: What the Gospels Really Teach about Jesus's Final Days in Jerusalem* (HarperOne, 2006), p. 215.

Politics means how we live together. The word comes from the Greek polis, meaning "city." Politics has to do with our civic life. What kind of community we engage in, how we treat our neighbors, whether we look after one another or not. The principal thing now for a Christian in the light of the resurrection is to determine the conditions of relationships in a world in which God's will is done; then help redeem these relationships.

Some years ago, a youth minister in North Carolina met with parents, and they decided to try something to get their affluent children to understand the state of the world and how other people live with great inequality. So they planned a banquet of all the kids' favorite foods along with other basic foods. They printed play money and distributed it to the kids in about the proportion to how resources exist in the world. Two kids were given a hundred dollars in play money to share, more than enough for them to fill their stomachs many times over. Ten were given forty dollars, barely enough that if they chose carefully, they could each get enough to eat. The final group of twenty kids was given only a few dollars. The money would be only enough to buy rice, and then only for enough that each kid would get just a bite.

They stationed a parent as cashier at the end of the food line. When the kids reached her and pulled out their money to pay, she noticed that every kid's plate was full to overflowing and that each kid had plenty of money to pay with. The youth minister was upset that the experiment wasn't working. The kids had somehow spoiled it. Turns out one of the kids had stopped by the church office the day before, saw the play money on the youth minister's desk and got wind of what was coming. He copied the money and passed out lots of it to everyone before the dinner. While the youth minister stewed, one of the parents looked over and saw all the kids eating together, enjoying each other, and actually throwing the play money up in the air in defiance of the order that it be divided according to the scarcity of resources. That gave them a second thought. Maybe that is the true picture of the politics of Jesus. Maybe the kids understood that abundance, not scarcity, should be the rule in the world, and class or wealth should no longer divide people.[29]

When enough of us accept Jesus Christ as our personal and our political Lord and Savior, maybe then more of the world will get what we celebrate at Easter. Maybe they will join us in saying, He is risen, indeed.

---

29 Thanks to Amy Butler for citing this in *Practicing Resurrection: Justice* (https://web.archive.org/web/20080705093217/http://www.calvarydc.com/Sermons/080413.html).

17

Not Fake News

Watch and listen to "Not Fake News" by following this link or scanning the QR code with your phone: youtu.be/Hv16q6Y6-ms. Sermon begins at 34:05.

January 21, 2018
Third Sunday after Epiphany
Mark 1:14-20

The news is the first rough draft of history. That's the money line in the movie *The Post* that Meryl Streep, as Katherine Graham, uses to speak about the role of journalism. She's quoting her late husband, Phil Graham, from whom she inherited the role of publisher of *The Washington Post*.

Graham didn't invent the phrase. Alan Barth penned it in the late 1940s before going to work for the *Post* and introducing it to Graham. Just a little research I did to honor the journalism profession in a time when it is under fresh attack from the powers that be. President Richard Nixon had tried to conceal the so-called Pentagon Papers in his time, hiding the truth from the American people and protecting his power. But the *Post's* decision to publish that account of America's shenanigans in Vietnam is timely today.

The current president announced his Fake News Awards this past week—to limited fanfare, don't you know?! Happily. The *Post* is one of his favorite targets, along with CNN and *The New York Times*. "Fake news" has become a mantra for the comments by anyone who doesn't like a reported story, whether it's true or not. We live in a time when no one trusts any news he or she disagrees with. We prefer propaganda to truth. Maybe it's always been that way.

Jesus went around Galilee proclaiming the truth of *the good news of God*. It shouldn't surprise us that it was controversial. In fact, if it isn't controversial to us as we read it here in Mark's Gospel, we haven't understood it. You see, the good news of God is the first rough draft of the in-breaking kingdom of God through Jesus.

Journalist Jack Shafer calls this phrase "the first rough draft of history," a perfect formulation. Not only the sense of the words, but the sound of them. *The single-syllable words fall like hammer blows driving a nail*, he says. *Its artful redundancy makes it resonate.* First, rough, *and* draft *all have separate and distinct meanings, yet they all point to a morning greenness, a raw beginning where truth originates.*[30]

The gospel points to the morning greenness of what God is doing in the world. It's a raw beginning where truth originates. Have you ever thought of the good news of God that way?

But if it is such good news, why is it controversial? Because it's not good news to everyone. It's good news to those who find themselves ensnared in the clutches of the powerful and who suffer under their reign. It's bad news or fake news to those who want to control people by the laws they pass and enforce for their own benefit rather than for the benefit of *all* the people. This is why Supreme Court Justice Hugo Black once wrote that the purpose of a free and unfettered press is "to serve the governed, not the governors."[31]

Mark sets the context right away: *Now after John was arrested, Jesus came to Galilee, proclaiming the good news of God.* Why did Mark tell us that Jesus started preaching publicly about the good news of God immediately after John the Baptist had been arrested by the Roman authorities? How was that the cue that the time was fulfilled and that the kingdom of God had come near?

It is hard for people like me to understand this conflict of kingdoms in the time we live in today. Almost everything about the social, economic, and political world we live in favors me. Name the legislation, name the politician, name the issue: More than likely it's all designed to reinforce my place in the world. And that's why people like me keep supporting people like me who favor people like me.

But that pretty much puts me on the side of the empire of Caesar in Jesus' day rather than the kingdom of God. It makes me likely to look at people like John the Baptist as a nuisance and a protester threatening my privilege with his moral messages about the rich and powerful. I wouldn't care much about him if he were simply preaching about people's souls being saved for the next life. But his message challenged the powerful in this life, so he was arrested and beheaded. This was fitting, of course. A man who had lost his head by preaching about the injustices of this world instead of staying in his lane and talking only about heaven—well, off with his head.

I posted something on Facebook this week that seems to have struck a nerve with some of you. Archbishop Oscar Romero of El Salvador was the spiritual leader of the people of that lately disparaged country from which two of our church employees and their families come. The people there were being exploited by a dictator propped up by U.S. foreign policy that saw any attempt to remake society in favor of the lower classes as rooted in communism. Romero served the people, not the palace. On Sunday, March 23, 1980, he delivered a sermon calling on Salvadoran soldiers, as Christians, to obey God's higher order and to stop carrying out the government's repression and its violations of basic human rights. The next day he spent time with some other priests, considering the nature of their call. He

---

30 https://slate.com/news-and-politics/2010/08/on-the-trail-of-the-question-who-first-said-or-wrote-that-journalism-is-the-first-rough-draft-of-history.html

31 http://www.gainesville.com/entertainment/20180102/movie-review-meryl-streep-stands-tall-in-journalism-drama-the-post

celebrated mass, then walked out from behind the altar toward the center aisle. A car then pulled up in front of the open doors of the chapel and a gunman got out and fired a shot right into his heart. The assassin was never caught. Romero had said this: *The transcendence that the church preaches is ... not going to heaven to think about eternal life and forget about the problems on earth. It's a transcendence from the human heart. It is entering into the reality of a child, of the poor, of those wearing rags, of the sick, of a hovel, of a shack. It is going to share with them. And from the very heart of misery, of this situation, to transcend it, to elevate it, to promote it, and to say to them, "You aren't trash. You aren't marginalized. It is to say exactly the opposite, 'You are valuable.'"*

This is why John was arrested and beheaded, preaching in this way. And this is why Jesus was arrested and crucified, preaching like this. So, here's my question to myself in these days when we are trying to renew the Jesus movement in our time: If that's what the good news of God entails, is it any wonder why I'm uncomfortable preaching it and you are uncomfortable with me preaching it? I don't want to get arrested for protesting unjust laws. I don't want to be a rabble-rouser. I want to be a respectable preacher who talks about God in quiet tones, one who uses polite words and doesn't offend. The problem is that this approach violates the very thing I pray for in baby dedications, that the child will have a good life, not an easy life. It turns the good news into fake news. It becomes a gospel of niceness, not a gospel that saves anyone.

This is why I guess we have to continue to talk about what it means that when Jesus finishes telling us to repent and believe the good news, he calls four disciples and changes their vocations from being fishers of fish to being fishers of people.

Here again, I have to confess that I have always had a little trouble with this call of Jesus to become fishers of men, as the King James version of the Bible puts it. Partly this is because I'm not a fisherman. Oh, I've fished a few times in my life, but to say that this makes me a fisherman is like saying I'm a singer because I sing in the shower. When I hear Jesus call these professional fishermen into the alternative vocation of fishing for people, my shallow understanding of this call is to feel sorry for the people they are going to fish for.

This sends me into all sorts of criticisms of how Christians do evangelism—the word that literally means to announce the good news. I object to the fishy way that some lure people to faith, bait the hook and catch them unawares, the way they reel them in from their natural life-giving habitat in the water that they had no desire to be saved from in the first place. That's the way we think of evangelism. We try to rescue people who don't want to be rescued. But this approach misses the meaning of what Jesus is calling these four—Simon, Andrew, James, and John—to do as his followers.

First, we don't all of us follow Jesus in some general or abstract way. We follow him out of the particulars of our own lives. When Jesus calls them to become fishers of people instead of fishers of fish, he is honoring their skills and training. He is simply redirecting their attention and ambition.

It's the same for the rest of us. As biblical commentator Debi Thomas puts it: *To the engineer, maybe Jesus says, "Follow me and build my people." To the visual artist,*

"Follow me and paint the colors of the kingdom." To the stay-at-home parent, "Follow me and nurture my children." To the dancer: "Follow me and dance to the Spirit." To the physician, "Follow me and heal broken souls." To all of us: "Follow me and I will make you ... ." This is a promise to cultivate us, not to sever us from what we love. It's a promise rooted in gentleness and respect—not violence and coercion. It's a promise that when we dare to let go, the things we relinquish might be returned to us anew, enlivened in ways we couldn't have imagined on our own.[32]

So, if you sense that God is calling you to drop your nets and serve God in a more deliberate way, it's probably only so that you can pick up other kinds of nets.

The second thing we have to realize about this is that the fishing business which the four disciples were engaged in was no small independent family business at the time they were called. It had been taken over by the government. "Caesar owned every body of water, and all fishing was state-regulated for the benefit of the urban elite. Fishermen couldn't obtain licenses to fish without joining a syndicate, most of what they caught was exported, leaving local communities impoverished and hungry, deprived of the dietary staple they had depended on for centuries, and the Romans collected exorbitant taxes, levies, and tolls each time fish were sold. To catch even one fish outside of this exploitative system was illegal."[33]

So, when Jesus had them drop their nets and offered them another way to think about the work they were doing by serving God and not Rome, he was offering them a different way of conceiving how the world should be ordered. And that different way of ordering life is called the kingdom of God. It's the way of the Beloved Community, as Martin Luther King Jr. called it. It's a world in which every person is cherished as a child of God with gifts to offer and needs to honor.

This is not fake news; it's good news, the good news of God that we embrace with joy when we repent, believe, and answer the call to follow Jesus. It doesn't just criticize; it advocates and elevates.

It may get us arrested; who knows? It may get us criticized—probably. But announcing the good news of God is our calling. And that always means acting in solidarity with those who need us most and standing up with them and for them, whether it's comfortable or not.

People will believe that God cares for them when they believe that we care for them. We may even find that we, as well as they, are being saved ourselves along the way.

---

32 https://www.journeywithjesus.net/essays/1623-fishing-for-people
33 Ibid.

18

Ambition

October 19, 2003
Nineteenth Sunday After Pentecost
Mark 10:35-45

It's hard to know how hard to be on the Sons of Thunder—James and John. On the one hand, they look like dimwit glory hounds so thickheaded and headstrong with ambition that we rightfully scorn them. Jesus has just finished delivering a speech on how he is going to Jerusalem and will suffer and die there as a rejected messiah. As if they hadn't heard a thing he said, they still try to weasel for special privileges when he succeeds in reigning over the kingdom. It's about like taking aside Governor Gray Davis just before the recall election in California and saying, *Hey, when you win this thing, can we be in your new cabinet?* What dunces!

But James and John are not the only dunces, are they? We are just like them, aren't we? We all struggle with ambition: too much, too little, mostly wrongheaded.

The very word *ambition* has a chilly October feel to it that keeps us from saying it too often. From the Latin *ambitio*, it originally referred to politicians ambling about the streets soliciting votes. *Webster's* definition is even November darker: *an ardent desire for rank, fame, or power*. And that seems to be what we have here with the Sons of Thunder. They are looking out for themselves. And after all, isn't that what we assume we need to do—look out for ourselves?

Well, we do, but maybe our sacraments should remind us otherwise. *Can you drink the cup I drink?* Jesus asks. *Can you undergo the baptism I undergo?* The boys in his band think they can, but, like us, they take the communion cup for after-dinner port rather than the thick vinegary wine in the Passover cup of suffering. We take baptism to be a blessing, a refreshing dip, something like the Nestea plunge, rather than drown our selfish ambitions in baptismal death for the love of God and the world.

William James was one of America's great philosophers, a father of modern pragmatism, and the author of the book *Varieties of Religious Experience*, which has had a deep effect on the spiritual perspective of Americans today. James was honest enough with himself to admit that he wanted to be both a saint and a millionaire—anyone else?—but he worried that what it might take for him to be the latter could disqualify him from being the former. He developed a threefold hierarchy of ambition. The lowest level is material self-seeking, in which we aim to gain wealth and accumulate property and things. This is rooted in the desire for self-preservation that affords us security and comfort. But it can also separate us from our neighbors because we have to protect what we have from loss. We become more interested in what our wealth can do for us instead of what we can do for others with our wealth. And the sad thing is that people of great wealth are not usually more comfortable than those with less who don't care about how much they have.[34]

The second level is social self-seeking. Because we are all social selves, we want to please others and be pleased by others. The ambition to achieve a level of social distinction does not always go with material success, and James thinks it progresses to this. To be well known and to have the power of esteem in a group or of a group is part of this.

The phenomenon of celebrity is an example of social ambition. We see it in people who are willing to go on TV and do just about anything to be widely noticed. Fifteen minutes of fame, don't you know?! Celebrity has its privileges, though. Like this past week, when Al Biernat's restaurant hosted Goldie Hawn and her longtime beau, Kurt Russell, for dinner. Aside from the special table and doting service, Al kept the place open for them until 1:00 a.m. so that Dallas Stars star Mike Modano could come and dine with them after the game. Now, that's nice, of course. But I'm just wondering, what if you or I were meeting a friend who couldn't get there until late? Would Al keep the place open for us until 1:00? Pay the staff overtime for us? I don't think so. That's celebrity power. Who wouldn't want it? But consider what they did to get it. I'm not saying they are wicked, but have they contributed to a richer humanity or a healthier planet? They have made a name for themselves. They sit at the right hand and the left in the kingdom of entertainment. The very word *entertainment* tells us something. It comes from the Latin, meaning *to keep someone in between*. It's a suspension of real life. Yet we exalt people for helping us escape life, more than teachers or scientists, or social workers, say, who try to make real life better.

Sadly, social ambition invades the church also. Martin Copenhaver is a colleague of mine in the Boston area, a pastor of a Congregational church that has also received a Lilly grant to operate a residency program for young pastors. He was once pastor of a New England church that had elderly members who remembered the day when wealthy families would send their cooks to serve alongside church members in preparing food for the needy. The tradition passed into modern times with the deacons helping out themselves. But the deacons always balked, because the bylaws said they were responsible for the "spiritual leadership" of the congregation. At one deacons' meeting they complained they were not able to fulfill this

34 Cited by Brian Mahan, *Forgetting Ourselves on Purpose: Vocation and the Ethics of Ambition* (Jossey-Bass, 2002), pp. 45-49.

high calling, because they were too busy delivering food to homeless shelters and washing dishes after communion. Said one deacon: *I feel like a glorified butler.*[35]

Said Jesus: *Whoever wishes to become great among you must be your servant, and whoever wants to be first among you must be slave of all. For the Son of Man came not to be served but to serve, and to give his life as a ransom for many.* A butler might be a good image for any deacon, pastor, or even lay minister.

The highest level of self-seeking is spiritual, according to James. This is the life of intellect and aesthetics and morality. The spiritual life concerns not just what it can do for the self, but more so what it does for others. The spiritual self-seeker is willing to give up material privilege or social prestige for the cause of loving God and neighbor. This faith sees beyond present struggles to the rewards that come from self-sacrifice.

And maybe this is where we might give the Sons of Thunder some slack. Maybe they have more faith than we realize but simply do not understand the cost of that faith. Close as they are to Jesus, maybe they truly believe that even though it will be tough sledding in Jerusalem, Jesus will prevail in the end and reign over the kingdom somehow, someday. Maybe they have more faith than any of the other disciples. Maybe they are saying what many of us hope for: Faithfulness will surely be rewarded, whether in this life or the next.

And yet James fretted over the fact that even in this dimension of ambition, noble though it may be, we are still *SELF-seeking*, still thinking in terms of personal reward, even if we are willing to delay glorification by serving now. If the last shall be first, then our strategy to be first is to be last ... for now. We are counting on a payday someday.

All of this fails the Jesus test. Jesus himself—though elevated by God after the crucifixion and resurrection—is still now and will forevermore be a servant. He is not sitting on his throne all day and night receiving glory now that he has done his bit. He intercedes for us now. He is still giving himself sacrificially to the world. It's simply his nature. And he is trying to get our self-seeking nature shaped into his image.

To do that, we need to practice what the late monk Thomas Merton called *self-forgetfulness.* That is, we leave worries about ourselves to God. We simply learn to serve, no matter the cost. We don't worry about how much we make or who notices us. We don't worry about rewards in heaven. We simply serve others and find that life is a gift that comes in community with others, not by distinguishing ourselves from others.

When your daughter turns twenty, as mine did this week, and you see more hair growing out of your ears than your brow, you start to think about ambition differently. I can't speak for you at whatever stage of life you are in, but all my life I've had the next thing to reach for: a football scholarship, a college degree, a master's degree, a doctor's degree, a big and good church, a great family, things like that. Then you wake up and realize it's all good, Martha. You have climbed every mountain in the range. What now?

---

35 Cited in *Pulpit Resource* 31.4 (Oct.-Dec. 2003): 15-16, from *The Christian Century*, Oct. 5, 1994: 893.

What I am learning is that the point has not been about my climb at all. It has been about learning from others how to climb so that I can help others climb, too. In fact, mountain climbing is probably not the right metaphor at all. I find myself more interested nowadays in judging my ministry by how well you are doing yours. I want to see a new generation of ministers hone their skills and ply their trade, and to do it better than I. I want to help shape a Baptist church that is so true to its heritage that it is not a prisoner to it. The Baptist vision has a continual reformation embedded within it. I want to see Baptist Christians learn to read the Bible intelligently and spiritually so that we can avoid the cul-de-sacs of fundamentalist fear and liberal license. I want to see the day when every child in Dallas is ready to read when he or she starts school. Things like that capture my heart these days, and they make worrying about myself seem downright petty.

This is the twenty-fifth anniversary of Pope John Paul II's papacy. Even a Baptist has to admit that he has been the most formidable figure in world Christianity for this generation. You may disagree with him on certain things—and I do, on birth control, the all-male unmarried priesthood, hierarchical church governance, the inability to see non-Catholic churches as part of the true body of Christ in the world—small things like that. But he has also been a consistent voice for the poor, a reconciling agent with Judaism, an unflinching critic of godless communism, fascism, terrorism, and even dehumanizing aspects of capitalism. He has been a peacemaker everywhere.

But when they handed out the Nobel Peace Prize last week, the committee passed him by. The winner was a deserving Iranian woman who has fought for human rights and women's rights and democracy in her country. But what the committee values most is only instrumental for the pope. They celebrate freedom as the highest value. He wants always to see freedom lead toward a dignity of human life and a spirit that is pleasing to God. In this sense, he is far beyond the Nobel folk. What's more, he doesn't care a fig about awards. He is ailing badly—Parkinson's disease most likely; but while many think he ought to step down and retire, he considers his suffering as an opportunity to serve the Lord in weakness. The shepherd will not leave his sheep. Nice.

The only ones privileged to be at the right hand and left of Jesus in this life were two bandits on crosses next to his. I suspect that isn't what James and John or we are ambitious for. Maybe we ought to rethink our ambition.

19

Journey Back to Love

Watch and listen to "Journey Back to Love" by following this link or scanning the QR code with your phone: youtu.be/kFiOJZ3PgBw. Sermon begins at 25:35.

March 27, 2022
Fourth Sunday in Lent
Luke 15:1-3, 11b-32

It's almost always called the Parable of the Prodigal Son. And you can understand why, right? The most ink is spilled on the character of the younger son in the parable. He asks his father for his share of the inheritance, runs off to a distant country, squanders his wealth in riotous living, finds himself eating humble pie in a pigsty, wanders home with his tail between his legs and a tale to tell his father, and the father takes him back without a hint of scolding.

It's a story that has long captured the imagination of artists and preachers both. Preachers have used it to describe how we rebel against God, mistreat God's love, ruin our lives, but finally repent of our sin and find that God is forgiving and kind. So, if you have rejected God's loving ways and left the house of God, found yourself far from church and feel as if all is lost, come to your senses, and return to the God who is waiting for you with open arms.

That's not bad, don't you know?! And it's not wrong, either. But it's also not exactly what's going on in this story.

There's also the part about the elder son who never leaves home and resents his father when the father welcomes back the younger brother and throws a party that he can't bring himself to attend. The moral of the story we tend to draw is that we should be like the prodigal son who repents of his sinful life and is reconciled to God and not like the judgmental elder brother who can't celebrate a sinner's repentance and would rather feast on his sour grapes.

And that's not all wrong either. It's just not likely what Jesus has in mind here in the telling.

The key to interpreting the parable properly is in the setup Luke gives us. Jesus, we are told, is scandalizing the guardians of goodness by welcoming tax collectors and sinners. He eats and drinks with them, thus compromising his own moral integrity by failing to call them to repentance. The Pharisees grumble about this.

Now, as I am not always wont to do, I want to say a good word for the Pharisees. We tend to use them as foil for those who love the law more than the Lord. They are legalists who miss the good news because they care more about morality than forgiveness. They are stand-ins for hypocritical religion. But that isn't quite true to who they really were. Jesus is closer to the Pharisees than any other group of Jews in his day. They share many of the same concerns. They both love the Lord and are faithful to the law of God. They both believe in righteousness and resurrection at the last day. But it is as true of them as of any of us that sometimes the good becomes the enemy of the good news. It's like what one wag said about someone: "He's a good man in the worst way." We can all be that way—whether Jews or Christians.

So, back to the parable. This is the third parable Jesus tells in response to the Pharisees' grumbling. The first is the Parable of the Lost Sheep. Jesus tells of a shepherd who goes after one wayward sheep and leaves the other ninety-nine. When he finds him, he brings him back to the flock with joy. The second parable is the lost coin. A woman loses a coin and desperately cleans her house to find it. When she finally locates it, she celebrates having found it. If the parable of the lost son here is seen in light of the first two, we see something we might have otherwise missed. Neither a sheep nor a coin can repent. They are simply lost and found. The focus is not on the repentance of the wayward ones; it is on the joyous spirit of the one who finds them.

So, if we look at this parable in that light, we see something curious. When the prodigal son finds himself hungry in the distant country, it says *he comes to himself.* We rush to think that means he comes to his senses and repents. But there's no clear sense that that's what he does. It may just as well be that he's up to his old tricks of looking out for himself. He conjures a story of how to get back into his father's graces. He comes ready to fall on his knees and beg to be made a servant so that he can eat something more satisfying than the pods the pigs were eating. But the father won't have any of that. The father goes running toward the son, won't let him finish his rehearsed speech, and lets him know that nothing has changed in his relationship to the boy. The relationship is what matters. It's what has always mattered. And it's time for that to matter most to the boy, if only for the first time.

The same is true for the elder brother. Nothing has changed as far as the father is concerned. His boy is his boy, and everything the father has is his, just as it always has been. The relationship is what matters. It's what has always mattered. And it's time for that to matter most to the boy, if only for the first time.

The one constant in this story is the father. And while it seems obvious that the father stands in for God in the parable, it's more likely that it's supposed to be Jesus who resembles the father. He is the one who is accused of welcoming sinners. He is the one against whom the elder brother Pharisees grumble on account of his generous love. If Jesus is the real issue here, it's also the church now that should see itself in this role. What is the church's attitude toward sinners? What is the church's attitude toward those who refuse to celebrate the reconciliation of sinners to the community?

In another sense, though, we should see that both sons are lost, despite their differences in the story. And both must take a journey back to home to find the truth that they have always been, are, and always will be loved.

Oddly, the younger son makes that journey that the elder son refuses. But all of us must make that spiritual journey if we are to know who we really are in the eyes of God.

The Franciscan friar Richard Rohr in his book *Falling Upward* talks about how easy it is for us to think that being at home with God is about never failing or falling, never leaving the safety of home. But really, the spiritual journey is about maintaining a hunger for being at home with God, regardless of whether you roam far from the house of God or stay close to it.

To repent really means to return—to return to your right mind, to return to the truth, to return to the God who never left you. You don't have to run off the rails to return, but it's often only those who do who realize they need to make the journey home. Only those who venture the journey discover the hidden truth buried right beneath our feet, wherever we are.

There's a Hasidic tale that illustrates the spiritual journey. Rabbi Bunam used to tell young men who came to him for the first time the story of Rabbi Eisik, son of Rabbi Yekel in Kraków. After many years of great poverty which had never shaken his faith in God, Rabbi Eisik dreamed someone bade him look for a treasure in Prague, under the bridge which leads to the king's palace. When the dream recurred a third time, he prepared for the journey and set out for Prague. But the bridge was guarded day and night and he did not dare to start digging. Nevertheless, he went to the bridge every morning and kept walking around it until evening.

Finally, the captain of the guards, who had been watching him, asked in a kindly way whether he was looking for something or waiting for somebody. Rabbi Eisik told him of the dream which had brought him here from a faraway country. The captain laughed: *And so to please the dream, you poor fellow wore out your shoes to come here! As for having faith in dreams, if I had had it, I should have had to get going when a dream once told me to go to Kraków and dig for treasure under the stove in the room of a Jew—Eisik, son of Yekel, that was the name! Eisik, son of Yekel! I can just imagine what it would be like, how I should have to try every house over there, where one half of the Jews are named Eisik, and the other Yekel!* And he laughed again. Rabbi Eisik bowed, traveled home, dug up the treasure from under the stove, and built the House of Prayer which is called Reb Eisik's Shul.[36]

As Rohr puts it: *Great love is always a discovery, a revelation, a wonderful surprise, a falling into 'something' much bigger and deeper that is literally beyond us and larger than us.*[37] That something is really Someone. Someone who never leaves us and always waits at the end of our journey to welcome us back to love.

36 https://www.learningtogive.org/resources/treasure
37 Jossey-Bass, 2011, p. xxvii.

May your Lenten journey in this season of the soul lead you home to God where you will find what was always true, what is true, and what will always be true for you—that you are a beloved child of God over whom God rejoices. Amen.

PART III

Always on the Way

Mission of the Church

"The focus of the church is the world. Whenever the church is in the world, God is in the church. Whenever the church is not in the world, God is not in the church."

~ **Kennon Callahan**

"What makes the gospel offensive isn't who it keeps out, but who it lets in."

~ **Rachel Held Evans**

"You are here because you have found a place at the table of the Lord. It's a table that welcomes EveryBody, as we like to say. There is room here for everybody because the heart of God stretches to make room for everybody. But EveryBody is not just about welcome; it's about the privilege of doing our part. You're on the team. You have a uniform. No one is sidelined. The coach has called your number. Time to get in the game."

~ **George A. Mason**

Preface by Gary Simpson

This section is aptly named. As people of faith and people seeking faith we are "Always on the Way." When we think we have arrived, we are indeed lost. George's quote that begins this chapter is a succinct capturing of his preaching essence and passion.

The Reverend Dr. George Mason and I met in the typical gathering of curious faith leaders.

"George, just George," he said when I asked how he preferred to be called. I knew then we were going to get along. Too bad we are in a profession teeming with pretense and airs. Now with many years of many earnest and honest conversations and visits, George and I are friends and brothers, inseparable despite all of the things that should divide us. We have shared tears and laughter. Prayers and pains. Our families might even tire of our countless references to each other at meals. (Not really, our families love our relationship!)

"Just George" has managed to bring his hope for common good and a holy dissatisfaction to settle for anything less in his sermons. While there are those who browbeat and pound Christian virtues into their pulpit talk, George has a vision for the church that is so compelling and inspirational it is hard to listen to him and want to remain as you are. He invites you to come sit with him in the company of his friends. Who are George's friends? I am sure this is not an exhaustive list: Jesus, familiar biblical characters, biblical characters we have forgotten or passed over, peoples of all faiths, playwrights, bestselling authors, scientists, artists, musicians and composers, young people getting ready for baptism, strangers who show up on the door of Wilshire, faith leaders, world citizens, and faceless nameless people who are hurting.

George spends his sermons introducing you to his ever-increasing group of friends. As both a scholarly pastor and a pastoral scholar, George is incredibly well read and well versed. As a deftly gifted pastor he manages not to alienate his listeners with his knowledge. He spends his sermons introducing you to the vast universe of his friends and inviting you as a listener to come to the table. George does not read without becoming familiar. I used to hear Gardner Taylor speak of the great preachers throughout history. He spoke with such intimacy that it felt like he just shot marbles with each of them that morning. George has this gift in his sermons. He knows no strangers.

When you hear his sermons, you hear the heart of a pastor, the passion of a church leader who wants us all to do better. From his sermon, "the church is a laboratory of learning that allows us to prepare for our life in the world."

To appreciate the quest for meaning that good preaching provides, one must cultivate a palate for nuance and the careful turn of phrases. In this section, George reminds us that we cannot be a community centered on the "love of power" but on the "power of love."

While scrolling through social media, whenever I see a good thing accomplished or celebrated by congregants, I simply respond, #PastorProud. I want congregants to know; first, I see you and second, that I am heartened by the good you accomplish. George's sermons exude this love for the people of Wilshire where there are no great or small, just people striving together to be people of good faith and works. I believe the word is "EveryBody."

Throughout these sermons his understanding of Jesus is that of a Christ who himself struggles to get beyond his familiar to be actively present in the struggle of "the other" and respond to their pains with passion and transformative friendship. Quoting again from a sermon in this section, "the world is larger than your heart." George's approach to the gospel makes Jesus accessible. His Jesus is himself a student of life, as seen most vividly in his sermons on the Canaanite woman and the Good Samaritan, learning from those who are outside his familiar stretching for a view of kin-dom that reaches beyond the comfortable.

Thank you George, just George.

Thank you, just thank you.

Gary V. Simpson is leading pastor of the Concord Baptist Church of Christ in Brooklyn, New York. He is Associate Professor of Preaching and Pastoral Formation at Drew Theological Seminary and serves as the chair of the Ordination Council of American Baptist Churches of Metropolitan New York.

20

They Call That Church

May 25, 2003
Sixth Sunday of Easter
1 John 5:1-6; John 15:9-17

Dr. David Kuhl has written a book called *What Dying People Want*. He offers practical wisdom for the end of life, wisdom that has grown out of his personal experience with people who are dying. He has learned that listening—really listening—is the mode of presence we must bring to the bedside. What concerns dying people most surprises us sometimes: it is often not their own suffering or the fear of what will happen to them; it is what will happen to the people they love when they lose influence over those lives upon their death.

Alice was the patient that taught him most about this. As a palliative-care physician, Dr. Kuhl spends his life trying to relieve the suffering of those who are dying. He had tried everything he knew to try on Alice. The pain in her chest persisted as she lay in the St. Paul's Hospital in Vancouver. Her lung cancer was progressing, but for all his efforts to make her comfortable, she was getting no relief. He finally asked her if the pain in her chest might have to do with her heart, not her cancer. Her eyes brightened, as if he had finally pushed the right button. She opened up. *Yes, the pain is in my heart. It has to do with my daughter, Ruth. She is marrying a man I do not approve of, and I told her so. My daughter, my only child, did not want to hear that message. I had to tell her because by the time she realizes that he's no good for her, I will no longer be alive. I don't ever expect to be free of this pain, and what's more, unless circumstances change for Ruth, I don't want this pain to be taken away.*[38]

My pastoral experience confirms the point. Most people can handle their own dying, but they worry about those they will leave behind. Jesus is doing much the same thing in our text today from the fifteenth chapter of John's Gospel. This is part of what scholars call the Farewell Discourses. Jesus faces his own death by passing on to his loved ones, his disciples, what is most important for them to know after he

---

[38] *Public Affairs*, 2002, p. xvi.

is gone. While he is with them, his own love for them can control their behavior to some extent, but after he is gone he knows that, his Spirit's presence not withstanding, their love for each other will be the controlling mark of his success.

Rick Warren is an innovative pastor in Southern California. He has written a new book called *The Purpose Driven Life*, which is a sequel to *The Purpose Driven Church*. Rick says he found his own purpose from his father's deathbed. The elder Warren was a Texas-born Baptist preacher who helped start 150 churches over fifty years. With his body ravaged with cancer, he talked about what mattered to him the most—building churches. Rick sat by his father's bed and heard him say in his sleep over and over, *Gotta save one more for Jesus. Gotta save one more for Jesus.* He said it nearly a hundred times in the next hour, Rick says. And then, before he died, he laid his hand on his son's head and said, *Reach one more for Jesus.*[39]

Well, Jesus himself said some things about that to his disciples in the other Gospel records. *Go ye into all the world and make disciples of every nation.* Matthew 28. And where the passing of the word is the main thing in churches, there is good energy around bearing witness to those who do not know Christ. And yet, when that becomes the main thing, it is also an invitation to dissension. *The Word*, Martin Luther said, *is the one perpetual and infallible mark of the church.* And when that is so, doctrinal correctness becomes the all-important issue. And that leads to loads of conflict over who is interpreting things aright. This is the very thing that the battling Baptists have gotten caught up with over the past twenty-five years or so. And when some of us have tried to say that that isn't the Baptist way, we have not been trying to exclude our fellow Christians, we have been trying to say that fellowship itself is the true mark of the church. How we treat one another, in other words. There is no way ever to know for sure whether we get our doctrine right, but there is no doubt about whether we love one another.

And just this is what Jesus emphasizes in our text. *This is my commandment, that you love one another as I have loved you.* Not *this is my commandment, that you get an A+ on every Bible quiz.* Neither did he say, *this is my commandment, that you do everything right all the time.* No, good theology is a good thing, and personal holiness, too. But the church demonstrates that it knows Jesus by the way it loves.

I visited with Taylor Little this week before her baptism this morning. I asked her about what it means to be a Christian. I didn't ask her to recite the Ten Commandments, The Lord's Prayer, or The Four Spiritual Laws. We read this passage together. We talked about how no one has greater love than to lay down one's life for one's friends. We talked about how Jesus had done that for us. And then I asked her if she knew anyone else who might love her enough to die for her. She said that she and her mom had talked about that recently, and that she thought her mom and dad would do that for her, and that she thought she would do that for them, too. I told her that that's the kind of love God has for her and for everyone. And that's the kind of love God wants us to show for others as the church Jesus left behind.

---

39 *The Dallas Morning News*, May 24, 2003, 5G.

Try to imagine a church like that—a church where people took loving each other to such extremes as giving their lives for each other. It certainly wouldn't be a church fighting each other all the time over whose theology was right. It wouldn't be a church where a few people tried to control all the committees. It wouldn't be a church where everyone was trying to find out who had been misbehaving so they could tell others about it. It would be a church that astonishes the world by the way they welcome people, forgive each other, find ways to pick up those who have fallen and restore their lost luster. It would be a church where people would recognize Jesus.

We've had a task force at work in our church in recent months trying to come up with a way to interpret to our community what kind of church Wilshire is. Our middle name, Baptist, does not turn up in *Roget's Thesaurus* as a synonym for love. The group kept bumping up against stereotypes of Baptists as small-hearted, narrow-minded, petty, chauvinist "only-we're-going-to-heaven" types. They started out with the slogan, *We're not that kind of church.* But the more they talked about their experience among us, the more they leaned toward a more positive motto: *We're that kind of church!* The kind of church that wields hammers to build houses for the poor rather than shaking fists at each other. The kind of church where women know their place, which may be behind the pulpit or the communion table as much as in the kitchen or preschool department. The kind of church where singles of all kinds are as much family to us as married people, and even those married more than once. We're that kind of church—the kind of church that loves each other enough to honor Christ by the way we treat each other under any and all circumstances.

Next to our Gospel reader today, Allen Walworth, who is one of the best preachers and storytellers I know, don't you know?!, the beloved Fred Craddock is a source no sermonizer can resist quoting. He tells about being the pastor of a small church in Appalachia years ago that had a wonderful custom. They would gather new converts on Easter eve at sundown by a nearby river. Craddock would wade out to a sandbar with the candidates, as the congregation met around a fire and sang hymns. Once everyone was gathered, a man named Glenn Hickey, and only he, would introduce the new folk and share what they did and where they lived. Glenn would then work his way round the circle. Every member would give his or her name and say something like: *My name is _____ if you ever need somebody to do some washing and ironing. My name is _____ if you ever need somebody to chop wood. My name is _____ if you ever need anybody to repair your house. My name is _____ if you ever need a car to go into town.* Once they were finished, they would sit down to a huge meal, pull out the banjos, and some would take to dancing. When darkness and cold got the better of them, Percy Miller would kick dirt over the fire, and they would head home ready for Resurrection Sunday. Craddock remembers the first time he was part of all that. Percy was standing behind the dying fire and said, *Craddock, folks don't ever get any closer than this.* With his usual flair, Craddock concludes: *In that little community they have a name for that kind of experience. I've heard it in other communities, too. In that community, their name for that is church. They call that church.*[40]

40 Cited by Mark Barger Elliot in *Lectionary Homiletics* (Apr-May 2003): 63.

Nice. Do they call this church? If we love one another like that, we will have no worry about how others perceive us. They will know that this is where they can come in from the world when the wind chill of broken relationships and life disappointment leaves them cold and alone. They are not out there searching for perfect theology, people; they are looking for love. They are not searching for perfect people, people; they are looking for love. They are not searching for the perfect building or music or preaching or parking, people; they are looking for love. They are looking for imperfect people who will not quit practicing until they get their love down perfectly.

An old African king is dying. He calls his people to his side and gives each of his many offspring, wives, and relatives a short, sturdy stick. *Break the stick*, he tells them. They each strain at it, but they all snap their sticks. *This is how it is when a soul is alone and without anyone. They can easily be broken,* he says. Next, he gives each of them another stick and says, *This is how I would like you to live after I pass. Tie your sticks together in bundles of twos and threes.* He waits as they arrange themselves according to his wishes. *Now break these bundles in half,* he says. No one can break the sticks, no matter the effort. The old man smiles: *We are strong when we stand with another soul. When we are with others, we cannot be broken.*[41]

What Jesus wanted is for his disciples to live like that after he was gone. He wants that still. We can't control what others do, but let it be said of us that this is a church that loves. It's that kind of church.

---

41 Kuhl, p. xxviii.

21

Love Power

Watch and listen to "Love Power" by following this link or scanning the QR code with your phone: youtu.be/_1-Y0zBZ7So. Sermon begins at 29:15.

October 2, 2016
Twentieth Sunday after Pentecost
2 Timothy 1:1-14

Sometimes we make too much of the differences between the culture of ancient times and today's. There are differences, for sure. Rome had an emperor, while most monarchs we have left in the world today are figureheads, with political power now diffused among the people. Women were considered the property of their husbands back then, just a notch above slaves, while today whatever remnants of those hierarchies still exist are generally considered morally wrong. Children weren't cherished then the way they are today, as their significance was more about the legacy of the family than who they were themselves.

But these differences are more degree than kind. If we have eyes to see, we can spot in our passage from 2 Timothy how we continue to wrestle with some of the same issues. The church struggled then and struggles now to find its place in a society that values strength and power more than anything else, and this is more or less tied to lingering notions of honor and shame.

Listen to how this comes through in the text. Timothy was Paul's younger protégé with the churches in Ephesus. It was hard going. In a Roman culture, being successful and respectable was everything, and yet the churches were small, and they mostly met in the houses of wealthy widows. The new religion worshiped a savior who was shamefully crucified as a criminal, and the foremost apostle of the church, Paul, had also been a prisoner. Suffering was a sign of divine disfavor. It proved a person's unworthiness. No respectable Roman would willingly sign on to a life characterized by weakness or shame.

Timothy's courage was apparently flagging. Paul had to remind him that *God did not give us a spirit of cowardice, but rather of power and of love and of self-discipline.* He went on to tell him not to be *ashamed* of the gospel or of Paul's having been a prisoner. Instead, he urged him to lean in and accept that this was the revolution that God was bringing about in Christ Jesus, one that would transform the world from the bottom up. This is the reason why God sent Jesus to be among us as a human being who endured shame and death. He removed the stigma that attaches to the loser and the failure, the low-brow and the low-born, the has-been and the never-was.

But this view is hard to accept even today. Our culture has made great progress in human rights and in understanding the mysteries of nature. Yet we still value success and power so highly that values like these become calling cards for us in social settings and qualifications for public office. We still too often think that honor is attached to wealth and beauty and youth, to intelligence and athleticism and heritage, to achievement and fame and self-esteem—and shame to their opposites.

The church is still struggling with its place in the world, trying sometimes to argue for power and prestige in worldly terms that seems odd when we consider what our text is saying to us. Some Christians today consider the church weak if we do not achieve worldly power. They read a passage like this about God not giving us a spirit of cowardice, but of power, and they think that means we need to assert ourselves boldly and to claim our place among the strong.

For instance, one local Baptist preacher has recently said, *I am getting sick and tired of these namby-pamby, panty-waisted, weak-kneed Christians.* He wants a manlier Christianity and a more militant faith that conquers culture and takes control of the public square for God. Another form of this faith involves those who believe that God has secretly anointed some special Christians to be in charge of the world in the seven mountains of culture—family, religion, education, media, entertainment, business, and government. They are to rule the world until Christ returns victorious at the Second Coming to reward the righteous and to condemn sinners.

This is not what Paul is calling Timothy to, and it's not what God is calling the church to today. It's a misunderstanding of our faith and witness. The way Christ defeated the powers of sin and death and brought immortality to light was through the gospel. And the gospel works by subversion—subverting the powers of the world by refusing to play according to their rules. Salvation comes through suffering on behalf of the lowly, not through success by lauding it over the lowly. God vindicated Jesus and raised him from the dead on account of his self-sacrificial life of love.

Jesus redefined courage as the power of love, not the love of power. He called us to *love* power, not to love *power. Love*, not *power*, is the proper noun of Christian faith. Said another way, love qualifies power instead of power qualifying love. Love is willing to suffer on behalf of others in order to demonstrate its power to redeem. Power is willing to make others suffer in order to prove its superiority to them.

Real courage is the power to endure suffering out of love, not the capacity to defeat others by force of power. This is where self-discipline comes in. God has given us a spirit of love and power *and* self-discipline. We discipline ourselves to exercise power in the service of love, not the other way 'round.

And if you think of it this way, the question, then, is where you learn this kind of love power. Paul begins by telling Timothy to fan into flame the faith that was first in his grandmother, Lois, and then also in his mother, Eunice. In other words, he turns to the women of Timothy's family as models of what kind of faith he should exercise. This is exactly contrary to anything that would have seemed laudable in the ancient world, where masculine virtues were superior to feminine ones. But maternal strength is hardly namby-pamby, panty-waisted or weak-kneed. It's a love power that begins with enduring the pain of childbirth, continues with the letting go of weaning, and never ceasing in prayer and love. If motherhood represents weakness to the world that is passing away, then it's the kind of weakness that God sees as strength for the world that is coming to be.

I was with Tony Campolo a couple of weeks ago. He's a well-known and highly respected inspirational speaker. His wife, Peggy, stayed home to raise their two kids while he traipsed around the world speaking. On the rare occasions when she did travel with him, she often found herself in conversations with some of the most accomplished, impressive, influential, sophisticated people in the world.

After one such trip, Peggy confided in Tony that she sometimes found herself intimidated and questioning her self-worth. Tony suggested that she come up with something she could say when she met such people that would let them know how she valued her role. Not long after that, when the Campolos were at a party, a woman said to Peggy in a condescending tone, *Well, my dear, what do you do?*

Tony heard his wife say, *I am nurturing two Homo sapiens into the dominant values of the Judeo-Christian tradition in order that they might become instruments for the transformation of the social order into the kind of eschatological utopia God envisioned from the beginning of time.*

The other woman said: *Oh my, I'm just a lawyer.*

Motherhood is a powerful job that God uses to shape the love power of Christians in the world. Timothy was called to remember and draw upon that female family faith when he was feeling shamed by the power values of the world or intimidated into thinking himself insignificant.

That's not to say that men and fatherhood aren't important, too, but the point is that women as well as men have a capacity to teach their children what it means to be Christian leaders. Women's Lives Matter, don't you know?!

The larger point is to point to the role of the family itself in Christian formation. I'm afraid that this is sometimes as neglected today as it was then. We have a way of outsourcing and delegating too much in our parenting. We want teachers and role models for our children in school and church, and we forget that we are the first line of faith development for them.

The difference in whether a child learns and achieves in school often comes down to how involved the parents are. Do they model reading and self-discipline for their children? Do they read to their children when they are young and set high standards for them? It's the same with spiritual education. Shall we neglect to model Christian practices of prayer and worship, generosity and service? Ask yourself: What kind of Christian will my children be if we as parents are their primary role models of faith? Would someone be able to say to them, as Paul did to Timothy, in a crucial time of self-doubt in life, to remember the faith of your parents and grandparents? Will they have a legacy of faith that they can fan into flame when the going gets tough?

This is a resource I have because of my parents' faith and faithfulness. To be able to honor and not shame the faith of my parents is a rich and important gift, and I hope it's something my children and grandchildren can say about Kim and me as well.

But the church also plays a key role. Paul told Timothy to also remember the gifts that were his through the laying on of hands by the church. The family and the church are the two spheres of influence that shape the faith lives of the next generation.

This is one reason we make a conscious effort in the faith formation of children from birth onward. We don't see it as our job to entertain children at church. They have plenty of that in the rest of their lives. And when they are youth, it's not all fun and games. It's about teaching them to be still and know that God is God. It's about building into them an awareness of who they are as children of God. It's about teaching them that the main purpose of their life is to serve and glorify God with the gifts that are given to them.

That also involves spotting those like Timothy, who have gifts for serving the church. Our ministers and Sunday school teachers keep an eye out for those who show a keen interest in spiritual things. And we tell them when we see that in them.

Our pastoral residency program is the icing on the cake, through which we train young ministers for service. I was moved by the testimony of our newest residents at deacons' meeting last week. They said how honored they were to be among us during this time. They named the challenge they see the church going through now in our inclusion and diversity discernment. They don't need us to be a conflict-free zone in order to learn the love power of ministry. They need us to be the kind of people who persevere together in seeking the will of God and honoring one another as we do.

The church is a laboratory of learning that allows us to prepare for our life in the world. If we are faithful to God and to each other when times are tough, we will give young people the resources they need to be faithful to God and one another when their turn comes.

If the church is in love with power, we have little to offer them that the world doesn't have. But if the church practices the power of love, the world will have a witness to the saving grace of Christ that endures forever and ever. Amen.

22

Learning Outside In

Watch and listen to "Learning Outside In" by following this link or scanning the QR code with your phone: youtu.be/Dm_onwKHbp0. Sermon begins at 12:50.

September 5, 2021
Fifteenth Sunday after Pentecost
Mark 7:24-37

His name is Byron. I found him sitting alone in the South Atrium when I came into the church building this week. I introduced myself and asked if I could help. He greeted me warmly and said someone was already helping him. At that moment, Heather Mustain appeared, accompanied by our pastoral intern, Lindsay Bruehl. They had been working on what we could offer him.

Byron had fled New Orleans with his family ahead of Hurricane Ida. He was quick to make his Baptist connection to us. He is a member of a church in New Orleans, one of the most prominent African American congregations in the Southern Baptist Convention. The pastor was the first Black president of the SBC. I told him it didn't matter what church he went to; we would help. I also let him know we are not part of the SBC for several reasons, including the way they deal with race and women. We stand for the full humanity and total equality of Black people and women in all aspects of church and society, I told him. He seemed surprised. I passed him to Heather and Lindsay, exhibits A and B in my case for equality. I later learned Byron spent a fair amount of time carefully telling his story as one who was worthy of our help, as if he needed to convince us. I know why. It's because that's the way things usually work when someone has a desperate need and comes to someone who has resources to help. And let's be honest. Tragically, internalized assumptions about race are a factor. This was a Black man asking for help from a white church.

Last Sunday we talked about *living inside out*. Jesus challenged the purity culture of his Judaism, saying that it isn't things that come from without that defile a person but things that come from within, from the heart. This week, we find Jesus learning from someone who is on the outside and changing his mind about what he would do based on his encounter with a pagan woman. The story of Byron and this—do note!—*unnamed* Gentile woman teach us a lot about how God can use outsiders to help us learn, even changing our minds if not our theology.

Jesus has left the region of Galilee where he had grown up and started his ministry among his own people. He is in the northeastern coastal city of Tyre, a Gentile town where he planned to rest, to get away from the press of the crowds. He is in the home of a pagan, eating.

Jesus is willing to eat with and be in contact with people who are "other" to him as a Jew. This itself is scandalous. But he has already said that being in contact with the unclean doesn't make you unclean.

This Gentile woman approaches Jesus because her daughter has a demon, and she wants him to heal her. She falls at his feet and begs Jesus to heal her girl. The humiliation is complete. In the face of it, Jesus' response to her sounds so—what shall we say?—un-Christlike. *Let the children be fed first, for it is not fair to take the children's food and throw it to the dogs.*

We don't expect this from Jesus, do we? We think of him as the perfect and finished product of humanity from the moment of his birth. He says and does all the things we are supposed to say and do to reflect God's concern for every person without respect to gender, race, social or economic status, moral character, or religion. Jesus is our model: he bears the divine stamp. Listen to Jesus and act accordingly.

But Mark presents this story in a way that shows us how even Jesus learned the will of God through his encounters with people, including outsiders. Up until now Jesus has viewed his messianic role primarily as a ministry of and to Israel. He had his eye on the imminent coming of the kingdom of God that would come about through Israel. He is laser focused there. Israel first, don't you know?! When all was accomplished, the Gentiles, as well as the Jews, would be fully brought into the universal reign of God. But this was *Israel's* divine mission, not a general philosophy that could be gained from anywhere if you were sincere.

Jesus' retort to the woman represents the prevailing understanding of Jews toward Gentiles, whom they considered something less than human because of their idolatry. Rabbi Eliezer had said: *He who eats with an idolater is like one who eats with a dog.*

Jews thought of themselves as children in the household of God and the Gentiles as dogs, regardless of whether they were wild or domestic pets. They were outsiders and unclean. Dog is clearly a derogatory term, no matter how you try to clean it up. At one level, then, Jesus echoes the Jewish sentiments of his time.

But stepping back a bit, consider first that Jesus has put himself into contact with people others kept themselves away from. This is the first thing to see.

Some of us Christians today do everything we can to steer clear of people whom we view as different, if not less than us. In fact, even though Christianity is the majority religion in America, many of us feel like we're the victims in a secular culture that disrespects us. Like Jews in Jesus' time who really were the minority, we think of ourselves as the elect of God who are discriminated against by people who don't share our faith. Contact is the first thing we must risk if we expect God to teach us anything from outsiders.

But in doing so, it doesn't mean we have to compromise our own faith. Like Jesus, we can hold our convictions strongly that we are children of God. We can believe that God has entrusted us with the message of salvation. Jesus held the view that God's purposes for the world were going to be worked out through Israel, not around it.

Having this risky encounter and dialogue with this Gentile woman shows us something we must have: a commitment to compassionate listening. We can learn from outsiders, and particularly from those who are in oppressed circumstances we don't fully understand from our positions. But we have to lean in to learn.

Considering recent developments in our state, it's clear to me we have a lot to learn. My understanding of racism has not improved one iota only by listening to white people who are sure they know the experience of Black Americans and what they are going through. We need to listen to Black people. My understanding of women's experiences in the world has not improved one iota only by talking with other men or about women as a man. We need to listen to women. My understanding of immigration has not improved one iota only by studying the history of America's immigration laws. We need to listen to immigrants. This litany could go on and on and on.

This is our great challenge today—to pay attention to and learn from those who are most affected by the circumstances of life that we cannot understand because of where we stand. Only by coming to know those whose experience is raw and real and different from ours can we learn what God is up to in the world and what God is asking of us.

This is hard work, whether we are talking about the things I just mentioned, or about other religions, or—and this is particularly important now more than ever—with people who differ from us politically. We can do hard things. We must. The only way we will ever heal our deep divisions is to risk painful encounters with others that lead us into compassionate listening.

One way to do that is to find the common humanity in others. Sometimes that can be as simple as saying to yourself, *I wonder if he likes carrots.* This is a technique Shakil Choudhury suggests in his book, *Deep Diversity.* We need to find ways to break through our biases about others.

My wife, Kim, is retired now from her career as a dental hygienist. She had one patient who always intimidated her. He came for a cleaning every three months. Three-piece suit. Always prompt. Never said a word. One day she couldn't take it anymore and she asked him: *John, what were you like as a child?* He was taken aback by the question, but he began to open up and relax. They became closer and Kim came to look forward to their visits. When she retired, he brought her gifts and expressed his thanks not only for her work but for who she was to him.

The woman's daughter in our story was afflicted. This may be the humanizing element that moves Jesus. The woman herself oddly seems to accept what Jesus says. We don't know if this is an example of internalized oppression. It could be. People who have been abused or traumatized often think they deserve their status, as tragic as that seems. But even then, they may call out to us, like this woman. Admittedly, this can be annoying and exhausting. But we are most like Jesus when we hear them as if God is speaking to us through them.

Even the dogs eat the crumbs from the children's table, she says. And with this, Jesus is converted by her argument. He not only heals her daughter, he reframes his understanding of his messianic mission. God isn't waiting until the end of time to include Every Body.

Contact, compassion, and conversion. Those are the three C's of learning outside in. God not only wants us to teach others what we already know but to learn from others what we don't yet know.

I wonder what God wants the church to learn these days from outsiders. We know how. Jesus showed us.

Now it's up to us. Amen.

23

Getting Straightened Up at Church

Watch and listen to "Getting Straightened Up at Church" by following this link or scanning the QR code with your phone: youtu.be/FQxs2xqwX-s. Sermon begins at 27:15.

August 21, 2016
Fourteenth Sunday after Pentecost
Luke 13:10-17

If only Jesus would have stuck to teaching. Everybody loves a good teacher. It's when that teaching goes to healing that it disrupts the fellowship and things get tense.

Like the story Luke tells of Jesus teaching in *some* synagogue, when *some* bent-over woman catches his eye, and then *some* man who was the leader of the synagogue starts fuming because Jesus should have known better than to do things the way he did when there would have been a better time or place to have done it—if it really needed doing at all.

Oh, my, do we understand why Luke doesn't name these people? He names people in other stories. He names all the key players in the birth narrative: We have Mary and Joseph, Elizabeth and Zechariah, the Angel Gabriel, and so on. The two sisters from Bethany, namely, Mary and Martha. The tax collector who was the wee little man, Zacchaeus. But here we have a powerful story of all unnamed people. I wonder why. I wonder whether Luke just wants us to crawl into this story and find ourselves in it, name ourselves—our church even. Just wondering.

He also doesn't tell us why this woman in the synagogue that day was so bent over. He says she couldn't stand up straight for eighteen years. She was so bowed from the waist that she looked like a walking jackknife.

After our children's moment this morning, I got to thinking it might have been a condition of *backpackitis*. I live across the street from an elementary school. I see kids getting out of their parents' cars every school day, and they hoist their heavy backpacks filled with books and other burdens. I sometimes worry that they'll fall over backwards, except for the forward lean they use to balance their march to school. After eighteen years of bent-over walking like that, maybe they won't ever be able to straighten up again. What do you think? Be careful, kids.

To everyone else's eye, this woman suffered from a physical ailment. She was so bent over that she probably leaned on a cane and would have gotten used to talking to your knees. Today we might call it ankylosing spondylitis—a condition that causes people to be locked in a bent-over position. I've seen people who suffered from this in their later years. I always think, why can't some doctor do something about that?

Then it occurs to me: I'm a doctor. When my kids were little and their friends found out that their daddy was a doctor, they were often quick to clarify: *Yes, he's a doctor, but not the kind that can do you any good.* But that's usually because we think of illness mostly in physical terms. Luke was himself a physician, and he tells us that this woman had been crippled by a *spirit* for eighteen years.

Now that may conjure up some scary movie about demonic possession that makes you spill your popcorn in your lap just thinking about it. But even now, when we talk about people who suffer emotional or psychological trouble, we say things like, *she struggles with personal demons.* And those demons can become squatters in your life that make themselves at home without your permission. They become hard to live with. They reside in your head or heart, and you can feel powerless over them: helpless, hopeless.

But here is the Great Physician, Jesus himself, untrained in the medical sciences but with a keen eye for what ails people from the inside out. Something spiritual is crippling her more than something physical. Even that has a medical name now: conversion disorder. In other words, sometimes something we have done, or something that was done to us, or something that just is us and we have a hard time accepting it, becomes so paralyzing that it affects us physically.

I know a woman who has a hard time looking any man in the eyes because of what one man did to her against her will—let's just say—eighteen years ago. I wonder about that woman in Luke's story. What happened to her?

Truth to tell, lots of us in this room today know how this woman might have felt. Let's do an experiment, shall we? Are you up for this? All right, now, let's see whether we can imagine how this woman felt when she went into—let's just say—church that day. Stand up if you are able. Good. Now bend over at the waist. Go ahead. Now hold that position. How does it feel? Vulnerable? Humiliating? Painful?

Now, let's say that a spirit has you in that position. Mostly I'm thinking of a spirit inside you that makes you feel like you are bent over all the time. What is it? Are you bent over inside because of some memory that brings you shame and you don't know how to look people in the eye because you feel dirty or unworthy? Have you done something you can't forgive yourself for? Is anger just tearing you up on the inside? Are you depressed for reasons you don't understand? Have you just wanted to be some definition of normal all your life and you don't know how to deal with your difference? What is your bentness about?

All right now, before you sit down, I want you to imagine that Jesus is here right now. He is. He sees you as you are from the inside. He sees the spirit of infirmity that keeps you crippled. Now listen: *Woman, man, you are free from your ailment.*

Boom. Mic drop. Did you hear that? You are free. Now feel his hands on your back, straightening you up. Straighten up right now.

There. Beautiful. How do you feel? Listen, this is no parlor trick. And, no, we're not going to pass the plate again. This is the good news. God does not want you to be knotted up with guilt, bent over in shame, torn up with worry or fear about who you are in the eyes of heaven. Jesus is the liberator of all things that bind us and keep us from knowing that we are children of promise.

That's why, when Jesus had to deal with the synagogue leader about this, he reminded the man that this woman was a daughter of Abraham. That means she is a child of promise. And so are you. Don't let anyone tell you any different. When Jesus finishes telling you the truth about yourself, you are free. Now don't start bending back over again to any evil spirits. Stand up in the sanctuary. Throw your heads back in gratitude. And praise God from this point on.

Of course, there's more to this story. Action and reaction. It's Newton's third law of motion: For every action, there is an equal and opposite reaction. We didn't need a genius physicist to tell us if we were just paying attention to life. Here we see it again. Jesus sees someone in need of healing on the Sabbath day. He has compassion for the person, and he heals her. Immediately the guardians of all things religiously proper throw a fit. In this case it's the leader of the synagogue. He knows the Law of Moses, and the law of the Medes and Persians, and I wouldn't be surprised if he hadn't memorized Robert's Rules of Order, too, don't you know?!

He is right in everything he says. And he is wrong in the most important way. He never takes time to take in what it might mean to this woman to feel like a full and dignified daughter of Abraham again. He doesn't run right up to her and sing harmony in her hallelujah chorus. He won't let himself cry tears of joy for one who is able to hold her head high now among the people of God. He goes straight into fixing blame and finding fault, not, mind you, with what was done, but instead it was all about how and when and why. Sigh.

What Luke wants us to see, I think, is that while the woman needed straightening up, the man needed straightening out. The woman needed less humiliation; the man needed more humility.

Let's look at the man's argument. Work is forbidden on the Sabbath day, according to the law. Healing is work. Therefore, Jesus is guilty of working on the Sabbath. He is sinning, in other words. And, maybe what's worse, he is messing with the orderly rules of the community that the leader is sworn to watch over.

But before we get to what Jesus says, please note that the man doesn't actually accuse Jesus himself; he blames the woman for putting herself in the position to be healed on the Sabbath. Here we go again—it's as old as the Bible and older: Always blame the woman. Can we just stop that now, people? I mean, really, once and for all.

Jesus reminds the man that the law may be strict but that accommodations are made for reasons of mercy. For example, feeding your animals on the Sabbath is work, but you get excused for that. And aren't people more precious than pets? Apparently not to all of us. Jesus is telling the church where to focus.

People. The focus is people, people! We are to be a healing community that seeks the full dignity of every child of God, every son and daughter of Abraham in our midst. Compassion is the hallmark of a spiritual community that invokes the name of the All Merciful God of Jesus Christ. We can be so right sometimes that we're wrong. We've got to straighten out our hearts so that people can straighten up and claim their places of honor.

The 1958 book *The Ugly American* tells the story of an American engineer, Homer Atkins—a man with an ugly face—who was sent to the fictional Southeast Asian country of Sarkhan to build dams and roads for the military. Atkins refused to build the dams and roads until the military first solved some of the everyday problems of the people. At the suggestion of his wife, Emma, he designed a bicycle treadmill pump to get water up to the hillside paddies on which the people depended for food. For centuries this water had been laboriously carried by pails.

Emma was also curious about the fact that every woman over sixty had a bent back. Then she noticed that after the monsoon season, the sweeping of debris from the streets was done by older people who used brooms with short handles. Since wood for longer handles cost too much and was in short supply, Emma found a long-stalked reed and planted shoots from this reed by her door. She tended these reeds carefully. One day, when neighbors were in her house, she cut a tall reed, bound coconut fronds to it and began to sweep with her back straight. When the people questioned her concerning the reed, she told them where they could find them growing.

Four years later, when Emma and Homer were back in Pittsburgh, they received a letter of thanks from an elder of the village. The letter read: *In the village of Chang Dong today, the backs of our old people are straight and firm. No longer are their bodies painful and bent. You will be pleased to know that on the outskirts of the village we have constructed a small shrine in your memory ... at the foot are these words: 'In memory of the woman who unbent the backs of our people.'*[42]

Would that they could say about Wilshire someday that because of our acts of compassion, the backs and the souls of many people have been unbent.

---

42 https://www.sermons.com/sermon/straight-backs-and-rekindled-dreams/1347593

24

Going Deeper

Watch and listen to "Going Deeper" by following this link or scanning the QR code with your phone: youtu.be/duEHZI-AcN0.

March 23, 2014
Third Sunday in Lent
John 4:5-42

The well is deep, and you have no bucket.

Little did she know what kind of bucket Jesus carried around with him.

But before we go there, we might start where she did, sensing the most immediate problem that Jesus had and that we so often have ourselves.

The well is deep, and you have no bucket.

Your health is failing, and you don't have what it takes within you to make yourself well. You are over your head at work or home or school and don't have any idea how to face the problem. You are staring at your credit card bill, and you look at your bank balance, wondering if you will ever be out of debt.

The well is deep, and you have no bucket.

Jesus has just left Jerusalem, where he had talked at length with Jewish religious leader Nicodemus. He is heading back now to his home in Galilee, but he has to go through Samaria to get there. Now, when I say he has to go through Samaria, that isn't exactly true. That's the straightest route, but many Jews actually took the Samaritan bypass east of the Jordan River in order to avoid Samaritans. That would have sent them through Gentile territory, though, which would have been a problem itself.

But you know, this is the way people think when they start out by making others "other." Instead of seeing people as people and recognizing that they are merely different in their look or dress or culture, we see those differences as threats to our own purity. Sometimes you have to pick your poison: Would you rather go through dreaded Gentile territory or hated Samaritan land?

We know what this is like. Would you rather your white daughter date a person of color who is a Christian or a person who looks like your family but is hostile to the Christian faith? Would you rather hire a hardworking single mom who might have to miss work sometimes because of her kids or a gay man who is always punctual and will work overtime anytime? Most of the time it's not about choosing between the two; it's about dealing with the one challenge right in front of you. Your daughter doesn't give you the choice. You may have only one applicant. What are you going to do with that situation?

Jesus had to decide whether to take the path that led through Samaria. Would he take it or avoid it? As the poet Robert Frost put it, *The best way out is always through*. And Jesus always takes the throughway because he goes deeper than most of us are willing to go. He goes deeper than skin color or dress, history or stereotype. He sees Samaritans as people that God loves. And he even made one of them the hero of his most famous parable.

Nicodemus comes to Jesus at night. The Samaritan woman came to him at noon. We should probably make something of this contrast. The learned Jewish man who should have seen the light comes at night. The unnamed Samaritan woman who should be in the dark comes to Jesus at midday. He hides, she steps right into view. The social elite is fearful; the social outcast is fearless.

Isn't that the way it is with so many of us spiritually? Those who have the most to lose by coming to Jesus have the hardest time engaging him. Those who have the least to lose are quicker to embrace him.

Well, this unnamed woman didn't seek Jesus out; she was simply coming to the well to draw water, and Jesus was sitting there thirsty.

The well is deep, and you have no bucket.

No, he has no bucket, but for heaven's sake, he is Jesus. He's the one who has already turned water into wine and who will feed the five thousand from five loaves and two sardines. Think that's a real problem for Jesus? Deep well. No bucket. No problem.

But remember that Jesus' miracles were materially and spiritually motivated at the same time, while many who were the recipients were only marveling about them on a material level. Here again we see how Jesus is *crossing the planes*. He sees the material through spiritual eyes, not the other way around. And so even his thirst becomes, by his willingness to delay gratification, an opportunity to go deeper.

Jesus makes himself vulnerable to this woman of Samaria. If we ever want to lead people to faith, we need to learn this. God came among us as one of us, with no attitude! When we Christians take an arrogant posture toward others, as if we're insiders and they're outsiders, we're superior and they're inferior, we're somebodies and they're nobodies, they can smell that a mile away. But when we take the Jesus approach, it sometimes shocks others right away and draws them deeper.

Look at how this conversation progresses. To begin, it's a two-way conversation. Jesus is the protagonist. He initiates the whole thing. He goes to Samaria and sits down at Jacob's well.

Which, by the way, I got to do a few weeks back—sit down at Jacob's well. I guess it's Jacob's well. At least that's what the locals say. It's now located behind and beneath the altar of a Greek Orthodox church. I drank water from it after our guide cranked the wheel for what seemed like forever to reach the underground spring far below. The water was good to drink. Whether it was really Jacob's well or not, who's to say? Like so many things in the Holy Land, don't you know?!

But here is Jesus at the well talking to this woman. The contrasts couldn't be greater, as the conversation reveals. Just follow along. We've already established that Jesus is a Jew and the woman is a Samaritan. It's obvious also that she's a woman and he is a man. Not sure the scandal then was much greater than now. We still have a hard time believing that men and women can be friends at anything but a superficial level if they aren't married. It's like Jesus is at lunch alone with this woman. What will people say? Well, that's the problem, isn't it? Most of what people will say is based on making sure that men and women don't engage at a deep level because to do so will always end badly. Jesus doesn't let that deter him, and to her everlasting credit, neither does she.

So Jesus says to her, *Give me a drink*. His request doesn't sound respectful or polite on the surface. We think he might have asked rather than commanded. He might have said please. But maybe being direct is most respectful of her since he goes below the surface this way. He gets straight to the point, and she appreciates it.

The conversation proceeds quickly past the initial stage, her wondering why he could want to be there with her at all, to Jesus saying: *If you knew the gift of God, and who it is that is saying, 'Give me a drink,' you would have asked him, and he would have given you living water.*

See what he's doing? He's going deeper. Things start superficially, and then he goes beyond ethnicity and gender as if he doesn't pay any mind to these things that divide people. He crosses the material plane and goes beyond literal water to living or flowing or spiritual water. The woman is stuck at first on the material plane and wants literal water that will allow her not to have to keep going to the well.

Jesus next addresses the woman's relationship status. I have no idea how he knew that she had had five husbands and the man she was living with then was not her husband. Here's one of those times I just have to say, *That's Jesus for you. He knows us better than anyone else.* But there's also no judgment implied in his knowing. Women in that day had limited agency in relationships. The fact is, if she had been married five times it was likely that she had had little choice five times and that her husbands had either died or divorced her. She would have needed a man for protection and provision, because there was no such thing as an independent single woman in that Samaritan or Jewish culture. She would have lived with her father or some other man. Again, though, Jesus doesn't exclude her because of her relationship history.

Next, they talk about the differences in religion and place of worship. She sees that he wants to talk about deeper things, and she shows that she knows some things herself, though no man had probably taken her seriously enough before now to engage her. But Jesus won't even let religion divide them. He doesn't try to make her a Jew in order to be saved; he goes deeper. He goes to God being spirit and not being tied to geography or religion.

And then things get really personal. She admits that there are limits to what any of us can know, and that we will have to wait for the messiah to come to straighten things out. Jesus finally has her where he wants her. *I am he*, he says, *the one who is speaking to you.* And I think the last part of that is the most interesting: the one who is speaking TO YOU. In other words, he is the one who breaks down every barrier, the one who breaks below the surface to the deepest places of the human heart, the one who knows you better than you know yourself—*I am he. I am the one who has the bucket to draw the deep water of eternal life.*

The disciples arrive on the scene with food, and they are aghast that Jesus is talking to a woman. They don't say anything to him directly. I think John wants us to see that we're in church at this moment. This is the way church people act toward one another. Those who are closest to Jesus and should have had the easiest time seeing that Jesus defies social conventions instead also have a hard time giving up superficial barriers that never adequately define us.

She then runs off to town to give her personal testimony of her encounter with Jesus. Some believe in him because of her words. Some are curious enough to go deeper and hear him out for themselves. And so Jesus has taken the matter deeper than we could ever have imagined.

Listen, people—people will not come to Jesus by our reinforcing all the social, ethnic, gender, sexual, religious, and national borders that we try to enforce to keep people apart. Unless and until we present Jesus the way Jesus presented himself, we will only be ghettoizing the church among our own kind.

The deep wellspring of eternal life can be reached only by a bucket that Jesus always has. The well is deep indeed, and Jesus has a bucket. Do you want this water of eternal life that Jesus wants to give you, or would you rather live on a superficial level forever?

There's one thing I am still wondering about regarding this story. Did Jesus ever get that drink of water from the woman, or did her faith quench his thirst in the end, the way our faith does for us? Just wondering.

25

Inseparable

Watch and listen to "Inseparable" by following this link or scanning the QR code with your phone: youtu.be/toVykKDc0l8. Sermon begins at 21:08.

October 25, 2020
Reformation Sunday
Matthew 22:34-46

I don't know if you remember it, but to me it's unforgettable. In 1991, Natalie Cole released an album of cover songs originally written and performed by her late father, Nat King Cole. Songs like "The Very Thought of You," "Straighten Up and Fly Right," and "Our Love Is Here to Stay," just to mention a few. The concluding song utilized digital remastering technology to produce a duet of father and daughter. Nat's 1951 recording was remixed with Natalie's 1991 voice, producing an unforgettable remake of the song "Unforgettable."

I kept coming back to that "coming-togetherness" when reading this passage from Matthew's Gospel today. Jesus is asked by a lawyer of the Pharisees which commandment is the greatest, or some say he was asked to choose one type from among the commandments that is more important than the others.

Jesus' answer isn't remarkable in itself, or unique. The command to love God above all else is the undisputed greatest. It is the prayer spoken twice a day by observant Jews and a confession of faith said in Jewish worship week by week. The so-called *Shema*. That is, *Shema, Israel*—as in *Hear, O Israel, the LORD our God, the LORD is one. You shall love the LORD your God with all your heart, soul, and might.* This beautiful admonition from Moses in Deuteronomy 6:4-5 combines the oneness, holiness, and wholeness of God with the oneness, holiness, and wholeness of human response.

For Jesus to say the *Shema* is the greatest commandment, the one that would stand at the top of the list of all the others would have been enough to validate his authority among the Pharisees. They agreed. Nothing is more important than loving the one, holy God wholly. Nothing to see here. Move on.

But then Jesus moves on and says the second is like to it, *Love your neighbor as yourself.* This second one is also from Scripture—Leviticus 19:18. Combining these two can be found in the teaching of rabbis before him. By connecting this to the *Shema*, however, Jesus combines the love of God and the love of neighbor, the vertical and the horizontal, inward faith and outward works.

Makes sense. But then what does he mean by "second" and "like"?

In the midst of COVID and our political distress, I have been seeing an interesting renewal of this debate about what Jesus means by second and like. Some theologians and pastors who oppose liberal things like the Black Lives Matter movement and LGBTQ inclusion and Christian advocacy for things like more humane immigration and asylum policies, say that when Jesus says second, he means secondary in importance. That is, second means something like don't get too active in these things because they will distract you from your first priority as a Christian, which is to worship God with all your heart, soul, and might. The things that matter most are eternal and not temporal. The gospel is about making sure you are welcome in heaven someday more than welcoming heaven to earth today. Hmm.

It's true that you can be a passionate advocate for justice and yet have no active spiritual life that includes God in your thoughts and desires. Sadly, many people live as though God doesn't factor into everyday life. Social movements are everything. Politics brings meaning and identity. This fails to honor what Jesus calls the first and greatest commandment.

Our worship and prayers draw us deeper into communion with God. They allow God to deliver us peace, inspire us to act, and sustain us with hope. Giving God room to speak to us, listening to the voice of God, especially as we hear it in Scripture that is filtered through the Spirit of Jesus: This is the beginning of wisdom. And doing all of this with siblings of spirit in the church encourages us and keeps us on track when our thoughts and values can drift under the force of worldly winds.

But the real force of Jesus' words in this passage is the way he adds the *love your neighbor as yourself* commandment to the love God commandment. "The second is *like* it" means, I think, that the love your neighbor part isn't optional or disposable or secondary; it's inseparable from the love God part. The greatest commandment is singular but twofold: love God *and* love neighbor. These are two sides of the same coin. You can't have a coin without both sides of it.

Jesus is saying you can't truly love God if you are not truly loving your neighbor. And loving your neighbor, who is created in the image of God just like you, is the surest test of whether you are loving God.

So, how do we honor Jesus' commandment to love our neighbor as ourself today in order to demonstrate that we understand the inseparable nature of love for God and people of all kinds?

First, we have to be honest with ourselves about implicit bias that produces our lack of love for some people. Jesus was radically egalitarian in an era that wasn't. Try to name one time in his ministry when he operated off of bias of hierarchy where some people were by nature superior to others. His biggest scandal—including, I might add, what's behind this encounter with the Pharisees—is his love for Gentiles. And the greatest breakthroughs in the early church after Jesus were in breaking down hierarchies between Jews and Gentiles, men and women, slave and free, clean and unclean, and so on.

And yet, we seem to persist in trying to get Jesus to fit our prejudices instead of allowing him to fix our prejudices.

I mentioned Isabel Wilkerson's new book *Caste* a few weeks ago. The main argument she makes is that race is only the façade of the house of American discontent; caste is the internal framework that holds it up. She says this: *We cannot fully understand the current upheavals or most any turning point in American history, without accounting for the human pyramid encrypted into us all. The caste system, and the attempts to defend, uphold, or abolish the hierarchy, underlay the American Civil War and the civil rights movement a century later and pervade the politics of twenty-first-century America. Just as DNA is the code of instructions for cell development, caste is the operating system for economic, political, and social interaction in the United States from the time of its gestation.*

If you listen carefully to our political talk these days, you will hear versions of caste embedded within it. The most prominent is the longstanding version that has white European Protestants at the top and in charge of the country, while Blacks of African descent are at the bottom, and Asians, Latinos and others are in between. There are variations in each caste that involve men being superior to women, straights to gays, and so on. Maintaining that social order is behind many political slogans. We can deny being racists all we want, but until we honestly examine our hearts about our need to be on top by keeping others below us, we will not be able to love our neighbor AS OURSELF. We may love our neighbor, but we will not love our neighbor as ourself until we see ourself in our neighbor.

But second, and here's the most uncomfortable part for me, we have to love our neighbor who disagrees with us. Sometimes that's a family member or dear friend who is close to us. One of the worst things about this time in our country is how politics has driven a wedge between people we consider loved ones.

There's a strange new caste-like system at work in this. People who agree with me are on top with me. I may even justify my disdain of those below me by dismissing their opinions as being beneath me. This cuts both ways. For some, it's a caste system based on education, and for others, tradition. Progressives side with those who seek social progress; conservatives side with those who seek social stability. Universities tend toward liberal-mindedness, and people in the media generally side with intellectuals and academics. You might imagine I feel more at home with these people. Which makes me less at home with those who believe their longstanding values are under assault by cultural elites who look down on them, even if they are white, which is a violation of our American caste system. On the other hand, people who have felt put down their whole lives for not fitting into the dominant profile of America because of their race or ethnicity or religion or sexual orientation likewise feel disdained and dismissed by traditionalists.

The church has to stop this. We have to practice mutual respect and empathy. We can't depend upon others to bring peace if we are not willing to do so ourselves.

All of us have to be part of the connecting work of loving God and neighbor, no matter how hard the task.

The next few weeks will be pivotal for our country, no matter how the election turns out. I am not telling you that only if my candidate wins will things get better. I am telling you that either way, we have to cure this caste thinking that is undermining our inseparable duty to love God and one another.

The title of the album Natalie Cole put out that closes with her duet with her late father is *Unforgettable … with Love*. Think about that: "with love." It all comes down to that in the end, don't you know?! Love. Love for God; love for Every Body.

Imagine conservatives and progressives singing the same gospel song together. The conservatives would be singing the melody in the voice of the departed that sounds across the ages. They keep the gospel song the same song. The progressives would be singing harmony in the voice of the hopeful that sounds forth from the future. They keep the same gospel song ever new. Like Nat King Cole and Natalie Cole singing the same song together, as if they are inseparable.

It would be, I tell you, unforgettable. Amen.

26

On Not Passing by Life

Watch and listen to "On Not Passing by Life" by following this link or scanning the QR code with your phone: youtu.be/uL0XykI0mOY. Sermon begins at 27:56.

July 14, 2019
Fifth Sunday after Pentecost
Luke 10:25-37

This is the fourth time I have preached a sermon at Wilshire on the Parable of the Good Samaritan with the title *On Not Passing by Life*. It's only the second one I remember, so that ought to tell you something about how memorable my preaching is even to me or how bad my memory is. I'm counting on the same from you today.

The first time I preached on this text and title was thirty years ago this month when the pastor search committee put me before you as their candidate to be the next pastor of Wilshire. I don't have a transcript of that sermon, because in those days I wrote out my sermon longhand on a yellow legal pad. Just as well for you since I can't imagine my preaching back then. But I do have a copy of the last two times, one from twelve years ago, shortly after my oldest daughter's wedding; the other time three years ago, fresh off the death of my father.

I keep coming back to this title, I think, not just for nostalgia, but because there's a kind of drumbeat in the way Jesus tells the story that makes this phrase pop. The priest and the Levite see the man in the ditch, and they *pass by* on the other side. The Good Samaritan sees the man and turns toward him, going out of his way to help. It turns out the difference between passing by and not passing by is a matter of life or death. It is for us, too.

To understand why, we need to go back to the setup of the story Jesus told. A lawyer approaches Jesus to test him. It turns into a test for him too, as he was really wanting Jesus to give him a passing grade on his life.

We all do this, not just lawyers, of course. In those days, a lawyer was a person of religious earnestness, someone scrupulous about keeping the law of Moses. So, let's assume that would be people like you and me. It's time we stopped scapegoating the lawyers.

The man comes to Jesus and asks him a question that concerns every one of us: *What must I do to inherit eternal life?* After two thousand years of church history and four hundred years of Baptist altar calls, we might expect him to have told the man to profess his faith in Jesus himself as his personal Lord and Savior and then get baptized by immersion in the Jordan River. Jesus doesn't say that. What he does say is what all of that is supposed to mean, if we understand it rightly.

He asks the man what God requires. The man answers well. *You shall love the Lord your God with all your heart, and with all your soul, and with all your strength, and with all your mind; and your neighbor as yourself.* Jesus tells him he's right. *Do this and you will live.* To that, the man answers in a way that shows that while his head is on straight, his heart is still bent. Wanting to justify himself, Luke says, the man asks Jesus, *And who is my neighbor?*

The question, *Who is my neighbor?* was common for ages among Jews who debated the law of neighbor love. Asking it in this case wasn't just about the man himself. It reflects our human tendency to look for loopholes, to limit our obligations to our neighbors.

Curiously, the man doesn't ask about the limits of his love for God. This is true about us too. We see it in the story Jesus tells about the two religious men passing by the desperate neighbor on their way from church, so to speak, in Jerusalem. We think we can separate our love for God from our love for neighbors. And Jesus simply won't let us do that.

The priest and the Levite both see the man in the ditch and pass by on the other side. Now, it doesn't say they were headed from the Temple per se, but that's the implication. They were going *down* the road, Luke says. You go down from Jerusalem and up to it. So, probably they'd just done their loving God best—the priest and the Levite being somewhat like a pastor and a deacon, don't you know?! They then chance upon a man who gives them a chance to round out the Great Commandment by loving their neighbor. They pass. They pass by on the other side of the road.

When the Samaritan sees the man, he has compassion for him. He takes pity. The word used in the Greek is interesting. It literally means that the man's entrails were disturbed by the sight. His bowels were moved. Too much information? But the point is that the man was sick to his stomach to see this other man in such a mess. He felt in his deepest parts that he had to do something.

I think the Samaritan acts on behalf of the man in the ditch because he sees himself in him, even though the victim is presumably a Jew. The Samaritan understands that "there but for the grace of God go I."

Samaritans were the most reviled class of people to Jews. Better you were a dirty Gentile than a Samaritan. Samaritans were the remnant of the northern kingdom of Israel that had set up their capital in Samaria, not Jerusalem. They were Jews, in other words, tracing their history to Moses as all Jews did. Yet, Jews hated Samaritans, and vice versa.

So, for Jesus to make one of them the hero of his story says something to all of us about what matters to God. What matters is not the purity of your bloodline, the clarity of your culture or the sanctity of your heart. It's the quality of your mercy.

When Jesus finishes his story, shockingly making the hated Samaritan the model of virtue, he turns back to the man and changes the question. The man had asked: *Who is my neighbor?* Jesus asks him: *Who was the neighbor to the man in the ditch?*

This is the decisive move. Jesus always puts the onus back on us. It's not about who the man is in the ditch; it's who we are in the face of the man in the ditch.

We've all been horrified by the terrible conditions on our southern border. Central American refugees have been traveling by foot for a thousand miles, running away from thieves and thugs in their homeland, seeking shelter and safety in a country that has long shined a light to the world beckoning those to come who seek life, liberty, and the pursuit of happiness.

We have political challenges about immigration policy that have no simple answers. If you have a simple answer, you haven't looked deeply enough into it. But here's the point: The church's job isn't to get lost in the national debate about who is our neighbor, joining the chorus of those who want to define neighbor by ethnicity, country of origin, or legal status. Because when we do that, what we are really doing is the same as the lawyer in Luke's story: We are trying to limit our obligations. Instead, the church's contribution is to raise the matter of spiritual and human conscience. We keep Jesus' question before the world by asking it of ourselves over and over: *Am I acting as a neighbor?*

Christians have a long history of missions. We care about people all over the world. We send missionaries to places like Central America to bring them the good news of Jesus Christ. When missionaries go there, they join the people right where they are. They live among them, bearing their burdens, relieving suffering, employing and deploying every resource to declare in word and deed that "God so loved the world."

There's even a Christian compassion ministry called Samaritan's Purse that collects material goods to distribute to needy people in some of the harshest places on earth. Some of you have contributed to the Christmas boxes. But now that the same people who received this charity are coming to our borders, something has changed. These same Christians are often heard defending the right to treat these same people inhumanely. This is nothing more than being the priest or the Levite in the story, passing by on the other side of the road.

It's as if we have fallen back into adjudicating the question the man asked Jesus: *And who is my neighbor?* We've lost our sense of who we are, which is supposed to be determined by Jesus, not our allegiance to political leaders. We should be asking the Jesus question of ourselves: *Are we acting as a neighbor to these people?*

A friend of mine, who used to be a member of our church, told me about coming to Dallas years ago. He and his wife visited a church that had a denominational middle name on their sign that was the same as the one he had come from in another state. When the pastor came to visit them to talk about his vision of the church, he told them in so many words that the church existed to serve "people like us." My friend took that to mean respectable, white, upper middle-class Christians like them. He knew in his bones that that wasn't what Jesus was asking of the church, and this family instead changed denominations and ended up here with us, even though being Baptist wasn't foremost in their minds.

The church in America has been seduced into joining a culture war that draws lines of us versus them. But our responsibility is culture care, not culture war.

The Samaritan looked at that Jew who had been traumatized by thieves and saw himself in that man's eyes. He knew what it was like to be despised and rejected, to be "othered" by people who shared the same DNA and the same ancient story of faith. He took this man to heart. He didn't just feel, he acted. He acted in a way that honored the humanity of the man in the ditch.

And the result was not just that the man in the ditch was saved; the man who stopped to care for him was saved, too. This is the point so often missed in our charity. You can give to the church or to a Good Samaritan-like organization and do a lot of good for people who have been unjustly victimized by rogues on the road of life. But you can do all that and remain unchanged yourself.

Brian Stevenson, the author of the book *Just Mercy* and the head of the Equal Justice Initiative in Montgomery, Alabama, talks about becoming "proximate to pain." We have to get involved. We have to side with those in the ditch or detention centers. We have to become vulnerable. We can't pass by on the other side if we expect to find life.

Dietrich Bonhoeffer, the German pastor and theologian who was martyred by Hitler just before the end of World War II, said this: *[We] have for once learned to see the great events of world history from below, from the perspective of the outcasts, the suspects, the maltreated, the powerless, the oppressed and reviled, in short, from the perspective of the suffering.*[43] And to do so requires our advocacy, our willingness to put our own lives at stake with theirs, the way Bonhoeffer did.

It is, as he put it, "the cost of discipleship." It may cost us our life, as it did his. But if the cross of Christ means anything, it means that that's precisely where life itself is to be found.

Let's not be found passing by life on the other side, lest on the other side we find life passing us by. Amen.

---

43 Dietrich Bonhoeffer, "An Account at the Turn of the Year 1942–1943," *Letters and Papers from Prison* (Fortress Press: 2015), 20.

PART IV

Christian Civility

Church and Contemporary Culture

"The church must be reminded that it is not the master or the servant of the state, but rather the conscience of the state. It must be the guide and the critic of the state and never its tool."

~ Reverend Dr. Martin Luther King Jr.

"The shape of obedience ... must always be cruciform—cross-shaped. We love God (vertical arm of the cross) and we love our neighbor as ourselves (horizontal arm). We are not here to occupy America, conquering culture in order to rule the country on behalf of Jesus. We are here to serve it for Jesus' sake. This is the way we serve Christ and the gospel rather than our own designs."

~ George A. Mason

Preface by Amanda Tyler

Jesus taught us that we have dual citizenship (Matthew 22:15-22). We owe offerings to both Caesar and God. Our allegiance is to God first and to our national identity second. But since our Scriptures don't provide an instructional manual on how to do that in our modern society, we need prophetic preaching to help sort out our allegiances and offerings to our political communities. In this section, Dr. George Mason instructs how to engage in politics and society, while maintaining an authentic Christian witness.

First, what do we mean by "politics" and "political engagement?" To be political does not necessarily mean to be partisan. Rather, politics gives definition to the rights and responsibilities of citizenship, that is, what is required of us in our civil organizations, institutions, and governments. George rightly speaks to politics while not straying into partisanship; the latter is a polarizing, divisive, and distracting force in our religious spaces that is best avoided for the health of our communities. But I would argue that we can't follow Jesus without "getting political," that is, without applying the gospel to meet the needs of our unjust world.

I appreciate how George calls us to be grounded spiritually and biblically both before and while we take political action. In "Faithful Betrayal," he points to the example of Jesus prefacing his public theology with a sermon in the temple, reading from the scroll of Isaiah. Jesus provides the ultimate example of a biblically grounded advocate. While we are politically engaged, George warns us in "Bearings" not to be tempted away from our values and mission by partisanship or greed, not to choose "self-serving power" over "self-sacrificing love."

As Christian citizens, we are powerful, but our power comes from the waters of baptism, not the anointing of political leaders. George counsels that "Christians serve the state best when they serve Christ first" ("Christian Civility"). This theme of recognizing our relationship to power emerges again in "Drawn to the Light," in which George preaches to the church's mission to be light to the world and speaks this truth: "Every time a nation tries to become Christian by use of worldly power, the light of Christ is dimmer." Amen to that.

Once we are spiritually grounded and recognize from whom our power comes, George turns to the way that we witness in politics. A key ingredient to Christian engagement in politics is humility—holding fast to our theological convictions while holding space for the truth that we may be wrong ("Pass the Salt, Hold the Whine"). When we take on a humble posture in our advocacy, the natural consequence is a tone that is compassionate and inclusive rather than judgmental and divisive.

Political engagement, when done responsibly, also requires a great deal of self-awareness. George preaches in "Slaying Giants" that we must discern when we are David and when we are Goliath. While we often want to think of ourselves as David, in reality some of us find ourselves more often in the role of Goliath, with the power advantage on our side. Recognizing our privilege as a byproduct of oppressive systems gives us the moral clarity, as George puts it, to be morally courageous to work for justice and peace. When we take this humble posture, we can also recognize our own complicity in the perpetuation of unjust and oppressive systems. "Deep Cleaning," preached just weeks after the January 6th attack on the Capitol, calls us to "recognize that we all need [Jesus's] deliverance." We are better able to confront evil in society when we confront it first within ourselves. This kind of self-reflection is exactly what the Christians Against Christian Nationalism campaign calls its network to do—to clean our own houses first by learning how Christian nationalism has infected our own theologies and worship practices. Only then are we prepared to do the hard but necessary work of dismantling Christian nationalism from the rest of our society.

While his sermons are thoroughly modern and responsive to current events, George uses examples from the rich Baptist heritage and history of advocacy for religious freedom for all. We are reminded of the long line of Baptists who have fought for religious freedom for all—from Roger Williams to Martin Luther King Jr. In "Pass the Salt, Hold the Whine," George points to examples of Baptist persecution in the past to contrast with the overblown and false claims of persecution by some modern-day American Christians who confuse Christian privilege with Christian nationalism.

George names Christian nationalism as an enemy of democracy, religious freedom, and a faithful Christian life. We can reject Christian nationalism while embracing a healthy sense of patriotism. In "Christian Civility," George preaches a model sermon for a Sunday close to the Fourth of July. He rightly counsels that patriotic celebrations don't belong in a Sunday worship service, while modeling some appropriate ways to celebrate American citizenship in the community.

Woven through all these prophetic sermons are not just wise words but examples of real people doing the work. He personalizes the call in a way that inspires the listener or the reader to take action to be a better Christian citizen. We all have daily opportunities to live out our dual citizenship in a way that honors God and contributes to our communities. These sermons help us discern how to do that faithfully.

Amanda Tyler is the executive director of BJC (Baptist Joint Committee for Religious Liberty), an advocacy and education nonprofit headquartered in Washington, D.C. and dedicated to defending religious freedom for all people. She is the lead organizer of Christians Against Christian Nationalism and serves as co-host of the BJC's "Respecting Religion" Podcast series.

27

Christian Civility

July 6, 2008
Eighth Sunday after Pentecost, Religious Liberty Sunday
1 Peter 3:13-17

It's been a red, white, and blue week. Wednesday night we were feeding 720 members, neighbors, and friends at a church barbeque dinner on the grounds, followed by a patriotic concert featuring our own Wilshire Wind Symphony. The place was packed. The music was boisterous. The goosebumps were popping up in every pew as the band played "Stars and Stripes Forever," "America the Beautiful," "My Country 'Tis of Thee," the theme songs for each branch of the military, and "The Star-Spangled Banner." Then Friday, many of us found a parade to attend, celebrating our national blessings and our pride in being Americans. We polished it off with fireworks all over town—a tradition that should remind us of the rockets' red glare as ships fired cannons in colonial harbors and John Paul Jones uttered his defiant reply to a British captain's demand to surrender: *I have not yet begun to fight.*

All in all, it was a great week to remember who we are as a nation and to be glad for the freedoms we enjoy and must be vigilant to defend. But among those freedoms is the most important, the first freedom—religious freedom. And when we get to this freedom today, while we can celebrate it uniformly as Americans, it increasingly makes some people think they are in uniform and others not.

We hear lots of talk from some quarters about how Muslims have a grand plan to take over America and establish an Islamic state here with no religious liberty, but the greater threat has always been from within. Will we hold to the high ground of complete religious liberty, or do we only think this country is supposed to tolerate any religion other than Christianity? Furthermore, is the church supposed to respect civil authority and honor those who serve the general good, or is the church supposed to serve the country and be the public agent of patriotism? I am pretty clear that we are not very clear about this anymore, if we ever were.

I spoke on the phone with my parents on the Fourth, partly to wish them a happy Fourth and partly to wish them a happy fifty-fourth wedding anniversary. Yes, it's hard to be much more patriotic than getting married on the Fourth of July, especially when it was a Sunday and you had to be insistent about the date. And when my parents built the house I grew up in on Staten Island about fifty years ago, they chose the street number seventy-six, and we had an ironworks sign on our walkway lamppost that read *The Spirit of 76*. But when I asked how their church was last Sunday—which is something preacher sons always ask about, don't you know?!—Mom said, *Oh, George, I was livid*. She went on to tell me about how the whole service was one big patriotic event. The color guard marched into the sanctuary with the flag, they said the Pledge of Allegiance, sang the national anthem, and proceeded to have a whole service that seemed to worship the nation. There were no Scripture readings or sermon lifting up the Lordship of Christ over all nations, no exaltation of God as supreme over all the earth, and no call to give up everything and follow Jesus. *I am as patriotic as anyone*, Mom said, *but that was not right to do on a Sunday morning in a church worship service.*

Amen, Mom. We are in a strange time in American life when it seems the church is being asked to carry out patriotism as another one of its duties to society. Baptists have long held up the doctrine of the separation of church and state as the best model for how to be a faithful Christian and a loyal citizen at the same time. But it is always a balancing act.

Thursday night Kim and I borrowed a couple of kayaks from two generous friends and set out across White Rock Lake to listen to the music coming from the arboretum. I was wet by the time we got there. I am not a novice boatman, my father having been a ship pilot and all. But for some reason, a short way out into the lake I found myself listing—weighting my "argument" more to one side than the other, no doubt. I'll let you guess which side I fell to. Before I knew it, I was in the water and trying awkwardly to get back into the boat.

This is the kind of problem we face as Christians when we try to balance our Christian commitments on the one hand with our civil duties on the other. It's an act of moral strength that takes diligence and vigilance.

When St. Peter wrote to Christians dispersed in small bands around the Roman Empire, he laid out a good outline for the church's relationship to the state that we would do well to attend to today. I'll try to restate it without putting words in his mouth.

Number first. *Christians serve the state best when they serve Christ first.* When we baptize people here on Sundays, they speak their confession of faith: *Jesus is Lord*. It's not just a personal statement of opinion; it is a political declaration of independence from the powers of the world and of dependence upon Jesus. It doesn't mean that Christians disrespect worldly authorities; it means that all authorities are subjected to Christ. In the fourth century after Christ, Emperor Constantine made Christianity the official religion of the state—a disastrous move that haunts us still. The forced baptism of all who served the emperor was a shame to conscience and a blurring of the line between God and king. Soldiers inherently knew that they could not serve Christ and Caesar as if they were one and the same. So, when many of them waded into the streams to be baptized, they held up their swords while the rest of their bodies went under the water.[44]

When the church becomes an unbaptized arm of the state, we become complicit in any violence that public officials do. We serve the state best by being a living alternative to the state that reminds it that it is sinful as we ourselves are. We will not sanction national ends in the name of God. We exist to keep alive a witness to the Christ who died at the hands of the state. Any time the church gets too cozy with the nation, as if the nation is somehow composed of a special elect who are made by God to bless the world, the church gives up its role to secular authorities. We lose our identity and our prophetic witness.

We must accept and respect all human authorities—including those of other nations. They have a role to play in God's ecology of creation. They help to keep chaos at bay. They help clear space for people to live in freedom and dignity, including Christians. By promoting the well-being of the civitas—a wholesome civil society—we show our fear of God and honor of human governors.

Number next. *Christians should engage actively in making civic life better.* In a democratic republic we have the rights and responsibilities to participate in public life. And we should want it to be the best it can be. We should vote. We should argue and lobby for the most just and equitable society possible, not only for ourselves but for everyone.

Honor everyone, Peter says. And honoring everyone means not using our freedom in this democracy to advance our own personal rights and well-being at the expense of anyone else. That would be using our freedom as a pretext for evil. And evil is always a matter of depriving others of what is good for some selfish purpose.

It's easiest to see this by looking at the behavior of our enemies. When terrorists use the freedom they enjoy in this country to murder innocent Americans in order to further their religious ends, we rightly call that evil. None of their rationalizations or justifications can change that. But we Christians must actively call upon our fellow citizens to maintain the same standards of judgment in dealing with other people and nations. If we fail to do so, we are failing our faith and adding our ultimate loyalty to a state that can never save.

I think we need to ask more from our civic life, not less. For instance, have you noticed how it seems to fall to churches nowadays to promote patriotism in our communities? Why is that? In the 1957 Broadway musical *The Music Man*, the writers Wilson and Franklin Lacey situate the Independence Day festivities in River City in the high school gymnasium. That's the kind of public setting it belongs in. The schools and civic centers and parks and government buildings belong to all of us, regardless of faith tradition. Why are they not open for such events anymore? Because it costs too much to cool them on a holiday? Because it costs too much to staff them and patrol them? Well, we need patriotic rituals to be able to tell the stories and celebrate our history and bind us together. But whose responsibility

---

44 *Uncivil Religion*, July 1, 2005. https://bjconline.org/wp-content/uploads/2014/03/Charles-Foster-Johnson-Uncivil-Religion.pdf

is that? Certainly not the church's. There is greater cost to our original American experiment in religious liberty when we move these festivities into Sunday-morning church. People need ritual, and they need ways to exercise their patriotic feelings. But we do not need to put the church in the position to look as if it is patriotic or not by whether we have such services held here.

Number last. *Christians must teach civility by our way of life.* My colleague and friend Charlie Johnson has said it well: *Religion in the public square has been stripped of its civility. A disease of uncivil religion has infected our land. This disease has been incubating for twenty-five years but has reached epidemic proportions in our current time of terror. The motivation of uncivil religion is not to recognize God in our national life, but, rather, to represent [God]. The high priests of this uncivil religion desire not so much to speak to God in the public square, but, rather, to speak for God.*

It is God's will, Peter says, *that by doing right you should silence the ignorance of the foolish.* But what if we are the foolish? Who will silence us? We have to model civility for the world. This means we do not use our freedom to speak as a means of demeaning others. We should represent the positions of those who disagree with us by using fair-minded words. We honor Christ by refusing to use slander or libel to win our way. So please remember that the next time you are tempted to forward some tripe about McCain or Obama that is meant to undermine their character.

We must pray for and honor those in authority. We must show our fear of God by loving our brothers and sisters in the faith and by respecting those who live next door or who worship or don't worship at the church, synagogue, or mosque down the street.

The last word on this should go to the first Baptist in America, Roger Williams. He founded the community of Providence, Rhode Island, after having been expelled from the Massachusetts Bay Colony for his Baptist ideas. In 1644 he published the small book *The Bloody Tenet of Persecution for the Cause of Conscience.* In it he declared that "true civility and Christianity may both flourish in a state or kingdom," even where consciences are protected and differing opinions are allowed to be entertained.[45]

Let us commit ourselves to that and no other end in our witness for Christ and in our love of country.

---

45 Brent Walker, *Reflections*, June 26, 2002. https://web.archive.org/web/20080724232548/http://bjconline.org/resources/articles/2002/020626_walker_baptists.htm

28

Pass the Salt, Hold the Whine

February 15, 2004
Sixth Sunday after Epiphany
Matthew 5:9-14

Thirty-four days ago, forty-two-year-old Baptist pastor Sergei Besarab knelt to pray one morning in his home, as was his custom. Before he could say amen, a religious zealot in the Republic of Tajikistan burst into the adjacent churchyard and sprayed his window with bullets, four of them fatally finding their target. Sergei was converted to Christ while attending prayer services in a prison chapel. After being released, he and his wife, Tamara, spent ten years in prison ministry before sensing a call to start a church in the town of Isfara. They understood what they were getting into. Nine Baptist Christians from the same family in a neighboring church were martyred for their witness in 1993. An American Baptist missionary teacher at our seminary in Prague says that Basarab's death reminds us *that the cost of discipleship and faithfulness in some contexts today may be martyrdom.*[46]

In some contexts, yes. Real persecution. My colleague and friend Terry York, who teaches Christian ministry and church music at Baylor University and Truett Seminary in Waco, was in Russia a few years ago. He said he never felt so American, so distant from the everyday struggle of faith that some Christians face in parts of the world. He was standing in one of their churches, looking at a wall of pictures of men in suits. He asked the man who was hosting him, *Are these your former pastors?* "No," the man replied, "these are our martyrs." If you go down the far south hall in our church, you'll see pictures of men in suits. These are our pastors, not our martyrs. Of course, that's a good thing, especially since I am one of them, don't you know?!

Christians came to these shores looking for freedom from persecution from King James. Same King James that gave us the eloquent English Bible. Go figure. The Pilgrim Puritans. The Mayflower. It's all part of our American religious

---

46 Wesley Brown, quoted on a Baptist World Alliance website news report.

consciousness. But today, if you believe some Christians who are always squawk-ing in the public square, it's all slipping away. I got a booklet from a well-known Christian conservative this week that talked of the "ever-increasing assaults on reli-gious freedom here in the United States." Anti-Christian forces "are determined to remove God from all aspects of American life," she said.[47] There's a new book on the market by David Limbaugh entitled *Persecution: How Liberals Are Waging War Against Christianity.*[48] He presents a similar case that a sinister conspiracy of the Evil One is at work in America to rob our country from its rightful Christian owners.

So, do we want to go back to Pilgrim days? Never mind we learned in those colonial times that religious liberty is not for politicians to grant or withhold; it is a human right endowed by our Creator, a gift from God. Every colony back then had an established church. Baptists weren't established among any of them. But we shouldn't feel singled out. Jews didn't have a place. Native Americans didn't either, even though this was their place first. If the majority decided that the Church of England or the Congregationalists or the Roman Catholics ought to be preferred, the rest were out of luck.

Roger Williams was dragged out of the Massachusetts Bay Colony by horseback for the crime of being a Baptist. He survived the winter in the New England woods with the help of Native Americans. Then he purchased a plot of land and set up the first colony of true religious liberty on earth. He called it Providence because God saw him through. He formed the first Baptist church on this continent there, and then invited Jews and Christians of every flavor to worship freely. Throughout early America, Baptists took a beating from other Christians in public matters. Our preachers were thrown in jail for preaching without a license. Our people could not hold government office because the ruling church did not authorize them. That was discrimination, if not persecution. At last, the Constitution encoded toleration, which was a step forward; and then the Bill of Rights guaranteed full religious liberty. This liberty allows Christians a level playing field with others, which is just what some Christians decry as persecution. But the gospel that proclaims the power of God that raises the dead and transforms people's lives doesn't need government props to stand; it can stand on its own because it is true. That we have to contend for it in the public square is what witnessing is all about!

How we witness matters, too, though. The spirit we bring to our witness needs to be the Spirit of Christ, not the spirit of contention and disrespect. If we are to be called by his name, we must turn to Christ Jesus' words for guidance in this and all matters. In his Sermon on the Mount, Jesus outlines our approach to the world and what to do with reproach from the world. We begin with the basic approach of the beatitude, *Blessed are the peacemakers, for they will be called children of God.* Now the word for peace that Jesus would have used is the biblical *shalom.* It is an active peace, not passive. It is a holistic peace that will not be confined to inner serenity. The geometry of peace is a circle—a comprehensive well-being in every direction and relation. Peacemakers are reconcilers; they promote community rather than discord.

47 Shirley Dobson, "Let Freedom Ring," *National Day of Prayer 2004 Resource Guide.*
48 Regnery, 2003.

And yet today, what we see of the church of Jesus Christ is an approach to the world more confrontational and divisive, more committed to claiming and widening our own space by defeating others rather than making space for them in our circle of care. Edwin Markham's verse comes to mind here: *He drew a circle that shut me out—heretic, rebel, a thing to flout. / But Love and I had the wit to win: / We drew a circle that took him in.*

The fear of many in the church these days is that if we do that, we are denying the truth of Jesus Christ and diluting our message. Tolerance is unfaithfulness. By allowing everyone's view to be heard without fear of reprisal, we are treating every view as equally true. That need not be so. People are allowed to be passionately and sincerely wrong, and they are entitled to be, just as we are, entitled to engage the debate about that. We also may be wrong about some things. But if we believe in the God that sorts all things out in the end, then it is not our mission to do the judging for God now. It is our mission to live in such a way that our beliefs are believable. When we are constantly griping about losing our privileged place in society, we push people out of our way and maybe away from Jesus' way.

We are seldom really persecuted in this country for our faith. But if you read the Christian literature and hear the whining, you'd think we were being martyred left and right. We don't seem to know what it is to truly suffer for our faith anymore. We consider persecution not to be able to pray with government sponsorship in public schools or display a Ten Commandments monument in the Alabama Supreme Court lobby. We feel under attack by the forces of secularism because we cannot pray before high school football games, as if God cares who wins or people have come to the game for religious exercises. Please! Some Christians feel the need to feel persecuted in order to feel faithful to Christ. So they prick the culture to get a rise; and when they do, they feel justified that they are doing the Lord's work in the world. But are they?

It's like the Australian man who was swimming in the ocean off Sydney this week and was bitten in the leg by a two-foot carpet shark. He couldn't shake the shark for anything, so he swam to shore, walked to his car, and drove to the lifeguard station. He strolled in with this shark hanging on his leg and asked for help. The lifeguards said they didn't have anything in their manual for it, but they poured fresh water in the shark's gills, and it finally let go, leaving the man bleeding from seventy teeth marks. The shark died, no doubt thinking himself a martyr.[49]

This is the way much of the world looks at our approach to them as Christians—as sharks instead of lifeguards. They feel our teeth biting into them, and we won't let go. When they try to shake us off, we think they mean us harm. Webster defines persecution as the effort "to pursue in such a way as to injure or afflict." I often wonder who is doing the more persecuting, Christians who seem to need an enemy in order to believe they are standing for the truth or those who want to marginalize Christians and challenge our beliefs. I am not saying we do not suffer any indignities or offenses in America today. But when we do, why whine about it, when Jesus said to "Rejoice and be glad"? This is just our opportunity to prove how our gospel

---

49 *Dallas Morning News* (Feb. 13, 2004): 29A.

way of salt-and-light peacemaking might commend to the world a suffering Savior who loved to death even those who rejected him.

In France last week, the National Assembly made a disastrous decision for religious liberty. They prohibited school children from wearing any religious garb: no Christian crosses, no Jewish skullcaps, no Muslim girls' headscarves, and no Sikh turbans. They want a completely secular society with laws that are hostile to religious practice. That is not the American way. We promote laws that protect religious expression and maintain neutrality toward religion.

George W. Truett, the late great pastor of the First Baptist Church of Dallas and a founder of the Baptist World Alliance, said in his address from the steps of the Capitol in Washington, D.C., in 1920: *It is the consistent and insistent contention of our Baptist people, always and everywhere, that religion be forever voluntary and uncoerced, and that it is not the prerogative of any power ... to compel people to conform to any religious creed or form of worship, or to pay taxes for the support of a religious organization to which they do not belong and in whose creed they do not believe. God wants free worshipers and no other kind.*[50]

Well, that is sadly no longer the consistent and insistent contention of our Baptist people, always and everywhere. But if we follow Jesus' words, we will accept reproaches from those who disagree with us as opportunities to demonstrate God's grace by our good works rather than as violations of our rights that must be redressed. We are not blessed when we are persecuted for our lack of fairness and generosity to others.

You are the salt of the earth, Jesus says. *You are the light of the world.* We remind you of this in baptism each time we take another one under. Salt does not exist for itself. And Christians do not, either. We are only useful when we are in contact with others, when we are in relationship to others, when we can penetrate whatever is bland and spoiling in society with our good taste and gracious works.

Likewise, we are lighthouses, sending beams of God's love to those who find themselves in distress on the stormy seas of their lives. But our light is not from within ourselves; we are reflections of the Son of God, who is the sun of righteousness. Therefore, we do not claim to see everything with perfect clarity. We do not throw the high beams in the face of those around us we think are in darkness. *Excess of light blinds*, said the philosopher Immanuel Kant. It blinds those who think they see truth without doubt, and it blinds those who come into contact with them.

Faith and humility go hand in hand for followers of Jesus. We may or may not suffer for our faith, but the way we live either way says as much about the God we worship as what we say we believe. So, let's pass the salt, for God's sake ... and hold the whine.

---

50 See *Christian Ethics Today*, Vol. 32. for the entire text.

29

Drawn to the Light

Watch and listen to "Drawn to the Light" by following this link or scanning the QR code with your phone: youtu.be/70f5E1m348E. Sermon begins at 19:49.

January 3, 2021
Epiphany Sunday
Isaiah 60:1-5a; Matthew 2:1-12

Epiphany is January 6, but on this Sunday before it we focus on the words of Isaiah and the Magi following the star. We are called to be a light to the nations. Epiphany means manifestation and it refers to the way Christ is made known to the Gentiles.

First, a word about our texts from the prophet and the Gospel. Israel has finally returned to their homeland after seventy years in Babylonian exile. They are despondent about the condition of the land and their feeling of lost glory. Isaiah declares the word of the Lord: *Arise and shine, for your light has come.* They are to lift their heads and set about the work of being a people worthy of admiration. It won't happen all at once, but if they will attend to the law of the Lord, the peoples of the earth will note their witness to the way of God.

And then we see that the one who is himself the Light of the world is born in Bethlehem. Wise men from afar see the light in the night sky and follow it to him. Christ is born to Israel and the light of God shines from and through them. The nations worship the child, bringing gifts of gold, frankincense, and myrrh. It's a beautiful picture: the election of Israel to be a light to the world and the coming of the light in Christ through them.

So, here's the question of the day for this new year: If the church today can rightly claim to share in the promises of God to Israel that the glory of God will shine upon us and radiate through us so that the nations will be drawn to our light, how will we rise and shine in these dark days of discouragement so that we will be an Epiphany Church?

I wrote a whole sermon on this subject that addressed the state of the church in America right now. I scrapped it altogether and started over because it sounded more like a screed than a sermon. Guess I needed to get it out of my system, don't you know?! I have a humbler aim in this one: to call on us as a congregation to do what we can, since we can only control our own obedience. Baptists always start with the small "c" church before moving to the big "C" Church. So, let's focus on ourselves today, Wilshire, and find ways to contribute to the renewal of the Church by aiding the renewal of the Baptist church in our time.

Using images of light, I want us to attend to a few things. First, *keep a steady flame.*

I don't know if you caught it, but in our prerecorded virtual Christmas Eve service, we had trouble with the Christ candle. The wick had burned to a nub and the fire kept going out. On the other hand, some churches will gather all their Christmas trees on Epiphany for a huge bonfire to symbolize the church's being a light to the world.

A healthy church lives between these extremes. We need the Spirit's Pentecostal power among us that keeps the fire going, but we don't need bonfires of vanity that call attention to ourselves. The constancy of spiritual fire will do just fine to bring warmth and light to the world.

Every church is facing the same challenge of staying connected during this time of COVID restrictions. Ours is no different. It's easy to lose touch with one another when we can't come together to worship and pray and study the Scripture as we always have. It's too easy to lose touch with God as well. Our spiritual lives require attention, and our communal life is God's way of keeping us alive in the Spirit.

The church exists as a reminder that God's light shines through a people dedicated to being light. The state is not the light, and individuals are not themselves the light. If we remain connected to Christ and to each other in these times of discouragement, the world will see a way forward through us.

And that leads to the second thing: *our relationship to power.* The church gets its power to bear the light from Christ, not from Caesar.

Baptists came into being as a form of church that refused to grant spiritual power to the government or to seek power from of it. We pioneered the idea of the separation of church and state. We believed government should establish and protect religious liberty—not just for us, but for every other religion and for those with no religion.

How things have changed. If you ask the average person whether Baptists stand for religious liberty today, they will look at you as if you are crazy. Too many Baptists nowadays long to be powerbrokers in Washington. They like to go to the White House and secure the special favor of the president. These Baptists want religious liberty for themselves and want to deny it to others. They have fallen into the idolatry of Christian nationalism and the light of Christ has dimmed in proportion to their increased secular power.

Every time a nation tries to become Christian by use of worldly power, the light of Christ is dimmer. When King Ferdinand and Queen Isabella in the fifteenth century set upon to make their country a Christian nation, they wanted to make Spain a light to the world to the glory of God. But to do so, their Reconquista forced all Jews and Muslims to convert or be tortured and killed. They set Columbus on his journey to find gold and bring it back to them, rather than have the nations bring their gold of their own accord. Their Conquistadors enslaved native peoples and raped the riches of their lands. Today, you can go visit Spain's empty cathedrals and find a country where the light of Christ is barely a flicker.

One of our most visionary Baptists, the Rev. Martin Luther King Jr., got it right when he said: *The church must be reminded that it is not the master or the servant of the state, but rather the conscience of the state. It must be the guide and the critic of the state, and never its tool.* There's a reckoning coming for Baptists who have lost our way in this regard. We have to return to our calling to live as the light and not try to blind others by it.

We do that by serving the common good, tending to the poor and marginalized in society, loving our neighbor. Our politics should be the politics of Jesus—rescuing the perishing, caring for the dying, liberating the oppressed, standing for justice, offering profligate mercy and kindness to all.

Which leads to this: Light is a metaphor for truth, and *we must be committed to the truth* wherever we find it.

For one thing, that means not falling for or promoting conspiracy theories based on lies or claiming that inconvenient truths are just hoaxes. Facts are stubborn: They should never be bent to fit what we want them to mean. Being light should lead to enlightenment, never to making the clear unclear for our own benefit. If the church won't bow to truth, we shouldn't expect people to bow to the one who says he is the way, the truth, and the life.

That also means trusting science, not denying it. Science is another way God is making the truth known. Too many Baptists think they have an absolute purchase on the truth because the Bible tells them all they need to know about everything. They are suspicious of science and see it as a secular means of denying the church its freedom.

We see some Baptist churches declaring the coronavirus a hoax and holding services without masks, only to see their own people come down with the deadly virus. The reports of subsequent deaths just break my heart. Take away just these Baptist skeptics from the last nine months, never mind all the other Evangelicals, and we might have seen a different result from all the illness and death that has plagued us as a nation. All truth is God's truth wherever it is found and by whatever means.

Just this past week, we have seen another sad example of denying truth when the six presidents of the Southern Baptist seminaries declared critical race theory to be contrary to biblical truth. It must be rejected by Christians, they say, because it was developed by non-Christians using tools of social analysis. Critical race theory points out how racism is embedded in systems of law, education, economics, and politics and must be addressed as such instead of just directing people to change their hearts. Black pastors and churches are leaving the SBC in light of this rejection and calling for the church's repentance for its complicity with white supremacy. It's about time.

This is a far cry from the declaration of the English minister John Robinson who preached to the departing Puritans in a sermon in 1619 before they boarded the Mayflower: *For I am very confident the Lord hath more truth and light yet to break forth out of His holy Word.* More truth and light! God is still shining more truth and light to us if we would only look and listen.

We can't answer for all Christians or all Baptists, but we can answer for ourselves. We can keep a steady flame by staying connected to God and one another. We can choose the politics of Jesus over worldly power. And we can embrace the truth wherever we find it and whatever it costs us.

I am proud of this church. Wilshire means something to people. It gives them hope. And it gives me hope for the church to be your pastor. Let's continue to rise and shine, people of God. Your light has come. Amen.

30

Slaying Giants

Watch and listen to "Slaying Giants" by following this link or scanning the QR code with your phone: youtu.be/PrcV_ZmHTbs. Sermon begins at 41:15.

June 24, 2018
Fifth Sunday after Pentecost
1 Samuel 17:1a, 4-11, 19-23, 32-49

The David and Goliath story is so well known it's become shorthand for any underdog challenging a powerful opponent. Unfortunately, it's also misused by anyone who says God is on their side and their opponent is the enemy of God. As we've learned this past week, even people acting as Goliath can use the Bible to justify their actions.

During the Civil War, President Abraham Lincoln was asked if he thought God was on his side. His reply is always a quip to quote: *Sir, my concern is not whether God is on our side; my greatest concern is to be on God's side, for God is always right.*

Today we need to work through the David and Goliath story carefully enough to make sure we're on God's side. There are still giants in the land, Goliaths spewing hate, demeaning dignity, and threatening freedom. These giants need slaying, but how to slay them is as important as their being slayed.

David is depicted here as a young boy. He is dispatched to the front lines of Israel's army to bring lamb sandwiches or some such to his brothers. More than likely, his father Jesse just wants to know that his sons are alive and well.

David is the eighth son. The number eight may be more than literally significant; it could stand for the Hebrew notion of the eighth day of creation—that is, the beginning of the new creation. And in fact, when we get to Jesus, who is called the Son of David, Christians claim he is the fulfillment of the promise of God to be the head of an everlasting kingdom in the name of David. So, David is important not only in his time, but also in ours. It's not just that he won a battle with Goliath; it's how he won the battle that tips us off to something enduring for anyone who wants to claim they are on God's side. There are some moral marks to note as we try to understand this epic tale.

Goliath is the champion of the Philistines, a people whose kingdom covered the coastline of what is now Israel. It includes the current Palestinian territory of Gaza. During the reign of King Saul, the children of Israel were at war with the Philistines repeatedly. Things come to a head when they put Goliath forward to challenge them mano-a-mano. And what a challenge it is. Goliath is enormous. Depending on which text of the Bible you follow, he is either 9'9" or 6'9" tall. Even if the latter, given how small in stature people were in that time, he is a giant either way. On top of that, he is equipped with the latest and greatest armor and arms. Think Ironman with a spear the size of a sawed-off telephone pole. This guy is scary by any definition. And the Israelites are immobilized by fear, shaking in their sandals.

It was common enough to have a warrior champion of one people face off in a winner-take-all match to the death with the champion of another people. In Homer's *Iliad*, we have a similar contest between Paris of Troy and Menelaus of Sparta, the winner taking Helen for the prize. And then later, Hector squares off with Achilles in a fight to end the siege of Troy. Moving forward in biblical history, Christians claim that Jesus in effect does the same, representing humanity against the forces of evil.

Well, nobody was volunteering to represent Israel in the contest against Goliath. Clearly, the Philistines have the upper hand and the existence of the people of God is threatened by this bully who curses Israel and its God.

The first moral point that emerges in the storytelling is clarity about who needs defending. God takes sides with the weak and calls us to take sides with them against those who would terrorize them. When one person or people humiliates another, holds them in contempt and dehumanizes them by calling them animals, as Goliath did, they lose all claim to God being on their side. Unlike so many myths of ancient valor or imperial histories of conquest, the Bible is written from the underside. It gives voice to the voiceless and face to the victims. The David and Goliath story is a prime example.

And yet, we have to be careful with it because we are all sometimes David and sometimes Goliath; we can't just pretend always to be David.

Take the current situation in the Holy Land. Both Palestinians and Israelis like to cast themselves as David with their opposite being Goliath. Palestinians see their homeland threatened by a nation with the military support of the United States and all traditional power on their side. They believe their cause is just. Their *intifadas*, which are stone-throwing events in the streets by children and youth, are just David with his five smooth stones and slingshot—the little guy against the giant. Israel counters that it is a small nation surrounded by Arab countries that want to drive it into the sea. It feels threatened by every neighbor, especially Iran and Syria and their surrogate terrorist parties, Hezbollah and Hamas.

You see how easily we can make ourselves David? But when we do, we overlook the ways we can be Goliath, too. Our identification with David can be justification for evil, like Palestinian suicide bombers, or cruelty, like Israeli occupation and embargoes that choke off hope.

We see this on our southern border. When the most powerful country in the world, which boasts a booming economy right now with the lowest unemployment in recent memory, pulls back from trade agreements because we want better deals for ourselves, this undermines the progress of countries like those in Central America whose people are crossing our borders illegally, desperate for work and eager to flee violence and corruption often rooted in poverty. When we then talk about these migrants as an "infestation," we dehumanize them. When we criminalize them so that we can then separate children from parents as a deterrent to others who might attempt to come, we lose the right to play the David card. We are Goliath.

The first thing then is moral clarity. If you want to be David, you have to act with compassion toward those whose lives and hopes are threatened. You can't claim to be David and act like Goliath. Empathy requires that you see and feel the pain of others, identify with it, and then move toward it to get personally involved. David was outraged on behalf of the weaker party, and it moved him to act.

Second is moral courage. Yes, David had experience as a shepherd protecting the sheep from *lions and tigers and bears, oh my!* And yes, this did teach him that victory was possible when all seemed lost. But he still needed courage to stand up and enter the arena.

Sometimes we need courage not just to face Goliath but to endure criticism or ridicule from the people closest to us. The edited passage we read from 1 Samuel this morning was long enough, don't you know?! But one part cut out was when David's eldest brother, Eliab, accuses his little brother of grandstanding. Eliab says he should have stayed with the sheep and left the battle to others. He just wanted attention.

This is often true when you speak up and stand up the way David did. You may feel sucker-punched by your own family or those you are fighting with and for. Pastors hear this when they speak up for justice in the public sphere: *Why don't you just go back to tending the sheep? You just like being in the media.* Women hear this when they speak up against domestic abuse or corporate sexual misconduct: *Why are you causing trouble like this? You'll destroy your family if you speak up. Or, you'll destroy the company and hurt innocent investors and employees.*

But courage comes from faith, faith that God is with you, even when it feels like everyone is against you, even those who should be for you.

Michael Gerson was a speechwriter for President George W. Bush. He knows the struggle pastors feel in these days. So, this week he offered preachers some words for their Sunday sermon, calling on us to have the courage to speak. I'm not used to letting other people write my sermons, but this is worthy of hearing. Here's what he said I should say to you: *There are many political and policy views among Christians, and many represented here in this sanctuary. But our faith involves a common belief with unavoidably public consequences: Christians are to love their neighbor, and everyone is their neighbor. All the appearances of difference—in race, ethnicity, nationality, and accomplishment—are deceptive. The reality is unseen. God's distribution of dignity is completely and radically equal. No one is worthless. No one is insignificant. No one should be reduced to the status of a thing. This is the changeless truth in our changing politics. You can argue about what constitutes effective criminal-justice policy—but, as a Christian, you cannot view and treat inmates like animals. You can disagree about the procedures by which our country takes in refugees—but you can't demonize them for political gain. And you can argue about the proper shape of our immigration system— but you can't support any policy that achieves its goal by purposely terrorizing children.*[51]

Finally, moral clarity and moral courage need moral cunning, too. Fear has a way of exhausting the imagination and limiting creativity. When David chose five smooth stones and slung one at Goliath, finding the one vulnerable place in his armor, he was undermining the prevailing system of worldly violence and showing that God does not work through fire and fury. *The Lord does not save by sword and spear*, David declares.

Which means, if the people of God are going to engage the world's Goliaths as true Davids, we need to be smarter, not stronger. We need to find slingshot-like ways to undermine violence by reducing violence, not by adding to it.

The whole humorous scene of Saul outfitting David with his armor and seeing it ill-fitting was more than just a way to move the story forward; it was a way of showing that our methods matter. We need moral means, not just moral ends.

Most of you sitting here today probably feel like you are too small to matter. What can you do to make a difference? Uh, hello, isn't that the David and Goliath story? Whoever you are, you have a voice and a vote. You have time to volunteer and a dollar to give. But more than all that, you will be on God's side and God will direct your slingshot service to just the right spot to slay giants.

The traditional media, social media, business community, and religious world cried out this past week and changed a heartless public policy. It isn't over yet by a long shot, but when airlines refused to transport separated children, when flight attendants refused to work flights that did, when religious leaders took planes and buses to see and photograph separated children in cages at the border, when ordinary people took to Facebook and Twitter and Instagram to speak their mind, giant injustices began to be rolled back.

Our own Cheryl Allison went to McAllen wearing her WOW shirt—Women of Wilshire. She met with Sister Norma, played with children, bought food we helped pay for, and in her own way stood up to Goliath.

You may not think you have much power to change the world, but sometimes all you need is clarity, courage, and cunning. Or said another way, when you feel like David before Goliath, remember God is there, too. Just don't forget your slingshot.

---

51 https://www.washingtonpost.com/opinions/a-case-study-in-the-proper-role-of-christians-in-politics/2018/06/21/39acd0bc-7578-11e8-b4b7-308400242c2e_story.html

31

Faithful Betrayal

Watch and listen to "Faithful Betrayal" by following this link or scanning the QR code with your phone: youtu.be/4jBIN5i4eNU.

February 3, 2019
Fourth Sunday after Epiphany
Luke 4:21-30

Don't you wish you could have been there to see how this went down? I mean, what was the feeling in the room that day? Did Jesus know it would go this way or did it take a turn he didn't expect?

To review, we are near the beginning of Jesus' ministry, fresh off his temptations in the Judean wilderness. He's been working miracles and teaching in the town of Capernaum, which is on the north shore of the Sea of Galilee, about forty miles from Nazareth. Now, like any good politician who is announcing his campaign, Jesus returns to his hometown folk to launch his formal messianic mission.

Last week, we looked at the first part of this scene. Jesus is invited to read the Haftarah portion of Scripture, which is from the prophetic books that come after the Torah, the first five books of the Bible. Law, then prophets. He takes the Isaiah scroll and turns to places near and including chapter 61.

> *The Spirit of the Lord is upon me, because he has anointed me to bring good news to the poor.*
>
> *He has sent me to proclaim release to the captives and recovery of sight to the blind,*
>
> *to let the oppressed go free,*
>
> *to proclaim the year of the Lord's favor.*

It's as if he is saying, "If you want to know what I'm about, this." This signals his commitment to enact in his ministry the so-called Jubilee, the time of joy that was to come every fifty years in Israel, but that also came to symbolize God's dream for the conditions of the whole world that will be in full effect when God's will is done on earth as it is in heaven. This is a big vision—not a little policy statement, not an outline of how to make Israel great again; it's a grand description of the good news of God that brings people together in one great experience of true equality, shared prosperity, and unending peace.

He sits down. The people are transfixed. They must sense this is not just about Isaiah. It's about him. They assume it's about them, too. And then he says this: *Today this scripture has been fulfilled in your hearing.*

That's where we pick it up again today. *Today this scripture has been fulfilled in your hearing.* Hold that thought.

At first the people seem proud and excited if we are reading them rightly. All spoke well of him and were amazed at the grace coming out of his mouth. Grace. If they only knew, Jesus must be thinking. He's about to let them in on just how right they are.

Is this not Joseph's son? they ask. Hmm. Is that what sets him off? Does he sense in those words their pride in raising such a fine young man or does he hear them wonder whether he's getting too good for them?

We don't know, but all of a sudden, it seems like Jesus picks a fight. *Doubtless you will say 'Doctor cure yourself,'* and *'Do for us here what you've been doing in Capernaum.'* The second part of that probably shows that the first part doesn't mean they're telling him that he needs to heal himself as much it means they want him to start at home taking care of them. He reminds them that the greatest prophets of that region, Elijah and Elisha, didn't stay on their Jewish side of the border, so to speak. They attended to the needs of those outside of their tribe. They did miracles and cured the illnesses of people considered their enemies.

He's poking the bear now, and the bear starts to growl. He hears their spirit rising against him and reminds them that no prophet is without honor except in his hometown.

I can almost see his mother and brothers cringe. "Did you have to say that, Jesus?" Or, "It's not what you said, Jesus, it's your tone."

The people get so mad at him that they try to throw him off the cliff the town is built on. He gets away, but not without us seeing something deeply disturbing that we continue to deal with any time we speak or act in the spirit of Jesus.

It's what I call *faithful betrayal.* The good news of God that Jesus announces is profligate grace. It can never be limited or controlled by insiders. It can't be ours if it's not all of ours. It's for everyone or no one. The real test of whether we get it is if we are willing for everybody to get it.

I've been reading up on Robert E. Lee this week. You know we finally got the statue of Lee taken down in Lee Park and have gotten the name of the park returned to its original name, Oak Lawn Park, before the effort of the Klan and the Daughters of the Confederacy to revive the spirit of the South in Dallas under the guise of acknowledging history—which is really only one side of history, don't you know?! Instead of contrition, they began a propaganda campaign to reestablish the nobility of their lost cause. We still have massive monuments to white supremacy in Pioneer Plaza downtown that need to go if we are ever to signal to our whole community that we intend to be whole. As of now, our leaders are still dithering and failing to act.

General Lee was asked to lead the Union forces in the Civil War, but he declined. He had sympathy for the Union and didn't want to see its dissolution. At times he spoke against the evil of slavery. In an 1856 letter to his wife, Lee wrote that *slavery, as an institution, is a moral and political evil in any Country.* But he neither released his own slaves nor fought for their freedom, even if he believed it was wrong. Why? He told his sister Anne Lee Marshall, *I have not been able to make up my mind to raise my hand against my relatives, my children, my home.* That, even though many members of his family were for the Union and against secession.

When he accepted the charge to lead the Confederate forces, the secession convention president, John Janney, remarked to him: *We pray God most fervently that you may so conduct the operations committed to your charge, that it will soon be said of you, that you are 'first in peace,' and when that time comes you will have earned the still prouder distinction of being 'first in the hearts of your countrymen.'*[52]

No matter how much any may admire Lee as a gentleman and soldier, the bottom line still and always will be this: At the crucial moment in this country's history, Lee chose the wrong side of the faithful betrayal dialectic. In doing so, he conducted the bloodiest war of our nation's story, one we have still not recovered from. Instead of setting the captives free, he fought to protect and defend the captors. He cared more to be honored in his hometown than to call his hometown to see the higher moral cause of freedom and his countrymen to live up to the words of the Declaration of Independence that said, *We hold these truths to be self-evident that all men are created equal, that they are endowed by their Creator with certain unalienable Rights, that among these are Life, Liberty, and the pursuit of Happiness.*

Imagine the course of American history if Lee had chosen otherwise, if he had been faithful to the Jubilee vision of Isaiah and Jesus even at the personal cost of betraying those closest to him?

The gospel of Jesus Christ calls us time and again to test whether we are working with God for the vision of a world that includes all of us or only those of our group. We all face this in small and large ways at times in our lives.

This week, the president of the Southern Baptist Convention, J.D. Greear, spoke bravely and boldly about the reality of white privilege and called on his conservative Christian tribe to acknowledge it. *Whatever privilege you have,* he said, *it is your responsibility to leverage it to help others who are not as privileged. Whether you are progressive or conservative, as a Christian ... you must want to see all people in our culture treated with dignity and experience the same privileges that any of us experience.*[53]

Just saying that, which may seem so obvious to people in this room, will leave some of his supporters feeling betrayed. They may not try to throw him off a cliff, but he will lose friends and feel the weight of their rejection. Some of us know what this is like and the pain that comes from decisions like that that amount to faithful betrayal. We must praise him and pray for him.

---

52 https://www.historynet.com/a-question-of-loyalty-why-did-robert-e-lee-join-the-confederacy/
53 http://www.bpnews.net/52327/greear-white-privilege-should-extend-to-all-race

That's the courage the gospel calls for. It's the kind of courage you need when you see a classmate being bullied and you have to decide whether you want to be liked by the group doing the bullying or you will risk yourself to stand up for the kid being picked on. It's the kind of courage needed in the boardroom to stand up for principle over profit, to protect whistleblowers instead of those being called out. It's the courage needed to stand with anyone who is marginalized, an outsider or different. Being faithful to the gospel will often feel like betrayal to some who want to retain their privilege and protect the status quo. But our call to follow Jesus will sometimes involve that choice.

When Jesus said *Today this scripture has been fulfilled in your hearing*, the verb tense he used is interesting. It's the *present perfect progressive tense*. That is, in hearing him read Isaiah's prophetic words in that moment, those words were perfected, that is, they came to fulfillment. But in doing so, those words didn't come to an end; they came to a beginning. The progressive part is that the force of their being actualized continues. Jesus is saying that this is the direction of the reign of God in every time to come. This is what we are being called to as the church every time we hear these words.

The Recovery Café Network started in Seattle, Washington. It's a place of healing and wholeness for individuals who have experienced trauma related to homelessness, addiction, and other forms of mental illness. In her book, *Descent into Love: How Recovery Cafe Came to Be*, Killian Noe tells about what brought this movement about:

"We needed to stay conscious that planting ourselves in the soil of community and showing up daily through meditation or contemplative prayer as a means of surrendering our lives was not just about our own self-actualization but was for the sake of a wounded world desperately in need of healing and justice. That healing and justice can flow through us but is not from us and is certainly not 'about' us.

"The Sufi tell a story about a spiritual seeker who was distracted by the sick, crippled, and beaten down who continuously passed by as he tried to pray. Finally he cried, 'Great God, how is it that a loving creator can see such things and do nothing about them?' Out of the long silence, God said, 'I did do something about them. I made you.'"[54]

The present perfect progressive tense of living out the call of God's grace for others will sometimes make us tense with those closest to us. It may mean sacrificing our comfort for the sake of relieving the suffering of others. It may mean suffering loss for the sake of others' gain. But how will people ever come to know the Jesus we read about in this story if we don't join him in living out his story?

Frederick Buechner puts Jesus' Jubilee message this way: ... *in the long run, there can be no joy for anybody until there is joy finally for us all.*[55]

Amen.

---

54 https://inwardoutward.org/i-made-you-jan-14-2019/
55 *The Sacred Journey: A Memoir of Early Days*, (Harper & Row).

32

Deep Cleaning

Watch and listen to "Deep Cleaning" by following this link or scanning the QR code with your phone: youtu.be/CrPCpcIOO_w. Sermon begins at 29:16.

January 31, 2021
Fourth Sunday after Epiphany
Mark 1:21-28

I like to keep things neat and orderly. If you look at my desk at home or at the office, you'll find that books and papers are arranged just so. The clothes in my closet are lined up logically, facing the same direction and grouped by types—not just shirts and pants, mind you, but dress and casual sections, too. Oh, and golf clothes in their own section. Even the sock drawers are systematized. Yes, I did say drawers, plural. It's a mild sickness, don't you know?!

But for all that, I perpetually fail my wife's test for housekeeping. Kim's a deep cleaner. I like to see things properly placed. But I don't see dust, apparently. Now and then she will invade the sanctuary of my spaces with her alternative authority and give it all a good scrubbing. She goes beneath the appearance of things to make things shine.

We have a story today about Jesus doing that kind of work on a man with an unclean spirit. Jesus is a deep cleaner: he exorcises the demon and sets the man free. But before we get there, there's much to look at. And it will take eyes more like Kim's than mine to see it.

Mark's Jesus gets to the bottom of things. He takes us beneath the surface. He confronts the invisible, demonic world that hides in plain sight and disrupts the intentions of God for humanity. And in doing so, he invites the faith community to join him in his ongoing work.

After being baptized in the Jordan by John the Baptist, Jesus heads north and begins to call his disciples by the Sea of Galilee. Then he goes to Simon Peter's home village, Capernaum, and enters the synagogue on the Sabbath—holy space in holy time. This is a subtle clue to what is happening.

He begins to teach, and his teaching catches their attention. It isn't so much what he says but the authority with which he says it. Now, that doesn't mean just that he had a strong gift for teaching or was especially charming in his style. It's that, unlike the pattern of the scribes who taught by referring to various interpretations of the rabbis, Jesus gave his own interpretation. He didn't couch what he said to show his mastery of the tradition and gain their admiration. He spoke as though he knew the meaning of these texts for the spiritual life and mission of the people of God. So, right off, the contrast is made between Jesus and the scribes.

Just then, a man with an unclean spirit speaks up. Note: He didn't burst into the synagogue; he was already there. We aren't told if everyone already knew that he had an unclean spirit. But he was there among them as one of them.

Now this is important because of our tendency to "other" this man right off. The good, unsuspecting worshipers are on one side with Jesus and this one oddball luna-tic is threatening the peaceful assembly. If this were to happen on a normal Sunday here at Wilshire, the ushers would rush to escort him out so as not to disturb the peace. Then we'd go back to worship as usual. But we have already seen that this was not worship as usual in Capernaum that day because Jesus taught with "authority."

So, if we're not supposed to see this man as a weirdo to whisk away, a one-off mentally disturbed person that Jesus would deal with individually so that the good folk could get back to being good, how should we understand him as possessing an unclean spirit? I want to suggest to you that this man possessed a spirit that was also present throughout the assembly that day but was most acutely manifested in the one man. He symbolically represents the social arrangement between the oppressive Roman Empire and the complicity of the scribal authorities who had settled for a life of quiet acceptance of their domination and had lost the sense of God's power to resist it.

Look at what the man says. *What have you to do with US, Jesus of Nazareth? Have you come to destroy US?* Who is the US here? Isn't he a single individual? Well, yes and no.

This man has been more thoroughly taken over by the same spirit that was present to a lesser degree in all the people gathered that day. Why him more so than others? We don't know. But we do know that when an abusive environment exists in a family, say, there is usually an identified patient, one member of the family who takes a disproportionate amount of the abuse and internalizes it. It's not that only that person is sick, though; the whole family is afflicted. The individual needs to be set free from this unclean spirit, but so does the family.

Look how the man with the unclean spirit speaks. He speaks first in the plural and then the singular. That is, he speaks as if he is representing a spirit that has taken them all hostage. He is no longer defined by his own unique voice but by the voice of the oppressive force that has taken control of him. And when he does use the singular—*I know who you are, the Holy One of God*—it's as if he speaks now in the collective voice of that invisible power that is in mortal conflict with the invisible God.

This is the nature of the demonic. It lurks in ideologies and systems of oppression. It hides in plain sight. It speaks in a way that makes sense in one sense to everyone who is wittingly or unwittingly caught up in it. Until, that is, the Holy One shows us how to speak with authority and break its grip on the minds of the people.

Is this not what we are seeing in our American churches today? We have some among us whom we have known for years but who have been seemingly taken over by spirits that have changed them. They have imbibed the false narrative of Christian nationalism or American exceptionalism or white supremacy or cultural entitlement to the point that we hardly know them anymore.

The Southern Baptist research group, LifeWay, released the results of a study this week that found that in churches of more than 250 people, 61% of pastors said they are dealing with members who are spouting conspiracy theories. *While hundreds of people stormed the Capitol*, the report says, *there are millions of Americans who share their views. There is no doubt: The United States has a serious problem with pathological political delusions.* It continued pessimistically: *Once people have gone far enough down the rabbit hole of conspiratorial thinking, it can be nearly impossible to get them back out.*[56]

Nearly impossible, but not impossible. Wherever Jesus is present, deliverance is possible.

And I want to hasten to say, not because I just want to be fair and balanced, but because it is true, that it's not just the far-right radical element of Christians that is susceptible. We all are, even people with a more progressive view of politics and theology. Rome, so to speak, seeks domination of everyone and everything. Groupthink is dangerous and demonic, whether from the right or left. It robs people of compassion for others and divides us from one another. We all need to be delivered and set free.

Jesus rebukes the unclean spirit and casts it out of the man. Which is something the community had not done itself because they lost touch with the power of God to identify and defeat the demonic.

But the unclean spirit wasn't cleansed easily. It came out convulsing and crying loudly. This is because it had such a foothold on the man's personality.

James Baldwin said that *people are trapped in history and history is trapped in them.* We see that with racism, Blacks as well as whites. We internalize it all until we can't even see that it's there, let alone get free of it. It has taken up residence in us. The rabbis said this about the Israelites after they left Egyptian slavery: *You can get the people out of Egypt but it's harder to get Egypt out of the people.*

So, how do we do this? First, trust the power and presence of Jesus among us that is always trying to free us and never leaves us helpless.

Second, recognize that we all need his deliverance. When we see someone who seems to be far gone in our eyes, see ourselves in that person. Don't write off the person and act as if we are fine and the problem is only with him or her. We will never come together and experience salvation and renewed community if we scapegoat others and demonize them as the enemy while letting ourselves off the hook.

---

56 https://baptistnews.com/article/half-of-pastors-say-their-congregants-are-spreading-conspiracy-theories/#.YBTRVi1h1qt

Third, we can't settle for worship without dangerous encounter with the presence of God. We need word *and* deed, enlightenment *and* exorcism, illumination *and* transformation. We need Jesus to shake us and change us, all of us, even if that is uncomfortable. The church has to address the demonic within the community with honest interrogation of our hearts if we are to live as free people.

Finally, address those who are most disturbed among us with power and grace at the same time. See beneath the surface to find the tender humanity in them.

Jesus isn't satisfied with being among nice people who have adjusted to the cultural and political powers that hold us hostage. He goes deep and he calls us to join him.

Thomas Troeger wrote a hymn on this passage that carries the truth of it: *"Silence, frenzied, unclean spirit!" cried God's healing Holy One. "Cease your ranting! Flesh can't bear it. Flee as night before the sun." At Christ's words the demon trembled, from its victim madly rushed, while the crowd that was assembled stood in wonder, stunned, and hushed.* Amen.

33

Bearings

Watch and listen to "Bearings" by following this link or scanning the QR code with your phone: youtu.be/sx6gk5CrmFI. Sermon begins at 17:35.

August 30, 2020
Thirteenth Sunday after Pentecost
Matthew 16:21-28

Pigeons. Have you ever seen how those incessant birds in parks and plazas head in one direction for a time, and then turn and go another way, and then another like they're always fall-down drunk? There's a reason for that. As long as pigeons are in motion, they can't see their surroundings clearly. So, they frequently stop, pivot, and cock their heads as if to take bearings, and then they're off again. Canadian bird scholar B.J. Frost says that *the momentary stillness of their heads allows pigeons to become aware of movement around them, while the motion of their bobbing heads enables them to detect depth and distance.*[57]

Pigeon-walking and head-bobbing helps these creatures get their bearings. Best we can tell, though, birds have no lofty ambitions. They use their faculties for survival: to find food and to fend off enemies. Humans, on the other hand, are strategic. We have a sense of the future, and we desire to be part of something enduring. We find meaning in joining movements we think are going somewhere. But how do we keep our bearings, so we don't get lost?

A disciple is someone who follows a master. In our text today from Matthew's Gospel, the disciple Peter has just confessed that his master is the messiah of God, the one God would use to redeem Israel. Jesus praises Peter for his insight, albeit crediting God for giving it to him more than Peter himself for having it. And yet, Peter—whether him personally or the faith he confessed in Jesus being the Son of God—is declared to be the Rock on which the church will be built.

Peter is in that moment perfectly aligned with Jesus. But no sooner is that blessing given than Peter loses his bearings and Jesus needs to get him back in line.

---

57 Cited by Leonard Sweet, *Quantum Spirituality: A Postmodern Apologetic* (Dayton: Whaleprints, 1991), p. 56.

This is true for all of us who follow Jesus as his disciples. We love associating ourselves with Jesus and his mission to save the world. We want to be on his team. We walk the aisle and sing, *I have decided to follow Jesus, no turning back, no turning back.* We are baptized in his name, drowning our self-centeredness and re-centering ourselves in and around him. But we lose our bearings so easily.

Look how this happened with Peter. Jesus starts to tell Peter and the other disciples what it means for him to be the messiah. He must go to Jerusalem, suffer at the hands of religious leaders there, be crucified … and on the third day rise from the dead. I'm sure by the time Matthew got around to writing this half a century later it was easier to remember that Jesus added that part about rising from the dead. At the time, though, he and the others heard nothing but the part about suffering and dying.

None of us wants that part. We want victory without struggle. We want light without the darkness. We want the world fixed without the sacrifices that go into fixing it.

We've just finished two weeks of political conventions that laid out plans for "saving the soul of America." Not that politicians are ever given to overstatement, don't you know?! Now, you probably resonate more with one party than the other. Most do. I won't debate you here about that, no matter how strongly I feel personally. I must warn you, however, about not losing your bearings as a disciple of Jesus in your political partisanship.

It's easy to confess Jesus as Lord until it calls on you to question every other loyalty. Jesus' words to Peter and the disciples—that is, to us—amount to this: Curb your enthusiasm for personal glory and for stitching your faith to a flag. There are two key bearings you need to get right if you will be in proper alignment as a disciple: *behind Christ* and *under your cross.*

Getting behind Christ is our first and ongoing duty. Notice again this encounter between Jesus and Peter. Jesus asks the disciples, *Who do you say that I am?* Peter answers correctly, saying, *You are the Christ, the Son of the living God.* He gets the doctrine right but not the discipleship.

When Jesus starts to talk about suffering and dying, Peter objects. *Mercy, me,* he says. *Lord, have mercy, no, not ever,* is what he means. And Jesus hears him speaking with the voice of Satan rather than the voice of God. God revealed to Peter the true identity of Jesus, but then Peter tries to take over as his campaign manager. He goes from being an ally to an adversary. The word Satan means adversary. Jesus has heard this tune before and knows it isn't the song of the Savior.

When Jesus was tempted by the devil in the wilderness, the essence of all three temptations was the same: *You deserve not to suffer. Get behind ME and I will give you the world.* Jesus rejected that then and he hears in Peter's words a repeat of the same temptation. So, he says to Peter, *Get behind me, Satan.*

The proper place for Satan and true disciples is the same: behind Jesus. Jesus tells us to get behind him, not to get out ahead of him. Disciples follow; they don't lead. And followers of Jesus do not try to direct him or co-opt him to follow their agenda.

For Jesus to be the Christ means he will save the world by going through, not around, suffering. He will take up his cross, be true to God's loving solidarity with the suffering and neglected of the world. He will win by losing.

This is where we can find God at any time. God is with us all and for us all in the pain and loss and struggle of life. As Richard Rohr says: *There is no nonstop flight to salvation. You can't skip over the suffering and dying.*[58]

Which is why Jesus then turns to the disciples and tells them that this is true for them as well. We are to get behind him, and we are to get under our own cross. You see, some people seem to think that since Jesus died for the church, the church doesn't have to die to itself. We can have all the power and glory associated with his resurrection without following the same path of self-denial he followed. But that isn't how it works.

Jen Hatmaker is a powerful voice for us in our day. Her appeal has been mostly to Christian women, but her experience encompasses all of us. She's been going through some hard, personal family struggles of late and this week she posted this: *Quite a while ago, I lost my tolerance for Christianese. The platitudes, the trite phrases, the simplistic way of viewing life and loss and complexity. I left that behind and chose a wider, less formulaic faith that made actual sense in the real world.*

So please trust me when I tell you that Jesus is real in suffering. Not in a "let go and let God" way. Ugh. Because what does "let go" even mean pragmatically in a lived experience of loss and grief? I hate that [stuff]. Everybody, stop saying stuff like that.

No, I mean in the actual darkest, pitch black night of the soul, there is a comfort in the weird, miraculous proximity of Jesus who loves us. He doesn't even suggest "letting go and letting God" or give any sense of hustling through suffering.[59]

We each of us have a cross to bear in our lifelong calling to follow Jesus. I don't know what the nature of your cross will be, but the crux of it will be the choice between self-sacrificing love and self-serving power. You will either follow the path of the suffering Savior or of some self-styled Sovereign. One path will soften your heart and the other will harden it.

The shooting of Jacob Blake seven times in the back by a white police officer in Kenosha, Wisconsin already had me reeling again. He was unarmed, but now they are doing what they always do—trying to justify the shooting of a Black man by saying he had a weapon. Which was a knife on the floor of his car! But then when a seventeen-year-old white boy showed up with an AR-15 and killed two protestors, the police watched him walk away and cross the state line before being apprehended. I am beside myself as a Christian. If you want homework on what Jesus is saying to Peter, you can use this as a test case. Are you more passionate about protecting property or people? Do you care more about law and order or about justice? Are your sympathies directed toward defending the powerful in their use of deadly force or the powerless who are continually hunted down and killed?

---

58 https://email.cac.org/t/ViewEmail/d/8058BBABE52BB3052540EF23F30FEDED/164215EB34D30C
FE6E6039C17E42EE19
59 Facebook post, August 22, 2020.

In his new book *Scandalous Witness*, Lee Camp talks about how Christianity should bear witness to an alternative use of power that brings peace, not more power. He cites the historical marker in Nashville, Tennessee that shows the tragedy of how people who called themselves Christians ended up reversing the biblical vision of beating swords into plowshares. The marker reads: *Site of a farm implement factory operated by Messrs. Sharp and Hamilton, previous to the War Between the States. With the outbreak of hostilities they reversed the Biblical injunction and produced swords of excellent quality for the Confederacy. With the coming of the Federal Army, the making of swords was discontinued.*[60]

Our partisan loyalties can lead not merely to ignoring the call of the gospel but inverting it and perverting it. There is only one way to transform the world for good and for good, and it's by winning with love. The kind of love that refuses to play the self-justifying power game. The kind of love that gets behind the King of Love and carries its cross rather than nailing others to it.

It's always hard to keep our bearings *behind Christ* and *under our cross*. But there's no other faithful place to be.

Amen.

60 Eerdmans, 2020, p. 176.

PART V

Who(se) Are You?

Calling and Vocation

"Tell me, what is it you plan to do with your one wild and precious life?"

~ Mary Oliver

Preface by David Wood

In one of the sermons that follows, George recounts a conversation where he was asked what the difference was between an occupation and a vocation. Here is how he answered: "an occupation is something you *can* do; a vocation is something you *can't not* do. And what a joyful thing, what a happy union, when those things come together." Anyone who reads these sermons on vocation will sense what those personally acquainted with George know to be true: George experiences the pastoral life as the overflow of that happy union between an occupation and a vocation.

Most pastors I know don't want their children to grow up to be ministers. George is not like most pastors—nothing would make him happier than to see his children answer a call to ministry. Of George's three children, his oldest has her Master of Divinity (MDiv) and is pursuing the path to ordination, his son works in commercial real estate, and his youngest is currently in seminary studying for her MDiv degree. George sees all of these as vocational callings in their lives and a gift beyond measure.

While George clearly has a love of pastoral ministry that informs his thinking and speaking about vocation, his theology of vocation is expansive and inclusive. "The first calling is the calling of God to come follow Christ," George declares, "Everything else follows from there." Every life is to be lived in response to what God is asking of us; all our work is to have a vocational character. A calling from God is inclusive of (for example) the stockbroker, the teacher, the banker, the salesperson, the homemaker, the businessperson, and the architect—"Those callings are only secular renditions of spiritual gifts that God has given to each of us and all of us for the purpose of building up the church and serving the world."

That being said, George is keenly aware that in discerning one's call, the cultural drift is one that draws young people away from a serious consideration of ministry as a calling. This awareness weighs heavily on him and explains why his preaching on vocation so often highlights the call to ministry in the church. At times his tone turns emphatically prophetic, like a voice crying in the wilderness. Nowhere is this tone more evident than in his sermon, "Call Answerers," when he calls out parents for their unwillingness to counter that drift.

> *You parents offer your children to God in one dedication service after another. You acknowledge that their lives are not their own, that they belong to God, that you are only stewards over their childhood. You promise to keep them within the precincts of the temple in order that they may learn the sound of the voice of God. But then when they show the least interest in the ministry, do you celebrate that and nurture them toward discernment or do you figure they can never make enough of a living in the church to take care of you in your old age? Do you worry they might be making a mistake? Do you worry just as much if they go to business school? Listen, we don't want young people in the church world that God has called into the business world. But neither should we want young people in the business world that God has called into the church world. We want every person to answer the unique call of God to each one. All we're saying here is that we may need to help our kids get the wax out of their ears that builds up with our built-up expectations of them doing anything but ministry in the church.*

For George, if vocational formation is a family matter, it is no less an ecclesial matter. It is the liturgical and relational life of the congregation that amplifies and mediates the callings of God to each of us. Again, this becomes most explicit when he speaks to the challenge of raising up the next generation of ministers for the church. He believes that, for Wilshire, it will be "one of the finest measurements of our success as a church—whether we can pass the mantle successfully to the next generation." This conviction had a formative impact on the life of Wilshire—most explicitly in the development, under George's leadership, of the pastoral residency program in which young pastors are mentored into ministry by the congregation.

And finally, for George, the familial and ecclesial dimensions of vocational formation come to their finest point in the personal. Vocational formation is a matter of the heart. One must listen to one's life. Personal stories drawn from Scripture (Jeremiah, Samuel, Elisha), from individuals within his congregation, and from his own life animate his articulation of what it looks and feels like to listen for God in the midst of one's life. Discerning God's intentions for our lives is not a matter of doing one's duty and learning to love it. It is more like acquiring the kind of self-knowledge that comes only through love. All of George's preaching on vocation is rooted in a profound experience of the love of God. That experience is the heartbeat of his theology of vocation.

David J. Wood recently retired from pastoral ministry and now lives in Waldoboro, Maine. He served for almost forty years in various congregations, most recently as Senior Minister of Glencoe Union Church in Glencoe, Illinois. In the early 2000s, he served as the National Coordinator for the Lilly Endowment funded program, Transition into Ministry. Wilshire Baptist Church was a grantee in that program.

34

Perfect Submission, Perfect Delight

May 19, 2002
Pentecost Sunday
Jeremiah 1:4-10; Ephesians 4:1-8, 11-13

Jeremiah's call to be a prophet is just the focus I need today to keep from thinking too much about things like my daughter's graduation from high school. Hard to imagine a man as young as I, don't you know?!, having a child that old. Well, like the rest of her class, she's been practicing answers to two questions everyone has been asking for nearly a year: Where are you going to college, and what are you going to study?

But those are not just questions we ask high school seniors; we ask them of ourselves. A lawyer friend of mine was thinking out loud with me about this recently. He's hit fifty and he still hasn't finished answering the questions: *Where am I headed? What am I going to do when I grow up?*

I think the first thing that would help is to realize that it is your life we are talking about and not someone else's. A sure-fire way to miss your future is to live someone else's future on their behalf. Parker Palmer is a Quaker writer and teacher. He quotes these lines of William Stafford: *Some time when the river is ice ask me / mistakes I have made. Ask me whether / what I have done is my life.* "For some," says Palmer, "those words will be nonsense, nothing more than a poet's loose way with language and logic. Of course, what I have done is my life! For others, and I am one, the poet's words ... remind me of moments when it is clear—if I have eyes to see—that THE LIFE I AM LIVING IS NOT THE SAME AS THE LIFE THAT WANTS TO LIVE IN ME. In those moments I sometimes catch a glimpse of my true life, a life hidden like the river beneath the ice. And, in the spirit of the poet, I wonder: *What am I meant to do? Who am I meant to be?*"[61]

We are talking about "calling" here, vocation. Vocation comes from the Latin *vocare*, to call. Now if someone is called, that suggests someone or something is

---

61 *Let Your Life Speak: Listening for the Voice of Vocation* (Jossey-Bass, 2000), pp. 1-2, emphasis added.

doing the calling. There are lots of voices that call you to do your particular work in the world. It's your job to sort through those voices to make sure they are not the voice of your mother who wants you to be a doctor, your father who wants you to go into the family business, or your Fuehrer who wants you to give up your life for the Fatherland. What we're after here is to discern the voice of God amidst the voices all round us that have agendas for our lives. God's agenda for our lives is what we are really after because we believe that when we find it, we will find our true selves. *Perfect submission to God's call will lead to perfect delight.*

But maybe you think the whole idea of calling is only for prophets like Jeremiah or preachers like me, that we can't generalize the calling stories of the Bible to think that God might also actually call someone to be a stockbroker or a Head Start day-school teacher or a banker or a salesperson or an architect or a businessperson. But all of those callings are only secular renditions of spiritual gifts that God has given to each of us and all of us for the purpose of building up the church and serving the world. You don't have to be a paid Christian to have a calling.

Sometimes we get off track early on because we haven't learned to listen to our own life carefully enough, to hear the voice of God calling to us from within the snap, crackle, and pop of our hard-wiring as it fires off its unique music within us. And that leaves us vulnerable to hearing only the calls of the world.

There's a teaching shortage right now; isn't there always. Everywhere you turn you hear appeals for people to go into teaching. Now, that's good, because teaching is a good and noble calling, and because sometimes the way we hear the voice of God calling to us is through the voice of someone else. Just because we desperately need more and better teachers in our schools doesn't mean that's your particular calling. It's the same with going into a field because you think you can make good money. That makes about as much sense as eating the newspaper every morning because you need a little roughage to make you regular. There are better ways to make a living than just doing something to make you more money. *Think about making a life more than making a living.*

A friend of mine, Carl Reeves, came to grips with this ten years or so ago. He was a banker and made a good living for himself and his family, but he woke up every morning thinking he was living someone else's life and not his own. He realized that at heart he is a nurturing caregiver. After much prayer and consultation with his family, he and they agreed that he would quit his job and begin nursing school. It was a hard midlife correction, but today he gets to do a job he believes God made him for. He attends especially to patients in the latter stages of cancer, and he gets to see them through their final journey to God. Carl and his family ended up with less money, but they and many others ended up with much more that money can't buy.

May Sarton begins one of her poems with these lines: *Now I become myself. It's taken / Time, many years and places; / I have been dissolved and shaken, / Worn other people's faces ... .* It's a lot to ask of seventeen and eighteen-year-old young people to know right off what they are to do with their lives and who they are to be. We all tend to wear other people's faces until we find our own in the mirror and can say at last, *Now I become myself.* But it's never too early or late to begin.[62]

I think there are two great paradigms of calling that have dominated the soul-scape of Western thought. The first is duty and the second, love. The first involves God calling us to something that we have to submit to in obedience, though we probably will not like it or want to do it, but if we really love God and not the world, that's what we will do. The second is to be guided by love as a gift of God and be obedient to it as it leads us back to the God who is love. Let's look at them in turn and see if they have to be at odds with one another.[63]

Perfect Submission

In Virgil's classic epic story *The Aeneid*, the hero Aeneas has lost his beloved kingdom. Troy has fallen to the infamous Trojan Horse. Aeneas and his comrades set sail for an uncertain future. After seven years, the gods conspire against him and he ends up shipwrecked after a terrible storm. He and his surviving band wash up on the shores of North Africa where they are welcomed in the city of Carthage by the fair Phoenician queen, Dido. Their chemistry is immediate and their love intense. But the gods have other plans for Aeneas. He is destined for greatness, fated to found the Roman Empire. But to do so he must leave behind his heart. He must love country, and duty to the gods, more than a woman. Brokenhearted, Dido cries to him: *Can our love / Not hold you, can the pledge we gave not hold you, / Can Dido not, now sure to die in pain?* Aeneas, in good hero fashion, fights down the emotion in his heart: *Apollo tells me I must make for Italy, / Named by his oracles, There is my love; / There is my country. ... So please, no more / Of these appeals that set us both afire. / I sail for Italy not of my own free will. ... Then, duty bound ... though he sighed his heart out, shaken still / With love of her, / yet he took the course heaven gave him / and went back to the fleet.*[64]

When we think about this in a Christian context, we are prone to think that submission to the will of God will always involve something we will not want to do if we had our choice. It would always be against our deepest love and desire, or it wouldn't be heaven's call. But while sacrifice in the service of heaven is always part of any vocation, spiritual duty need not be in conflict with our deepest affection.

That is hardly my own experience. People talk about surrendering to the ministry, as if God is putting a gun to your head. Surrender nothing, I would volunteer. I get to do this. And I don't know when I feel more alive than when I am standing here before you.

When God called Jeremiah, God formed him in the womb for this purpose, he says. He has a sense that he was set up for his calling. Although many times in his life he suffered on account of it, Jeremiah knew in his bones that this is what he

62 Also quoted by Palmer, p. 9.

63 I am indebted in what follows to Gilbert Meilaender, "Vocation: Divine Summons," *Christian Ethics Today* (Oct 2001): 11-15.

64 *The Aeneid*, trans. Robert Fitzgerald (Vintage, 1990), pp. 106-110 passim.

was made for; to choose otherwise would go not only against God but also against himself.

Perfect Delight

Which leads to the other view. In his masterpiece allegory *The Divine Comedy*, the Florentine poet Dante travels in three movements toward heaven. He descends into hell, climbs the mountain of purgatory, and finally rises to heaven. The self-same Virgil has been his guide through the inferno and the transition world, but he gives way to the lovely Beatrice who carries him straightway to the face of God. Beatrice was the love of Dante's life, though she belonged to another man. We do not know the extent to which they came together in life, but his heart remained fixed to her after her death. When he considers the journey of his soul to perfection, he believes that the love he has for her is the same love that God has given him to draw him back to God. Following that love is what leads him to the One who is love, who is passion personified. And when Beatrice brings him at last to that pure experience of God, Dante honors her again by calling it the Beatific Vision. He ends his work *Paradiso* with these words: *High phantasy lost power and here broke off; / Yet as a wheel moves smoothly, free from jars, / My will and my desire were turned by love, / The love that moves the sun and the other stars.*[65]

Here Dante claims that God calls us to follow our hearts' desires, for when they are in the service of God, it is God who works in us through them. Here is the duty of love, rather than the love of duty. Here is where perfect submission and perfect delight are joined in marital bliss. Here is where surrender to God's will is surrender to your secret joy.

Frederick Buechner says it this way: *The kind of work God usually calls you to is the kind of work (a) that you need most to do and (b) that the world most needs to have done.* So, if you love what you do but what you do is push pills to preschoolers on the playground, you can't claim that is God's call. Likewise, if you work in a homeless shelter and feel noble yet depressed and grumpy all the time, odds are that isn't what you're supposed to do either and you probably aren't helping anyone much anyway. *The place God calls you to is the place where your deep gladness and the world's deep hunger meet.*[66]

One last word: No one ever feels fully qualified to answer God's calling. Not to worry. Just as God put words into the mouth of the prophet Jeremiah, so God will equip any of us for the work God calls us to. *God doesn't call the qualified; God qualifies the called.*

So, do what God calls you to do; duty demands it. But do what your heart commands too, for the love of God compels it. When these two come together, when duty and love meet, you have found your calling.

---

65 *The Divine Comedy 3: Paradise*, trans. Dorothy L. Sayers and Barbara Reynolds (Penguin, 1975), p. 133.
66 *Wishful Thinking: A Seeker's ABC*, revised and expanded (HarperCollins, 1993), pp. 118-19.

35

Call Answerers

January 19, 2003
Second Sunday after Epiphany
1 Samuel 3:1-10; John 1:26-31

It's a quaint custom we get a glimpse of in 1 Samuel. A relic from a distant past. Something inconceivable to us moderns. The idea that Hannah and her husband should offer their firstborn child to the priesthood in exchange for God giving them a child, well, it's just un-American, I tell you. We want to say, *Shouldn't the boy himself have some say about what he will be when he grows up and how he will serve God?* He might want to be a shepherd or a tentmaker or something the world needs even more of—a golf caddie! Why should he be thrown into the temple and raised to be a priest against his will? Isn't that just complicating things for him all his life as to who's the one calling him—God or his mother?

Well, maybe, but let's look at the other side of the coin. Would you agree that the most important priority in time and eternity is the kingdom of God? And would you agree that the church is the chief agent of the kingdom in this life? And would you agree that the church thrives when it has many and able servants of the Word of God that equip and enable the ministry of all the people of God? And would you agree that God would not leave the church without the leadership necessary for it to be at its best in the world? If you answered yes to all those questions, then you must believe that God has called enough men and women in our time to serve as vocational ministers in our churches. Right? All right, then why is it that only about 5% of all Christian ministers in North America today are under the age of thirty-five? Is God planning an ensmallment campaign for the church of the twenty-first century? Has God quit calling people into the ministry? Or did we hear Willie Nelson wrong? Did he really sing: *Momma, don't let your babies grow up to be preachers. Don't let 'em drink grape juice and baptize ole drunks; let 'em be doctors and lawyers and such ... .* Well, judging by the number of young people applying to law school and medical school compared to divinity school, we're doing a pretty good job of directing our kids away from the ministry.

Now, you could say that the church hasn't needed any help directing young people away from career ministry. We've done a good job of looking like the last place young people might want to land. Scandals and slanders left and right from the left and from the right; infighting and backbiting; too strict on some things and too loose on others; too out of date in some ways and too up to date in others; too worldly and not enough at the same time; we get it wrong in lots of ways. But then again, excuse us, please, but we church people—including us paid Christians—are plagued by the same tragic flaw of flesh and blood as every other profession, we're just flesh and blood human beings, for God's sake. On the other hand, that's all God asks us to be is human beings—for God's sake! We are sinners in the hands of a loving God, nothing more or less. So, find a profession free of sin and go into it. Otherwise, consider the church a live option.

There's plenty wrong with the church, but take it from one on the inside, there's plenty right with it. I see all the problems; heck, I see them all the clearer up close—in the mirror! But this is where people find the life that really is life. This is where everyone is treasured for who they are apart from the size of their treasure. This is where we stand up for justice and speak up for the voiceless. This is where we practice on each other how to love our neighbor so that we'll do better next Friday when the guy next door leaves his trash in the alley ... again.

Imagine this weekend if Martin Luther King Jr. had not answered the call to preach. How different would our world be? It's a curious thing that Martin Luther, the great reformer of the church and the loudest voice for the priesthood of all believers over against the clergy, spoke plainly to his congregation about this very problem in his day. One Sunday he looked out over the pulpit and said this: *It is your fault. You could have done something about it. You could have helped to maintain them [churches] if you had allowed your child to study. And where it is possible for you to do this but you fail to do so, where your child has the ability and the desire to learn but you stand in the way, then you—and mark this well!—you are guilty of the harm that is done when the spiritual estate [clergy] disappears and neither God nor God's word remains in the world. To the extent that you are able, you are bringing about its demise. You refuse to give one child—and would do the same if all the children in the world were yours. So far as you are concerned, the serving of God can just die out altogether.*[67]

If you think that sounds harsh, you ought to hear it in German! In the Middle Ages families were urged to offer one of their sons to the church as a tithe of the womb. One of the reasons for the idea of a celibate priesthood is that often the firstborn would be offered to the church, and with it the inheritance. If there were no offspring the church would gain the property. And you thought that unmarried priesthood thing was all theological?

But let's look into the matter of calling a little deeper. You parents offer your children to God in one dedication service after another. You acknowledge that their lives are not their own, that they belong to God, that you are only stewards over

67 *Luther's Works,* Vol. 46 (Philadelphia: Fortress Press), pp. 222-223

their childhood. You promise to keep them within the precincts of the temple in order that they may learn the sound of the voice of God. But then when they show the least interest in the ministry, do you celebrate that and nurture them toward discernment or do you figure they can never make enough of a living in the church to take care of you in your old age? Do you worry they might be making a mistake? Do you worry just as much if they go to business school? Listen, we don't want young people in the church world that God has called into the business world. But neither should we want young people in the business world that God has called into the church world. We want every person to answer the unique call of God to each one. All we're saying here is that we may need to help our kids get the wax out of their ears that builds up with our built-up expectations of them doing anything but ministry in the church.

Hannah offered young Samuel to God and put him in the hands of the old priest Eli. She prayed for him to serve God. That's all she could have done, and I don't fault her for it. She had every reason to shy away from the temple. Eli's sons were immoral rogues. The priesthood was in a bad way. A religious vocation was hardly attractive then. But God moved in Hannah's heart to offer her son. And God spoke a word to Samuel himself, a word for him and only him. Eli helped him discern the voice of God in the night.

This is one of our great tasks in the church: to help each other recognize the unique call of God to each soul. We only want people to serve by God's design. We want them to find the gifts God has given them and the way to use them best that God has made them for. That will likely mean that most people still won't go into full-time church ministry; but it will likely mean that many more will than have been until now. I am happy to say that this church has been catching a vision of this duty of calling out the called—whether to clergy work or other spiritual work in the world. (Serving by God's Design is a specially designed class for just this purpose, and it's going to a church near you on future Wednesday nights. Check your local listings.)

We have a developing community of call answerers here in our church. Currently, ten Wilshire members are at either the master's or doctor's level of theological studies. Four more are headed to seminary next fall, two others are going back to do Ph.D. work, and several more in high school and college are exploring their call even now. They are doing it with the help of parents and ministers and friends who are helping them discern the voice of God calling them in the night, the way God called to Samuel.

We believe in a living God who knows your name and mine and is keenly interested in your finding out how you were made for the sake of the kingdom. Whether you are made to do church work or the work of the church in the world, God has designed you with gifts and desires that can only be satisfied fully when you tune in to the frequency of God's voice and turn on to the frequency of daily service of God's world. The church is here to help you tune in and turn on. This is what we do: it's one of our callings to answer for the world.

But let's not get too far ahead of ourselves. I've not been able to resist this morning riding my hobby horse about clergy calling. Our texts just happened to saddle me up, don't you know?! Shame on me if I didn't trot him out of the carnival corral for a while. If any of you think this was for you, then hop on the back and we'll ride the wide-open spaces together. The point of these texts is not only to say that God has a special calling of vocation for some of us, or that God has a unique ministry for each of us, though that word is here too. The first calling is the calling of God to come follow Christ. Everything else follows from there.

And if you look at the story of Jesus calling his disciples in John's Gospel, you see that again God uses human friends to interpret the voice of God's call to faith. Philip goes and finds Nathaniel. And we go and find our sisters and brothers and mothers and fathers and friends and neighbors. God knows their name and is calling them to faith—whether from a bed in the nighttime or from under a fig tree in the daytime. God knows who you are and where to find you. But we know that it may take lots of cups of coffee, a few books, a night under the stars on the back patio, and lots of secret prayers before the sound of God's voice rings clear in the ears of someone who is ready at last to be a call answerer.

The beautiful thing is that Christ himself is our spiritual friend, seeking us out, standing beside us, and speaking up for us all in the midst of times when we cannot discern the voice of God from the voice of our nighttime fears.

My good friend Barry McClenahan was a helicopter pilot in Vietnam. He flew important missions rescuing wounded soldiers and bringing in medical supplies. One night a ruckus broke out in the officers' club after too many drinks. They hauled the lot of them off to the brig, which was one of those huge metal containers they stored cargo in on freighters. They had replaced the doors with iron bars and *voila!*—a makeshift jail. After a frightful, sleepless night, Barry was roused the next morning by the sound of his commanding officer's voice: *McClenahan*, he said, speaking loudly and directly to the MP in charge. He insisted that Barry be released immediately. When the man resisted, the CO said he needed him right away to perform important missions. *He belongs to me*, he said.

My friends, you belong to Christ! He has won your life at the cost of his own. He comes to call you to himself. And he has important things for you to do. Answer the call to faith and find your true life in him. Answer the call to service and find your true life work with him. Answer the call, for God's sake and yours. But answer the call. Amen.

36

Who Are You?

Watch and listen to "Who Are You?" by following this link or scanning the QR code with your phone: youtu.be/EyDizICtSbA. Sermon begins at 25:45.

December 26, 2021
First Sunday after Christmas
Luke 2:41-52

"Who are you?" That may seem a deep question for the day after Christmas, but our Gospel text indirectly asks us to answer it today. A sound sense of identity is a component of any healthy personality. When you know who you are, you can live with confidence and freedom. When you lack it, you will search for it all your life long.

But how do you discover your identity? You could go to 23andMe.com and search your genetic history, but that will take you only so far. It can tell you a great deal about where you came from—not only who your parents were, but also further back in time to the branch of the human family you come from. I did it, by the way. And what I found should not surprise you: I am very white. Mostly Anglo and Scandinavian. But DNA isn't the whole answer to who we are. Biology needs theology to finish the job. We are spiritual beings as well as physical.

We see this in our text today. Now, I know you think, wasn't Jesus born just yesterday on Christmas? And here we are picking up his story at age twelve? Yeah, well, kids grow up fast, don't you know?!

Mary and Joseph have taken Jesus with them in a large entourage that went up from their home in Galilee to Jerusalem for the Passover feast. A day's walk toward home, they realize that Jesus isn't with them. This is every parent's nightmare. They have lost their child. They rush back to Jerusalem and look for him everywhere. The text says three days, but they are probably counting the way the Jews did at that time—one day since they left, one day to get back, and on the third day they find him. When they find him, he's in the temple among the wisest teachers of the faith. All who heard him were amazed at his understanding.

His mother scolds him for worrying them so. I get that. If I'm Joseph, I'm thinking: *Son of God or not, as long as you're living in my house, you're going to respect your father.* Then Jesus utters those lines so familiar to us but so perplexing to his parents in that moment: *Did you not know that I must be in my Father's house?*

Twelve-year-old Jesus already understands the key spiritual thing about his identity. He is the child of God, the Son of his Heavenly Father. And he is, in fact, respecting his Father.

Since Jesus' conception and birth are still fresh in our minds from this weekend, and since Mary and Joseph have lived this story for twelve years now, we should all have figured that this moment was coming. But we should think more deeply about how Jesus came to understand himself.

Sometimes we think of Jesus as this one-off character on the stage of history who only appeared to be like one of us. Secretly, though, from the manger onward, even when he was in those swaddling clothes, he was concealing all the knowledge of the universe and trying not to out himself to the adults. That is exactly *not* what our faith requires us to believe. If Jesus were unlike us in that way, he would be too unlike us to redeem us. He had to learn who he was just the way we do. Or maybe better, we have to learn who we are just the way he did.

Imagine the awkwardness of all this for Mary and Joseph. I'm thinking they haven't had the talk with him yet. I don't mean the birds-and-the-bees talk; I mean the angels-and-the-shepherds-and-the-wise-men talk. I'm guessing they never knew whether they were supposed to, and if they ever started it, they didn't know how to finish it. I mean, how would you do that? And would you even want to? But they must have known that sooner or later, somehow, they would have to face this day—the way some of you do when you present your baby to be dedicated and I tell you in no uncertain terms that this child is not yours but God's. And then I ask you if you are willing to keep your child within the precincts of the temple so that they may learn the deepest truth—that they are a child of God first and last.

This is hard for all of us parents. But it is absolutely crucial. We all have to come to learn this bedrock truth about ourselves, without which we will struggle on and on. You are a child of God. And wherever you live in the world, you are most at home only when you feel yourself at home in the house of God.

I love that my mother is in our congregation. And my dad was too until his death. They worshiped here with me, and before that they brought me up in the church. I am honored to be their son, to be a Mason. My family has given me much of my identity. I am named George Mason, as was my father and my grandfather. What's more, I am the son of a son of a son of a sailor—my father was a ship pilot, my grandfather a docking pilot, and my great-grandfather a barge pilot in New York Harbor. I am not. I could have been. It was somewhat expected. But my parents made the mistake of taking me to church. Whatever their own dreams for me, they kept giving me to the Lord. What I learned from all that is what Jesus learned from his parents' faithfulness: I belong to God, and I am most at home in the house of God.

You are, too. You may not know it yet, but this is indispensable for you to learn. It's no side note to say that everything we've been up to in becoming a more inclusive church over time here has been to make sure you know that, whoever you are. No matter how great your genetic inheritance, no matter how virtuous your parental upbringing, you will never know yourself rightly until you know yourself as a beloved child of God. And if your nature or nurture was not all that great, you need to hear this in *all caps*: YOU ARE A CHILD OF GOD.

When Jesus returned to Nazareth, he was obedient to his parents and his mother pondered these things in her heart. Luke tells us that Jesus *increased in wisdom and in years, and in divine and human favor.* The language is the same as in the Old Testament story of the prophet Samuel. Jesus knew this Bible story. So did his parents. Why? Because they took him to church, so to speak. Please hear me about that, parents.

But knowing that we are children of God is not enough. It's what we do about it that matters most, because in the end "who we are" is as much about where we are going as where we have been, maybe more so. We are what we become, and we become what we do.

When the King James translators phrased Jesus' retort to his parents, they put it this way: *Do you not know that I must be about my Father's business?* The word translated *house* can also be translated *business* because it literally reads in the Greek: *Do you not know that I must be in the things of my Father?* In other words, Jesus gets that he is his Father's Son, and therefore he must be into or about his Father's interests.

In the same way, whoever you are and whatever you do with your work in the world, it must proceed from a conscious awareness that you are a child of God and must reflect the passion and compassion of God, the giving and forgiving of God.

Victor Hugo's classic *Les Miserables* is still playing on a stage somewhere. It's a movie now, too. In many ways it's nothing but the retelling of the Gospel. The protagonist, Jean Valjean, has come to know himself as a thief on the run. He can never escape his past until he is welcomed in from the cold by a kindly priest. The lesson of forgiveness he learns goes straight to his soul. The church—and I love that he learns it in church—teaches him that he is a child of God. And it sends him back into the world to live out his truest identity.

What follows in *Les Mis* is nothing less than what we learn from Jesus as he ventures forth in the remainder of Luke's Gospel. If you are a child of God, you must live like one if you are to know the wonders of God's world and be welcomed home to God in the end.

Jean Valjean is confronted over and over with what identity will rule his decisions. Will he be 24601, the convict who can never escape his fate? Or will he be the man that the church has told him he is—a child of God who need never escape his faith?

The song "Who Am I?" comes at the moment in the story when another man is accused of being Valjean. If that man is sentenced, Valjean is free. But Valjean knows he himself will never be free that way. *How can I ever face my fellow men? / How can I ever face myself again? / My soul belongs to God, I know / I made that bargain long ago / He gave me hope when hope was gone / He gave me strength to journey on.*

You are God's child. And if every day you choose to live like it, you can count on God giving you the strength to journey on. Now, go be about your Father's business. Amen.

37

Fingers, Hands, and Toes:
The Anatomy of Leadership

January 7, 2007
The Baptism of the Lord, Deacon Ordination
Acts 8:14-17; Luke 3:15-17, 21-22

The church calendar is an experiment in time travel. Jesus was born only thirteen days ago, wrapped in swaddling clothes and lying in a manger. During the twelve days of Christmas, he aged thirty years. Today we pick up his story with the beginning of his public ministry. John the Baptizer baptizes his second cousin Jesus in the river Jordan. On this same Sunday of the church year, we see where two apostles of the early church go and lay hands on newly baptized believers in Samaria in order that they might receive the Holy Spirit. Fast-forward another three years. And here on our own calendar of church life, nearly two thousand years hence, we celebrate the ordination of five people to deacon ministry with the laying on of hands.

The theme of leadership fills both our texts and temple today. If we pay attention to the anatomy of fingers, hands, and toes in both text and context, we'll pick up on some things.

First, kids, let me ask you a question. If you were going to draw a picture of the relationship between John and Jesus, how would you draw it? Maybe some of you budding artists will get to work on it right now and show it to me later like you often do after church. Now, lots of people have painted this picture of John baptizing Jesus. All of them have him pouring water over his head as he stands in the Jordan River. We Baptists would like to see them have John take Jesus all the way under, don't you know?! I guess we have to pass that off to artistic license, else the "sprinklers" be right that they actually baptized that way. But my favorite picture of John and Jesus picks up on this sense of the scene and imagines John at the crucifixion of Jesus. John was already dead himself by that time, but in this painting, he is standing by the cross, pointing a bony finger away from himself up to Jesus.

The German Renaissance painter Matthias Gruenewald's most famous work is the altarpiece of the Isenheim church of the hospital of St. Anthony, completed about 1515. I almost never wish we had big projection screens in the sanctuary, but I would love to show you a picture of it. Jesus hangs lifeless on a cross made of still-green rough-hewn wood, the crossbar bending with the weight of his arms and the sins of the world. Off to the painting's right of Jesus is John, pointing his finger at Jesus with one hand, and in the other hand he holds a book. The words of John 3:30 are printed in the background: *He must increase, but I must decrease.*

Remarkable. Just remarkable that John should think this way about Jesus. Our text from Luke expresses a similar sentiment from the mouth of John. *The one who is more powerful than I is coming,* he says; *I am not worthy to untie the thong of his sandals.* That John should point away from himself by fingering Jesus as the rightful focus of attention is an act of true spiritual leadership.

Christian leadership involves this very move time and time again. Every time someone tries to make you the point, you point to Jesus.

Consider how difficult this must have been for John. You may think he knew who Jesus was and had no choice but to give way to him when Jesus' time had come, but God does not force any of us into the roles we play as if it is all preordained that we act this way or that. The very fact that God comes to the world as a human being in the person of Jesus reveals something about the nature of God's relationship to the world all the time: God does not operate in the world with a heavy hand; God participates in the world with us by offering a hand and asking for one.

John was on top at the moment when Jesus approached him to be baptized. His popularity was high. Many wondered whether he was himself the messiah, not just the fingerer pointing to the messiah. John had to give up the spotlight and give way to Jesus. He had to move to the wings so that the Christ could take center stage in salvation history. And John had such a different temperament from Jesus'. He was far more conservative than his messiah cousin. John's ministry was known more by what he did not do than by what he did; he called for a holiness that avoided sin rather than one that embraced sinners. When Jesus came eating and drinking with sinners, John thought there must be some mistake. Even at this early stage, it's all the more reason to marvel at John's willingness to point his finger to Jesus and tell us to follow him.

When we look at the church, this becomes vital. This is not my church. This is not your church. This is Christ's church. Yes, I am responsible. And, yes, you are responsible. But listen again to that word—responsible. We do not take matters into our own hands; we offer our hand to Christ. We seek the mind of Christ because we are always pointing toward him in what we do. Which is why I tell new members not to be carried away with the formal truth that a Baptist church is a democracy, in which we each have a voice and each get a vote. The deeper material truth of things is that we don't care what you think; we care what you think Christ thinks. We don't want to know what's on your mind; we want you to tell us what you think Christ's mind is on a matter. The only vote that counts in the end is the one Christ casts with an X—with a cross, that is.

Our duty as Christians—whether ordained pastors, ordained deacons, or any other laypersons ordained to the ministry of Christ in their baptisms—is to seek the will of Christ and do it. When we agree to be a leader in his church, we agree to decrease in order that he may increase. You deacons here today feel honored and lifted up by the privilege of being called upon for this service, but keep in mind that your service is always to point your finger to the Christ among us. And to the extent that you do that well, you will fulfill your calling.

The finger that points to Christ is connected to the hands that bless and empower others for the sake of Christ. Our text from Acts preserves one act of the tradition of the laying on of hands. Our context today preserves another act of hands being laid on others. In each case something powerful is happening, even if the power of it is unseen by the naked eye.

Let me ask you deacons: did it make a difference to you in your experience to have these hands laid upon you as we prayed for you this morning? Would it have meant the same to you if you had just sat in the pew and heard a prayer on your behalf? There is something in the touch blessing that comes from those we admire and trust that transforms us.

We have an odd story here from the early church in which some people north of Jerusalem and south of good reputation have come to believe the good news of Jesus the Christ. And yet Luke tells us they had yet to receive the gift of the Holy Spirit, even though they had been baptized in Jesus' name. What could be the meaning of this? Does this mean that we need two baptisms, so to speak, as our Pentecostal friends claim: one in the name of Jesus with water and another in the Spirit with the laying on of hands? Or does it mean that baptism with water must include the name of the Holy Spirit as well as Jesus in order to be complete? Is God that legalistic and mechanical? Isn't it enough trouble convincing the rest of Christendom that they're supposed to be put all the way under the water, do we now have to make sure they get the words just right, too?

I think the issue here is again the way God works in the world. The Spirit of God had come dramatically, with tongues of fire at Pentecost, and loosened the tongues of the apostles to point to Jesus with their witnessing words. The church was born when the Spirit came upon them and brought them together. Jews from all over the world were charter members of the church. But what of Samaritans, those half-breed Jews who came from intermarriages? Would they be welcome in the church? Would they receive the same powerful Spirit? God wants them to experience the inclusive spirit of the Spirit of God, and they do so when these former enemies extend hands of blessing to them. They experience the power of God's reconciling and blessing presence.

Friends, the church does not exist for itself. We do not possess the Spirit of God for our own privilege; we are channels of the Spirit's blessing. A broken world needs signs of wholeness; it needs signals of God's acceptance and love. When the leaders of the church go out of their way, whether to Samaria or Somalia, to lay hands of blessing and inclusion on those who have lived on the margins, we honor the leadership of the early church and show that we are connected to them still. When we hold and protect our fellowship against outsiders as if it belongs to us, we do not lead in the way of ancient leaders.

Finally, when John says that he is not worthy to untie the thong of Jesus' sandals, he must have his head down. To untie the thong of someone's sandals in a day when the roads were all dusty and the feet were filthy meant that one put oneself in the category of a slave.

Christian leadership not only points a finger to Christ and holds out hands of blessing and empowerment, but it bends low to touch the toes of others and wash their feet in love and care.

In a former church I served as pastor, a certain deacon I admired represented the meaning of humble service. If you had just met him and asked what he did for a living, he would always say he worked for the gas company. You might have left the conversation thinking he was a meter reader, when in fact he was the president of the huge public utility. You could never tell how important he was at church, either.

President Gerald Ford was buried this week. He may have been the nicest and humblest president in recent memory. Shortly after my football playing days at the University of Miami, I was with the former president at a fundraising event for the school. He had lost the election two years before to Jimmy Carter, and my best memory of that election occurred when the two of them appeared afterward and reporters peppered Ford with questions about his defeat and whether his pardoning of Nixon had done him in. Carter was standing next to him, and Ford deflected the questions, accepted defeat graciously, and said that the praise needed to be given to his opponent, Jimmy Carter, for running such a good and honorable campaign. He might as well have said, *He must increase, and I must decrease.*

President Ford spent about ten minutes with me that night, while shooing away his handlers. Having played football himself at Michigan, he wanted to know what I planned to do next. He listened more than talked. He told me why he went into law and politics. He urged me to a life of service, something I have tried to remember.

Focus on Christ, commit to building up others, and live a life of humble service. These are the marks of Christian leadership. May they characterize your life and ministry.

38

Your Call

August 22, 2004
Twelfth Sunday after Pentecost
Jeremiah 1:4-10; Luke 13:10-17

Something tells me that when Jeremiah was a boy, sitting in the pews, watching his father conduct services as a priest of Israel, he wasn't dreaming that one day he might be a prophet. Something tells me that most of you sitting in the pews today have not been dreaming about God calling you into some special ministry.

When I was growing up, becoming a pastor—Baptist, Lutheran, Presbyterian, or any other flavor—was the furthest thing from my mind. I was all about sports. I dreamed about playing professional football. Along the way I had to give up that dream—until recently when I heard that the Cowboys are now going with a 40-something University of Miami quarterback. *Put me in, Coach!* With a business degree in my pocket, acceptances from business school, law school, a coaching offer, and some other job possibilities, I headed to seminary to study for the ministry. Why? Because God called me, of course. *But, George, how did you know it was God calling? What did that sound like? Was it a voice you heard in your ears or in your head? Was it like it was with Jeremiah?*

Well, yes and no. All of our calls are alike, and yet each of our calls is unique. What's alike is what Jeremiah learned: God knows you, God made you, God has a purpose for your life, and God wants you to know the joy of living out that purpose. The particulars are the hard to figure parts.

For many, our work will be the work of the church in the world, while for some it will be church work. There is no greater or lesser to this, even though we like to say that the ministry is a "higher" calling. But the whole notion of higher or lower callings suggests that the woman who changes the sheets in your hotel room is less important to the kingdom of God than that good and gentle man who wears the pointy hat in Rome. The pontiff has a more strategic role, perhaps, but not a higher calling if both he and she are doing all they can in the places they are called to serve the Lord.

We should not compare ourselves to others vocationally, because someone will always make us feel superior or inferior, instead of just what we are meant to be. There's a lovely and simple parable in Karen Santorum's book *Everyday Graces* that gets this right. "Once upon a time there was a king who had a beautiful garden. One day, he went there and found everything drooping. He asked why. The vine said it couldn't grow tall and strong like the pine tree, so it saw no use in trying. The pine tree, in turn, couldn't produce tasty fruit like the apple tree, so why bother? The apple tree produced only small, simple flowers, unlike the beautiful flowers on roses that everyone loves.

"Finally, the king came upon the pansy. It had avoided this trap. The king asked how. *I am happy because I know that when you planted the seed out of which I grew, you didn't want a pine or an apple tree or a rose. You wanted a little pansy. So, to please you, I am going to be the best pansy I can be.*"[68]

I'll resist the temptation of urging you all to become pansies. But to turn this another way, some are called to raise their children as homemakers, volunteer at school, and spike the spirit of the community; some are called to raise shopping malls where people will be employed and goods sold and the economy expanded so that many may prosper; and others are called to raise the spiritual maturity of a generation of Christians who are called to a thousand kinds of ministry. One is not better or worse than any other.

Even within church ministry, though, we are tempted to compare ourselves wrongly. I would love to have the voice of my preacher friend Joel Gregory, the former pastor of First Baptist downtown. But one of the finest preachers in America, Fred Craddock, is a slight man of about 5'5" and voice he describes as the sound of "wind whistling through a fence post." No one can tell a story like Fred, though many of us try to tell Fred's stories. All of us envy his gifts. God gives each of us and all of us unique gifts with which to work for God's glory, the world's benefit, and our delight. Our pastoral residents will have to find their own voices and avoid too much George creeping in.

But how do you get to the point where you think you really are doing what God has called you to do with your life? Jeremiah's call is a template for our own. If we wonder about whether God might call us to be prophets or priests or teachers or mothers or bankers or bakers or whatever in order to glorify God in the world, then notice how the call story begins with Jeremiah saying, *The word of the Lord came to me.* God takes the initiative. If there is a calling, there is a Caller. And God is far more interested in our knowing our call than we are in knowing it. So, God comes to us, in various ways, through various events, in the sound of various people's voices. Jeremiah doesn't tell his whole story, but my guess is that he had been hanging around the temple a whole lot of his life, smelling the incense, watching the sheep slaughtered for sacrifice, seeing his father do his work. He had an idea

---

68 ISI Books, 2003. Thanks to Carl Reeves for this citation.

about what a religious vocation might be like—and maybe even whether the voice he was hearing, probably in his head, sounded like it could be God.

When we dedicate babies here, we ask parents to keep their children in the precincts of the temple. We want our kids to get acquainted with the interests of God, to learn what God cares about. We want them to know that if their greatest ambition in life is to be rich and lazy and care about no one but themselves, they cannot possibly call that a spiritual calling. If they cannot see that the Sabbath was made for man, not man for the Sabbath, if they cannot see that healing the bent-over woman is more important than keeping things under control, then they cannot blame that on God or claim to be doing God's will. But if they find something they are clearly good at doing—speaking in front of people, say, caring about fairness among classmates, making friends with newcomers other people don't bother with, listening to the problems of others with genuine concern—well, there may be something to that.

We love to see the human dramas unfold in the Olympics at this quadrennial time. The beautiful movie *Chariots of Fire* told the story of Scottish runner Eric Liddell, who competed in the 1924 games in Paris but would not run on Sunday out of spiritual commitment to keep the Sabbath holy. His sister Jennie didn't understand his desire to run at all. She thought it undermined his higher calling to become a missionary—something Liddell would go on to do in China some years later. His wise preacher father said: *You can praise the Lord by peeling a spud if you peel it to perfection. Run in His name and let the world stand back in wonder.* And later, Liddell explained to her in his own words: *I believe God made me for a purpose. But he also made me fast, and when I run, I feel his pleasure. To win is to honor him.*

Jeremiah says that God knew him before he was born, that God had formed him in the womb and consecrated him and appointed him to be a prophet before he ever took his first breath. What Jeremiah is saying, I think, is that his calling was not his idea. He was not self-appointed. He did not seek the role of prophet for some selfish reason of putting himself above anyone else. He just felt in his bones that this is what he was meant for; that it all came together for him when he was speaking the truth to power, calling upon a nation to wake up, suffering their rejection even in doing it. When you discover your calling, the matter of whether it is hard or easy is beside the point. The point is that this is what you must do because it is who you are.

When I was wrestling with my call to ministry, I finally took a long look at how my life had been shaped. I remembered how I was the boy who won the competition in the fifth grade for speaking the longest in front of the class on a subject I knew nothing about. Some of you think I still do that, although I have learned how to stop, don't you know?! You have Kim to thank for that. I was the boy who loved to go to church, who could memorize Scripture without difficulty, who always was called upon to pray, and who hated to choose up sides in games because someone would always be chosen last. I was also the young man whose pastor told him he ought to consider the ministry, because that older man saw the gifts that seemed to fit the ministry calling. In other words, when I was really honest with myself, I was most at home in the world in the church. I still am. Especially here in this church. It fits in a way that makes me feel like I was made for this.

And that's why we are beginning a new program for teenagers called YourCall. You can read about it in the *Tapestry*, but the gist of it is that we want to introduce high schoolers to the possibility of God's call to ministry in the church or for the church in the world. And then we are offering again the class "Serving by God's Design" in order for adults to reflect upon the way God has formed them in the womb and called them to serve until they settle in the tomb.

Someone asked me a while back how to distinguish between a vocation and an occupation. I am not sure I want to squeeze all the mystery out of it, but my immediate answer still makes sense to me: An occupation is something you *can* do; a vocation is something you *can't not* do. There are many ways to make a living for any one of us. But circumstance and abilities might dictate or allow that we can do the kind of work that best fits how we are made. That's what you can't not do. And what a joyful thing, what a happy union, when those things come together!

Anyone who feels called by God to do anything will feel also the humbling inadequacy that goes with it. You might feel as Jeremiah did that you are too young, or that you are not from the right school or the right stock or the right sex. Those things too are beside the point. The humility is a good sign, however, since it makes you depend upon God. God will put words in your mouth, as Jeremiah learned, if you are called to preach or teach or speak for a living. God will give you a heart for children if you are called to work with little ones. If God has called you, whatever the field of service, God will empower and sustain you. God's adequacy, not yours, is the issue. If God has called you, you are up to it. Period. There is no need to fear and no cause for arguing the matter with God or running from the call. But it's your call. Are you answering your call?

39

Transfer of Power

February 26, 2006
Transfiguration Sunday
2 Kings 2:1-12

It was his first Sunday as the new pastor. The eager young successor to a beloved long-term pastor went to the main entrance of the sanctuary and greeted people atop the front steps as they entered the sanctuary for worship. Seeing an elderly woman climbing the stairs with some difficulty, he quickly went down to help her make her way up. She took his arm, and they slowly made the climb together. When they finally reached the top of the stairs, the old woman collected her breath, straightened up, and adjusted the tilt in her hat with her white-gloved hands. *Thank you*, she said. *Now, could you tell me who's preaching here this morning?* The new pastor told her the name of the new pastor without revealing that he was the new pastor. Whereupon the elderly lady turned round nimbly and said, *Well then, could you please help me back down the stairs?*

What I didn't tell you is that the church was Wilshire. And the young pastor none other than ... Willsie Martin. Oh, yes, and the church was actually Wilshire United Methodist in Los Angeles, California. Got you![69]

But I know a little how the good Reverend Martin felt that day. Since nearly seventeen years have passed since my first days at this Wilshire church (and since most of the elderly ladies of those early days have climbed up the stairway to heaven, don't you know?!), I can tell you that I had some interesting experiences in trying to follow the beloved long-tenured pastor Bruce McIver. Some didn't give me much more of a chance than the California woman. Most didn't tell me directly, but word gets back. *He's not my kind*, one would say. *He doesn't tell enough stories*, another opined. Most didn't come right out and say, *He's a Yankee*, but the implication was there when they spoke of my being too direct or assertive. I got a letter from one man who left in the first few weeks, telling me he just didn't like my style. I don't

---

think he meant the cut of my suits, do you? One woman took twelve years to transfer her loyalties. In the receiving line after Bruce's memorial service, she looked at me and said, *Now you can be my pastor!*

Well, you can probably tell from the tone of my voice that I don't harbor any resentment toward anyone about any of that. The fact is, I had one of the easiest goes of it anyone could have when following such a warm and loving man as Bruce McIver. The transfer of power, so to speak, went without a hitch between us. It was the people that had a harder time of it.

And these are the same dynamics at play in our text today from 2 Kings. The prophet Elijah was a proven man of God. He led a company of prophets for some years during a time when such spiritual leadership was crucial for Israel, because it didn't come from the White House. Kings like Ahab, who was married to the Phoenician queen Jezebel and introduced Baal worship to Israel, were threatening the integrity of Israel's faith in the one true God. Elijah led Israel to walk with God in the same way Moses once had. But now, after a successful and dependable tenure of service, Elijah knew that his time had come to depart this life.

Earlier in his ministry Elijah had been passing a field and saw Elisha working his plow with a team of twelve oxen. He tossed his mantle upon him, symbolic of a call to join him in his work. Elisha left everything to follow in the steps of the great man and train to be a prophet. Elijah tried to stop him, telling him to turn back, just as he does over and over in our text today at the end of his life. Elisha will have none of it. He slaughters his oxen, using the plowshare as a sword, and throws a going-away feast for his friends and family. He never looks back once he gets his call. And he doesn't look back or turn back at the end of Elijah's life either, even though he wonders whether he will be up to the task of succeeding the great man.

After Elijah parts the waters with his mantle rolled up like Moses' rod and they go to the other side together, Elisha asks for a double portion of Elijah's spirit. This doesn't mean he wants to be twice as powerful as his mentor; it means he wants to be Elijah's principal heir, inheriting the two-thirds share of his father's wealth that would go to a firstborn son. He is asking for a spiritual inheritance. He wants to be a worthy successor to Elijah.

Elijah does something important and curious. He points away from himself to God. He tells Elisha that he has asked a difficult thing, which is to say that he has asked something that is not in the power of one man to give to another. If Elisha is to be God's man to follow him, the gift and call will have to come from God. He will have to experience God for himself and carry on in the power of God's spirit.

After Elisha sees his mentor taken up to heaven in the chariot of fire, he uses the mantle to part the same Jordan River and cross back over to where the company of prophets awaits. They see that he has performed the same wonder of the waters that Elijah had, in the same way Joshua had done after succeeding Moses. They could sense that he was indeed called to lead them. But even after that, oddly enough, the verses that follow in our text say that the prophets went looking for Elijah. He had gone up to heaven, but they had a hard time letting go of him. It took time for them to transfer their loyalties.

Now, there are so many things to learn from this wonderful narrative. Transfer of power from one generation to another is no easy matter. It depends on all the parties involved working together.

A secular if not spiritual miracle over the past two and a quarter hundred years of human history has happened every four to eight years in the American experiment that is our democratic republic. When you look at how difficult it is to see a peaceful transfer of power in Iraq today, consider how remarkable it is that every time a new president is elected—even when that president comes from the opposition party, and even if the vote is highly contested, as it was in the Bush-Gore election of 2000—a commitment to our system of governance and a determination to preserve the principles of democracy allow us to move on without violence.

Family businesses have succession problems, too. A father, say, builds a good company, and then a son comes along, and everyone hopes he will be up to the job of taking over for the next generation. But just having the same last name does not mean it will work out. Even if he gets a double portion of the inheritance, he has to have his own experience that matches the father's commitment; he has to work hard and use good sense himself if one expects him to succeed.

One of the reasons we have an estate tax in this country is that we have said we want to avoid the inertia that comes from primogeniture. The old gentry system of Europe, for instance, where wealth is inherited and the kids feel entitled to it without doing anything themselves for it, works against the American spirit. Our idea of opportunity for each new generation to do something for itself builds responsibility. People should be rewarded for their own labor, not just live off someone else's.

Iraq is on the brink of civil war today. What are the roots of this? You can say that our intervention is the cause, but that would be too shallow an analysis. Sunni and Shia Muslims have been fighting each other for the upper hand in Muslim identity for centuries. This goes all the way back to the seventh-century argument over who was to succeed the Prophet Muhammad as leader of Islam. Sunni Muslims, who constitute 90% of Islam worldwide, believe that Muhammad's lieutenant and father-in-law, Abu Bakr, was the legitimate successor, because he was chosen by the community of elders in the culturally customary way after the prophet's death. The Shia, however, believe that the prophet had specifically anointed his son-in-law Ali as the worthiest successor, and that Abu Bakr had obtained the office through trickery and political deceit. The animosity between these groups therefore has a long history, one that shakes up others in its tragic wake.

These days some of us are working with diligence to call and nurture the next generation of church leaders who will follow us. While we cannot and should not appoint our successors, we can and should look for those women and men of good gifts and graces to answer this call to serve the church with all their hearts and souls.

For our part, ministers must do as Elijah did and cast our mantle freely upon others who seem spiritually fit for the work. We must not withhold our blessing or think only about our own legacy. I can tell you that at this stage of my life, I am far more interested in what happens in and through the ministries of our residents as they leave this place than I am about myself. I am going to die one day, like all the rest of us. I am not counting on anything like a sweet chariot to swing low and carry me away. But I am counting on many young ministers to take up the work and do wonderful things much greater than I ever could. That will be one of the finest measurements of our success as a church—whether we can pass the mantle successfully to the next generation.

And it's okay for someone to want this as much as Elisha wanted to follow Elijah, even if he is confused about where the prophetic power truly comes from. Some people say that if you want to be a minister, if you seek ordination, you must not be truly called. But don't tell Elisha that. Elijah kept telling him to turn back, but Elisha understood that he did not have a choice deep in his soul. Taking up this work was something he could not not do. He only knew that he needed greater power than his own to do it.

Our job is to bless those who come after us. Ministers must not withhold our blessing from those who would be our younger colleagues. Parents must not compete with their children for supremacy of significance in the family. Parents do well to remember that they will die, and they should want every one of their children to live as if each is specially favored with a double portion of spiritual inheritance. If you favor one of your children over another, shame on you. They will carry their competition with one another way beyond your lifetime, to the detriment of your family legacy.

But at the end of the day, this transfer-of-power work must come from below, so to speak. The community must accept the leadership of one coming along after another. They cannot hold on forever to the leader who has gone to be with God forever. And the best way to do that at pivotal moments like that is to practice now.

Your acceptance of our young ministers and the encouragement you give them now is indispensable to their future leadership of the church. Any time you praise a teenager or spot a child with spiritual gifts and say a word to her or him, you transfer power more than you know.

God is at work in the world and in our lives in ways that defy mundane description. Mantles given and taken, chariots of fire that make thin the visible and invisible worlds, and miracles of water parting and people sensing God in one another: These are all examples of a mystifying holiness and holy mystery. If you are not caught up in it all yet, you are missing in action, and, what's more, you are missing the action. Isn't it time to join in?

PART VI

Blest Be the Tie

Pastoral Care

"Christ plays in ten thousand places
Lovely in limbs, and lovely in eyes not his
To the Father through the features of men's faces."

~ Gerard Manley Hopkins

Preface by Amy Butler

When I was in college at Baylor University I was dating a young man whose family lived in north Louisiana. The whole experience of moving to the middle of Texas to go to college from my home on the islands of Hawaii was culture shock enough. But holiday visits to north Louisiana felt almost like traveling to a completely different country.

Whenever we'd go to visit, we would attend church with his family. And after a couple of years of traveling to his home on the same holidays: Mother's Day, Thanksgiving, etc., I realized that the pastor of their church had a year-long set of sermons he repeated in rotation every single year.

That realization dawned on me the second Mother's Day we visited, when the preacher repeated his admonition from the year before: *it is wrong for women to walk around the house wearing curlers in their hair.*

Of course, I wasn't a pastor then, or even really a feminist, and I didn't have a clue where my life's path would eventually take me, but I knew enough to be outraged by the curler comment.

I remember, however, feeling even more outraged by the fact that this preacher used the same sermons over and over, year after year, feeding his people the same tired repetitions because he was too burned out or too lazy or not skilled enough to do the constant and critical work of grappling with the text, the life of the church, and the events of the world, then weaving them into something engaging, instructional, and worshipful. This is a skill that takes considerable talent and a lot of work, and not many preachers do it well.

The sermons that follow in this section, "Blest Be the Tie," span in time over the course of almost twenty years. In reading them you can see George's progressive development as a homiletician, but you will also notice some of the qualities of his preaching and leadership that remain consistent and strong throughout.

What you won't see are the same sermons year after year, and at least in this selection of sermons, no mention of women wearing or not wearing curlers (though I would have loved to comment on a sermon like that!). But you will see some qualities that identify George as an extremely skilled preacher.

For church leaders, you'll see a master at work, a preacher weaving together some teaching, some storytelling, some pushing the limits to make us think. And the qualities I enumerate below are essential elements of excellent preaching; look for them here and then evaluate your own sermons to make sure you're including these essential pieces.

For church attenders, paying attention to some of these qualities will help elucidate how George maintained meaningful leadership at Wilshire for over three decades, what kind of formation his sermons were offering to those who listened to him preach, and whose lives were changed by that listening.

First and foremost, woven through each of these sermons is the serious work of a theologian. The best pastors take their responsibility to be the "theologian in residence" very seriously. That means, of course, introducing and explaining the work of other theologians and including theological concepts with language and explanation that make them accessible to the average listener. But most of all, an excellent theologian in residence is always invitational. By that I mean she is not the "holder of the wisdom," but rather someone who speaks of theology in a way that makes it accessible and even exciting to someone who is not a professional theologian: "I am the resident theologian, and I am inviting you to join me in the work of parsing concepts about God in the text we're studying today." You'll see this quality of George's preaching over and over in the sermons that follow. Only a preacher with confidence and skill will welcome the theological pondering of his people, and George certainly has that confidence and ability. He is widely invitational in his work of applying theological concepts throughout his sermons.

A second quality you'll notice in these sermons is a skillful weaving together of stories, of the story, and of our own stories. Using illustrations from outside the life of the congregation is an important skill necessary to garner the attention of listeners, but many pastors never go beyond engaging storytelling. A skillful preacher, however, will use an outside illustration and soon after, weave the text at hand into the story he's telling. And an exceptional preacher will bring the stories full circle, adding to the sermon a shared story of the congregation, something almost all the listeners share in common. George does this in all of these sermons with what seems like effortless skill.

Third, the world is in crisis always and forever, some catastrophic events impacting the life of the congregation more than others. George deftly names the shared pain of the community and owns it himself in a way that helps hurting listeners feel accompanied in their grieving. Good preachers always speak from their scars, not their wounds, otherwise they inadvertently rely on the congregation to be their therapeutic listeners. Sitting in the pews and watching the pastor actively grieve is deeply uncomfortable, but a pastor who ignores corporate pain is ineffectual. Watch George here as he skillfully names shared areas of pain without bleeding all over the congregation. This is an advanced skill more pastors need to learn.

Finally, these sermons encompass times in the life of the Wilshire congregation when the church was navigating difficult and divisive decisions. A good pastor knows that, during those necessary and painful times in the life of a congregation, there are always some who will not be able to come along the path the church chooses to go. When that happens the pastor is almost always the recipient of ire, which is hurtful and discouraging. One of the most healthy ways to navigate divisive issues from the pulpit is to prophetically tell the truth and to name the reality that some will not be able or willing to make the move and remain part of the community. George addresses this truth with candor and grace in these sermons, skillfully demonstrating for any pastor navigating congregational division, healthy ways to use the pulpit during times of conflict.

Read carefully for these qualities and more in the sermons that follow, and let your life be impacted by George's words. They spoke to the Wilshire congregation, but they speak now to us, so listen closely.

Amy Butler is the founder of Invested Faith, a fund set up to receive the assets of institutions and organizations at the end of their life cycles and offer small grants to faith-rooted social entrepreneurs. She has served churches in New Orleans and Washington, D.C. and was the first woman and seventh Senior Minister of The Riverside Church in the City of New York. Her first book will be released by Random House in October 2023.

40

Birth:
The Labor and Delivery of New Life

January 11, 1998
The Baptism of the Lord
Matthew 2:1-2, 10-18; Revelation 21:1-6a

Amistad is history. I wish it were just a movie. Captured Africans on a slave ship successfully free themselves from their chains, kill their oppressors, but end up in America anyway, standing trial for murder. They can't speak English and their captors can't speak Mende, their African tongue. In one scene, Christian abolitionists on the jailhouse steps sing hymns, protesting and demanding their freedom. One of the Africans grabs a Bible out of the hands of a churchman. He cannot read the words, but he studies the pictures in the Book. He studies them well enough to make out the essential outline of the Gospel story. In the jail cell, he shows the pictures to the group's chieftain figure, Cinque. When he gets to the Bethlehem scene, he explains, *And then he was born, and everything changed.*

Indeed it did. As any birth does to some degree. I remember when each of my children were born, driving home from the hospital and thinking about all the dim-witted people on the streets, *You don't get it, do you? My kid was just born. The world will never be the same.* And while that is true, the birth of the child of Bethlehem changed the world in ways we can hardly imagine. It was not the birth of any child, it was the birth of a new world. That one new life brought new life to a dying world. But if we understand it rightly, if we understand ourselves in light of him, as we have begun to do in this series of sermons, we have to do what we normally don't do; namely, see his birth in all of its gory as well as its glory. For the labor and delivery of new life to the world was not just Mary's but God's.

Mary first. Have you ever really thought about the travail of this woman? God certainly didn't make it easy on her. Unmarried. Pregnant. And no matter how much faith she or anyone close to her might have had, she cannot avoid the scandal of that. Glen Schmucker rightly pointed out a few weeks ago that with all God's connections, you'd think this could have been done with more aplomb. But God chose to be a scandalous stumbling block to the world as it was, right from the start. God chose to save the world from the bottom up instead of the top down. God chose the hard way instead of the easy way. God chose to enter the mess of humanity in a seemingly illegitimate way. God chose to right the world in what seemed the most wrong way.

Mary bore the indignity of seeing her waistline swell for the first five months or so of her marriage. People could tell time even back then. She went off to visit her cousin for a spell, giving some relief from the whispers. Then came the bad news that would be providentially good news that Joseph would need to go to Bethlehem for the census. Now Mary had an excuse to escape the embarrassment of a seemingly six-month birth. She could stay gone awhile and no one would be the wiser. But nine months pregnant and a ninety-mile journey riding a donkey over rugged terrain—oh, boy, great news. When Kim was two days late with Cameron, I had her eat pizza and jog up and down the street. I know, I'm a slug. But it worked. Apparently so did the four-to-five-day donkey ride.

Jesus was born in a stable of sorts. Probably more like the bottom floor of a house where the domestic animals were brought in from the cold for the night, heating with their smelly bodies the upper chamber where the people slept. Nice start for the Son of God, eh? Feeding trough for a cradle. Hay mattress. God among us. Amazing. And the salvation of the world would begin there! Go figure.

For all of you who feel like you will never amount to much because you grew up on the wrong side of the tracks, because you have parents who to this day embarrass you in public, because there's only so much a blue-collar kid can achieve in a white-collar, blue-blood world, think again. God chose to enter the world in the lowest, humblest way humanly possible.

Still, there was great rejoicing in heaven and on earth over this birth. No matter what the rest of the world thought, angels in the realms of glory sang the good news, just as I think we are to imagine they did over your birth and mine, too. For we are all of us created in Christ Jesus for God's good pleasure.

What's more, some in the world shared the joy of heaven and the holy family. Shepherds came to pay respects, and wise men, too. People of all classes celebrated the birth of this new life. The wise men even threw the first baby shower. Gold, frankincense, and myrrh. Typical Crate and Barrel gifts, don't you know?!

But all the sounds of the first Christmas were not joyful. Matthew tells us that Mary's pain of labor and delivery to bring new life into the world are exceeded by the pain of other mothers in Bethlehem. King Herod was old and cranky by the time of Jesus' birth. He had years ago been dubbed King of the Jews, and he liked his title real well. After a glorious start that included the rebuilding of the temple in Jerusalem, Herod gradually turned on everyone, including his own family. He had his own wife murdered and grew more paranoid with time. He suffered from hardening of the arteries and distemper. Toward the end his insides began to rot away, including his private parts. He was so worried that no one would mourn his death, he gave orders that when he died, all the leaders of Judea were to be gathered in the great hippodrome in Jericho, and when the doors were closed, the archers were to fire their arrows and slaughter the lot of them. If no one would mourn his death, at least many would mourn on account of him. No wonder in such a state he could issue a decree that all boy babies under two years old in Bethlehem should be killed, just to make sure the Christ child should have no claim to his title. Fortunately for Jesus, God intervened in the angel's warning, and the child went safely in his parents' arms to Egypt.

But his good fortune did not extend to the babies of Bethlehem slaughtered on his account. We think of this in biblical proportions as thousands, but in truth it was likely more like about twenty or so, judging by the size of the little town of Bethlehem. But few or many, even one is enough to make us rear our heads for the moral injustice of it. A cry was raised in Ramah, Matthew says, Rachel weeping for her children. And she would not be comforted. The reference is to the town where the exiles were gathered when the Babylonians were deporting them. Mothers lost their babies, just as Jacob's wife, Rachel, lost her own life in childbirth "on the way" to Bethlehem.

Rachel's cry is the cry of every mother who has lost her child. It is one of the hardest things I do as a minister; forget as a minister, as a man—to be in the presence of a mother who has lost a child. There is no human comfort. There is nothing to say. And there is no way to dry the tears. Every time I am with a mother like that, I hear Rachel weeping. Every time I sit in a hospital waiting room and hear the news that the baby didn't make it, or that one of the two or three didn't survive, as has happened more than once among us in recent times, I hear Rachel weeping. And I know I cannot expect to comfort her. Nor can I explain why it had to be so.

I can explain it no more than I can explain why when God chose to come into the world in the form of a baby in Bethlehem, God almighty couldn't find a way to protect the other innocents in that town from the evil madman. Why did God's child survive and those others die? Were they not God's children, too? Would it have killed God to send an angel to them, too? If God goes to such trouble to see us all through conception, labor, and delivery, and if we believe as I said last week that God really is involved in all of that, then how can God allow this to happen to others?

I feel a kind of survivor's guilt every time I sit in the presence of Rachel. Here I am, here are my children.

Why should I have made it? Why should my kids have so far survived Herod and others died? I have no explanation. All I can do is weep with Rachel and know that there will come a time, from which neither I nor my children will be able to escape, when we know her tears as our own.

And I live with that foreboding like the other shoe is ready to drop at any time. I carry babies down the aisle, often amid tears. You join me in the joy. But if you look round the room, you will see another kind of tears; and if you listen closely, you can hear Rachel weeping.

Why? Why must it be so? Dostoevsky asked the same thing in *The Brothers Karamazov*. The intellectual agnostic brother Ivan asks his more spiritually sensitive brother Alyosha, *What about the children? How will we ever account for their sufferings?* He was willing to accept that maybe human beings suffer for their sins and even for the general rebellion of the human race. But, Ivan says, *If the suffering of little children is needed to complete the sum total of suffering required to pay for the truth, I don't want that truth, and I declare in advance that the world is not worth the price.* We cannot afford that truth, he says. And if believing that is what is needful for a ticket to heaven, Ivan wants to give up his seat. Him we understand.

But we have to wait; we can't look at this as though the whole story is here. The boy who got off safely with angel warnings would grow to refuse all angel help in keeping him from his appointed unjust death. He would not live a privileged life, but instead would seek out Rachel wherever she might be found. He too would die at the hands of evil forces and even staring into the heavens begging to know where God was in his time of death. In the end, he was not delivered from evil either. His mother, the lucky woman smuggled off to Egypt with her baby safely snuggled in her arms, would stand before the cross on which her son was hanged. She would weep with Rachel after all. As we all will. And in that moment, we see her son care for her. He asks John to comfort her as his own mother. He could do no more then. But gospel logic says that God, in saving the one child of Bethlehem, in time saved them all by dying with them all.

The slave in *Amistad* went on to show the pictures of the haloed Christ child as he grew. *The sun follows him everywhere he goes,* the man said. And when he was beaten and nailed to the cross, the slave saw that he too was, just like them, a slave unjustly treated. This child died but was raised up to the skies. He could be trusted to save them.

Dostoyevsky has Father Zossima comfort a grieving mother in the novel this way: *Weep, but every time you do, remember that your little son is … looking down on you from where he is now, … he sees and rejoices in your tears and shows them to God … You will shed a mother's tears for a long time to come, but in the end your weeping will turn into quiet joy.*

Which, after God's labor and delivery of a new world into this one, is what we get. Quiet joy; no more tears. Behold, I am making all things new, says the Lord, the Alpha and Omega, the Beginning and the End. Beginning even before the birth in Bethlehem and continuing through his death and resurrection. Including all of our births and deaths, too. The mystery of your life and mine is found in, and only in, this story of new life. His birth changed everything indeed.

41

Life in the Valley of Death

May 22, 1994
Pentecost
Ezekiel 37:1-14

Close your mind's eyes and dream with Ezekiel. God gave the prophet a vision and if we are to see it with him, we'll have to close our eyes to usual ways of seeing first.

Now imagine yourself as Israel and walk with me and Ezekiel as God takes us to the valley of dry bones. We don't know where it is, this valley, but it seems familiar. It looks like the Valley of Jezreel, but it's hard to tell, it's been so long since we've seen it, since we've laughed and played in it, since we've felt at home in it. We've been away so long. Babylon is our home now, they tell us. And how many times have we wanted to sing the songs of Zion but have forgotten the tunes? Long ago we hung up our harps on the willows of the rivers of Babylon, and there we wept. We wept for what we once were. We wept for who we'd become. We wept for home. But Babylon is our home now. We have lost the song in our hearts of our home in Zion.

Lord God, why this cruelty? Why not let us alone? Leave us to work out our sadness and grief and loss. Why take us to the valley of Zion and show us these bones? O God, look at them. Thousands of them. Skulls bleached white. Skeletons. Knee bones disconnected from the thigh bones. Just a pile of bones. No sinew, no skin, no life. Just death everywhere. Dry bones. Where once blood coursed through those bones and cartilage held them together and breath gave them life and hope gave them reason to live, now they lay still. My God, why this nightmare? There's not a blessed thing we can do about it. We missed our future. We blew it. And now just let us sleep without these haunting reminders.

Now walk with a young couple into the back yard of their home. See them holding hands, holding each other up, holding back tears. No luck, the water comes pouring down their cheeks like the rivers of Babylon. The swing set is still. Where there was once a smiling, happy child, pumping through the air and yelling, *Watch me, Mommy and Daddy,* now there is only the loud silence of her absence.

Now walk with me down the aisle of the church and find a seat in the pew near the man who's come alone. He shouldn't be alone. This should be a happy day. See his daughter is getting married. She doesn't know he's there. Another man—she calls him Daddy now—is walking her down the aisle. He remembers the day he stood up there at the front with the woman smiling in the second row. He remembers seeing her walk toward him that day, so much like this one. God, she was beautiful. He bows his head. How could he have done it? How could he have left her? O God, he looks so sad.

Off we go now to high school. It's been twenty years. Look at them filing into that gymnasium like it was prom night. There's a guy sitting in his car, watching. Is he waiting? Or is he deciding whether to go in? He's balding, looks a little on the paunchy side. Could that be Cleve? I think it is. Wow, has he changed! Back in high school, he was really something. Quarterback on the football team. Won the state championship. All the girls wanted to date him. Went off to some big college on scholarship. Busted a knee, they said. Dropped out after that. Been married twice, I hear. Kicked around from one job to the next. Wonder what he's doing now? Must be hard on him tonight. Wonder if he'll go in? Wonder if he can imagine being there without his letter jacket and stand all those stories about his glory days that only make him feel like life has passed him by?

So, so much pain in life for so, so many of us. And if you don't know any of it firsthand yet, you haven't lived long enough yet. So much goes wrong in this world, so many dreams of yesteryear dashed. When we feel the rush of memories that call us back to those happier times, we sometimes waken ourselves and block them for fear that it will only make us hate the present more. When we feel led back to uglier times, we close the door quickly to those thoughts, lest we fall into depression over what we cannot any longer control.

We don't deal too well as a society with death and all its impersonators: failure, sin, loss. When someone dies, we dress him up in a suit and have the embalmers make him up to look really good. Better usually than he looked the last few years. But they can't warm him up, give him breath, bring him back. We're only kidding ourselves. Underneath it all are bones drying out. Hope winging its way to worlds unknown, but without us for now.

God is not being cruel to make us look upon the dry, lifeless bones in the valley. God means to heal us and give us back our lives. But that doesn't happen until we look upon our loss and accept it as it is. That doesn't happen as long as we pretend that it isn't so. Which is why it's so important to look upon the bones, to stand before the still swing, to sit in the pew and sob over our sin, to get as far as the parking lot of the high school and come to grips with what's become of us.

Jesus didn't get raised until he was dead and could do nothing about it for himself. Israel didn't return to their homeland until they accepted the fact that they could not return in their own strength. And the rest of us have to get this truth if we have any hope of getting beyond the pain to new life.

We are trained to be socially courteous when people ask questions like, *How are you doing?* Eight out of ten probably expect you to say, *Fine, good,* or some such answer that lets them off the hook. Ten out of ten probably want you to answer that way. Boys used to be taught to be tough, not to show too much emotion. Some still are. Women are feeling the need more and more to suppress emotions in an effort to be more like men, so that they will be treated as equals and be taken seriously. Churches want preachers to be light and sweet, even if life for those very people is heavy and bitter. Oh, how we hide!

But God takes us by the hand and leads us through the cemeteries of our memories. God wants us to read the gravestones of loss and pain and realize that we can't turn back the clock, we can only turn back to God. Before we can move forward to life, God has to take us back just long enough to bury the dead in us.

This is the prelude to hope in the vision from Ezekiel. God makes him look upon the bones and asks him, *Mortal, can these bones live?* And the obvious answer is, from a mortal point of view, NO. It is perfectly clear that those bones have no chance at coming together, undoing their undoing, making fresh flesh and fresh breath reappear in them. They lie still and dead and hopeless.

This is why we only baptize the way we do as Baptists. It's not because we think everyone who sprinkles is sinning. Why, even churches who baptize infants use the same words we do about death and burial with Christ. And I'll tell you a little-known secret, even the first Baptists in the seventeenth century probably didn't go all the way under the water. They stood in the water and had the final wetness poured onto their heads. The key issue was less the form and more the fact that these were people old enough to make their choice for Christ. They were able to look upon their life as a valley of dry bones and consider themselves dead. Going under the water altogether most vividly depicts the breathlessness of our state before God. The Apostle Paul is even more blatant about it in his language than we: He says we have really died with Christ in baptism. We are a little more inclined to say that we are acknowledging our deadness in baptism. But then again, we do more in a wedding ritual than merely express our love in public; we, by virtue of our public vows, participate in a new reality that is formed between God and our partner and the families and the whole community. We die to the way life was organized before, and we come alive to a new way of life together.

God is calling you and me to join Israel in seeing that the way of organizing our lives on our own terms leads us to the valley of death. And we have no way to fix things ourselves. We must depend upon God.

Notice also that God does not linger with the prophet in assigning blame or finding fault. That's one of the few things we do better than God. God doesn't get as much practice as we do in the matter of settling who's responsible for this mess or that. God is in the business of forgiveness and resurrection. And God is much too busy with those things to spend the time we want on sorting out liability.

Did you hear God's question to the prophet? God didn't ask, *Mortal, whose fault is it that Israel is here in exile? Who's to blame for these dry bones? What is the root cause of this condition?* Have you ever noticed how the best way politicians evade doing something about problems that face us is by claiming that we don't yet know the root causes, and until we do, there's no sense throwing good money at bad? The root problem with that root cause approach is that no human being is ever going to get straight to the root of any complex issue enough to be able to fix blame.

I was talking to the director of the local chapter of Habitat for Humanity the other day. Jim was telling me about the problem he encountered in Memphis when his church tried to renovate a low-income housing project. They found that poor people stay poor not because they are frivolous and ignorant, but because there are unseen forces that keep them from making progress. Some of the volunteers had been mentioning how they didn't understand why people on food stamps would go into the grocery stores and buy frozen pizzas and TV dinners and such that cost much money and don't keep and are less than nutritious. Then they went into their apartments and found that most of them had vermin crawling through their pantries and broken ovens. Some of them had only one working stove burner out of four. Do you think the landlord would fix any of that or have regular exterminations?

Listen, if you spend your whole life trying to figure why your father did this to you or failed to do that, why people don't give you a chance or how you can ever have a half decent life after blowing it in your first marriage, then you'll never get done analyzing and you'll never get done drying out in the valley and you'll never get to the question that God wants you to answer. *Mortal, can YOUR bones live? Can YOU breathe free ever again? What about it?*

And the answer you must give is the answer of Ezekiel. *O Lord God, you know.* In other words, it's out of our control. The only hope is if God so wills. And the grand news of the gospel is that GOD SO WILLS!

The Stephen Spielberg cinematography of the bones rattling and the sinew and flesh growing at rapid speed, and the winds gathering to fill the lungs of these people is the image of you getting to your feet. It's the image of God giving the couple in the backyard a reason to say yes to life again without their little girl. It's the image of a man in the church pew raising his head and saying yes to the future. It's the image of an old football hero getting out of his car and going into the reunion because he believes he can be a "will be" instead of a "has been."

It will never be what it once was. It will be different. It will never be what you wanted and maybe want still if you could just turn back the clock. But then again, the choice is not between *what might have been* and *what might be*, the choice is between *what is* and *what might be* by the power of God.

Been to Arlington Stadium lately? It's a valley of dry bones. Games used to be played there. Life once roamed the diamond in that place. More hope than wins took place between the lines of that field, I grant you. But today it awaits demolition. You can still go there if you want to. You won't see baseball. Or you can walk across the street to a veritable cathedral of baseball hope. The Ballpark in Arlington is something new and something wonderful that defies imagination. There's plenty of life there if you are willing to go there. And more hope than pitching, don't you know?!

So, what's it going to be for you? Dry bones or the miracle power of new life? Mortals, can these bones live?

42

Gone Today, Here Tomorrow

May 20, 2001
Sixth Sunday of Easter
John 14:23-29

In the last chapter of John's Gospel, Jesus tells his disciples that he is here today and gone tomorrow. He is going away, and they cannot go where he is going. Then in this chapter 14 he says he is going to the Father and coming back to take them to where he is. They tell him they are already feeling lost at the prospect of being left behind and don't know the way to where he is going. He says not to worry; they do know the way because he himself is the way. Later, in our text today, he tells them again he is going but coming again, yet not to worry—he'll soon be gone today, but he'll be here tomorrow.

All this talk of comings and goings reminds of the puzzled little boy saying to his mother, *Is it true that we are all made from dust, Mom?* "Well, yes, honey, that's what the Bible says all right." *And Mom, is it also true that we are going to be dust again someday?* The mother was impressed by her son's Bible knowledge. "That's right, from dust we have come and to dust we shall return," his mother said. *Well, then, Mom, I don't know whether he's coming or going, but there's a big fellow under my bed.*

We all live between our coming and going. Life is about living well in the in-between times.

We say a ceremonial goodbye to many of our high school graduates today. They have been with us, some of them all their lives. They are headed out for a new place, an exciting place, but a place that will not include us. They will be on their own, and one of these days, after the excitement settles down in Oz, they'll look at the dog and say, *Guess we're not in Kansas anymore, Toto.* (Except for Katy Kirkham, of course, who is going to the University of Kansas.) The question they will ask themselves in quiet moments is, *Am I ready for this being on my own?* The question their parents will ask is, *Are we ready for this being on our own?*

I watched the videotape this week of Bruce's [McIver, pastor emeritus] last sermon as pastor of our church on December 18, 1988. For thirty years he had served faithfully, and the church had come to depend upon his leadership. Now he was leaving and trying to help his church believe that even if the search committee came back with a frightfully young, overconfident, long-haired, ex-Lutheran, Yankee New Yorker as the next pastor, maybe things would still be all right. (The jury's still out, don't you know?!) Over and over, he reminded you and himself that God wants us looking to the future. But in the meantime, he reminded the church that it has resources in Christ to manage whatever may come.

This is what Jesus is dealing with in his last hours with his disciples. He knows he is going to die, and they will not be able to go the way of the cross with him. He knows they have leaned on him for direction, and they know they will feel lost without their North Star to set their life compasses by.

Any of you who have lost your parents know this feeling, even if your parents were elderly and you hadn't needed them much in the last years. The thought that you are the oldest generation now, that there is no one to turn to for advice who has lived it all longer than you—it's a bit scary. Same thing with a divorce. The wife is especially vulnerable if she hasn't had a strong part in financial decisions. Maybe she married right out of school and never really had to set up house and live on her own, and, all of a sudden, at middle age she is forced to do it all, maybe with kids to boot. How will she manage? What resources can she depend upon?

Or maybe spiritually you feel in-between. The simple and certain faith you were brought up with has broken down. You've learned things in college or in the school of hard knocks that make you certain now of only one thing—that the simple answers no longer suffice. You feel the absence of Christ today more than his presence. You wonder if you will ever feel his presence as thick again as you once did. You are trying to figure out how to live in the in-between time of faith and doubt.

If our text tells us anything today, it is that Jesus knows all this. No matter what your situation in life, Jesus has anticipated it and wants to bring you good news of comfort and hope today.

The first thing to notice here is that Jesus tells us that his going from us is good for him and good for us both. He is going to be with the Father, and that ought to make us glad. His going makes possible our growing.

Any parent knows this hard truth. You want your kids to grow up, so you have to give them space. You can't hover over them forever, take care of them, house them and feed them, or you'll be changing their diapers at 37. If they are going to come into their own, they need the right measures of guidance *and* freedom.

I remember leaving for college in Miami, Florida, at age 17. By myself. Very alone. Excited and scared to death both. I pulled out of my driveway in Staten Island in my 1972 Toyota Celica that always pulled to the right because the previous owner had bent the frame in an accident. I pointed the wheel southward and held against the westward drift. It was a clear and sunny July day, but I kept the windshield wipers on all the way down the New Jersey Turnpike because I couldn't keep the rain out of my eyes. Twenty-seven years later, I can say how good that was for me.

Jesus knew that if he was leaving them, he also had to leave something of himself to keep them company. He promised them not only that his leaving would be good for both of them and that he would come again to be with them; he promised them a new kind of presence in the meantime. He would give them the Advocate, the Holy Spirit.

It's an interesting term he chooses: Advocate. In many ways it is exactly the opposite of the meaning of the term for Satan in the Bible. Satan means "adversary" or "accuser." Devil's advocate is the name for one who always takes the other side of things. Deacon is another name. (Only kidding.) What Jesus knows is that we will all of us have many times before we have a clear and confident sense of Jesus' presence among us when we will feel accused, alone, made to feel guilty by forces inside us and outside us. And when we stand at that bar of judgment, we need someone to stand alongside us.

The word John chooses to describe what Jesus is saying is *paraclete*, which means "one who is called alongside another." *Advocate* is a term used for lawyers. Now there are lots of lawyer jokes out there, and maybe they deserve them—as much as preachers deserve preacher jokes! But just go to court and stand before a judge or jury, hearing the charges filed against you, and suddenly no more lawyer jokes. You are glad and not a little comforted to have someone next to you speaking for you, giving you confidence against the charges.

This is what Jesus does: He gives us the Holy Spirit to be with us, when our conscience accuses us, when we feel inadequate, powerless, attacked. Jesus promises that when we cannot see him standing next to us, he is there on the sly, shy, but working within us nonetheless. So, when you begin to doubt yourself, when you hear things about you that make you feel inadequate, when you begin to play the tapes of your father or teacher or boss that make you feel like you're not up to whatever life brings you, listen to the voice that speaks quietly in your soul, a voice that sounds curiously and coincidentally like Jesus himself. Trust that voice.

The Holy Spirit will not only stand up for you and reassure you, though; the Spirit will also teach you new things and remind you of what you already know about Jesus and how to keep your promises to him.

In his autobiography *Climbing the Mountain*, Kirk Douglas tells of accepting a bit part he had agreed to play in a Sylvester Stallone film. In the opening scene he plays a dying father on his deathbed. His son Angelo (Stallone) is nearby, and Douglas' character says weakly, "My son, come closer."

Stallone leans over. "Closer." Stallone is inches from his face. Crack. His father gives him a solid smack on the side of the head. "Papa, what have I done?" his boy asks. "You gangster! You lie, you steal, you shoot people!"

"I don't shoot people." Angelo points to his henchmen. "They shoot people."

"Shut your mouth! You bring shame to the family!"

As the scene continues, the father extracts a promise from Angelo to go straight. Finally, he closes his eyes. Stallone, weeping, leans over to kiss him, and suddenly his father comes to life and smacks him again right across the face. Angelo is shocked. "That's so you don't forget." At that he dies.

Jesus doesn't slap his disciples around before he leaves them so that they'll remember who they are and how they are to live. He speaks to them tenderly and gently, and he gives them his very own spirit to guide them and assure them.

When we talk about the differences between one religion and another, we can talk about different sacred Scriptures, about views on God or the gods, about how to live in the world. But Christians claim the One they follow was not just a wise teacher who lived a noble life we should emulate; we speak of him in the present tense. We speak of Christ being present to us by his Holy Spirit. His resurrection from the dead sets him apart from all other teachers. Yes, he is with the Father in heaven and coming back to bring us to God. Yet because he is no longer confined to a single body, he can be present to many bodies at the same time. He can be with you and me spiritually so, making his presence strangely known in the midst of his apparent absence.

Let not your hearts be troubled, neither let them be afraid, Jesus says. As if we have some say about it. And we do. Because he is really with us, because we are not alone. Because he will lead us into a future filled with the promises of God—we can be at peace. Do you want to be? Trust in him today.

43

Lamentation and Loss

October 4, 1998
Eighteenth Sunday after Pentecost
Lamentations 1:1-6

Among the minor mysteries of the church—such as how the pastor gets from the baptistery to the pulpit so fast after getting wet and why his communion cup is so much bigger than everyone else's—is the matter of how the preacher decides what to preach on week to week. It might surprise you to learn that most of the year I follow a thing called the Revised Common Lectionary. Instead of just picking Bible texts that happen to strike my fancy, I try to discipline myself to listen to parts of Scripture I wouldn't preach on otherwise. The lectionary gives you in a three-year cycle an Old Testament reading, a Psalm, a Gospel passage, and an Epistle text for each week. So, I've been tracking Jeremiah the past month or so (have you noticed?), and today the wise ones who put this thing together have cast us into the companion to Jeremiah called Lamentations. Ever heard a sermon from Lamentations? I never preached one either, so we're even, don't you know?! The least they could have done was choose chapter 3, verse 22. Nice words about the endless mercies of God. Our old favorite hymn, *Great Is Thy Faithfulness*, comes from there.

But here today we enter into Israel's lament for the loss of her land. It's not a happy text. Nor is it ever happy for any of us who lose what was so much a part of us, we can't imagine ourselves without it.

A few years ago, Alvin Burns and I went to Israel with a dozen Jews and Christians. It was remarkable to me, the difference between us on the matter of the spiritual significance of the land. The Jews, even those who had never been to Israel, felt as though they were going home. They knew they were living away from the center of their universe. Judaism recalls the promise of God to Abraham that they would inherit a land of their own. And Jerusalem, affectionately known as Zion, is the center of the center. Christians, Protestants especially, are more oriented toward the word, toward a sense of life as a journey. Jews know about journeys too, but the idea of a homeland has always been their dream and goal. And if you need proof, just pick up the newspaper.

Judah had lost her heart's love. Jerusalem—that beautiful city of Zion had fallen to the Babylonians, and God's people felt the loss. *How lonely sits the city that once was full of people!* Listen to the phrases. *Like a widow she has become ... she was a princess ... she weeps bitterly ... tears on her cheeks ... no one to comfort her ... the roads to Zion mourn ... no one comes to her festivals ... her young girls grieve ... her lot is bitter.* They speak out. They grieve together.

The way a West Texas rancher might as the bank forecloses on the property. The way a Midwestern farm family might as they watch a three-generation farm pass from their control. The way my mother-in-law felt when she had to close her father's Five and Dime stores, as rising rents, Office Depots, and Walmarts made business impossible to sustain.

It's hard to deal with losses like that. You spend your whole life thinking something will always be there, and then it's gone. You count on someone always being there and then he or she is gone. Forty years of marriage, plans for retirement, trips to be taken, grandchildren to enjoy. Then a heart attack. A stroke. Cancer. And it's all over before you have a chance to get ready. The loss is so great you can hardly get out of bed in the morning. Suddenly, the land you live in is as foreign to you as Babylon to Zion.

What do you do? You don't just get over it. You don't make believe it doesn't matter. But there are healthy and unhealthy ways to grieve the loss. And here we have a good example of what to do. The Bible is full of unexpected types of literature like this, because we inhabit a world where the unexpected hits and hurts.

Lament is a movement in the grief process where you make your complaint to God. Lamentations, like some of the Psalms, are personal and public prayers in which God is either addressed directly or indirectly with the pain of Israel's loss. There's no stuffing it stoically or burying it under a smile. They face the loss squarely, admitting where they are responsible, accusing others of their part, grieving a past that can never be reclaimed. They acknowledge they have no future apart from God's making. They are powerless to fix things. And they write their poetry and read it out loud together. Remarkably, over time Israel and the church found this so appropriate, they regarded it as God-given and called it Scripture. So, we learn from it ourselves.

At a certain point in the grief process though, there must come a time of acceptance. Lament is a part of that, but acceptance moves deeper still.

Reinhold Niebuhr was perhaps America's greatest theologian. He authored the well-known 'Serenity Prayer,' which is repeated over and over again in recovery groups. *God grant me the serenity to accept the things I cannot change, the courage to change what I can, and the wisdom to know the difference.* At a point in the grief process, you have to come to grips with the reality of the loss. The past is past, what is, is. Just as acknowledging the loss through lament is healthier than denying it, so accepting it allows you to move beyond preoccupation with it.

I was talking this week to an older man who came to see me. He was telling me about his daughter, whom I know to be addicted to prescription drugs. She has been through at least two treatment programs and seems no better. She has lost her marriage and custody of her child. Her father told me of the help he has found through Al-Anon, the family recovery program. *It seems crazy to say this*, he told me, *but the greatest thing that has ever happened in my relationship to God has been my acceptance of being the father of a chemically dependent child.* Then he went on to tell me about the spiritual awakening that had taken place in him. He had always tried to fix things, take care of his daughter, feel responsible for her life. But he came to realize that only God could handle that much responsibility. He was learning to let God have it.

Later he came back with a gift. This tin can with painted angels on it is what he calls a God Box. (He also gave me one in these lovely fall colors.) The point is this: Whenever you bump up against a loss or a troubling situation beyond your control, you write it out and put it into the God Box. You give it to God, in other words. And then you let it go. Presumably the angels are there to carry it up.

Trying to hold on to something that is gone is an unhealthy attachment. The word attachment comes from the French, meaning literally, "to be nailed to." Some of us are nailed to our losses in ways that keep us stuck. A lost marriage that we just can't get beyond. An affair that changed the landscape and soul-scape both. An abortion we can't undo. A decision we ache to have made or to have made differently. We live in a land of *what-ifs* and *if-onlys*. Lost loves or lost dreams. We can either remain attached to them or let them go.

Remember the good news. Jesus was attached to our sin for us, nailed to the cross so that we would have hope. So we would not have to bear the pain of it alone. Because he bore our loss, we could gain a future through his resurrection power. We cannot experience that power, though, if we are intent upon crucifying ourselves for the rest of our lives. We have to let go and give it to God.

Ultimately, though, we have to find a way to go on with what is left of us. Sometimes the wounds are deep and remain, no matter the sense of relief forgiveness brings. God wants us to live hopefully and bravely and joyfully, even with our life-formed and sometimes sin-shaped limitations. And God will not fail to give us ample opportunity to do just that.

Vy Malcik, our good Wilshire friend who with her husband, Michael, has recently moved to Colorado, wrote to me about seven years ago as she was grieving the loss of their ten-year-old, Adam. Our Adam's Baskets remember his giving spirit. She told of the great conductor Toscanini, who was sitting at his podium before a concert one evening as the orchestra was warming up and tuning instruments just minutes before the performance. All at once a bassoon player approached him in a fearful panic. *Maestro*, he said, *I am very sorry, but my instrument has suffered an accident and the E-flat will not sound. I am afraid I will not be able to play tonight.* The great man went silent, his eyes closed for what seemed minutes. The bassoon player cowered in fear of his fury. Toscanini put his hands to his head and continued in silence, only adding to the poor man's shame. At last he looked up and said quietly,

Do not worry. E-flat does not appear in your music tonight. Toscanini had played through the entire concert in his mind and was able to reassure the bassoon player that E-flat would not be required of the bassoon for the symphony to come off.

Vy told me how that story kept her alive many days. She had been damaged by her loss, but she said that *God has looked at the song of life and assures me that the music he has for me to play can be played on what is left. ... There is still a place for me in the orchestra,* she said, *even as I wait patiently to be restored.*

Nice. But you don't get there until you go through lament and acceptance. There is no short cut to spiritual growth. Lamentations teaches us that you can't experience the good news if you are unwilling to acknowledge in your bones the bad news. After all, the good news is only good because it is such news. Amen.

44

Expectancy

June 22, 2008
Fifth Sunday after Pentecost
Genesis 18:1-15

When you make the decision to become a member of our church, you are soon invited to a fellowship, as we Baptists like to call it, at my house. (Now, just so you know, you can make that decision today. You can walk to the front at the end of the service, and we will welcome you then, or you can fill out a new-member card in the pew and hand it to me later, since the offering plate has already been passed. Actually, if any of you wants to rethink your offering and hand it to me later, I promise I'm good for it. And have I mentioned that summer is the best time of year to give generously to the church if you would like to prove to yourself and God how faithful you really are?)

Okay, so, back to the fellowship thing. A Baptist fellowship usually amounts to a social gathering that includes finger foods, sweets, nonalcoholic drinks, and lots of talk; sometimes it's just punch and cookies, don't you know?! (Oh, and you don't have to talk if you don't want to, and we won't call on you to pray or anything like that.) When you come to the Mason's for our new member teetotaling tête-à-tête, you will be welcome in the house that Kim and I built partly for the purpose of making you feel welcome in it. My mother-in-law's friendly little dog, Webster, will wag his tail and meet you at the door. We will let you sit and rest. We will feed you. And we hope you will feel at home with our hospitality.

But of course, in this case, you will be welcome because we know you and have invited you. If you just show up as strangers, I have to admit you would not immediately get the same treatment. When strangers come knocking, Kim and I go quickly into a covert operation. We do reconnaissance work to size up whether to answer the door at all. We hide. We peek. We profile. We check for Jehovah's Witnesses and Mormons on bikes, for underprivileged youth selling magazines we would never read, for Boy Scouts selling trash bags, and for Girl Scouts selling

Thin Mints. I open the door for the Girl Scouts selling Thin Mints. We know we shouldn't be that way, but we fall into a cocoon mentality in our own house.

Abraham had no permanent house. He was a nomad who must have called at the tent of many others as he moved his herd and clan from one place to another. There were no Days Inns back then. He knew what it was like to be on the other side of the door. So maybe he wasn't as given as I to vetting visitors. Unlike the custom in Dallas, hospitality to strangers was one of the chief virtues of Near Eastern culture. So, when three strangers show up at his tent, he goes out of his way to make them at home.

When the three men appear in Rublev's beautiful Russian icon *The Trinity*, we know who they are—Father, Son, and Holy Spirit. The writer to the Hebrews alludes to this scene and says they are angels. But when they first appeared at the oaks of Mamre, while Abraham sat at the entrance to his tent, he had no way of knowing that he was about to entertain the Lord, or angels, or both.

Abraham doesn't scrutinize them. He doesn't size them up. He just jumps up and welcomes them. He doesn't greet them with bread and water alone, only then to send them on their way knowing that he has done what is expected but nothing more. He welcomes these unexpected guests with an openness that defies our typical practice. He sees to their comfort; then he calls on Sarah and his servant to get to work. There's baking to be done. There's a calf to be slaughtered and a roast to prepare. There's milking to be done, and (even back then) cottage cheese on the side. Go figure.

Abraham prepares a feast for the three strangers. He opens his home and heart to them. Imagine what he would have done if he had known it was the Lord and two angels! Probably nothing different. And that's the point. Abraham lived with a sense of expectancy. He was open to life, open to what may come, open to God.

This is the challenge to us all, even to those of us in the ministry. I have just been with a lot of my minister colleagues in Memphis at our annual meeting of the Cooperative Baptist Fellowship. We swap stories about our churches. Some are good, others not so. Some of my colleagues are out of work now; they've been cut off by churches they once served—no longer welcome. Like Abraham, we ministers have all heard something of a call from God. It may have meant that, like him, we have had to be open to leaving behind a settled and more comfortable life for a life of itinerancy in which we have no confidence we will ever settle down with a people. I am one of the rare lucky ones who finds a church willing to go the long haul together. God knows that God's people are getting harder to settle down with.

I am wondering what is happening to the church these days. Several of my friends have been fired or have resigned lately under unhappy circumstances— including one of our beloved pastoral residents. He and his family will soon return to Dallas to regroup and restart after a church that he was serving actually resorted to anonymous notes in his home mailbox that read *Resign, or else.* I am mad about that, and sad. It's hard to keep your heart open to what God might want to do with your life when people who are supposed to be part of the family of faith would so cruelly turn you out. And the worst byproduct occurs when their turning them out makes the ministers turn in. Turn in their ordination papers, in some cases, or in other cases just turn in on themselves. It's hard to do ministry when you have to retreat inside a hard shell. Ministry is an affair of the heart.

But part of our call is to keep our hearts open anyway—whether we remain pastors of those churches or not. And the reason is not that it makes us more virtuous, but because it nurses in us an openness toward God of what might be possible if we would keep a spirit of expectancy. The more we protect ourselves against getting hurt, the more closed our hearts become. And the more closed we become toward the future, the more the future becomes closed to us.

Some of you have been hurt like that by giving your heart to someone who has broken, rejected, or ignored it. You said, "I love you" to someone, and maybe even "I do." Then came a time when you heard "I don't." He or she started to treat you like a stranger instead of a lover. Or it might have been a parent who deserted you or preferred your sister or brother or the stepsiblings. It might have been a church you once loved deeply as an active member, and then it went another direction and broke your heart. We all know something of the kind of pain that makes us want to close ourselves off to the unexpected, because the pain we know is safer than the pain we don't yet know that could be joy but might just be more pain.

Our text contrasts Abraham's expectancy and Sarah's. God has made this promise of a child to Abraham and Sarah—twenty-five years earlier. Nothing. Is she supposed to remain expectant when she is not expecting? Sarah laughs. She laughs at the idea of pregnancy after childbearing age, after even the times of sexual pleasure. Her laughter betrays her spiritual unexpectancy, we are told. She cannot see that nothing is too wonderful (or too difficult) for the Lord.

Settling down to the facts of life is safer than living expectantly. Living expectantly requires believing that God may work within you to bring about new life for you and through you. But to live that way, you have to be open to the possibility that it may yet come to you. The call still buried deep in your soul, the promise that beats ever so faintly in your breast that you have almost given up on but is still alive and still in force, no matter how long it has lain dormant inside you, no matter how barren you feel or how much you think God has teased you with desire only to deprive you of the offspring of your hope.

Now some people think, *If it is to be, it's up to me*. And others think, *If God wills it, God will do it, no thanks to me*. But these two extremes are not the way God works. God promises and God prompts; God elicits and God enlists. God does not intrude or ignore. The consummation of promise and fulfillment is the product of mutual faithfulness.

Becoming hospitable to God means embracing the unexpected moments and the means in which and by which God may come to us. Sometimes God comes calling in the disguise of people or things that don't look like bearers of good news. Like a pregnancy that makes you sick before it makes you a mother, the good news is sometimes found only in what seems like bad news.

Tony Snow had reached a high point in his professional career when he served as the press secretary for the president of the United States. He had beaten colon cancer the year before—or so he thought. Shortly after taking over the White House talking-head job, Snow found out that the cancer had returned with a vengeance, now including tumors in his abdomen. Cancer was an unexpected return visitor, and Tony knew he had a choice: He could turn inward and cut himself off from people he loved, or he could trust in God, welcome the challenge, and find God's new purpose for his life in it.

Here's what he says: "God relishes surprise. We want lives of simple, predictable ease—smooth, even trails as far as the eye can see—but God likes to go off-road. He provokes us with twists and turns. He places us in predicaments that seem to defy our endurance and comprehension—and yet don't. By his love and grace, we persevere. The challenges that make our hearts leap and stomachs churn invariably strengthen our faith and grant measures of wisdom and joy we would not experience otherwise.

"Picture yourself in a hospital bed. The fog of anesthesia has begun to wear away. A doctor stands at your feet; a loved one holds your hand at the side. It's *cancer*, the healer announces.

"The natural reaction is to turn to God and ask him to serve as a cosmic Santa. *Dear God, make it all go away. Make everything simpler.* But another voice whispers: *You have been called. Your quandary has drawn you closer to God, closer to those you love, closer to the issues that matter—and has dragged into insignificance the banal concerns that occupy our normal time.*"[70]

I daresay that accepting his cancer as a call has produced more children of faith than accepting his job at the White House ever did. He is a prophet of hope because he was a good steward of his pain.

How do you receive the unexpected strangers that come into your life? What if the greatest and noblest contributions of your life are to be found in how you welcome these uninvited experiences?

If we want to experience more of the power of God in our lives, we might start by cultivating Abraham's spirit of expectancy. Being hospitable even to the people and events that seem to lack the potency to give us what we dream of may expose us to the omnipotence of the Lord who wants to give us more than we can imagine. Who knows what kind of life may then be conceived in us, and begin to stir inside us, and be born at long last through us?

It could happen. Don't laugh.

---

70 "Cancer's Unexpected Blessings," in *Christianity Today,* http://www.christianitytoday.com/ct/2007/july/25.30.html.

45

Plain Talk

Watch and listen to "Plain Talk" by following this link or scanning the QR code with your phone: youtu.be/bmlvm6jtmPQ. Sermon begins at 41:36.

The following three sermons were delivered during a time of decision both for Wilshire as a congregation and for the nation, albeit on different matters. Having completed a time of study, Wilshire was embarking on a two-Sunday vote on inclusion of all persons as full members of the church, regardless of sexual orientation or gender identity. This pivotal vote coincided with the 2016 United States presidential election.

Together, these sermons give insight into the careful process of decision-making among the community of faith and offer a model for working through conflict in Christian community. Prior to this season of study, Mason led the Wilshire community through similar studies, sermon series, and periods of congregational discernment around the inclusion of women and divorced persons in ministry (in the 1990s) and recognition of different modes of baptism required for membership (early 2000s).

November 6, 2016
All Saints Sunday
Luke 6:20-31

Year after year after year, for 108 years, all they could do was hope. Those lovable losers, the Chicago Cubs fans, finally realized their fondest hopes this week: Their team is now World Series champions.

Our former pastoral resident Scott Dickison is a lifelong Cubs fan, as was his father before him. A year ago, the Cubs were swept in four games by the New York Mets in the National League Championship Series. The next night, Scott's two-year-old son, who had gotten used to watching his dad watch the Cubs go down to defeat night after night, asked, "Daddy, where baseball game?" Scott said: *I looked at him in a way I imagine my father once looked at me and told him those words that*

every Cub fan learns at far too early an age: "Son, there's no more baseball this season.
We'll have to wait 'til next year."[71]

Well, at long last, baseball justice has been done. Dreams have come true. And those fans who have gone on to their eternal reward without seeing victory in their lifetimes are now celebrating above as Cubs fans are below. For more than a century, Cubs fans learned that loyalty is not about what happens when things are going well, but when things are going badly. There's no such thing as a part-time Cubs fan: You're in for thick or thin, or you aren't in at all.

Today is All Saints Sunday in the church. We remember those who have gone on to their heavenly reward without seeing all the fruits of their faithfulness come to fruition in this life. They lived and died without knowing the full joy of their labors. But their lives inspire us still. And they inspire us precisely because of the way they lived when it was hard. It was their character that counted. And their character was proved by how they lived during tough times.

Our lectionary text for today is from Jesus' Sermon on the Plain in Luke. I told you last week about the contrast between Matthew's Gospel, which records Jesus' Sermon on the Mount, and Luke's version from down on level ground. Luke's Jesus has a variation on the Beatitudes that includes a series of woes with the blessings. Blessed are the poor; woe to the rich. Blessed are those who hunger now; woe to those who are perpetually stuffed. Blessed are those who weep now; woe to those who can't stop laughing in this life. Blessed are those who are hated and reviled in this life; woe to those who are spoken well of only now. In each case there is a promise of table-turning to come.

The Christian faith is always future-focused. God is doing something in the world to bring about a time of perfect peace and justice. The inequalities and injustices of this life, the losses and sorrows, will come to an end. The dream of God for all creation will someday come true. And those who lived loyally in pursuit of that dream will know the joy of it when it comes. Those who resist it and prosper now at the expense of others will be sorry later.

Jesus continues the Sermon on the Plain, or what I am calling Plain Talk, by giving explicit instructions on how to live in hope in the meantime. The summary of all he says is this: Live now as if the time of vindication has already come. Live now as if victory is finally yours. Live now as if God's will is done on earth as it is in heaven.

Listen again to these astonishing words of Jesus: *Love your enemies, do good to those who hate you, bless those who curse you, pray for those who abuse you ... Do to others as you would have them do to you.*

Up to this time in Jewish tradition, the prime directive was to love one's neighbor. Jesus also said that on numerous occasions. But the great debate among the rabbis was always the question, *Who is my neighbor?* That appears in Luke's Gospel in the remarkable parable that Jesus tells of the Good Samaritan. While tradition was always trying to limit who the neighbor was in order to know where to draw the line on love, Jesus erased the line altogether. Love everyone, he says. Love those

---

71 https://baptistnews.com/article/next-year-people/#.WB-vpXfMyV5

close to you. Love those far from you. Love those who love you. Love those who hate you. Love them all.

Amy-Jill Levine is Jewish, but she teaches New Testament at Vanderbilt Divinity School. One of the great gifts she gives to the church is to keep us mindful of the Jewish background and assumptions behind the words of the Christian Scriptures. But at this point, she finds no real parallel to Jesus' teaching that we love our enemies. This is an unprecedented "Jesus variation."

During the time of Jesus, we are told in the Jewish Talmud, a Gentile approached the two great rabbis of that time, seeking to convert but impatient with the long process of learning Torah in order to know how to live as a Jew. He challenged them: One was the strict Shammai, and the other—the more liberal Hillel—was to teach him Torah while standing on one foot. Shammai dismissed him as unserious. Hillel accepted the challenge. He said this: *Whatever is hateful unto you, do not do to your neighbor. This is the whole of Torah. The rest is commentary. Go now and learn.*

This is the religious version of the medical mandate called the Hippocratic Oath: *First, do no harm.* And the first way to do no harm in relationships is to resist the impulse to hate or to retaliate in any way.

Almost a decade before his death, the Rev. Martin Luther King Jr. preached a sermon on loving one's enemies at Dexter Avenue Baptist Church in Montgomery, Alabama. He actually believed that these words of Jesus were so important that he tried to preach on this subject every year, adding more and more layers to his understanding of it and trying his best to live it out amid the terrible times of hatred and persecution that he and Black Americans faced daily in those days. I read his 1957 sermon this week. In it he said that the first thing to do when you are inclined to hate and not love someone who has hurt or abused you is to look deeply and honestly at yourself. The reason, he said, is to remind yourself that it takes two to make for enmity. It is unlikely that all hatred and abuse springs solely from a guilty person or group that opposes or oppresses you. If you can own up to your own participation in the conflict, you will have greater sympathy for your enemy.

Next, he says, when you look at your enemies, look not only to that part of them that you deem evil; look at the good in them first. No one is all bad or all good. By refusing to treat someone who has hurt or harmed you in some way as pure evil, you create the conditions to one day find that person again in friendship.[72]

This is so important in our time. We are in an election week in our country and in our church. We will vote in both cases on matters that have divided us. We have different visions of how to fulfill our hopes and dreams, of what these communities should look like. And along the way, we have sometimes hurt one another and closed our hearts to each other. Some have determined that it is better to live without one another than with one another. Some would rather move to Canada than live in a future in our country under the administration of the one they didn't vote for. Some would rather move to another church than live under the conditions of

---

72 https://kinginstitute.stanford.edu/king-papers/documents/
loving-your-enemies-sermon-delivered-dexter-avenue-baptist-church

a future determined by a vote they didn't support. But by doing so, we only prove that the way the world operates is the only way open to us.

I am aware that this may be the last time many of us will worship together. If you are one of those who have already decided that you are leaving, I have something to say to you: thank you. Thank you for all the years of sacrifice and service. Thank you for the gifts of time, talents, and treasure that you have given to make us the church we are today. And if you wonder how you will be remembered after you leave, I will tell you: You will be recorded among the saints of this church. No one wants to be judged on the basis of one decision or snapshot of time in a life. So, we will bless you and miss you.

And for those of you who are undecided, I want to say that there is a place for you here. It may be hard, but it can be good. *A good life, not an easy life*, don't you know?! Let's prove the gospel together by staying together. But whether you leave or stay, don't let hatred or bitterness or resentment rule your heart.

Antoine Leiris lost his wife in the ISIS-inspired Islamic terror attacks in Paris last November. He was left with a young son who would afterward be motherless. Leiris wrote a Facebook post the next day that went viral. In it he defiantly declared, *You will not have my hate.* When asked a year later about it, he said this, referring mainly to his duty toward his son: *When you're a kid, what you need is protection and so I wanted to make sure he felt secure. And by secure I mean emotionally secure and secure because I took care of him. And if I let this feeling [of hate] enter into our lives, it would have taken up all the space in our lives ... In our hearts everything would have been heavy and I wanted our lives to be light again. ... He has the right to not worry about everything all the time. He's just a child. So I had to protect him from that feeling [of hate]. He's going to keep growing and growing, and that feeling cannot dominate his life.*[73]

There is a cost to us when we hate someone else. So first, as Hillel taught, do not do what is hateful. But there is more that Jesus offers. It isn't enough to resist hating or retaliating; you have to do good toward the one who has hurt or hated you. This is the positive content of Jesus' Golden Rule: *Do unto others as you would have them do unto you.*

In his second inaugural address, President Abraham Lincoln acknowledged something mystifying about those on either side of the Civil War: *Both read the same Bible and pray to the same God, and each invokes His aid against the other ... let us judge not, that we be not judged.* He then ended with these immortal words to heal the nation: *With malice toward none, and charity for all ...*[74]

Charity is a King James word for love. Divine love. The kind of love we are commanded to have for our enemies, who are really our fellows, whether we want to acknowledge them as such or not.

After another hard election in 2001, President George W. Bush said these profound words in his first inaugural address: *Sometimes our differences run so deep, it*

---

73 https://web.archive.org/web/20190105042031/https://www.onfaith.co/discussion/
onfaith-conversations-antoine-leiris-author-of-you-will-not-have-my-hate

74 http://www.nationalcenter.org/LincolnSecondInaugural.html

seems we share a continent but not a country. We do not accept this, and we will not allow it. Our unity, our union, [are] the serious work of leaders and citizens in every generation. And this is my solemn pledge: I will work to build a single nation of justice and opportunity.[75]

The words of these presidents echo the words of Jesus and the examples of the saints. Let us not give up hope and let us not give up on one another. The answer for the country and the answer for the church are the same: love.

At least that's what Jesus says. Now what do we say?

---

75 https://www.washingtonpost.com/opinions/one-final-election-plea-on-the-behalf-of-us-ideals/2016/11/03/4975a1c4-a1dd-11e6-a44d-cc2898cfab06_story.html

46

Opportunity

Watch and listen to "Opportunity" by following this link or scanning the QR code with your phone: youtu.be/GRR9-P4M5lo. Sermon begins at 36:05.

November 13, 2016
Twenty-sixth Sunday after Pentecost
Luke 21:5-19

This week, dear God, this week. *Now, George, are you talking about the election in our country or the election in our church?* Yes. Anxious times. Surprising turns. Bewildering feelings.

So here we are looking for a word from God again. And here I am again telling you that the way I choose a passage of Scripture to preach on is generally—like last week and this week—to accept what is chosen for me; that is, it's a text assigned in the lectionary for these Sundays in the church year. I didn't go looking for a text for our context. Apparently, the Holy Spirit has a sneaky way of pointing us to hope, wherever we look. This Sunday is no different.

I'll tip my hand to you about what that word will be by highlighting a few instructions from Jesus in the passage. Ready? *Don't be afraid.* Next: *Take this as an opportunity to testify.* Finally: *Hang on; you'll get through this because I will be with you.*

There now, we're done. Well, not quite yet. Let's see what's going on that would lead Jesus to tell us these things. We'll go back and forth between then and now.

Luke is writing in about AD 85, and he recounts the story of Jesus overhearing some people talking about the Temple in Jerusalem, about how beautiful it is. They figure that it will last forever. Jesus tells them not to count on it. As it turns out, of course, Jesus was right. About forty years later, in AD 70, the Temple was destroyed and, so they thought, was their world. They had always thought God lived in the Temple, and they'd been told by their Bible that only sacrifices made at the Temple in Jerusalem would be acceptable to God. Now there was no Temple. What now?

The rabbis led the Jews out of Jerusalem, and they wandered about for about twenty years trying to figure that out. They finally settled on a more portable religion that involved three things they could do anywhere and anytime: prayer, Torah (that is, Bible study), and acts of lovingkindness. Beautiful. Jews all over the world are still doing those things.

Christians remembered that Jesus had told them that he himself was the true temple where God and humanity came together. That would continue to be true forever, even after he died, because his resurrection meant that he could always be found in our every human interaction when we do what he commanded us by loving God and our neighbor as ourselves.

You see, we are always prone to think that our faith is tied to religious institutions, and sometimes to our buildings. Nothing lasts forever. Things change. Things fall apart. But we don't have to fall apart when things fall apart. Our faith is founded on the living Christ, and he won't ever fall apart because his broken body is eternally being remembered in his church as we come together literally and figuratively around his Table in sweet communion.

And that goes for us here at Wilshire too. Yes, we are going through a difficult time. It feels to some like impending doom as we look around at this lovely building, adorned by beautiful stones and built by sacrificial gifts from faithful members for more than sixty-five years, some of whom worry about its future. And yet the church is not a building. What we are building, as our mission statement says, is *a community of faith shaped by the Spirit of Jesus Christ*. And that will always be changing if we are faithful in our time. Gratitude for the past is proper, nostalgia not so much. Gratitude spawns hope; nostalgia fosters fear.

It's true that this disruption that many of us feel at this time is disorienting. But it's only the end of one way of being; it's not the end, as Jesus says. It may feel like an end, but the end is not yet. Jesus is Lord of his church, and in every end is a beginning. Jesus calls us to look for the new beginning, for what is coming to pass right in the very moment at which it feels as if something is passing away. He isn't finished with us yet.

And that includes our denominational entities. Baptist institutions are supposed to serve churches, not the other way 'round. They are supposed to protect, not undermine, Baptist principles such as religious liberty and local church autonomy, and to promote cooperation. When they fail in that mission, it is because they have decided to let worry and fear dictate their actions. Sad, but we have no control over that.

What about the nation? Jesus said that nations and kingdoms will fight against each other and that there will be great turmoil. And I think we can also say that within nations there will also be fighting. We are seeing that fact this week in the wake of our election. What we are told is that the election of Donald Trump to the presidency is an expression of antiestablishment sentiment. Our political dysfunction has betrayed many Americans, so many voted to try something different. Some think that this action was wise; others think it was unwise. But the point is that Jesus warned us against putting our faith in human orders that never last.

Keep this in mind, too: Since Jesus uttered these words, there has never been an extended time in history when people didn't think everything was falling apart. There have always been wars and rumors of wars. There have always been natural disasters and famines. And, yes, there have always been times when family members and friends were pitted against one another, even betrayed by one another—or at least feeling betrayed. This is the way of the world, people. It always has been, and it always will be, until the true end of all things comes, and the kingdoms of this world shall become the kingdom of Christ.

What does this truth mean for us today? It will mean the same as it meant in Jesus' day. Don't put your faith in politics. All politics is temporal. Only God's kingdom is eternal. And don't put your faith in politicians to be your messiah who will fix this mess, any more than you should put your faith in a preacher—present company included, don't you know?! Politics is something, but it isn't everything. The answers to our social and spiritual anxieties are not all with the state. When are we going to learn that?

On the threshold of the Cold War in 1952, Harry Emerson Fosdick, pastor of The Riverside Church in New York, was on the West Coast to speak to the Pacific School of Religion. After acknowledging the chaos and uncertainty of the time, he said these timeless words: *The highest use of a shaken time is to discover the unshakable.*

That is exactly what Jesus was saying in Luke 21 and is still saying to us now. Be still. Don't be terrified inside when things are terrifying outside. God is still God. And this is the moment when you can be a great witness.

I really hate it when I do research and find out that things I thought were so aren't so. Like the oft-repeated meme that there is one character in the Chinese language that stands at the same time for both crisis and opportunity. Sad to say, that isn't exactly true, although there's enough truth in it to extrapolate. But the idea that in every crisis is also an opportunity—that is true. And Jesus tells us that very thing right here.

In the face of shaken times for religious institutions, political culture, and the natural world, we have an opportunity to testify to the unshakable. Have we forgotten that testimony is our abiding privilege? We can do and say so much for Christ during these anxious times if we ourselves will not give in to anxiety because we are people of the living God.

I loved what Rabbi David Stern said this week in a letter to his congregation in the wake of the presidential election: *May we, who praise the God who upholds the falling and heals the sick, help bring healing to a nation sundered by toxic polemic. May we hold our ideals with deep commitment and daily humility. If we are to be stubborn, let us be stubborn about justice, compassion, and human dignity. If we are to be vocal, let us be vocal in the name of empathy and decency. If we are to be passionate, let us be passionate for the good of all.* Nice.

And then I quote from Russell Moore, the head of the Southern Baptist ethics agency, with whom I find myself surprisingly agreeing more often than you would guess. He also pointed to the church's role in these times as an opportunity to testify: *No matter what the racial and ethnic divisions in America, we can be churches that demonstrate and embody the reconciliation of the kingdom of God. After all, we are not just part of a coalition but part of a Body—a Body that is white and Black and Latino and Asian, male and female, rich and poor. We are part of a Body joined to a*

Head who is an Aramaic-speaking Middle-Easterner. What affects Black and Hispanic and Asian Christians ought to affect white Christians. And the sorts of poverty and social unraveling among the white working class ought to affect Black and Hispanic and Asian Christians. We belong to each other because we belong to Christ.

Can I get an amen?

So, what can we do? We can look for opportunities to testify. That testimony is first a witness that while others are flying off the handle in fear, we are holding fast in faith. We will not be afraid. Then we can testify by being the kind of church that embodies a witness of reconciliation in Christ. We can teach the world what it looks like to love across all our differences rather than pitting ourselves against each other.

But finally, we can take to the streets—not in unproductive protests of words that sometimes lead to violence, but in acts of lovingkindness that point the way to peace.

Our missions minister, Heather Mustain, posted a beautiful challenge to us on her Facebook page this week after the election. She quoted her aunt, who was disappointed in the election outcome but said: *If you are wondering what to do today, I suggest you grieve, yes, but also find something that needs to be done for someone else and do it.* Then Heather offered us these suggestions as opportunities to testify: *If you're worried about our children's education … then become a mentor with KidsHope or a reading tutor with Reading Partners. If you're worried about the lack of affordable healthcare … then become a volunteer with Healing Hands Medical and Dental Clinic or CitySquare's Health Clinic. If you're worried about the rights of women and girls … then become a HERO and champion with Genesis Women's Shelter. If you're worried about those who are hungry … then volunteer at White Rock Center of Hope's or the Wilkinson Center's food pantry or serve a meal at Cornerstone Kitchen or The Bridge. If you're worried about the status of refugees in the U.S. … then volunteer as an ESL teacher or throw a baby shower for Gateway of Grace. If you're worried about our criminal justice system … then volunteer as an executive with Prison Entrepreneurship Program and mentor a man into reaching his dreams. There's work to do, friends, and it's time to do something, to show up and to be present …*

Yes, it is. Our church's vision statement says it well: We aspire *to be a bold witness to the way of Christ in our time.*

Now is always the time.

47

Practice

Watch and listen to "Practice" by following this link or scanning the QR code with your phone: youtu.be/UAOK8fVIY1M. Sermon begins at 34:50.

November 20, 2016
Thanksgiving Sunday
Philippians 4:4-9

There's a new craze hitting social media called the mannequin challenge. Here's the idea: You get a group of friends or teammates or coworkers together and strike a pose that looks like you were caught in the act of doing something. Then make a short video clip of it, as if time has stopped. We could do it here. Catching Doug, say, in the act of singing or me preaching or an usher ushering, say. It's fun to see what people come up with.

What makes this interesting is the idea of still life, since life isn't lived like that. If you took a freeze frame of any particular moment in time in our lives, it wouldn't tell the whole story as much as a full-length film. Snapshots tell you something but not everything. They miss the flow of what came before and what comes after. And no one life is properly judged by a mannequin moment.

Take the church at Philippi, for instance. Overall, Paul seems to have loved that church. They supported him financially when others didn't. They prayed for him and honored him when other churches questioned his authority. And yet, in the mannequin moment we catch him writing to them, they are going through something challenging, and he has some words for them.

Seems there were these two women who couldn't get along. Go figure. We don't know anything about Euodia and Syntyche except that they were troubling the fellowship for reasons we also don't know, don't you know?! So, in the verses just before these, Paul tells them to get their act together and get together. And then he tells the church how to get its act together. These verses are filled with imperatives about what to do in order for the God of peace to reign in the congregation.

Last Sunday our church completed its voting on the question of whether all members of our church should be entitled to the same rights and responsibilities in Christ as every other member, regardless of sexual orientation or gender identity.

The answer was yes, but it was not, by a long shot, a strong consensus. Euodia and Syntyche still disagree. And the question is whether we're going to turn this into a mannequin moment and hold the pose forever, or, let go of the tension and relax into a new rhythm of life together.

Change is hard and it's painful. It always requires giving up something familiar. That's actually true for those who welcome the change as well as for those who resist it.

Those who resist the change have held a view that the way things have been is the way things should be from now until kingdom come. They feel a sense of loss and judgment upon them because they participated in the resistance movement to the change movement. They wonder if they will have a place in the new order, or whether they even want a place. Those who welcome the change have something to give up, too. For a long time, LGBTQ Christians have had to make themselves invisible in order not to be singled out. They have found ways to fit in, even as they have internalized a sense of being marginalized. Now they have to learn a whole new mode of being among us, and it's not like flipping a switch. They have to learn to trust us, to be open and honest among us, and they have to let go of the resentment that lived in their hearts for too long. So, can we find each other and live together in a new way now that reflects the way of Christ? Can we be OneWilshire?

There are people here this morning for the first time who want to know the answer to that before they move into relationship with us or stay away. There are people here this morning for the thousand and first time who want to know the answer to that before they stay in relationship with us or move away. Look around. Every person you see in this room is someone God loves as much as you that Christ died for them, too. They are your sisters and brothers, and they need to know you know that as much as you need to know they know that about you.

I want to remind all of you that we were not a perfect church at any time in the past, and we will not be a perfect church at any time in the future. We are all only imperfect people striving toward a greater sense of unity with Christ and one another. Our mission statement is constantly on my lips in these days: *The Wilshire mission is to build a community of faith shaped by the Spirit of Jesus Christ.* If we are forever building it, that means we are never finished with it.

This reminds me of one of the most curious lines in the preamble to the Constitution of the United States of America. The authors included this oddly phrased justification for the constitution: *We the people of the United States, in order to form a more perfect union,* etc., etc. I always smile when I think of that phrase *more perfect union.* Can perfect have a modifier? Isn't it like the word unique? Something either is unique or isn't, but it can't be really unique or sort of unique. And something is either perfect or it isn't. But I still like the phrase, because I think our founders were saying something about this project that is America. The previous union we had established under the Articles of Confederation wasn't yet quite right. By establishing the Constitution, the people were working to perfect a union that would never be perfect. And when President Obama was a candidate in 2008 and needed to address questions about race in the campaign, he called his speech *A More*

Perfect Union. Slavery is our original sin, and racism is its legacy. Owning up to our sin and making racial justice a reality is a work in progress. Our country is a project we are working to perfect. And the church is no different.

So, what shall we do? The first thing Paul says is to *rejoice in the Lord.* Actually, that's the first and second thing he says: *and again I say, rejoice.* It's like he knows we aren't given to rejoicing in moments of conflict and change. But notice, he doesn't say get happy even if you aren't. He says to rejoice *in the Lord.*

Look, if you favored our decision, you may be elated today, but I would urge you to do so *in the Lord,* which is never at the expense of your sisters and brothers. I truly believe God is doing a new thing among us that honors the gospel and will prove to be a witness of grace that will save lives and souls both. But Paul immediately after this says: *Let your gentleness be made known to all; the Lord is near.* That word gentleness may also be translated forbearance. Which means that we will hold off dancing in someone else's end zone as an act of Christian grace. On the other side, those of you who feel like you lost something in all of this are also told to rejoice in the Lord. You don't have to be happy about an outcome you opposed, but you can rejoice for those who are rejoicing in it. That may seem unnatural to you, but hey, that's what rejoicing *in the Lord* is about; it's a spiritual response, not a natural one. Nobody said it's supposed to be easy, this Christian thing.

Then Paul tells us *not to worry about anything,* but instead to *pray with thanksgiving.* In other words, we are to give all this to God to sort out. We've got to give up the illusion of control. And that requires practicing gratitude rather than complaint.

I tell couples I am counseling about marriage that there will be things about their partner that will annoy them. They have a choice about what they do with that: They can either focus on the annoyance, in which case the distance between them will grow until their hearts are cold and brittle; or they can pray with thanksgiving for their partner. I don't mean pray that God take away the annoyance, because then you're still focusing on that. I mean pray with thanksgiving for all the things you love about your partner. And when you do, it will change the way you see him or her.

And that plays right into what comes next. Paul says, *whatever is true and honorable and just and commendable and excellent and worthy of praise, think on these things.* Ponder the good. Meditate on the noble. Contemplate the virtues. We could all do with more of that right now.

Right now, in the wake of the election, some people are protesting in the streets, too many are yelling screeds at one another, and still others are taking moral license to push vulnerable people more into places of fear. We can do better.

I was reading the incredible words of Dean Acheson this week from back in 1952 when Adlai Stevenson lost the presidential election to Dwight Eisenhower. Acheson had been secretary of state under Harry Truman, and the Democrats had had a long run in power with FDR and Truman covering twenty years. He talked about how change is a normal part of life, even political change, and I would say spiritual, too. He then said: *From this moment you should not go on fighting battles that have been lost ... Do what nature requires, that is to have a fallow period. Just let the field of your emotions stay barren, let new seeds germinate ... Have different activities; think of something else. Don't read* The New York Times *from cover to cover every day.* And I would add, don't let cable news and social media run your day or it will ruin your day. I think that should go for all parties right now.[76]

Have different activities, he said. And think of something else.

Father Joshua Whitfield of St. Rita's Catholic Church writes an occasional column for *The Dallas Morning News.* He wrote yesterday about taking his daughter to an art museum as a way of dealing with his post-election emotions. They took their time and looked at the works of Spanish artists like Miro and Picasso and Dali. They giggled at the nudes, and they tried at times in vain to figure out what this one or that meant. They just let the beauty take over their hearts for a while. *He said: I was there because of her and because of this new sadness. Many parents have wondered just what to tell their children; I chose art. Again, I didn't know what else to do. I could only think to find beauty and to be quiet there.*[77]

That's a good place to start: focusing on things that are good, true and beautiful. Let them nourish our souls right now as we find our balance again and walk into this future together.

Paul ends by saying that we must do these things. Another way to translate do is keep on doing. It's not a one-time thing. Not a mannequin moment. And another translation puts it this way: Keep on practicing these things.

Lawyers practice. Doctors practice. Christians practice. We don't practice because practice makes perfect; we practice because practice makes more perfect. As in a more perfect union. As in a more perfect church.

This week has been an emotional whiplash for many of us. High highs and low lows. Our hearts have soared, and our stomachs soured. But there's a promise tagged onto that call to keep on practicing these things: And the God of peace will be with us.

As we close today, let's practice that peace by passing it to one another as we typically do on Communion Sundays. And let's see if we can sense that the God of peace is among us.

---

76 https://www.washingtonpost.com/opinions/how-can-democrats-deal-with-losing-heres-what-trumans-secretary-of-state-said-in-1952/2016/11/18/9ab2bde4-acfd-11e6-977a-1030f822fc35_story.html

77 http://www.dallasnews.com/opinion/commentary/2016/11/16/took-daughter-art-museum-election

PART VII

Thanks Be to God

Stewardship

*"I would maintain that thanks are the highest form of thought;
and that gratitude is happiness doubled by wonder."*

~ G.K. Chesterton

Preface by David King

Most preachers dread talking about money. Thankfully for us, George Mason is not most preachers. He regularly addresses the topic in his sermons because the power money often holds over us is too strong to avoid. Avoiding the topic because it makes a preacher uncomfortable is nothing less than pastoral malpractice.

The sermons that follow address questions of stewardship with not only clarity about the consuming role money can play in our lives but also with an invitation to see a new way forward that is nothing like a fundraising pitch. With his ever-present but gentle nudge, George challenges us to take a step toward living lives of both generosity and gratitude. These two virtues go hand in hand, don't you know?!, and as virtues, generosity and gratitude are also essential practices to a life of faith. They are not a spiritual gift that we either have or do not. They are spiritual practices that take time, effort, and a community around us to nurture and develop.

As George highlights in the first sermon in this section, "being thankful often requires us to be thinkful." Gratitude does not simply happen. It is an intentional activity. Over decades of coming alongside a congregation from the same pulpit, George's preaching has been a regular reminder of how often we have to make a conscious choice to work toward practicing generosity and gratitude in our daily lives. For as George notes in the sermons that follow, gratitude and generosity are not simply attainable or required after one reaches a certain level of spiritual maturity as a duty or obligation, but rather they are necessary practices that allow for faith to grow and take root. They may not be easy, but they are intertwined in any honest journey of faith. Generosity is not the result of a mature faith. Gaining perspective on the proper place of possessions in our lives as well as learning how to both give and receive are core aspects of gospel living.

George also notes that not only are these practices difficult in our current world, but we cannot assume that they will naturally develop without attention and intentional effort. There's no setting autopilot for such virtues. In fact, our natural tendency in the busyness of life to set things on autopilot with little opportunity or margin for reflection may be one of the most difficult barriers to generosity. Breaking up the monotony of life and opening up our imaginations to see the world afresh is the gift that George's preaching has offered so many each and every week. Through literature, art, music, or simply stopping to attend to a story from our daily, ordinary lives, he offers us a new angle to see the world. Making space to breathe, refocus, and reflect on our lives is necessary to cultivate the virtues of gratitude and generosity that a life of faith requires. George's preaching gives us opportunities to find that space and gives us footholds to journey on without giving us any false hope that the road is an easy one.

Sometimes, in order to avoid talking about touchy subjects like money, preachers attempt to address stewardship and the virtues of gratitude and generosity by focusing on abstractions and feel-good stories to avoid particularities and the difficult work that these faith practices require. That is another temptation George avoids. He does not flinch from making the story personal—addressing the issue within his own personal and family life, and inviting us to do the same. He challenges us to make choices: Are we going to tithe off the firstfruits, change our habits of consumption, or live our lives in certain ways that free up resources to invest in the kingdom? At the same time, in a world where religious language like "tithe" is less and less understood by those in our pews, George illustrates the biblical tradition through approachable stories. While many people want to criticize the church as "always talking about money," most of us crave practical wisdom on how to live in the midst of consumerism, caring for one another, and teaching our children how to live responsibly. George models the many ways pastors must address our relationship with money and "stuff" for those of us who've heard too many stewardship sermons and those who have never heard of Christian stewardship, much less a pledge card or congregational capital campaign.

At the same time, while we cannot avoid talking about money, George knows a theology of stewardship is not just about money. We are also stewards of traditions, communities, and institutions of which we are a part. He challenges all of us to realize that this is our job as members of a faith community, and it must not just be the job of the religious "professionals." How do we acknowledge the saints who have gone before us and are still with us by building upon the foundations they have left us even as we seek to address the current context in which we find ourselves? This too is the work of stewardship. Again, this journey toward practicing gratitude and generosity leads to a transformation not only of us as individuals but also of our institutions, as we work toward justice and wholeness in the communities to which we belong.

The stewardship sermons that follow are invitations to a new way of living around some of the most difficult, practical concerns that keep us from a deeper life of faith. They address us as individuals and families, in our work and in our church, locally and in our visions of the larger world around us. With the wisdom of a seasoned pastor and preacher, George models the honesty and imagination necessary to address topics like stewardship in ways that cause us all to stop, listen, and maybe even make changes in the way we live.

David P. King is the Karen Lake Buttrey Director of the Lake Institute on Faith & Giving and Associate Professor of Philanthropic Studies at Indiana University Lilly Family School of Philanthropy. He is the author of God's Internationalists: World Vision and the Age of Evangelical Humanitarianism.

48

Being Thinkful

November 22, 1992
Christ the King Sunday
Deuteronomy 26:1-11; Philippians 4:4-9

There they were, all gathered round the turkey, in their best pilgrim dressing, ready to dig in. Father tucked his napkin in tight and folded his hands in pious preparation. The family took the cue and bowed their heads.

"We thank thee, O Lord, for these bountiful blessings. Make us to be duly grateful for thy provision. Amen."

A few minutes later the father and Uncle Bill started talking about how the world was going, about those "Gomers" in Washington, about how far behind last year's sales the father's company was, about how dry the white meat was and how watery the gravy.

Suddenly, the father's daughter spoke up. "Daddy, do you think God heard what you said a little while ago when you prayed?"

"Certainly," the dad replied with confidence.

"And do you think God heard what you said about the meat and gravy and all that other stuff?" "Probably so," he said, this time not so confidently.

"Then which did God believe?" [78]

The question of the day is, *How thankful are you this Thanksgiving season?* If we listened closely to your talk, would we believe that you are truly thankful? If God were listening closely, would God believe it?

So, what shall we do? Well, some people figure there's nothing to be done. After all, they argue, either you feel grateful or you don't. Either you are joyful or you aren't. You can't force these things. If times are bad and you have no reason to feel grateful, this is just a season of life that you have to go with.

---

78 Adapted from David Chancey, "A Life of Thanksgiving," *Preaching* (Nov-Dec 1992): 10.

But notice in our texts this morning—one from that older testament and one from the newer—that God does not ask you to sit around until the joy just bubbles up naturally before you are thankful. In Deuteronomy, the people are commanded to perform ritual acts of giving of the first fruits of their harvest to God, no matter whether the harvest looks hearty or not. In fact, since it is the first fruits, they wouldn't even know for sure how great the harvest would be. But that is apparently irrelevant to God's insistence that the people learn to be grateful. They are commanded to celebrate, instructed to rejoice.

That is just what that apparently Pollyannish Apostle Paul says to the Philippians when he says, *Rejoice in the Lord always, and again I say rejoice.* It is not a conditional suggestion but a determined decision to be made. "Be thankful!" is what he says, implying that we have a choice.

But we only choose when we have left that region of the emotions that operates on autopilot and ascend to that region of the mind which can see that things like our attitude about life does not have to be what it feels it is. In other words, being thankful often requires being thinkful! And would you believe that when you do a little lexiconical research, you find that the English word for "thank" comes from the same stem in the Old Anglo Saxon as the word "think." Thus, a spirit of thankfulness grows out of a practice of thinkfulness.

The first tip toward thankfulness for those of you who are having trouble with pilgrim pride this November is to think about what is yours, not about what is not yours.

The apostle says to rejoice always, and in everything to give thanks. Now let us wisely stipulate that Paul does not say that we are to rejoice *about* everything. Who among us is going to grit her teeth and be grateful for the day the telegram came with the news of her son's loss on the jungle battlefield of Vietnam? Or who would be callous enough to suggest that a man is to somehow by act of spiritual will interpret the tragedy of his wife's cancer as some hidden good yet to be revealed. God may be at work to help us become our best possible selves even out of the worst possible circumstances, but we are not to call evil good.

Instead, the apostle points us to something deeper—the determination to see all of life in a given moment, not just the part that most accosts us. In the midst of life we sometimes lose perspective about how things really are. Our natural inclination is to look at life from the point of view of deprivation rather than provision. Which is just a fancy way of saying that we have a "knack for lack," don't you know?!

This was true in the Garden of Eden, and it is true for us. Instead of seeing how much we have, we focus on forbidden fruit. We become preoccupied with it and feel ourselves somehow lacking unless we have it. Consumerism is bent on this false view. Advertisers try to convince us that we are deprived until we acquire this product or that. They seek to make us seek what we have not, for for them to cultivate in us an attitude of gratitude for what we already have is not profitable.

As a society, we are like Cinderella saying to the fairy godmother, "How is it that I must leave the ball at twelve?" Her godmother might answer, "How is it that you are going there till twelve?"[79]

Our lust for more and our disdain for life within limits creates in us a growing inability to be thankful. Since we're on lust, I'll do my Jimmy Carter impersonation and confess how I catch myself at times longing for what is not mine instead of what is. Read between the lines. But we married men (I think this is true for married women, too!) must think about what is, not about what is not. If you believe Madonna, the idea of marriage and sexual integrity only gets in the way of your human right to experience the limitless possibilities of your eroticism.

But in our lust for what we lack, we are drawn away from the extraordinary privilege of what is ours. When I awake from being intoxicated by our culture's bombarding of the senses, I am caused to wonder at the wonder of why one, even one, should love me like she does. This is not my right, this is my privilege; that Kim should love me like she does. To be ungrateful because thirty-seven nymphs of desire are not mine, too, is an unthinkable deception.

Besides, people who are dragged along by their lust for what is not theirs soon learn the awful truth of what Frederick Buechner has said: *Lust is the craving for salt of a man who is dying of thirst.*[80] We seek just what deprives us more.

The answer is first to think and then to thank. Like the man who called a real estate agent because he wanted to list his house for sale. He said he was feeling tired of his house and wanted a new one. The agent asked him to describe the house so that an ad could be placed. The man told about the new carpet, the recently replaced roof, the great yard, and the fruit trees. The agent wrote up the ad and called the man back to read it to him. About halfway through, the homeowner interrupted the agent. *You know, all my life I've wanted a house just like this. It was just now, listening to you describe it, that I realized how lucky I am to have this house. I've changed my mind; I'm not selling.*[81]

What about you today? Have you taken the time to ask yourself about what you have? The first step to thankfulness is thinkfulness about what is.

But that does not mean that you should become lax about your idealism. Certainly the pilgrims who made it through that first winter were not saying in their thanksgiving celebration that they should be content *with* the world as it was. They were only saying that they were content *in* the world as it was. And there is a difference.

When Paul says at first that we are to rejoice in all things and be thankful, he immediately says that we are also to pray, to make requests of God. Now why would you make requests of God if you are supposed to be simply thankful for what you have and not ask for something more? No, God asks us to do two things at once: to be thankful for what is, but to seek its improvement, too. And these are not two contradictory things.

79 G. K. Chesterton, *Orthodoxy*, (Image Books), p. 57.
80 *Wishful Thinking* (Harper & Row, 1972), q.v. "lust."
81 Chane Hutton, "A Holiday for Every Day," in *Dynamic Preaching* (Nov 1992): 43.

Consider my love for my daughter Cameron, who was just baptized this morning. I love her unconditionally, but I do not accept that my love should thereby make me think her totally accomplished as a person. No, I love her enough to want her to grow and to change, to want her to rely upon the gospel as a sure guide to her becoming her best self. I assume that none of us is perfect, that we all have work to do in kicking the worst of Adam and Eve out of the Garden of our souls.

Chesterton rightly says that *a man's friend likes him but leaves him as he is: his wife loves him and is always trying to turn him into somebody else … Love is not blind; … Love is bound; and the more it is bound the less it is blind.*[82] Obviously, we can become controlling and manipulative, never satisfied enough with our partner that it becomes sinful and ungodly. But all that shows is that we do not love truly. To love someone truly is to want to be a partner in that person's salvation, in helping that person become his or her best self.

This is why Christianity has been accused both of being too optimistic about the universe and too pessimistic about the world.[83] We are not afraid of paradoxes. We understand that "This Is My Father's World" on the one hand, and that this world has gone awry on the other. So, we cling to it and love it, and we seek its betterment, too.

This attitude is based on God's attitude toward us. God so loved us that God sent Jesus to die for our sins. God didn't wait to love us until we were more loveable. But then God doesn't leave us to ourselves as though we have already become all we can be.

I feel that way about you. Sometimes you may think, especially at stewardship time, that all I see in you is inadequacy and lack. But I want you to understand truly that what words of prophetic challenge I utter grow not from the heart of one who is waiting for you to change so that I can love you and be grateful that I am your pastor, but from the heart of one who loves you first and last, and because of that wants you to become your best self before God. I know that the grass is not greener under the next steeple. I am happy to nibble upon God's graces with you in this pasture. But that doesn't mean that we have arrived at the end of what it means to be the sheep of God's flock.

So, being thankful involves both being thinkful about what is and being thinkful, too, about what can be. Finally, being thankful grows out of a disciplined thinkfulness about what is good and true and beautiful.

This long list Paul gives, telling us to think about virtue, not vice, is intended to help us bridge the chasm between what is and what can be. Thinking about what is true and honorable and just and pure and pleasing and commendable and excellent and worthy of praise produces in us the character that is needed to live faithfully and thankfully in a world caught between the second and third chapters of Genesis, between creation and the Fall.

---

82 *Orthodoxy*, p. 71.
83 Also Chesterton.

When we do such things, when we consistently pursue such thoughts, God's peace is ours. This peace is God's gift that allows us to sing amid our grief and dance in the darkness.

Martin Rinkart was a German Lutheran pastor in the seventeenth century during one of the darkest periods in Europe's religious history. The Thirty Years War between Catholics and Protestants had devastated the continent. Rinkart's own village had been sacked three times. This man was responsible for about 4,500 burials in the year 1637 alone; some days as many as fifty! Others were poverty stricken and holding on for dear life. His sadness drove him to his knees in prayer. And when he arose, he had found the peace of God to pen our closing hymn.

Now thank we all our God / With heart and hands and voices / Who wondrous things hath done / In whom his world rejoices / Who from our mothers' arms hath blest us on our way / With countless gifts of love / And still is ours today.

Let's sing it together as a first act of thankfulness this Thanksgiving season.

49

Giving Thanks: It's More Than the Thought That Counts

November 22, 1998
Christ the King Sunday
Luke 17:11-19

Baron and Susan Hamman took along their two-year-old son Jack on a retreat for physicians and health professionals at DeGray Lake in Arkansas' Ouachita Mountains. On Saturday morning, little Jack—usually a sound sleeper and therefore a blessing to his parents—was up early. Baron got up with Jack, thoughtfully giving his wife the gift of sleeping in one day. Something Kim would tell you I do at least once a year. Key to a good marriage. Anyway, father and son headed for coffee and donuts before daybreak, and on their way something of biblical proportion happened.

What's that? asked Jack.

That's the sunrise, his dad replied.

Does it happen every day?

Every day.

Wow! [84]

We celebrate Thanksgiving once a year, I think, to remind us that sunrises deserve a "Wow." The older we get, the more sunrises we take for granted. And the more sunrises we take for granted, the more easily we lose our "Wow." Thanksgiving teaches us to practice our "Wow." It makes us *think* about sunrises and all other gifts we take for granted, but more so it bids us go beyond the thought to *give* thanks. Thanks to God, I mean.

Gratitude is the attitude necessary for faith to get hold of your heart. I think we see that in the story of the cleansing of the ten lepers. Jesus is going along to Jerusalem through a territory where you would find Jews comingled with Samaritans and Gentiles. In the social pecking order of Jesus' day, Samaritans fell below Jews, and then came Gentiles, women, and wild boars, in that order.

---

84 Thanks to Bobby Guffey, per email.

Reminds me of the Southern world of Mrs. Turpin in Flannery O'Connor's short story *Revelation*. She liked to keep the classes straight: most colored folk on the bottom, followed by white trash next, then homeowners, then home and land owners, then people with a lot of money and a lot of land. Of course, the problem was that people kept messing up their places. Like the colored dentist, for instance. Or people with money that acted like white trash anyway. It all gets so confusing.

Well, when you add leprosy to any of the classes in Jesus' day, you go right to the bottom and start over in the sub-classes. You had to even leave town, live outside the city gates so as not to contaminate others. Lepers found out they were brothers and sisters after all, whether they liked it or not. Leprosy didn't discriminate. So notice, when the ten lepers come to Jesus, there is no mention of any differences between them. It is only when they are healed that the differences resurface. Then we find out that the nine are presumably Jews and the one who returned, a Samaritan.

Before that, they were united in their misery. And perhaps in their unbelief. Suffering, especially unjust suffering, has a way of making atheists out of us. We wonder why God could allow such a thing as this or that to happen to us. If God even exists. Such a thing as atheism is more a modern possibility than ancient though. The lepers were more likely filled with resentment and despair, doubting whether God loved and cared for them.

And this is one of the biggest obstacles to thanksgiving. We allow ourselves to be overcome by the chaos in our lives, by the presence of evil or unjust suffering. *Why is there so much evil?* is a good question. But it isn't the only question. *Why did I get leprosy?* is a question not impious for ten lepers to ask. But there is another question we ask too seldom. *Why should I exist at all to have the opportunity to ask it?* When we *look at life from both sides now* (thank you Judy Collins), we have to look at why we are so blessed with sunrises to begin with. In a world in which so much bad takes place, why so much good? Why are any lepers healed? Why does someone like my wife love me as she does? Why do I get to enjoy the children who bear my name and even some faint resemblance to me (the girls mostly to Kim, praise Jesus)?

G. K. Chesterton once mused, *We thank people for birthday presents of cigars and slippers. Can I thank no one for the birthday present of birth?*[85] We ought to be thankful for so much, but especially for life itself. But there is a difference between wow and worship. You don't need a God to thank in order to celebrate your good fortune. But when you perceive that your good fortune is not just luck but a gift, then you must thank the giver.

And just this is what we learn from the one leper who returned to give thanks to God for his healing. Jesus told the men to go show themselves to the priests, and upon their obedience they were healed. They acted in hope, maybe desperation, and God made them well. God made all of them well, even though only one returned out of gratitude. You see, God doesn't wait to see if we are grateful before saving us, making us whole, cleansing our sins, or blessing us. Yet we need to give thanks in order to experience the joy of God with us and in us. The nine who didn't return were surely thankful that they were cleansed. But what are thanks if you don't have

85 *Orthodoxy in Collected Works* (Ignatius Press): 1:258.

anyone to thank? They are merely self-satisfied and on their way back to being self-actualized, as Maslow would say. But the one leper leaps and bounds back to Jesus. He goes to him, uses his feet, not just his mind. He falls on his face; he doesn't just acknowledge the gift mentally. He uses his voice and cries out to God in loud sounds of praise.

Giving thanks is more than just *being thankful.* It discloses the heart and closes the loop between the generosity of the giver and the gratitude of the receiver. Have you ever given a gift to someone who didn't acknowledge it? I fear to say I have probably been on the other side of that equation more often. But it takes something of the fun out of it for the receiver not to celebrate with the giver. And I think that's true for God, too.

Now you know the old saying, *Never mind a gift, it's the thought that counts.* I have always thought that a nice sentiment for everyone else's birthday. I was a real baby on my birthday this year. Kim and the kids kind of let it pass without much of a fuss. Now I know they love and appreciate me. But they didn't pay much attention to how to tell me. So, I moped about it and made them feel guilty, until Kim reminded me what we did for her birthday.

About the same. End of moping. Beginning of apologies. The real key to a good marriage, don't you know?! But the point is that a gift has a way of expressing your thoughts. It's not the thing in itself, it's that the gift is an expression of the thoughts. And without it, who's to know?

I have been in a quandary over what to do for some friends who married recently. Older couple. Grandparents both. Widowed each. Second marriage for the two of them. They don't need a thing. Got too much stuff between them anyway. So they insisted on no gifts. I know I can write a letter or send a card, but I feel kind of limited and constricted by that.

I am wondering, in your relationship with God, do you feel somehow limited by God in how to express your gratitude? Listen, I don't think God's done the limiting!

If all you were allowed to use in order to give God thanks were thoughts, how would you do it? Prayer and meditation maybe. If all you had were words, how would you say thanks? Poetry? A journal? Go out under the sky and yell "Wow!"? If all you had were your legs, would you run to Jesus and fall on your face? Would you dance? Skip? If all you had were hands, how? Applause? (Not in church please. Can't get too excited here.) Would you raise them up toward heaven? Maybe the charismatics have something here.

Now to the question you knew was coming? What if all you had to use to show God your gratitude for saving you and loving you and blessing you was your money? What would you do?

Oh, God doesn't need my money. God has all the money God needs. Besides, God knows how I feel. God knows my heart and my thoughts. And anyway, didn't God give me the money in the first place? Hmmmm. Sounds like nine-leper logic to me.

But honestly, I have seen and heard during this capital stewardship campaign 'round here the past few weeks much more one-leper logic prevailing. Some amazing things have been happening in people's lives. I have listened to some who have become aware for the first time of their need to give thanks. I have seen tears stream down their cheeks as they have counted their blessings instead of protecting their claims. Many have decided that one important way they can thank God is with the first fruits of their increase, as the Bible puts it. That is, by returning a tithe (10% of their income) to the Lord's work.

I have heard people say they were going to take a second mortgage on their home because they wanted to give more to the Building on Faith campaign, but they had so little in the way of cash reserves. Others are refinancing their homes at lower interest rates and giving the savings. Some are postponing major purchases like furniture for the house or new cars; others are making smaller adjustments in lifestyle to free up money. One person is forgoing a trip she longed to take, giving the value of the trip instead and waiting on God to see if another way opens for her to go later. An older gentleman on a limited fixed income who already gives beyond the tithe to the church and elsewhere, is planning to give ten dollars per month additional to the campaign, because he will not allow himself to miss the chance to be a part of it. I told him he is already doing more than God calls for, and he told me he doesn't want to sit in pews he had no part in paying for.

I honestly don't know when I have been prouder of a church, or when I have been so honored to be among such people. During an effort to raise funds, this church has determined to raise stewards. During a capital campaign, we have engaged in a prayer campaign. During a time when people generally cringe at all the subtle forms of manipulation that go on to get people's money, this church has willingly given thanks to God, fallen at the feet of Jesus, and acted the part of people who know the wonder of their salvation.

I am awed. And with you, I am going to use my thoughts, my words, my voice, my legs, my hands, and my money to give thanks to the Giver of all good gifts.

50

Money Matters

Watch and listen to "Money Matters" by following this link or scanning the QR code with your phone: youtu.be/RqUqryni_a4.

October 14, 2018
Twenty-first Sunday after Pentecost
Mark 10:17-31

The older I get, the more I look at my savings and wonder whether my money is going to last until I die. Anyone else? This wasn't a good week for that, what with the Dow dropping 1,300 points in two days. But we think we deserve it when the market goes up, and somehow we don't deserve it when it goes down. Keep in mind that the market has still risen nearly 6,000 points in the last two years! Money matters to us. Too much so, much of the time.

Money matters aren't only on the minds of people of advanced age, though. At every age, we worry about money, making it, saving it, spending it, and giving it. Judging by most of our stewardship records, maybe not so much the giving of it. And that's always been the problem for us humans: We're programmed consumers.

When I say programmed, I mean that we're wired in our DNA for that. Kim and I have been reading this book by Yuval Noah Harari titled *Sapiens: A Brief History of Humankind*. Kim came running in to tell me that it's not her fault, after all; it's out of her control. See, my ageless wife has a sweet tooth. She can binge on a whole package of cookies, and the worst part about it is that you can't tell. Not fair, I tell you. Forget the problem of evil—I want to know the secret of metabolism.

Anyway, here's her favorite passage in the book: *If a Stone Age woman came across a tree groaning with figs, the most sensible thing to do would be to eat as many of them as she could on the spot, before the local baboon band picked the tree bare. The instinct to gorge on high-calorie food was hard-wired into our genes. Today we may be living in high-rise apartments with over-stuffed refrigerators, but our DNAs still think we are in the savannah. That's what makes some of us spoon down an entire tub of Ben & Jerry's when we find one in the freezer, and then we wash it down with a jumbo Coke.*[86] See, it's not her fault.

---

86 Harper-Perennial, 2005, p. 41.

But here's the thing: God has been driving our human consciousness to the point that we don't have to be driven by our genes. We can recognize the impulses within us for self-indulgence and for saving ourselves, but we can choose to transcend them to fulfill a higher purpose.

This idea brings us to our text today. A certain man runs up to Jesus and kneels before him, asking him what he can do to inherit eternal life. It's a question we all should be asking, of course, but it's the kind of question we ask after we've gorged ourselves on figs, saved enough for the baboons, and have a little time on our hands while our bellies get to work on digestion.

Wealth allows us freedom from want so that we can think about things like the meaning of life. This is why so many of us come to midlife and begin to wrestle with the shift from success to significance. We realize that when success is measured only in terms of what we have, we will never have enough.

Jesus focuses on the question and offers a very un-Baptist kind of answer. He talks about obeying the law, keeping the commandments. That sounds a lot like works over grace, but don't jump to that conclusion too soon. The Law of Moses was meant to teach us what leads to a good life. And notice that Jesus lists only those commandments on the back end of the Big Ten that deal with the way we treat our neighbors. Jesus is making the way we treat other people a part of whether we inherit eternal life.

The man must be relieved by Jesus' answer, since he replies that he has done all these things perfectly since his youth. There's no need to ask forgiveness, in other words, if we've never done anything wrong. But mostly, I think, the man kept the commandments by keeping away from his neighbors, not by moving toward them. This is a typical Jesus trap. *One thing you lack,* he says to the man lovingly: *Go, sell what you own, and give the money to the poor, and you will have treasure in heaven; then, come, follow me.*

So, what should we make of what Jesus told this man? One strategy would be to blunt its impact on us by telling ourselves that this man was a hard case, unlike the rest of us. He obviously had such a problem with greed that he couldn't be generous. He probably wasn't even a tither at the Temple. But Jesus didn't tell him to go sell 10% of his holdings and give that amount to the unified budget. He told him to sell all he had and give the proceeds to the poor.

Selling all he had may have been the only answer for this man. He should not be advised to cut down to one fifth of whiskey per day instead of two. He should be told to cut out the whiskey altogether and start attending AA, where he will be in touch with other poor souls with the same problem.

Church is something like a rehab program for greedy would-be followers of Christ. We help each other learn how to let go of our wealth by giving, so that we can truly follow Christ. We need each other to help us believe we're going to be all right if we don't gorge on our figs and save them away in our 401(k) pantries.

One possible objection to Jesus' counsel is that he wants the man to give his money to the poor. I can't imagine they thought much differently back then than we do today about the poor. This action would be irresponsible, for we would be rewarding the poor for their irresponsibility. Imagine what they would do with our money. They would waste it in no time.

But would they? There's plenty of evidence that the poor are poor because they don't have enough money, not that they don't have enough money because they are poor. Studies show that if the poor are given enough money to do with as they please, they will make good decisions, just as those who have more than they.

Jesus is trying to teach us all something about what being rich and poor means, and how all that is related to what we all really want—which is what the man really wanted when he asked Jesus about eternal life. Barbara Brown Taylor puts it rightly, I think: *You have to be free to receive the gift of eternal life. You cannot be otherwise engaged. You cannot be tied up right now, or too tied down to respond. You cannot accept God's gift if you have no spare hands to take it with. You cannot make room for it if all your rooms are already full. You cannot follow if you are not free to go ... The rich young man walked away, sad about the invitation to have eternal life, because he could not believe that the opposite of being rich might not be [to be] poor, but free.*[87]

I heard about an expert in diamonds who happened to be seated on an airplane beside a woman with a huge diamond. The man introduced himself to her and said, "I couldn't help but notice your beautiful diamond. I am an expert in precious stones. Please tell me about that stone." She replied, "That is the famous Klopman diamond, one of the largest in the world. But there is a strange curse that comes with it." Now the man was really interested. He asked, "What is the curse?" As he waited with bated breath, she replied, "It's Mr. Klopman."

Before we can be free to experience the gift of eternal life that God wants to give us, we have to break the power our possessions have to possess us. Too many of us end by making decisions about our lives based on how to preserve our stuff, which means that our stuff rules us, instead of the other way 'round.

The only antidote for that, the only way to break the curse, so to speak, is to give. Generosity breaks the curse of greed. And the degree to which you give is the degree to which you will experience eternal life on both sides of the grave.

But giving to the poor is another way of saying that God wants us to be in relationship with the poor. This is another action the church helps us do. Most of us spend time and effort to make friends with the rich and avoid the poor. But since eternal life is a fellowship of the poor, we have to start now putting ourselves into proximity with the pain of the world. Those of us who can choose our relationships are called on to live in solidarity and friendship with the poor—not just to be charitable toward the poor, but to join the poor ourselves by learning to depend upon God. The church has a greater range of people across the economic spectrum than most of our neighborhoods. But then we are called to go out and create bonds of life in our community, too.

The Urban Institute has done a recent study on all the major cities in America about how the economic recovery has been shared. Unfortunately, it turns out that

---

87 *The Preaching Life*, (Roman & Littlefield), p. 131.

Dallas ranks 274 out of 274 in the sharing of prosperity across racial and economic lines. We have work to do.[88]

I was talking to some prominent business leaders in Dallas this week about what they could do to promote racial peace. I told them not to think in terms of peace; peace will be the natural consequence of a more just and generous community that includes people of color in the prosperity of our city. Those who are rich and powerful have to use their wealth and influence to create a new definition of what a successful city looks like. One of them said that this might be a hard sell, because it's hard for people to give up their privileges. And I could just hear Jesus saying how hard it is for the rich to enter the kingdom of God—like a camel going through the eye of a needle, don't you know?!

The kingdom of God is not a country club of the rich and famous, the wealthy and well-connected. It's a fellowship of the poor that the rich can join by choice because they can give up enough to be a part, whereas the poor cannot do the same in trying to join the rich.

The thing is, people, if we really do want to experience eternal life, and if Jesus is right that we have to travel light to do so, what's the point of holding on to our stuff?

An American tourist in Jerusalem met up with a monk. The monk offered to show him around the monastery of which he was a part. On their tour they came to the monk's room; the tourist noticed that there was no TV or radio, only one change of clothes, a towel and a blanket. He asked, "How do you live so simply?" The monk answered, "I noticed you have only enough things to fill a suitcase; why do you live so simply?" To which the tourist replied, "But I'm just a tourist. I'm only traveling through." To which the monk said, "So am I, so am I."[89]

Your money and possessions can't save you, but they could damn you to a life that is unable to experience the promises of God. Give as if your life depends upon it. Because according to Jesus, it does.

88 https://www.urban.org/sites/default/files/publication/97981/inclusive_recovery_in_us_cities.pdf
89 Wiley Stephens, "Sticker Shock for the Soul," Day1.org.

51

Re-generational Church

First in the series *Generations: Roots and Reach*

Watch and listen to "Re-generational Church" by following this link or scanning the QR code with your phone: youtu.be/lB_yO2YlsoM. Sermon begins at 43:30.

November 3, 2019
All Saints Day
Psalm 145:1-13; 2 Timothy 1:1-7

Someone has said: *Getting pregnant or making a child together doesn't make you a parent. Popping in for a few hours each year doesn't make you a parent. Having your child's name tattooed on your arm or in your bio doesn't make you a parent. Telling your friends that you have a child doesn't make you a parent. Being there every single day through the struggles, tantrums and tears, holding them tight, taking care of a child who isn't [even] your [own] blood ... that's what makes you a parent.* What's more, anyone who has adopted a child knows it's not the blood that matters most in shaping the soul of a child; it's the love and care, the daily faithfulness, the selfless service that makes all the difference.

I want to say the same thing to you today about the church and the task of passing on faith from one generation to another. These children may live with us, or they may live with others, but they are all God's children and therefore they are all also ours.

Martin Luther, whose Protestant Reformation we commemorated last Sunday, said that it's a strange thing that every twenty years or so God builds a new church out of children. The backside of that is this: The church is always one generation away from extinction. Every church has a half-life of one generation. That is, unless we re-generate.

The psalmist says: One generation shall laud your works to another and shall declare your mighty acts. That's the way it works. That's the only way it works. If we have a re-generational church, it will only be because one generation tells the next generation about God and teaches them by word and deed to trust the Lord.

We are calling our stewardship emphasis this fall Generations: Roots and Reach. The timing may seem obvious. I just had my thirtieth anniversary as your pastor, which means I'm more than halfway done, don't you know?! Before long, it will be my turn to turn things over to the next generation. Our Pathways to Ministry program has been one way for me to get a head start on that by helping to nurture the next generation of pastors.

But this is the church's work. Wilshire has always been a multigenerational church. My predecessor Bruce McIver was pastor here for thirty years and then pastor emeritus for twelve more. We've never been mostly young or mostly old. We've always been a church for the ages and a church for all the ages. And the way this works is for us to pass the faith from one generation to another.

Bill and Janice Jernberg have been doing this for more than forty years by teaching first graders. (They will be squirming in their pews to hear me talk about them, because they don't like attention focused on them.) But Sunday by Sunday for more than a biblical generation, they have been teaching children about the God in whose image and likeness they are made, about the God who knows their name and calls their name and promises to be with them through all the fires and floods of life that will come.

The Jernbergs' two children, Brad and Anne, grew up among us. They became residents in our Pathways to Ministry program, and they are serving churches today in Houston and Denver. But if you ask them (Bill and Janice) about the blessing of God on their lives, they will tell you story after story about their spiritual children too—kids who have passed through their Sunday school class and now teach Sunday school themselves. Some are deacons in our church today. Others are pastors and deacons and faithful Christians in churches all over America.

We honor saints on this All Saints Sunday. Most of the time we talk about saints who have gone to live with the Lord in eternity after doing their best among us. But there are so many among us now who deserve our notice. They are not asking to be praised. That would be precisely the opposite of what saints care about. If someone constantly wants your praise or praises himself, you can be sure his aim in life is not to make Christ more visible or to make the body of Christ—the church—more substantial. True saints are shy. They are preoccupied with being re-generative in others. As in generation to generation.

When the Apostle Paul wrote to his son in the ministry, Timothy, he told him to draw upon the faith of the saints in his life: his grandmother Lois and his mother, Eunice. Now, there's an old saying in the church that God doesn't have grandchildren; God only has children. Which is to say that faith isn't inherited by birth as much as it is adopted by new birth. Every generation has to have its own experience of taking up the faith.

And yet, how does that happen? Most often it's because of the example of parents and grandparents, whether those of our own nuclear family or those of spiritual family.

I sent a letter this week to members who are parents of grade-school age children. Some of you got the letter. Most of you who are here today probably didn't need it, because you are already in the habit of being here. But there is a trend among too many in churches these days of neglecting attendance in intergenerational worship.

That also extends to service. Our Associate Pastor Emeritus Preston Bright likes to say that the church is a weekly miracle. Every Sunday, the only way church happens is if somebody shows up to teach fourth graders, sing in the choir, collect the offering, and serve Communion. Even though we have some paid Christians who tee it up for you, church is essentially a makeshift, voluntary operation. We either take our places or our places will not be taken.

That said, churches like Wilshire are in danger of developing what Kenton Keller calls a "concierge mentality." We expect that in return for our membership, we will have staff and dedicated laypersons to cater to our needs. We want our kids to get a good Sunday school education, to learn about missions and Bible skills and music and handbells on Wednesday nights, but there are always other priorities that take precedence when we ask you to work with kids to achieve those ends. We run into the same thing with adult Sunday school. So, do we really want to professionalize the church so much that we have to pay Sunday school teachers to accomplish our mission? And wouldn't that actually undermine our mission?

Of course, all of this is magnified by the financial support of the church. Part of the miracle of the church is that we set a budget every year and pay as we go with no source of funding except what comes from you and me. I mean, if Wilshire is to exist even one more year, it will depend upon our commitment to give generously toward its re-generation.

Every year the church re-generates. We start with Genesis, so to speak, on January 1. And we hope to make it to Revelation by December 31. That is, to finish what we started, to fully fund our ministry year by year.

If that is to happen this year again or the next or the next, we have to develop the regenerative habit of generosity in all our members. It won't be the same amounts given by everyone, but it will be the same effort given by everyone.

We are not a nonprofit organization that goes out to find wealthy donors to float our mission year by year. We are a family of faith that pulls together year by year, doing our common chores for the household of faith: showing up to worship, learning and sharing together, serving one another, and giving of our means.

All this takes spiritual commitment. And I will tell you that it's always easier to get spiritual commitment out of fundamentalists than moderates or progressives. They have a commitment to underlying values of loyalty and authority that motivate them to faithful giving and serving. People like us like to say that we aren't legalistic—just doing things out of obedience to rules and laws. Okay, fine. We are motivated more by justice and joy, by freedom and love. Great. So, my question is this: Are we going to let our vision of the faith perish by failing to fund it generously? It's up to us.

Paul tells Timothy that *God did not give us a spirit of cowardice, but rather a spirit of power and of love and of self-discipline.* Cowardice is a harsh word. But it puts the matter of generational faithfulness in the context of courage. It takes courage to trust that God will take care of your needs when you give from what you have when you fear you don't have enough. It takes courage to support the church in a day when people are giving up on church all around.

You are here because you have found a place at the table of the Lord. It's a table that welcomes EveryBody, as we like to say. There is room here for everybody because the heart of God stretches to make room for everybody. But EveryBody is not just about welcome; it's about the privilege of doing our part. You're on the team. You have a uniform. No one is sidelined. The coach has called your number. Time to get in the game.

Molly Marshall is a friend of our congregation. She is the president of Central Baptist Theological Seminary in Kansas City. She wrote about All Saints Day this week and said this: *Saints inspire us to live more luminous lives. They light the pathway through their authentic faith, their love of God and others and their unnoticed acts of service. They bear faithful witness to the grace they have received.*[90]

I'm sure if we asked every single one of you this morning, you would be able to name those people of an older generation who were saints to you. They may have been in your family or in your family of faith. But the question now is simply this: Will you be that to the next generation?

In his will the American patriot Patrick Henry wrote, *I have now disposed of all my property to my family; there is one thing more I wish I could give them, and that is the Christian religion. If they had this, and I had not given them one shilling, they would be rich; but if they had not that, and I have given them all the world, they would be poor.*[91] We can give our faith. One generation can praise God's works to another.

Walt Whitman, in his poem *O Me! O Life!* reflects on all the challenges of being human, and then he concludes this way: *The question, O me! so sad, recurring— What good amid these, O me, O life?*

Answer.

That you are here—that life exists and identity, That the powerful play goes on, and you may contribute a verse.[92]

You may contribute. Will you? Amen.

90 https://baptistnews.com/article/saints-dont-have-to-be-dead-gratitude-for-regular-blessed-folk-through-whom-goodness-shines/

91 https://www.presbyterianfoundation.org/wp-content/uploads/2018/03/Sermon-1-WE-2018-new-logo.pdf

92 https://www.poetryfoundation.org/poems/51568/o-me-o-life

52

Generative Roots

Second in the series *Generations: Roots and Reach*

Watch and listen to "Generative Roots" by following this link or scanning the QR code with your phone: youtu.be/KFl9XvUlLMY. Sermon begins at 42:10.

November 10, 2019
Twenty-second Sunday after Pentecost
Psalm 1; Ephesians 3:14-21

I've been having fun with this Generations initiative in our church. I know that makes me a weirdo preacher because most preachers dread talking about money as much as most of you dread us talking about it. But the point is never money itself.

Money is the means, not the end. Money is the fuel, not the engine. Money is the light, not the photosynthesis.

Which brings us to a tree. (See what I did there?) A tree has been the symbol for our emphasis this fall on growing the church. Roots and Reach is the sub-theme of this Generations initiative. Today we're talking about roots.

The first hymn in Israel's hymnal begins with the image of a tree planted by streams of living water. A wise person, a righteous soul, is like a tree well planted. He or she will flourish, like a tree well planted that gets what it needs to bloom and grow.

And it's the soil it's planted in that matters most. You can't see what's going on underground, but you can tell everything about what's going on underground by the story the leaves tell above ground.

When we lived in Lake Highlands (in the house Julie Girards now owns), we had a tree that struggled for several years and was becoming an embarrassment. It had been transplanted into the front yard by the sidewalk where everyone could see it. We trimmed it and watered it. We would have danced around it and recited incantations over it if we thought it would have helped. But it only got scragglier and I finally gave up on it. I chopped it down right to ground level and forgot about it. And wouldn't you know, by the next spring it came roaring back. It shot up with healthy shoots and began to grow. In a few years it stood tall and strong.

You see, the soil was good. The roots were taking hold. The tree was getting grounded. But it was taking too much energy for the roots to send life up to the tree to make leaves. It needed to attend to the process of attaching itself more deeply to the soil and gaining strength below ground before sending forth its shoots.

The Apostle Paul wrote tenderly to the church in Ephesus with an allusion to a tree. He prayed for them to be strengthened in their inner being. With the power of the Holy Spirit coursing through them, and with Christ dwelling within them, they are, he said, *being rooted and grounded in love.* As the psalmist sees a flourishing person as a well-planted tree, Paul sees a healthy and growing church the same way. He wants them to attend to their inner life, that is, to the invisible places of the soul or heart where God's best work is done in secret. When that happens, the church grows and thrives. When it is missing, when the church is preoccupied with appearances, when the church worries about what it looks like more than being rooted and grounded in loving relationships, it declines and dies.

I had an interesting email exchange with a church on the East Coast this past month. They are searching for a pastor and wrote to me asking for recommendations of possible candidates. When I read their materials, I became concerned with the way they described their church and what kind of pastor they were looking for. So, I asked them for clarification, and, frankly, I was hoping they would take my questions more as a challenge to be bolder in their search. But this week I got an email back from them that told me they were doubling down on their approach. They are seeking a pastor to come in and reinforce their desire not to change. About half the congregation is over 65—which is getting younger to me all the time, don't you know?! They said they were sure I could understand that they wanted to make sure they didn't lose anyone in that demographic by calling a pastor who might say or do things that might cause discontent. I do understand, of course. And what I would say about that is that they are tending to the struggling branches and leaves rather than the roots, to the visible rather than the invisible. And it's a path of death for a congregation, not a prescription for life.

I've been reading a book Molly Shepard put me on to written by Hope Jahren and titled *Lab Girl.* Hope is a young woman scientist who tells her story of what it's like to do her work in what has traditionally been a man's world. Sound familiar, women ministers? Anyway, Hope is a tree scientist, and is the inspiration for our planting a tree this week as a symbol of our Generations initiative.

No risk is more terrifying, she says, *than that taken by the first root.* She describes the adventure of a tiny rootlet as if it has a mind of its own. In a sense, it does. See, when a root commits itself to anchoring in a place, it's there for good. And so, she says, *It assesses the light and humidity of the moment, refers to its programming and quite literally takes the plunge.*

Everything is risked in that one moment when the first cells ... advance from the seed coat. The root grows down before the shoot grows up, and so there is no possibility for green tissue to make new food for several days or even weeks. She talks about the decision to commit itself to a course as a great risk. *Rooting exhausts the very last reserves of the seed,* she says. *The gamble is everything, … but when it wins, it wins big.*[93]

I love this imagery for the church. I believe our church has set down roots just this way. Since 1951, we have been making decisions to anchor ourselves in this soil. But the soil is not only a literal spot on the map; it's also a way of being rooted and grounded in love. We have continually attached ourselves to any and all who want to join us in this flourishing work. Along the way, we have made decisions not to play it safe, to commit ourselves in ever expanding love that has called us to exhaust ourselves in service to others and to each other. This is what it means to be rooted and grounded in love.

Love is dogged connection through mutual giving and receiving. We nourish one another and are nourished by one another. We can't hold back individually, or we will be held back collectively.

So, here's the shift to the preacher talking about money. I had a conversation this week with one of our members. He and his wife have had a rough year, he said. She has battled a serious illness and medical bills have taken a toll on their resources. They have been tithers for many years, but three years ago they knew that we had lost a lot of faithful givers, so they gave more and have continued to do so, despite her illness. They love their church and they are continuing to do more. He told me that their relationships with people in the church have meant everything to them through this ordeal. And one small decision they are making to free up money to give to the Unified Budget is to do away with their landline telephone and give that extra amount. Love that.

When you are thinking about your giving, you might think about what you can give up in order to give more. Adjusting our expenses and our lifestyle is a beautiful way of demonstrating what it means to be rooted and grounded in love.

We need to tend to the soil of our growth by giving consistently and faithfully to the ongoing ministry fund of the church. We get no money from anywhere but each other. We will only have the church we decide to have, and the most significant decision we all make to make that happen is to give.

So, what are we asking of you? Let's grow our giving by 10% over the next three years. We have struggled to maintain our ministry without growing it for the past three years. It's time for us to commit to God and to each other to be the church we believe God has called us to be.

And speaking of 10%, that's the calculus for each of us as well as all of us. It's what the Bible calls tithing. It's the benchmark for faithful stewardship. If every member were to reorder their spending habits by following the spiritual wisdom of giving back to the Lord the first 10% of all that comes into the household, the mission of the church would be secure from generation to generation. I am calling on you to commit to that standard of giving.

Some of you are in a position to begin right now, even if it takes faith to do so. Some of you are in a position to commit to that as a goal you will work toward in

---

93 Vintage, 2016, p. 53.

the next year. And some of you are in a position to do more than 10% as your way of giving time for others to catch up to their desire to join you in this work.

One of our younger members has had an ongoing conversation with me about moving toward the tithe. He and his young family are excited about the progress they are making. When they came and joined the church, tithing wasn't on their radar. But as they became more deeply rooted and grounded in their relationship to the church, they have moved up their giving to the point where tithing is now in their sights. He told me that they are members of a country club and pay dues. When he thought about the relationships they enjoy at church compared to their club, they realized that they should be doing more giving voluntarily than they are required to do at the club.

Jimmy Allen died this year. He was one of the leading lights of Baptist preachers during the last generation, and he was the interim pastor of Wilshire before I got here thirty years ago. Jimmy was always ahead of Baptists and calling us to do better in racial justice and all sorts of ethical matters to make the church an agent of healing and reconciliation in the world. Two of Jimmy's grandsons died of AIDS, having received it from their mother who had gotten a blood transfusion when her first child was born at the beginning of the HIV plague.

Jimmy's son Skip was gay. He was a landscaper by profession. He did the landscape design work for our resident houses before his own death a few years ago. Jimmy learned a lot from Skip's work that he applied to the church. People around the state knew Skip as a person who could make things grow in the sandy Texas soil. It wasn't always easy work.

The key, Jimmy said, was that Skip kept bringing in new soil to mix with the old. He mulched, watered, and fertilized them together until it was the proper environment in which the plants could flourish. He knew that the key to a beautiful lawn and garden wasn't so much in what was planted, but in the soil that gave them nourishment and life.[94]

Wilshire, we are planted in good soil. But it's good only because we continue to mix in new soil, new people, who make it richer. And when we give generously, we are watering and feeding it to see it grow healthier and stronger.

This is generative work, and it never ends. Let's all do our part to stay rooted and grounded in love. Amen.

---

94 http://newbaptistcovenant.org/remembering-dr-jimmy-allen/

PART VIII

A Free Church

Baptist Roots

"It is the consistent and insistent contention of our Baptist people, always and everywhere, that religion must be forever voluntary and uncoerced ... God wants free worshipers and no other kind."

~ George W. Truett

"We believe in a free church in a free state. We believe in the separation of church and state—not the separation of God and government; not the separation of religion and public life; not the separation of the spiritual from the secular. ... The persuaded church is also the persuasive church: we make our case in the public square like everyone else. We vote our conscience and we appeal to the conscience of others. We trust in God's patient and longsuffering love to make the truth known through our Spirit-inspired witness to the world."

~ George A. Mason

Preface by Bill Leonard

The first three sermons included in this chapter were preached by George Mason at Wilshire Baptist Church (WBC) during the month of April 2005 as a series entitled Baptist Persuasions. The fourth sermon, preached in 2009 during the 400th year of the Baptist movement, revisits elements of Baptist belief and practice.

The sermons reminded the congregation of the biblical, historical, collective, and dissonant elements of Baptist identity. They were conceived a decade or so after the Southern Baptist Convention (SBC), the denomination with which WBC was originally affiliated and a powerful source of its Baptist identity, came under the control of a decidedly rightist theological/political Baptist faction. Mason's sermons were surely an effort to encourage Wilshire members to celebrate the historical roots of Baptist heritage as still significant and viable, even as they renegotiated the Baptist landscape of their own times.

The fact that the sermons are included in a book published almost twenty years later speaks to their historical relevance at a time when these formidable ideas are more fragile than they were when first preached. That George Mason maintained those views throughout his ministry is itself an affirmation of his sustained convictions as a prophetic gospel minister and a Baptist pastor given to the care of souls.

Reading these sermons two decades later we might call George "an old-timey Baptist" given that his affirmation of Baptist roots of religious liberty and uncoerced faith now seem strangely foreign to large numbers of Baptist individuals and groups. Then and now they stand in sharp contrast to what has evolved into the neo-establishmentarian efforts of the Christian Nationalist movement.

Mason captures the importance and distinctions of Baptist identity from the beginning. Unashamedly Baptist in its approach to issues of religious liberty, the first sermon introduces the topic within an ecumenical context by referencing the death of Pope John Paul II which occurred on April 2, 2005. While acknowledging the pope's many contributions to Catholicism and beyond, Mason acknowledges the boundaries between the two Christian groups, occasions when both communions have condemned the other as a "false church." He then proposes another way: "The day has come and is long past when we must stop the ensmalling language of us-and-them and work together toward the greater WE. To do so does not mean that we all become Catholics or Baptists. It means walking the salvation road together after Jesus Christ and learning from one another along the way."

Throughout the series, Mason highlights Baptist traditions regarding faith and baptism, mission and ministry, conscience and religious freedom, all within the larger unity in the Body of Christ, the Church.

Mason's sermons give substance to the classic statement set forth in one of the earliest Baptist confessions of faith, written by those English Separatist exiles who gathered in Amsterdam in 1609 to organize the first Baptist congregation. It declares: "That the church of Christ is a company of faithful people separated from the world by the word & Spirit of God, being knit unto the Lord, & one unto another, by Baptism, upon their own confession of the faith, and sins."[95]

In these sermons, George Mason articulates elements of that description four hundred years later. He reminds his listeners of the centrality of Baptist concern for persons to experience faith in Christ yet warns: "There may be and should be earnest and powerful persuasion to that end, but there must never be coercion. Coercion disrespects the dignity and freedom of each person before God. Coerced faith is no faith at all." That statement captures the historic foundation of Baptist views that religious freedom is essential for freely chosen faith. The early Baptists reacted prophetically against the idea of a "Christian nation" in which citizenship in the state compelled baptism into the church.

In the second sermon, Mason contrasts the position of a popular "TV preacher" who declares that Christians must work toward "godly dominion" over every element of national life, with the assertion of Baptist icon George W. Truett "that religion must be forever voluntary and uncoerced, and that it is not the prerogative of any power, whether civil or ecclesiastical, to compel men to conform to any religious creed or form of worship ... ."

The third sermon reflects on the Baptist calling to extend Christian faith to others, not through political or ecclesiastical coercion, but through faithful witness to the love and grace of God in Christ. As Mason says, "We trust in God's patient and longsuffering love to make the truth known through our Spirit-inspired witness to the world." The sermon concludes with this assertion: "So convictional faith and faithful community make up one grand experience of life in Christ."

The 2009 sermon celebrates four hundred years of the Baptist witness by reasserting the continuing importance of their commitment to religious liberty. Mason cites founder Thomas Helwys' declaration that Christians' relationship to God "is between God and themselves. ... Let them be heretics, Turks, Jews, or whatsoever,

---

95 "English Declaration at Amsterdam," 1611, in *Baptist Confessions of Faith*, second edition, edited by William L. Lumpkin and Bill J. Leonard, (Valley Forge: Judson Press, 2011), p. 111.

it appertains not to the earthly power to punish them in the least measure." Mason concludes that contemporary Baptists must not abandon those classic ideals from the distant past, but treasure and live them out here and now.

He asserts: "We have to continue to be passionately convictional people. This is the way we honor the past and our Baptist forebears. Not by doing only what they did, but by doing what we must do by the same gospel reasoning they employed." No doubt the first Baptists who gathered in Amsterdam four centuries earlier would recognize those words, a faithful witness to who they were and who 21st century Baptists, as George Mason understands them, should remain.

Bill J. Leonard is Founding Dean and Professor of Divinity Emeritus at The School of Divinity, Wake Forest University, in Winston-Salem, North Carolina. He is the author or editor of some twenty-five books, including: Baptist Ways: A History; Baptists in America; *and* The Homebrewed Guide to Church History: Flaming Heretics and Heavy Drinkers.

53

The Persuaded Church: Convictional Faith and Faithful Community

First in the series *Baptist Persuasions*

April 10, 2005
Third Sunday of Easter
Matthew 16:13-20

We have witnessed this week a remarkable moment in Christian witness. The death and funerary rites for Pope John Paul II produced an outpouring of love from tens of millions around the world. This pope served the Lord and the Church and the world with the kind of servant spirit and shepherd heart we long for in our religious leaders but seldom find. He was an example of true humility. He preferred the power of love to the love of power. His commitment to the reign of God in the world allowed him to see the bankruptcy of communism and consumerism alike. His commitment to life led him to oppose war and capital punishment as much as abortion and euthanasia.

Many Catholics disagreed with the pope on many things, and yet they respected and loved him for his faith and faithfulness. Baptists have reason to be thankful for him, too. While he never fully recognized us and other non-Catholics as being truly the Church per se, he reached out to us all in Christian fellowship. The truth is, Baptists and other Protestants have been taking our bearings from the Catholic compass since our beginnings. We would hardly know ourselves apart from how we are different from the Catholics. Our differences have too long defined us more than our similarities. Sometimes that has meant bitter and unkind rhetoric. We have been guilty of declaring ourselves the true church and the Catholic Church the false church in the very ways that the Catholic Church has done to us. Sometimes we have been all too sure that we are Christians and too unsure that they are, just as they have done to us. *But they did it to us first!* Not very Golden Rule of either of us, don't you know?!

The day has come and is long past when we must stop the ensmalling language of us-and-them and work together toward the greater WE. To do so does not mean that we all become Catholics or Baptists. It means walking the salvation road together after Jesus Christ and learning from one another along the way.

In that spirit, we begin today a three-week look at what Baptists might contribute to that conversation. This series of sermons, called *Baptist Persuasions*, was conceived before the death of the Holy Father and is not meant to be disrespectful to Catholics by its timing. But it helps us now and then to take a fresh look at what we believe about the church, about the church's relation to the state, and about the church's relation to the world and other religions. That is the brief outline of the series.

Our text today details the confession of Simon Peter that Jesus is the Christ, and it looks at how Christ conceived of and constituted the church from that moment forward. It begins with Jesus asking his disciples who people say he is. They answer John the Baptist, Elijah, Jeremiah or one of the prophets. But then Jesus puts the question to them more personally: *Who do you say that I am?* And this is the point at which Baptists jump out of their seats and say, "See, this is the point of it all. Christ poses the personal question to each of us and all of us. He puts us on the spot to see what our answer will be. No one can answer for anyone else. We can all answer only for ourselves." Peter answers for himself: *You are the Messiah, the Son of the living God.* Baptists believe this is the crucial moment. Peter's confession begins it all. But Catholics believe this is the crucial moment, too. Peter's confession begins it all. Catholics emphasize *Peter's* confession; Baptists Peter's *confession*. For Catholics Peter speaks as the head of the church, while for Baptists Peter speaks as one of the church. For Catholics Peter becomes the father of the church; for Baptists Peter is our honored older brother. The point is not Peter but Peter's faith.

Jesus declares that Peter did not come to this insight on his own but through God's act of revealing it to him. And we still believe that no one comes to confess the identity of Jesus as the Christ, the Son of the living God, without the Spirit of God opening the eyes of faith and heart of love to this truth. *We love because God first loved us.* That is always the order of things. We do not discover God; God discovers us. God discloses God's self to us. Our knowledge of God is really acknowledgement of God. And we believe that acknowledgement of God happens by the very active revelation of God to every individual, just as it did with Peter. We do not believe that a saving faith is ever secondhand; personal experience with the resurrected and ever-living Son of God is always firsthand faith.

One of our Baptist historians, Walter Shurden, puts it this way: *In the Baptist faith tradition, individualism in religious matters manifests itself at the very beginning of the Christian life. Baptists insist that saving faith is personal, not impersonal. It is relational, not ritualistic. It is direct, not indirect. It is a lonely, frightened, sinful individual before an almighty, loving, and gracious God.*

So faith is convictional. And this is the reason we do not baptize babies, although our baby dedication ceremonies are virtual dry baptisms. We believe someone should be convicted or persuaded to become a Christian by the mysterious work of God revealing Christ and by the church bearing witness to Christ and calling out faith. That's why when we baptize someone, we ask, *What is YOUR confession of faith?* "Jesus is Lord," the baptizand answers, and she answers in that moment for herself and only for herself.

As in infant baptizing traditions, we want parents and godparents and church leaders to pass on the faith to children, but with them we believe that faith must be received in order for it to be their faith. A pass needs to be caught. And that is what confirmation aims at in other traditions. The baptized come to belief themselves and take their public stand with the church that passed the faith to them.

We delay baptism until that profession of faith because we emphasize this persuasion principle. We believe people must be conscious enough to understand that they stand alone before God in this matter of the eternal destiny of their souls. No one can stand in for them except Christ, and they must open their hearts to him themselves. There may be and should be earnest and powerful persuasion to that end, but there must never be coercion. Coercion disrespects the dignity and freedom of each person before God. Coerced faith is no faith at all.

That's why a great Baptist preacher of the last generation, Carlyle Marney, put it pithily: *The rabbi begins, "Thus saith the Lord!" The priest begins, "As the Church has always said. ... " The average Protestant begins, 'Now, brothers and sisters, it seems to Me .... "* Whether it seems to you or not is, of course, the second-most-crucial matter. The first is whether it is so that Jesus is the Christ, the Son of the living God. But then it must be so to you for that to make any great difference in your life.

And this is what makes the church the church: that we each of us confess for ourselves that Jesus is Lord. It makes all the difference.

My colleague and friend Curtis Freeman tells about a curious experience with some neighbors that illustrates the point. "A few years ago, our family had some neighbors that were not Christians. They observed that there was something different about us. Then one day they made a connection: *These folks have something we don't have. They go to church. We will go to church.* So, they did—Sunday morning, Sunday evening, and Wednesday evening. They even began working with the preschool and apartment ministries. But it wasn't long before they dropped out. They gave the usual excuses: *The people weren't friendly; they were always asking for money; the answers just didn't work for us.* But the real problem is that they had missed the point of church. They had never taken the first step. They never professed their faith in Jesus Christ. Without that, the church is just another social club or service organization. You can never join up with this group unless you declare your faith in him as Lord and Christ. Without a personal, and indeed, embarrassingly public confession of faith, there are no living stones with which God can build the church. Our evangelical commission is to take this question to all creation: "Who is Jesus Christ to you?"

But there's more to faith than what it means to you as an individual. Faith is personal, but it is never private.

When Peter confessed his faith in Jesus, Jesus went on to talk of building his church on this foundation. Faith involves Christ being in you, but it also involves your being in Christ. And as such we are part of something more than a collection of believers: We are members of Christ's own body; we are signs of his presence on earth. And we are that together, not by ourselves as individuals.

But what is the foundation on which the church is built? The Catholic Church says it is Peter himself, and thus upon all the successors of Peter—those who sit in his chair, the popes of Rome. *You are Peter,* Jesus says, *and upon this rock I will build my church.* You are *Petros,* the Greek language has it; and upon this *petra* I will build my church. *Petros* is the proper noun and *petra* the common noun for rock. So is Peter the literal foundation of the church or the metaphor of it? Well, in the Aramaic language that Jesus would have spoken, the proper noun and common noun for rock are the same—*Kepha/kepha,* as in Cephas. So it's hard to say. And the truth is that the Catholic reading is possible. But later, Jesus goes on to grant the same responsibility for binding and loosing, for leading the church, to all the apostles. So it seems Peter is representative of something other than just himself. And Baptists say he represents anyone who confesses Christ in the same way Peter does. The church is made up of confessing Christians that believe and have been baptized.

Now, it is true that in some churches believing and being baptized do not happen in that order. And yet, wherever both occur, in whatever order, we are happy as Baptists to enjoy Christian fellowship, even if in most of our Baptist churches now that does not extend to church membership. Because of our commitment to persuasion in personal faith experience, we believe our pattern to be best, even if we do not believe that you have to do it our way in order to be right with God. So we admit that we might be a bit narrower on this point than God.

Baptists emphasize the individual, while Catholics emphasize the church. And we need each other to learn the proper balance. Baptists can become so committed to our individualism that individual Christians behave like churches unto themselves. Marney said that we are like tubs that sit on our own bottoms. But faithful community in Christ is more than a choice of whether you would like to be among some Christians or not. You may be personally accountable to God and in need of a personal experience of faith, but you are part of something that Christ created when you join up with him. You are a member of his body; you are baptized into Christ once you receive Christ into yourself. And as such you cannot go it alone without hurting Christ and yourself and everyone else joined together in him. You would be cutting yourself off from the body, spiritually amputating yourself. And you cannot live long or well apart from Christ's body.

So convictional faith and faithful community make up one grand experience of life in Christ. If you want to know more about it, you might with good profit ask a Catholic or some other kind of Christian for their take. But since you are here, I pray you will be persuaded by the Baptist persuasion that genuine faith is convictional faith, and a faithful community is a persuaded church. Or so it seems to me …

54

The Persuasive Church: True Freedom and the Freedom of Truth

Second in the series *Baptist Persuasions*

April 17, 2005
Fourth Sunday of Easter
John 8:31-36; 2 Corinthians 3:17-4:2

Congress shall make no law respecting an establishment of religion or prohibiting the free exercise thereof; or abridging the freedom of speech, or of the press; or the right of the people peaceably to assemble, and to petition the Government for a redress of grievances.

The First Amendment to the Constitution of the United States of America: it's not Scripture, but it's hard to imagine it springing forth from the human imagination without Scripture. We won't say after reciting it, *This is the Word of the Lord*, but we should say in unison and without hesitation, *Thanks be to God!*

The First Amendment guarantees freedom of religion, freedom of speech, freedom of the press, freedom of assembly, and freedom to pursue justice. It's not gospel, but it is good news. It's not the gospel truth, but the truth of the gospel leads us to these very truths of freedom.

The little-known secret of these words—inspired and inspiring (if not divinely inspired)—is that Baptists were the chief conspirators in their adoption. More secularly minded patriots joined the Baptists in taking the handcuffs off truth so that it could do its freedom work freely. We are more concerned, however, with how our Baptist forebears got to these truths of freedom from our understanding of true freedom, and how Baptists today may stay tethered to freedom's truths.

Virginia Baptist evangelist John Leland had been jailed in America for preaching the Gospel without a license. He didn't take it personally, but he personally took it upon himself to see that not only was he vindicated but that the whole idea of religious liberty was, too. Before 1791 and the passage of the Bill of Rights, Americans from one state or commonwealth to another suffered but did not welcome religious views different from those held by the majority. Leland saw, as did Roger Williams of Rhode Island before him, along with the first Baptists in England and their older Anabaptist cousins in Europe, that diverse religious opinions should not be tolerated but celebrated. If the Spirit of God wishes to do a new thing in the world, the voices of God's prophets must be heard with respect and not silenced by fear of the truth.

Leland threw his support to James Madison to represent Virginia at the ratifying constitutional convention only after extracting a promise to press for full religious liberty and not just toleration. Listen to Leland's view and see if you are his kind of Baptist still: *Government has no more to do with the religious opinions of men than it has to do with the principles of mathematics. Let every man speak freely without fear, maintain the principles that he believes, worship according to his own faith, either one God, three Gods, no God or twenty Gods; and let government protect him in doing so, i.e., see that he meets no personal abuse, or loss of property, for his religious opinions. ... [I]f his doctrine is false, it will be confuted, and if it is true (though ever so novel), let others credit it.*

Well, can you vote for that? Many Baptists and other Christians today cannot. One out of three teenagers in a recent study thinks that the First Amendment goes too far in granting freedom of religion and speech and press. They think some censorship would not be a bad idea. Now some of that can be accounted for by a lack of education and life experience. But sadly, plenty of well-educated grownups make the same argument today—and more tragically, some of them are Baptists!

The usual line of reasoning goes like this. Since Puritan Christians came to these shores seeking to set up a colony of heaven on earth based upon biblical principles, America is really a Christian nation, they say. America is true to its roots only when the government prefers the Christian religion, even if tolerating others. But the Massachusetts Bay Colony was a spiritual and political failure. The colonial idea of established churches in each state, where one church had the right to grant or limit religious freedom to others, was deemed wrongheaded. The Constitution and the Bill of Rights granted nothing: It only secured what was granted by God and should not be denied by any human authority. That we needed these documents to begin the American experiment in religious liberty only proves that the way forward is not back to the Puritan plan but to the Baptist idea.

So where do Baptists get this notion of civil liberty? What are the roots of political freedom? Baptists go to the Bible and reason from there. While others might point to the natural dignity of the individual, we point to the claim that every person is created in the image of God and is therefore responsible to God. That is, we are made as response-able creatures—able to respond to God. So to get between the God who calls us and the creature that responds to that call is to get in the way. It's to be where one does not belong—whether that one is a civil magistrate or a church minister. It's to put oneself in the place of the one mediator between God and human beings—Christ Jesus the Lord.

And this hones in on the matter better than anything. Jesus Christ himself is the agent of true freedom. We are not truly free just by virtue of our being human. Sin makes slaves of us all. Only Christ can set us free, because, as the Son of God, he alone has the power to make us also sons and daughters of God. But Christ does not force himself upon anyone. He gives himself to us and calls us to respond. And he does so persuasively, sending his Holy Spirit as a secret agent, working an inside job in pricking our consciences and nudging our wills and warming our hearts. At no time, however, does God coerce our belief. And Baptists believe that if persuasion is good enough for God in eternal affairs, it is good enough for us in temporal ones.

The government should never coerce citizens in matters of faith, nor should the church employ coercive power over the government to achieve its goals. The First Amendment strikes just the right balance in protecting the church from the state and the state from the church—thus the so-called "wall of separation between church and state." The phrase is rightly credited to Thomas Jefferson, but a Baptist named Roger Williams used the word *hedge* rather than wall a century and a half earlier. It fits the Baptist idea of the church being not just a persuaded church, in which each person must be persuaded in his or her own mind to join the church, but the church as also a persuasive church, bearing witness and making our case for the truth in the free marketplace of ideas.

Listen to the contrast between two Christian preachers, one who rejects this view and one who accepts it. *Our job is to reclaim America for Christ, whatever the cost. As the vice regents of God, we are to exercise godly dominion and influence over our neighborhoods, our schools, our government, our literature and arts, our sports arenas, our entertainment media, our news media, our scientific endeavors—in short, over every aspect and institution of human society.* And now hear these words: *It is the consistent and insistent contention of our Baptist people, always and everywhere, that religion must be forever voluntary and uncoerced, and that it is not the prerogative of any power, whether civil or ecclesiastical, to compel men to conform to any religious creed or form of worship, or to pay taxes for the support of a religious organization to which they do not belong and in whose creed they do not believe. God wants free worshipers and no other kind ... Christ's religion needs no prop of any kind from any worldly source, and to the degree that it is thus supported is a millstone hanged about its neck.*

The first preacher (who conducts a TV ministry from his large church in Florida) believes that the church must have dominion over the state and all its institutions, by means of coercive power if necessary, whether anyone agrees or disagrees with it. The second view was expressed by the late great pastor of the First Baptist Church, Dallas, Texas, George W. Truett. On the steps of the Capitol Building in Washington, D.C., in the year 1920, he recalled the history of our Baptist movement, emphasizing this principle of freedom in all things, and the idea of persuasive power as sufficient to achieve spiritual ends.

For the same reasons, Baptists promote freedom of inquiry in education and freedom of the press. If Jesus is the way, the truth, and the life, as he says, honest inquiry into any matter will finally end at the feet of the one who is himself the Truth. It may take time for the truth to become evident, but truth cannot be helped and can only be hindered by those who would control the search for it.

Some years ago, a prominent Baptist pastor declared that if the leaders of the convention should declare that "pickles have souls," then teachers in Baptist schools would be obligated to teach just that. That's a dilly, huh? Makes me a sourpuss just thinking about it. The same man once tried to convince a Baptist journalist not to publish the facts about a certain preacher's ethical lapses. He appealed to the scriptural story of Noah to say that a Christian reporter has the responsibility to "cover his brother's nakedness." Right. And what about the Apostle Paul's notion of the *open statement of the truth* being commended *to the conscience of everyone in the sight of God?*

Baptists have long held that we should *tell the truth and trust the people.* But these days principles of freedom such as these are under assault from within even our own Baptist family. Brent Walker, executive director of the Baptist Joint Committee, says that he is not sure that the First Amendment would stand the test of a vote among Baptists today. Which is why we need sermons preached and lessons taught and institutions dedicated to the advancement and preservation of the Baptist way.

This is why we have established and must support organizations such as the Baptist Joint Committee, the *Associated Baptist Press*, and the *Baptists Today* news journal, which keep these "first freedoms" ever before us. They tell us the truth unconstrained by political partisanship or personal agendas. They understand that true freedom is slavery to Christ, but that we must promote freedom for everyone or we will have freedom for no one. We must all do our part. We must tell the story of Baptists. We must call the world's attention to the truth that is in Christ, which is the world's last and only hope. But we must utilize the weapons of the Spirit and never the sword of the state to accomplish God's work in the world.

We have seen a remarkable example of this in our lifetime. While Baptists have long been at odds with the Roman Catholic Church over matters of religious liberty, the recently deceased Pope John Paul II showed why the persuasive way of witness to the truth of Christ is the only way that leads to freedom.

In 1979, the Communist government of Poland, fearing a backlash from the people and sure that they could contain the masses by controlling the news, granted the pope the right to visit his native country. That visit was the beginning of the end of the atheistic state in Poland. The pope did not call for revolt against the government; he merely charged the people to remember who they really were: They were to be a "special witness to [Christ's] cross and His resurrection," he said. The people erupted. *We want God!* they shouted. *We want God!*

Word about that powerful spiritual moment passed quickly all through Poland. But when people went home and turned on the news, the state-controlled media showed only a brief shot of the pope, without the crowds, and showed him speaking for only a second or two. The people compared the reality they felt at the Mass to the propaganda reported by the media. "It's all lies," they said. "It's over." When ten million Poles began to say it together, the house of cards that was communism fell at last.

The truth, and only the truth, shall set us free. And freedom to tell it truly is a human right that Baptists have an unending duty to protect and promote. Let us not faint or fail. Amen.

55

The Persuading Church:
Witnessing Faith and Faithful Witness

Third in the series *Baptist Persuasions*

April 24, 2005
Fifth Sunday of Easter
Luke 14:15-24; Romans 10:9-15

People inquiring about the Baptist faith ask me all the time what makes Baptists Baptists? What distinguishes a Baptist kind of Christian from other kinds? These days you almost have to go one further and ask what the differences are between one kind of Baptist and another. But we'll leave that for another day and concentrate on the more pleasant subject of Baptist identity in general.

Two weeks ago I made the point about the Baptist idea of the church as a believer's church. That is, we are always one generation from extinction, since only those who freely and publicly profess their personal faith in Christ Jesus become members of the church. We do not baptize anyone without their consent, but we persuade them to follow Jesus of their own accord. Thus, the church is itself a persuaded church.

Last week we looked at how the principle of persuasion applies to our view of religious liberty. We believe in a free church in a free state. We believe in the separation of church and state—not the separation of God and government, not the separation of religion and public life, not the separation of the spiritual from the secular. We simply believe that the state should be neutral and respectful toward diverse religious expressions, and that the church or any religious body ought not try to control the state. The persuaded church is also the persuasive church: We make our case in the public square like everyone else. We vote our conscience and we appeal to the conscience of others. We trust in God's patient and longsuffering love to make the truth known through our Spirit-inspired witness to the world.

And that brings us to the last of these sermons. We need Spirit-inspired witness. The persuaded and persuasive church is also the persuading church. We are mission-minded people, witnessing to our faith in Jesus Christ so that others might come to know the power of God's salvation.

Baptists have been a powerful missionary force in the world since at least 1792, the night a British cobbler named William Carey preached a sermon that birthed the modern missions movement. His sermon had two points: expect great things from God and attempt great things for God. He and Andrew Fuller began the Baptist Missionary Society, and the spirit of preaching the gospel to all the world became part of the DNA of Baptists from that time forward. Our heroes have always been missionaries. Our heroines, too, don't you know?! This is how women really made it. Like St. Lottie (Moon) and St. Annie (Armstrong).

Across the last century, Southern Baptists did nothing better than missions. And today the Cooperative Baptist Fellowship, of which we are a part, continues this work alongside them. Baptists have called out people from our own pews to give up everything and move to the darkest corners of the world for the sake of sharing the good news of Christ. We have built hospitals and schools and drilled water wells and fed hungry children and started churches and nurtured the faith in the cultures we encountered without imposing all our own Western ways on everyone.

These days it is fashionable in some circles to question whether missionary work is even legitimate. After all, some say, shouldn't we believe that all religions are essentially equal? Why should we be so narrow as to think that Christianity is an absolute religion and the only way to God?

Now, this strikes me as a peculiarly Western question, born out of the weariness of a culture that has grown up on Christianity and known its abuses and intolerance. But we do not expect Muslims to think of their religion as one option among many equally true ways to God. And God knows they don't think of themselves that way. So why should we think it wrong to claim the rightness of our faith in Jesus Christ? If we truly believe that God was in Christ reconciling the world, if we truly believe that the Son of God became flesh, suffered, died on a cross, was raised from the dead, if we truly believe that God's love can be poured into our hearts in order to transform our lives from the mundane to the meaningful, and if we truly believe that Christ now invites the world to share in the joys of life eternal, how can we think to keep that to ourselves?

Most of the time when you hear sermons about witnessing and doing missions work, they come from a call to duty. We are told that Jesus commanded us to witness, so we must. The Great Commission requires us to go to all nations and make disciples, so we must obey. But there is something deeper than duty that fuels our witness—it is astonishment or wonder or beauty or love. Call it by whatever name, it is the breathtaking experience of life from the dead that is too good not to be true.

I remember when my children were born. The world changed each time for me. I knew that nothing would be the same again. And I wanted everyone to understand that. First-time parents are the worst about this (or the best). They act as if everyone ought to see things the way they do. They think that their new child has altered the course of history for good. And they cannot understand how it is that others do not light up at the very sight of their child the way they do. And that is the very attitude that characterizes true witnesses for Christ. They can't help themselves because they are so carried away by the gift of life that comes through Christ Jesus.

Jesus tells a parable in Luke about a king who throws a banquet and invites his subjects. You would think a king would simply demand attendance, but instead he invites. When some who are invited unimaginably decline the invitation, as if they could have anything better to do, he sends out his slaves to recruit anyone who will come. And when there is still room at the table, he sends them back out again to the highways and hedges, to the back alleys and underpasses. *Compel them to come in*, Jesus says.

Compel them. Now there's a word that didn't take long before it brought great abuse. By the fourth century, St. Augustine appealed to this passage to say that the state has the right to make Christians of every citizen, that baptism of persons without their consent is permissible. Since eternity is at stake for every person, servants of Christ are authorized to use any means possible to bring people into the church. He even applied this parable to justify persecution. The Inquisition and the Crusades and the forcible Christianizing of the heathen were all part of this dreadful misinterpretation of Jesus' words. Today many Christians in America are still tempted to use whatever means possible to coerce faith or manipulate people politically to join the Christian cause. This is completely foreign to Jesus' meaning and is totally uncalled for in Christian witness.

The word *witness* in the Greek language is *martures*, from which we get *martyr*. Christian witnesses vow to live the gospel and to love the gospel even if it costs them their lives. They will never take someone else's life for the cause of the gospel, but they are always willing to give up their own, just as Jesus himself did. Christian witness is testimony to "the truth, the whole truth, and nothing but the truth, so help us God." We live it and we tell it with a view that anyone else and everyone else might know it for themselves. We do not believe it is our own private experience that might not be right for someone else; we believe that Jesus is Lord of all and that all should come to enjoy the fellowship of his table spread out for all eternity.

We use persuasion to tell the Christian story, not coercion. We invite people to share in the joy of abundant life through the risen Christ. We respect the right of others to reject the invitation to life, even if we can hardly imagine why they would. But we reject the idea outright that respecting others' right to reject should lead us not to invite!

And yet that's mostly what we do, isn't it? The Baptist idea of the church is that everyone is equally privileged to share in the sharing of the gospel. We don't delegate that duty to a few missionary professionals or overeducated preacher-types. But when we fail to live as if the gospel makes any difference to us, when we are more excited about telling people about our latest business opportunity or about our newest hobby or the NFL draft, why should anyone want to come and join us in the faith?

I fear that we are like those in Jesus' parable who found every kind of excuse for not dropping everything and going to the party. We have decided that other things are more important to us. We have to tend to business, to our family obligations, to our entertainment pursuits. The worship of God, serving the community, giving our money and time for the sake of showing the world what God cares about: These things can all take a back seat to our other preoccupations.

When is the last time you sought out a friend you knew was hurting and talked about what a difference faith in Christ could make? When did you last invite some-one to church with you? When did you decide to sacrifice something you wanted so that you could contribute more to the things that would bring glory to God?

We have some wonderful opportunities in this church. We are located in a place where we can make a great difference for Christ in Dallas and in the world. We have enormous resources in educated and talented people. We have loads of wealth, if we would only admit it and not try to protect it by denying how much we really have.

And yet we act more like our duty as Christians is to keep a secret rather than to publish it far and wide. Go figure. *Everyone who calls upon the name of the Lord shall be saved,* St. Paul says. But how will they call on one in whom they have not believed? And how will they believe if they have not heard? And how will they hear if no one tells them?

You'd think we were holding on to bad news, not good news. You'd think we have something to be so embarrassed about that we try to hide it.

Mostly when Baptists say why they are Baptists, it has to do with how nobody gets to have control over their souls. We are all priests of God. Yes, true, but I worry that we've got a largely retired priesthood! It's time to come out of early retirement and take our place among those with beautiful feet.

How beautiful are the feet of those who bring good news! It's not about having painted toenails that people notice; it's about being the kind of person that makes others always glad to see you coming. How beautiful are your feet? How beautiful? How beautiful?

56

The Baptist Witness: Making All Things New

400th Anniversary of Baptists

October 11, 2009
Nineteenth Sunday after Pentecost
Revelation 21:1-5

Turning and turning in the widening gyre / The falcon cannot hear the falconer; / Things fall apart; the centre cannot hold; / Mere anarchy is loosed upon the world, / The blood-dimmed tide is loosed, and everywhere / The ceremony of innocence is drowned; / The best lack all conviction, while the worst / Are full of passionate intensity.

When William Butler Yeats penned these opening words of his poem *The Second Coming* in 1919, he believed the world had reached a hinge of time. Change was at hand. Chaos had eroded the balance of creation and culture. The carnage of World War I had punctured modern confidence in progress, and what the future would hold was less certain than that there was no going back. A revelation of something new was at hand.

History has a way of doing that to us. It moves us through cycles of stability and instability until reaching a new stability. And in those chaotic times—as things are falling apart and the centre fails to hold—we wonder what is indeed at hand, what new creation is about to be born.

Four hundred years ago, John Smyth poured water over his own head and gave birth to something we celebrate today. It was, in a sense, a false start of the Baptist movement, as the local Mennonite community quickly persuaded him that he should be immersed by a church. That, itself, was a step in the right direction, as it should still warn us about the ever-present temptation in our tradition to make faith in Jesus Christ a wholly individual matter. The first correction in the Baptist vision then took place right away as Smyth and his persecuted band acknowledged that whatever else it might mean to be a faithful follower of Christ, it takes a church.

In an important sense, this was a way these first Baptists kept things from falling apart. Discarding the church altogether in favor only of personal experience and self-baptism would have loosed anarchy upon the Christian world. But instead, Smyth, along with Thomas Helwys and their brave brood, innovated. They proposed a gathered church of believers, a covenantal community, a church that depended only upon the kingship of Christ. They rejected papal rule and royal rule, opting for the rule of the resurrected and living Christ, and him alone.

This was a radical departure from anything they had known until then. It must have felt like the reinvention of the church. But, in fact, it was in their minds only the restoration of the church. Where did they find such a radical notion of a gathered believers' church? They went back to the Bible and read it for themselves without the aid or—shall we say hindrance?—of church authorities who had a vested interest in maintaining the status quo. They imagined themselves as the disciples of Jesus and heard his commands to his ancient disciples as commands to them afresh.

The times in which they lived were spiritually disorienting. Less than a century earlier Luther had initiated a Reformation that severed the link between faith and the authority of the Catholic Church. And once the spirit of division had entered the communion of Christ, all sorts of manifestations of church would follow. In addition to Luther, Calvin would render another reformed model, and Zwingli another still. The more radical Anabaptists would offer yet another rendition that would lay the groundwork for the new Baptist vision of the church Smyth and Helwys would give us. But in England, the divisive possibilities coupled with the king's appetite for new wives. You know the story: Henry VIII established the Church of England essentially under his own authority, thus securing a divorce from a complicit church.

Against the backdrop of such audacity, Helwys could see clearly what others could not. In his little book called *A Short Declaration of the Mystery of Iniquity*, Helwys took no prisoners, taking to task not only the Catholic Church and the Church of England, but also the Puritans and Separatists who failed to grasp the full import of what was at stake. Here's what he said to the same King James I who gave us the English Bible: *For we do freely profess that our lord the king has no more power over their consciences than over ours, and that is none at all. ... For men's religion to God is between God and themselves. ... Let them be heretics, Turks, Jews, or whatsoever, it appertains not to the earthly power to punish them in the least measure. This is made evident to our lord the king by the scriptures.*

Well, truth be told, it was not made evident to the king by the scriptures. But it was evident to Helwys and the Baptists who saw something in the scriptures others were not seeing, though they were reading the same Bible. These convictional souls were the best of men and women, though their low social standing left them unesteemed by the lords and ladies of their day. They were also full of passionate intensity, to cite Yeats's phrase again. Conviction and passion. Helwys himself suffered martyrdom for the cause of a believers' church and a free church in a free state, rotting away in King James' infamous Margate prison.

And what has become of the vision of these passionate convictional Christians called the Baptists? Well, we are not only here today preserving their view of the believers' church four centuries later, but their influence on all Christian churches has been profound and lasting. A few years ago the church historian Martin Marty coined the phrase, "the Baptistification of American Christianity."[96]

By that he meant that the democratic spirit of church governance had prevailed. Even if hierarchs technically rule churches, the people no longer believe they should simply defer to their spiritual betters who hold church offices. They will have their say in how things go. And, likewise, we see a development that has even reached the Catholic Church. The Methodist theologian Geoffrey Wainwright recently declared at a meeting between Roman Catholics and the Baptist World Alliance on the matter of baptism as the normative form of Christian initiation, the Baptists have won. He pointed out that even the Catholic Church now recognizes that the pattern of believer's baptism is biblically preferable, and that only that affirmation allows infant baptism as an exception to make sense.[97] Remarkable. Now if we could just find it in ourselves to be equally gracious about Catholics not being somehow dubious or incomplete Christians because of their different baptism.

So, good for us: We have made a great contribution to the whole of the Christian cause. But let's remember why and how. In the midst of turbulent times, we looked forward and backward at the same time. We innovated by digging deeply into our tradition to find the resources for change that would fit our vision of the coming kingdom. Baptists have rightly attended more toward the future than the past. We have seen ourselves as the vanguard of the coming rule of Christ. Our very existence as a church in the world, we have thought, is but a token or sign of what will be true for everyone when Christ's work is finished and God's will is done on earth as it is in heaven. This doesn't mean we are perfect or superior to everyone else: We know we are yet sinners and unfinished saints. But we do not see our role in the Christian world as preserving what has been in order to maintain order. We see our role as igniting the imagination of the world to what may be and will be.

Jesus talked in his parable about the scribe who goes to the treasure of Torah in order to bring out what is new and what is old—not what is old and what is new! The reason many could not understand Jesus' teaching is that their minds had become so fixed to what was old they could not see or accept the new. And in the vision of John in Revelation 21, the risen Christ says *Look, I am making all things new!* He is doing that even now. He is not waiting until the condemnation of the world to start over again by making all new things. He is making all things new now.

And this is what we have to look for today as Baptists in our turning times when the falcon cannot hear the falconer. While many about us and among us bemoan the chaos and lament the loss of our cherished ceremonies of innocence, we have to keep innovating. We have to continue to be passionately convictional people. This is the way we honor the past and our Baptist forebears. Not by doing only what they did, but by doing what we must do by the same gospel reasoning they employed.

We must not jettison tradition; but neither can we become slaves to it if Christ is indeed making all things new. The great Yale historian Jaroslav Pelikan summed up

---

96 "Baptistification Takes Over," *Christianity Today* (2 September 1983): 33-36.
97 Note the creation of the Rite of Initiation of Christian Adults. Curtis Freeman, *Does Your Baptism Hold Water?* (unpublished sermon preached at Georgetown College, KY, 12 October 2009).

the challenge neatly: *Tradition is the living faith of the dead; traditionalism is the dead faith of the living.*[98] We want a living faith of the dead, which means that we will continually go to the traditions of Scripture and church history to find the grounds for renewal in our day.

We have to fight the temptation of traditionalism. I've come to believe that for many in our day, Baptist tradition is nothing more than what you grew up with. If you grew up in Cross Switch, Texas at the First Baptist Church there (or maybe at the Second Baptist Church, since where there's a first Baptist there's always a second, don't you know?!—by whatever name)—well, that for you is true Baptist tradition. Everywhere the church is changing today we hear the hue and cry that this is not the church I grew up in. Hello, if it's a Baptist church, it shouldn't be. Our story of innovation cannot be only a history lesson; it must be a lesson to guide the future. We have to continue to be nimble and agile for the sake of the wider Christian world. We have to dig into our Baptist history and into church history in general and into the story of the church in the New Testament to find the shape of things to come for our day.

And we have been doing that. While some have retrenched to forms of faith that only want to guard the past and put up walls against the winds of change, we have been busy punching holes in those walls to let the Spirit blow through. When moderate Baptists could no longer accept the approach of those who controlled the Southern Baptist Convention, we formed a Fellowship instead of Convention. When it became clear that missions work had been overly outsourced by the churches to professionals, we brought it back to the pew and are recovering the missional church. When the training of ministers had become so academic that the pastoral imagination was lacking, we retrieved forms of mentoring in the local church for future pastors. When it became clear to some of us that men and women will serve in the future kingdom of God as co-laborers in the gospel without the constraint of roles that may be more old creation than new creation, we started ordaining women to the task. And in each of these things, we have found firm footing for the future in pockets of the past.

The 108-story Sears Tower in Chicago, now named the Willis Tower, is the tallest building in the U.S. They have now built three glass balcony enclosures that stretch four feet out from the building at the 103rd floor observation deck. You can walk out there and look down at Wacker Drive below and feel the sway of the building in the winds off the lake. But they warn you before you do that it can be quickly disorienting. The best way to go out there is to walk backward and keep your eyes trained on where you were. Then when you are better accustomed to the newness of your place in space, you can look out with less fear.

Many of us feel like we are standing out there feeling the sway of the winds of change. Only time will tell if these are the winds of the Spirit, currents of Christ's renewal of all things through the church. It's a fearsome place to stand, but with a little faith in the One who holds the future, it's also thrilling. Amen.

---

98 *The Vindication of Tradition: The 1983 Jefferson Lecture in the Humanities* (Yale Press, 1986).

PART IX

In One Peace

Ecumenism and Interfaith

"In essentials, unity; in non-essentials, liberty; in all things, charity."

~ Rupertus Meldenius

Ecumenism preface by Steven R. Harmon

As anyone reading this book is undoubtedly aware by this point, George Mason is a different kind of Baptist. But how does one name the different sort of Baptist that George is?

George Mason is an "other Baptist." My friend and fellow Baptist theologian Curtis Freeman, who also contributed one of the chapter prefaces to this book, has defined what he calls an "other Baptist" as someone who has "frustration with both lukewarm liberalism and hyper-fundamentalism; a desire to confess the faith once delivered to all the saints, not as a matter of coercion, but as a simple acknowledgement of where they stand and what they believe; a recognition of the Trinity as the center of the life to which they are drawn; a longing to be priests to others in a culture of self-reliance; a hope of sharing life together that is not merely based on a common culture or determined by shared interests; a commitment to follow the teachings of the Bible that they understand and being open to receive more light and truth that they do not yet understand; trusting in God's promise of presence in water and table; a yearning for the fulfillment of the Lord's prayer that the church may be one."[99] George fully fits this description of an "other Baptist," but the sermons in this section of this book in particular live into George's "yearning for the fulfillment of the Lord's prayer that the church may be one" and invite their hearers and readers to yearn for this, too.

George Mason's "otherness" as a Baptist can therefore be named with a label that will strike many as oxymoronic: He is a "catholic Baptist." The case of the term "catholic" is significant. George is not an upper-case "C" Catholic. He is not Roman Catholic, and his yearning for the oneness of the church is not one that envisions all

---

99 Curtis W. Freeman, *Contesting Catholicity: Theology for Other Baptists* (Waco, TX: Baylor University Press, 2014) p. 26.

other denominational traditions coming "home to Rome"—though he does dream of a future in which Roman Catholics and Baptists and all other Christians are visibly united with one another, with current barriers to full communion between the divided Christian traditions removed. He is a lower-case "c" catholic Baptist: a Baptist who belongs to the church that is "according to the whole," which is what the ancient Greek word that gives us our word "catholic" literally means. George believes that Baptists have distinctive gifts that have been preserved uniquely in the Baptist tradition that are shaped by the distinctive historical journey that Baptists have experienced as a people of faith, and that the whole church will be enriched by receiving these gifts of the Baptist tradition into their own traditions. But he also believes that other Christian traditions have their own distinctive gifts that could help Baptists become more faithful communities of followers of Jesus Christ if they were to welcome these gifts into their own tradition without surrendering the good gifts that Baptists have stewarded.

I have claimed the label of "catholic Baptist" in my own theological work, and, as I have read the sermons that you are about to read in this section, I have been reminded of how the beginnings of my identity as a catholic Baptist are intertwined with the pulpit ministry of George Mason. When I was a Master of Divinity student at Southwestern Baptist Theological Seminary in Fort Worth in the early 1990s, my systematic theology professor, David Kirkpatrick, told me about his former student George Mason who'd written a doctoral dissertation at Southwestern engaging the trinitarian theology of Jürgen Moltmann and was now serving as pastor of Wilshire Baptist Church. By the time I too was a Ph.D. student in theology at Southwestern, I was listening to the radio broadcast of George's sermons at Wilshire on the Dallas classical music radio station WRR early each Sunday morning while I drove to the church I served as part-time pastor and receiving printed copies of those sermons in the mail. I was focusing my doctoral research on patristic theology, the thought of the fathers and mothers of the church in the first few centuries after the New Testament period, and wrestling with the tension between the New Testament biblicism of my Baptist tradition and what I was encountering in the developing tradition of the church in a period Baptists had long ignored. At the same time, I was experiencing an attraction to the larger Christian liturgical tradition that began to develop during those centuries and that had been retrieved by many other Christian traditions through the twentieth century liturgical movement. The preaching and worship leadership of George Mason provided me with a model for how I might receive some of these gifts of the catholic church, the church that is "according to the whole," in my own ministry. My current work as a Baptist ecumenical theologian is a flowering of seeds that were planted during that significant time in my theological growth.

Another way of saying that George Mason is a catholic Baptist is to call him an "ecumenical Baptist." The term "ecumenical" comes from an ancient Greek word that referred to the whole inhabited world. Early Christians began to apply it to the extension of the one church through the whole inhabited world that they knew. While this term may be more comfortable for Baptists of a progressive inclination than "catholic," not everyone has the same sense of what it encompasses. Some conservatives distrust ecumenism because they equate it with religious pluralism. But strictly speaking, ecumenism is an intra-Christian attempt to address the ongoing divisions of the church in light of the prayer of Jesus in John 17 that his followers might have the same unity in their relationships with one another that marks the relationships of the life of God. Yet there is also a "wider ecumenism" that includes interreligious dialogue, which all Christians can embrace without relinquishing their commitment to the truth they have encountered in Jesus Christ. Even such a comparatively conservative Christian tradition as upper-case "C" Catholicism has affirmed the necessity of interreligious dialogue: with Jews as fellow people of covenant who share with them the Hebrew Scriptures and messianic expectation, with Muslims as sharers of faith in a monotheistic creator God, and with other non-Christian religions in light of the "common origin and end of the human race" and as expressions of the search for God.[100] George Mason, the ecumenical Baptist, is committed both to an intra-Christian ecumenism that remains unashamed of distinctively Baptist convictions while maintaining openness to other Christians with whom he has significant differences and to a wider ecumenism that, while rooted in a robust faith in the Triune God revealed in Jesus Christ, joins those who do not share this faith in seeking mutual understanding and pursuing together God's goals of a restored creation and a reconciled humanity.

As I read the sermons gathered in this section, I was deeply moved by George's ecumenical vision of a church "according to the whole" that receives from the Triune God the gift of communion so that together it may participate ever more fully in God's community-making work, offering this gift of communion to a divided world. These sermons have renewed my own "yearning for the fulfillment of the Lord's prayer that the church may be one," and I hope they'll have a similar effect on you.

Steven R. Harmon is Professor of Historical Theology at Gardner-Webb University School of Divinity in Boiling Springs, North Carolina. He is Co-Secretary for the Baptist-Catholic International Dialogue Joint Commission and the author of several books, most recently Baptists, Catholics, and the Whole Church: Partners in the Pilgrimage to Unity.

---

100 *The Catechism of the Catholic Church,* §§ 839-56 (Liguori, Mo.: Liguori Publications, 1994).

57

The Once and Future Baptist Church

First in the series *The Once and Future Baptist Church*

Watch and listen to "The Once and Future Baptist Church" by following this link or scanning the QR code with your phone: youtu.be/Q0Z5Y1bECg8. Sermon begins at 27:10.

October 4, 2015
World Communion Sunday
Isaiah 43:16-21; Matthew 13:51-58

God is always calling us to be more than we have been.

That's what Loren Mead said in his landmark 1991 book *The Once and Future Church*. Mead was a church consultant who could see the need for a great congregational renewal in the American church.

The situation is even more dire today than it was a quarter century ago. Church attendance is down all across North America. Denominations are splitting and splintering. People are either losing faith altogether or losing faith in the church and opting out. Many still claim to be Christians, but they have had it with the church.

Baptists have seen this situation ourselves. Southern Baptists have recently announced that they have used up all the reserves they can spare and they will reduce their missionary force around the world by up to eight hundred people. The number of new converts to Christ who are baptized has been dropping steadily for years, especially if you do not include the baptisms of children who have grown up in the church. Don't think I am pointing only to Southern Baptists; we Cooperative Baptists are faring no better. Every large church in our group is seeing fewer people in the pews week by week. We see it here at Wilshire, too. Although we have maintained a vital and vibrant church, it takes about 50% more people being involved today than it did twenty-five years ago to maintain the same attendance.

Some churches have reacted to this development by changing their style of worship, looking for a magic strategy that will compel more people to be engaged and grow the church again. That approach usually creates more conflict than growth. All of these changes have church leaders everywhere asking themselves about whether there will be a church for our children and grandchildren someday like the church we have known. And most of us have to honestly say no; there won't be a church like what we have known.

But in the midst of all this, I have to tell you that I am hopeful. I believe in God. I believe the Spirit is at work giving birth to a new church in the midst of these developments. I believe the body of Christ will stand at the end of time. And I believe Wilshire can be a key agent in the renewal of the whole church.

What do I base this belief on? Is it naïve optimism? Is it the vain hope of an institutional leader who just wants to give you a pep talk to get you to help preserve the church on our watch so that I can feel better about my time in the saddle? No, it's based upon something more and something different.

When Israel was coming out of exile in Babylon 2,500 years ago, the prophet Isaiah said: *Do not remember the former things or consider the things of old. I am about to do a new thing; now it springs forth, do you not perceive it?* God had not forsaken the people. Yes, they lost their former glory in the land of Israel when the nation fell, the Temple was destroyed, and they were left to wonder whether they could sing the Lord's song in a strange land. The answer was, yes, they could, but it would not be like the good old days. There would be good new days to come, but they couldn't receive them and know that new joy if all they did was pine away for the former things.

Isaiah asks a poignant question: *Do you perceive it?* Do you sense, in other words, that amid so much evidence to the contrary, God is doing a new and wonderful thing?

Phyllis Tickle died a few weeks ago. She was the founding editor of the religion division of *Publisher's Weekly*. A few years ago she wrote a book called *The Great Emergence: How Christianity Is Changing and Why*. She looked at the history of Israel and the Church and found something astonishing. About every five hundred years the people of God have experienced a traumatic upheaval in the way they have understood and ordered their faith and life. Israel's captivity in Babylon in the sixth century BCE was one of those. The monarchy of Israel five hundred years earlier under King David was another. Obviously, another one was the Great Transformation, as she calls it, when King Jesus gave birth to the church in the first century of the Christian era. The rise of the monastic orders and the preservation of important texts during the Dark Ages of the sixth century were next. The great schism that split the churches of the East and West into the Orthodox and Roman Catholic communions followed in the eleventh century. Then the Protestant Reformation of the sixteenth century that toward the end included the emergence of Baptists. And here we are in the twenty-first century, a half-millennium removed from that time. Things are now changing underfoot, even as they had been in each of those other times. All those changes in the Church were responses to good and bad developments of culture, changing the ways in which people understood the world.

Each time a change happened, some Church leaders despaired at the loss of all they had known. They responded by doubling down on the former things, trying to hold on, claiming that that was the only faithful path for the faithful. But a few perceived that God might be doing a new thing. They looked at the past creatively, trying to find again what was essential and what wasn't. They charted a course to the future that they believed the wind of the Spirit was blowing them toward.

These developments remind me of Jesus' words in Matthew's Gospel about the householder who goes into his treasury to find what is old and what is new. He does interpretive work to reclaim what is valuable in the old and to show the value of what is new. He was referring to the true work of the scribes and defending his interpretation of the Law of Moses. Those who could grasp only the former things rejected Jesus and claimed that anything new was wrong. They discounted him and his disciples because they knew them personally and where they had come from. They took offense at him, and he could not do many deeds of power among them because of their unbelief.

We face a similar situation today. The task of the church of Jesus Christ is to find the way of Christ in our time and to be bold witnesses to it, as our new vision statement says. So, when we think of the once and future Baptist church, we have to be careful to reclaim what is good and enduring from our history and be open to what is good and new in our day.

Think about how different things are just in our lifetime of being Baptists. Once upon a time you could go just about anywhere in the South and find a Baptist church that sang the same songs out of the same hymnal, that taught Sunday school classes from the same curriculum, that worshiped the same way, that did missions together in the same cooperative program. Nowadays, churches are all over the map about those ways. Some have no hymnals at all. Some have praise bands. Some have preaching that is more like teaching, with the pastor in jeans and a golf shirt going on for forty-five minutes or more. Some don't even have Sunday school. And some are only doing their own mission work from their congregation. These changes aren't wicked, but they are certainly different.

When some of you were young, intermarriage meant Baptists marrying Methodists. Then it became Protestants marrying Catholics. Now it is Christians marrying Jews or other non-Christians. Today parents are more concerned that their Christian children simply know Christ and continue in the faith, regardless of what church or what style of church they attend.

When you look at how the spiritual landscape has changed, there are now more Muslims than Methodists in the United States. You are about as likely to have a Hindu nurse from India in a Dallas hospital as you are a traditional Christian. When Kim and I moved our family to Lake Highlands twenty-six years ago, we had Jewish neighbors on one side, Pakistani Muslim neighbors on the other side, and across the street was an Iranian Muslim man married to a Tennessee Baptist woman. The times they are a-changin', don't you know?!

You see, the challenge is no longer how we distinguish one brand of Christianity from another but whether the one church of Jesus Christ will be able to meet the challenges of a pluralist religious culture. So, during the next few weeks, we are going to consider how to face this new day. The times of playing intramurals among

Christian denominations are over. The time of finding the center of the Christian tradition and living into it with commitment and joy is upon us.

We will look at what Baptists still have to offer to the larger Church and what the larger Church has to offer us. We will consider the four traditional marks of the church: one, holy, catholic (small c), and apostolic. We will ask how Wilshire can be part of the emergence of a new and authentic Baptist Christian witness in our time.

I like to tell newcomers that if they want to understand our church, they can consider our name: Wilshire Baptist Church. Church is the family name. It's where we begin. We are part of the body of Christ that is bearing witness to the resurrected Lord Jesus everywhere across the globe. Our first name, Wilshire, comes next. We are gathered together as a congregation that is the visible expression here and now of Christ's body, alongside many others. And our middle name, Baptist—just as many personal middle names come from someone in the family tree—indicates the stream of Christian tradition we identify most closely with.

We have a tag line we often use that we stole from Wake Forest Divinity School: *Christian by conviction, Baptist by tradition, ecumenical in spirit.* I think that this captures much of our character.

How can we meet this challenge? First, we can each of us take our faith in Jesus Christ with utmost care and commitment. We can't take it for granted. We have to live our faith with courage and joy. We have to make it the center of everything in our lives.

Second, we have to commit anew to our life together. Being a Christian is a team sport, not an individual one. We are none of us the body of Christ by ourselves. We are only the body of Christ together. And that means renewing our commitment to each other, to worshiping regularly, to serving faithfully and giving sacrificially. Our life together is not mere association or convenience; it is essential. We belong to Christ, and we belong to one another.

Today is World Communion Sunday across the world. When we come to the Table of the Lord, we come together here in this place. But we carry in our hearts all those other Christians around the world who come to the Table of the Lord in their places, too. We come with those we agree with and those we disagree with. We come with those we admire and those we struggle to admit are part of the family. We come with those who are losing their lives at the hands of enemies of our faith and with those who worship in comfort and freedom. We are all in this together. And only if we are in this together will the Church of Jesus Christ emerge on the stage of this new world as the beautiful people of God that the world will be drawn to.

God is always calling us to be more than we have been.

58

The One Church:
Baptists and the Unity of the Church

Second in the series *The Once and Future Baptist Church*

Watch and listen to "The One Church: Baptists and the Unity of the Church" by following this link or scanning the QR code with your phone: youtu. be/7Db8wTEaut0. Sermon begins at 36:10.

October 11, 2015
Twentieth Sunday after Pentecost
Ephesians 4:4-6; John 17:20-23

Listen carefully and see if you can tell me what ONE word seems most important in Paul's words and Jesus' words ...

Jesus first (Jesus is always first, don't you know?!): *The glory that you have given me I have given them, so that they may be one, as we are one, I in them and you in me, that they may become completely one ...*

Paul next: *There is one body and one Spirit, just as you were called to the one hope of your calling, one Lord, one faith, one baptism, one God and Father of all, who is above all and through all and in all.*

That's a whole lot of oneness. Seems pretty important for Jesus and Paul to talk about the oneness of the church. Why isn't it more important to us?

We began last week a series of sermons on The Once and Future Baptist Church. And today we look at the first of the four traditional marks of the church over time. The church is one, holy, catholic, and apostolic. And what I am saying about the Baptist church of the future is that it will need to lean into these historic identifiers if it is to renew itself within the whole Church that is the body of Christ.

For us Baptists, part of the problem with the oneness of the church stems from the circumstances of our birth. We came into being in the early seventeenth century in England. We were one among many groups that mourned the corruption of the Church of England. Some were Puritans who never wanted to leave the mother church but committed to "purifying" it. Baptists were more radical. We were separatists who said that the Church of England couldn't be saved because it rested on a false alliance with secular powers. As long as church and state were united, the church would never truly be the church of the New Testament. We were called dissenters. And we honed our dissenter identity. We became good at it. Everywhere we went, we pointed out what was wrong with other churches.

This little ditty one of our members sent to me this week represents that critical spirit. This man's grandfather was a Baptist preacher who bequeathed the poem to his grandson. In an act of delicious irony, one of his grandfather's parishioners added the last verse that turns the finger-pointing back on us.

I had rather be a Baptist with faith, love and hope
Than be a Roman Catholic taking orders from the Pope.
I had rather be a Baptist and with my Savior go
Than be an Episcopalian with all their pomp & show.
I had rather be a Baptist rejoicing every hour
Than be a Presbyterian and never feel the power.
I had rather be a Baptist and have a beaming face
Than be a Methodist and afraid I'd fall from grace.
I had rather be a Baptist and know that I am right
Than trust in the water and be a Campbellite.

Now here comes the rejoinder from the pew …

I had rather be a Christian and know that I am right
Than be one of those narrow minded Baptists always in a fight.

I often tell people in marriage counseling: You have to decide if you would rather be right or be married.

The need to be right ends in a fight. It turns love into a contest of wills over who gets to define the relationship.

And that's what's happened with our many churches. Instead of starting from an assumption of oneness that we get from Jesus and Paul, we broke off into our separate churches and claimed we're the one true church. If you want to be in the one true church, join ours because we have it right.

This was the problem with our practice of baptism for many years. We said that, in looking at the New Testament, it seemed that baptism always followed belief by those who were able to make that decision for themselves. And frankly, I think we are right about that. Amazingly though, since 1988 the Roman Catholic Church has said that the normative pattern for adult initiation into the Church is by the conversion of the person before baptism rather than after infant baptism. Here's how they put it: *The Church recognizes that conversion is a free gift from God which must be nurtured, supported and allowed to grow with the help of the Spirit until the individual is ready to take the final step of professing his or her faith and becoming a Catholic.* In other words, they agree with us at last! Now don't jump up and down too quickly: They aren't building baptismal pools in their sanctuaries. Although some are. St. Joseph's Catholic Church in Richardson, for instance, where my old friend Monsignor Don Fischer served for some time until his retirement, has one.

Now, they don't usually practice baptism our way, but, still, this is a sign of how we can grow toward each other. Reciprocally, while we continue only to baptize in the way we do, we now acknowledge and receive confessing Christians from other denominations who were baptized in other ways. You see, we can hold our convictions and be generous at the same time. All of which moves us closer to the answer of Jesus' prayer that we all be one, and closer to Paul's claim that there is only one baptism.

But how should we think of this oneness? Our children's minister, Julie Girards, was telling me about a conference speaker last week who put up a picture of a tiger in a jungle. She asked the group what they saw and they all said they saw a tiger. Then she made the point that in many cultures when this picture is shown, the people say they see a jungle. They see the whole first, not the part.

This would help if we could begin to see the whole Church. You see, when all we see is a part of the church, we foster the feeling that we are apart from the one church because we are by ourselves the one church. But as my friend and colleague Curtis Freeman likes to say, *the local church is wholly the church, but it is not the whole Church.*

Jesus says the oneness of the Church is grounded in the oneness of the divine love of Father, Son, and Holy Spirit. The triune persons live in and through one another. The Father is not the Son, and the Son is not the Father, but the Father is not the Father without the Son and the Son is not the Son without the Father. Likewise, with the Spirit. They are altogether one, because they are all together.

Jeremy Begbie was in Dallas the other night and made a beautiful point of how to look at this oneness. Begbie teaches music and theology at both Cambridge in England and at Duke. He said that when we try to imagine the Trinity, our head hurts because we always use visual images for it. The problem is that it ends up making it look like God is either one in three parts or three gods. The three can't occupy the same space at the same time without each diminishing the others.

But what if we considered the world of sound? Jeff, help me here. [Organist plays on cue.] Play a note for the Father. Now play a note for the Son. And one for the Spirit. Great. Three notes, three different colors (as organists like to call these families of sounds). But now Jeff, play the same three notes together as a chord. Beautiful. Do you hear it? Each note is still itself. And each note occupies one and the same world of hearing as the others. But now they are more together than they were apart. Each supports the other and the one sound they produce from their three unique sounds is a *unity in diversity.*

This is what we should be aiming for in our efforts to live into the claim of our truly being one Church.

Baptists don't need to stop being Baptists or Lutherans Lutheran or Methodists Methodist or Catholics Catholic (you can name them all). But we should be able to look *through* the different churches to see the whole Church. If we offer ourselves generously to each other and receive each other hospitably, we will produce a oneness that will point the world to a new way of unity.

The world we live in is socially dysfunctional. You can see it in our politics right now. Whether liberal or conservative, each thinks they have the solution and the other simply needs to give in. The problem is that we have a common life to live that doesn't bow to the left or right. And the world doesn't have the vocabulary for what we have in common, only for what we have in difference. So, think about this: If the church that is the one body of Christ in diversity and is grounded in the life of the one God who is three persons cannot find a way to show forth our unity, who will the world turn to to learn it? The hope of human unity is in spiritual unity, not the other way 'round.

What can we do then to help make the future Baptist church one that makes visible the oneness of the whole Church?

First, we can believe in our hearts what Jesus and Paul understood: There is only one church, and no one congregation or denomination is the one Church without all the others. We can make a commitment to look at other churches as sister congregations that make up the one body of Christ instead of competitors to the title of the One True Church. The oneness of the church is a fact hidden in the life of God. It's not up to us to make the church one; it's up to us to show it is so.

Then this: We can move from a mode of being Baptist that is always and only dissenting, to one that's including and assenting. We need to say what we are for and not only say what we are against. And we need to stand with the rest of the church in all its imperfections, not just stand apart from it and point out its flaws.

A wounded man in a war-worn uniform was sitting beside a river. He wanted to cross but lacked the coinage for the ferry. A group of soldiers came to the shore to board several tied-up boats. The man pulled himself up and inched his way toward one of the men and asked if he could catch a ride. When they disembarked, one of the soldiers caught up with him and asked how he had the brass to approach the president of the United States, Andrew Jackson, for a ride.

I didn't know anything about him being President, he said. *All I know is that some people have a 'yes' face and some have a 'no' face. He had a 'yes' face.*

I don't know about you, but I want our church and all churches to have a 'yes' face toward the world. I want the world to look at us and see welcome for sinners and hope of salvation. I want other churches to look *through* us and see the whole of the beautiful body of Christ they share in with us.

If that's the Baptist church of the future you want to see, come along with us and make it so. Amen.

59

The Holy Church:
Baptists and the Sanctity
of the Church

Third in the series *The Once and Future Baptist Church*

Watch and listen to "The Holy Church: Baptists and the Sanctity of the Church" by following this link or scanning the QR code with your phone: youtu.be/DPZSczq-kd0. Sermon begins at 35:25.

October 25, 2015
Reformation Sunday
1 Peter 2:4-5, 9-10; Matthew 13:24-30; Mark 5:21-43

A weird thing happened in Washington, D.C. recently. What? Weird things happen in Washington, George? Well, this one moves past the political to the spiritual. After Pope Francis addressed Congress, Democratic Rep. Bob Brady of Pennsylvania ran to the podium and snatched the Holy Father's half-drunk glass of water and whisked it away to his office, where he, his wife and Rep. Bob Casey and his wife shared a sip of what they considered to be holy water. When reminded by reporters that the tap water was not holy in the strict Catholic sense, Brady dismissed them by saying, *Anything the Pope touches becomes blessed.*[101]

    The question of what is sacred and what is profane, and what is holy or blessed in relation to the church, is as old as the Church itself. We've made it today to the third of our five-part series on The Once and Future Baptist Church: A Challenge for Our Time. We're looking particularly at the Baptist movement—where we've been and where we're going—through the lens of the four historic marks of the larger Church. The Church is one, holy, catholic, and apostolic. Two weeks ago, we looked at how we can be uniquely Baptist and still part of the one Church with a capital C. Today we consider what it means for the Church to be holy.

---

101 Sightings, http://us6.campaign-archive1com/?u=6b2c705bf61d6edb1d5e0549d&id=932fe71a06&e=f0c9027622.

The odd incident concerning the pope's drinking water has more of a popular superstitious underpinning to it than even the Catholic Church would accept. But it is true that the Catholic Church has claimed that the pope and ordained priests have power to make ordinary water holy because the Church they serve as Christ's representatives on earth is holy by definition.

This debate about how the church is holy was fierce in the fourth century in North Africa. A group called the Donatists claimed that the true Church was composed only of saints—that is, holy ones, not sinners. And they went so far as to say that only if you were baptized by a Donatist priest or received communion from one could you have been validly baptized or truly have received the body and blood of Christ in the Eucharist. This debate raged until the eminent bishop of Hippo, Augustine, made his defining argument about the Church in his book *The City of God*. Augustine cited a passage from Matthew 13 about how the wheat and the weeds grow up together in the field, and, while they are growing, they look so much alike that it is futile to try to pick out the weeds until the harvest. His point was that saints and sinners are both in the church until the final judgment by God, who alone has the power to tell one from the other.

This issue goes along with the Catholic Church's baptism of infants and calling on church members to be faithful all their lives long in order to be counted among the holy when the judgment comes. Augustine himself feared on his deathbed that he would not be judged to be among the holy.

In the sixteenth century, an Augustinian monk named Martin Luther was so tortured about his sinfulness that he confessed to his priest to the point of wearing him out. Today we join the rest of the Protestant world in commemorating Reformation Sunday. On All Hallows Eve in 1517, Luther famously nailed his ninety-five theses to the door of the Wittenberg church, hammering home his protest against this spiritual insecurity, among other things. Luther's great insight was that the church is holy because God is holy, not because Christians are holy. For Luther, everything came down to God's grace in Jesus Christ. It is Christ's righteousness that we receive in our relationship to him, not our righteousness that we achieve in order to be worthy of him. Our faith is Christ's faith that is granted to us, because whatever Christ touches is blessed. Whoever is in Christ is holy.

Luther said the church is not filled with sinners and saints but with people who are sinners and saints at the same time.

Baptists came along about a century later. Luther's ideas about holiness being centered in relationship to Christ were carried over to how the church is organized. Baptists were not Reformers like Luther or Calvin; we were Separatists. The first Baptists believed that the only way to have a holy church was for it to be composed of holy people. And they were only holy if they were first born again and then baptized. Baptists believe in what is called the regenerate church; that is, the church is holy because it is only made up of people who have been regenerated—the word means "born again" or "born anew"—by their profession of faith in Jesus Christ and their baptism thereafter.

The problem is what to do with those regenerate people who, after becoming regenerate become degenerate again? What happens when they keep sinning? Luther himself acknowledged this problem when he said that the old man who supposedly drowned in baptism seemed to be a pretty good swimmer. Baptists didn't have a tradition of confession to a priest, since we believed all Christians were made priests, so we assumed that we should confess our sins to one another. And the revival movement really drove this practice home, as many would publicly rededicate their lives to Christ at planting and harvest times again and again.

However, this habit wasn't enough for some Baptists who were so concerned about this that they believed such sinners had actually fallen from grace. The Church of Christ movement under the influence of Alexander Campbell and Barton Stone in the nineteenth century split from Baptists and said that only if you were properly baptized by a minister in a truly New Testament church could you be saved. And if you kept on sinning, you would have to be baptized again and again. Sounds a lot like the Donatists, doesn't it? What's old is ever new, don't you know?!

Baptists were losing so many members to the Churches of Christ that they developed their own theology of how they were the true church. These Baptists tried to trace their holy lineage all the way back through history in an unbroken series of landmarks of true Baptist-like martyrs—all the way to John the Baptist himself. The Landmark Baptist movement is what shaped some of you in your Baptist upbringing, although you probably don't know it. For instance, the language of joining a church by letter came from the idea that only if you had a letter from a Baptist church that said you were duly baptized by a Landmark Baptist pastor could you safely join another Baptist church without being rebaptized. Some of you may also have grown up in a Baptist church that allowed only members of that church to receive the Lord's Supper. Same movement. You see, Baptists have sometimes reshaped their theology to stave off losing members to more-conservative churches by inoculating the church with even-more-conservative theology. Go figure.

I believe we need to rethink today what it means to be holy. With Luther we can affirm that all Christians are holy—that is, saints—in the general sense that by virtue of the work of Christ, he makes us his own. If you have put your trust in Jesus Christ, you are already among the saints. As Baptist professor Curtis Freeman puts it: When individual members fall into sin and even when as a community it is unfaithful and in need of reformation and renewal, the church by virtue of its union with Christ and the indwelling presence of the Spirit remains holy. As Karl Barth observed, the church may become a beggar, a shopkeeper, or a harlot, but it is still and always the bride of Christ.

We are, as 1 Peter says, the people of God, a chosen race, a royal priesthood, and a holy nation. But here's the important thing Peter says that follows: ... *in order that you may proclaim the mighty acts of him who called you out of darkness into his marvelous light.* You see, our holiness is directly related to our purpose as the people of God.

This is where we have so often gone wrong. We have made holiness into something that must be constantly examined to see whether our status is sure and our salvation assured. We have defined holiness as sinlessness, as purity, as some kind of state of saintliness. And too often that idea has to do with what we don't do rather than what we do. You know the old saw among us: A good Baptist boy is someone who doesn't drink or dance or chew or go with girls who do.

But the point of purity isn't purity any more than the point of fitness is fitness. If you work hard to get into great shape by watching what you eat, lifting weights and doing cardio workouts, and all you do with that is to celebrate how great your body is and how good you look, that's vanity, not purity. The point of great fitness is what it allows you to do because of it. If an athlete is out of shape, she won't be much good on the field or the court. The point of self-discipline is what it allows you to accomplish with the instrument of your body.

Likewise, spiritual fitness—let's call it holiness—is about how Christ-like we are becoming in order that we may participate in God's great mission to the world of calling those in darkness into the light of God's love.

With Augustine, we can leave the winnowing work to God at the end of days and now just trust in Christ for our eternal salvation. This approach will free us to get on with the work we share with all other Christians of every stripe—that we proclaim the good news.

So how can we as Wilshire Baptist Church become part of this effort to interpret a holy church to the larger Christian community?

First, let's acknowledge that we are all of us sinners saved by grace and get out of the business of trying to figure out who's holier than someone else. We should leave the sorting to God and get on with the serving instead. We should focus on how each of us can be better spiritually prepared to serve.

And that's the second thing: As Mark Wingfield nicely put it in his *Tapestry* column today, we should attend to how the gifts the Holy Spirit has given to us can be used for holy purposes. What are your unique gifts and passions? How can God activate them in service in order that your purpose can be fulfilled?

An old American Express ad said, "Membership has its privileges," but the future Baptist church saying should be, "Membership has its responsibilities." Holiness is the means of achieving our mission; it is not the mission itself.

A holy man was praying on a creek bank one day when his eye caught a scorpion that had gotten stuck on a log trying to cross the waters. As the waters continued to hit the small creature, the holy man sprang to his feet, reached out his hand and freed it so that it could make it to the other side. In the midst of the rescue operation, the scorpion stung the holy man. A bystander noticed the goings on and asked the holy man, "Didn't you realize that it's the nature of a scorpion to sting?" The holy man replied, "Yes, but it's my nature to save."

Friends, as long as we are concerned with a holiness that protects us from dangerous encounters with others, the church is not really holy. The holy nature of the church is seen only when we are about the work of saving.

60

The Catholic Church:
Baptists and the Universal Church

Fourth in the series The Once and Future Baptist Church

November 1, 2015
All Saints Sunday
Psalm 133; Matthew 16:13-19; 18:19-20

One of my favorite memories of the otherwise terrible tragedy that was the Ebola crisis—which led to the death of Eric Duncan and the twenty-one-day quarantine of Louise Troh and the three boys—was something the Catholic bishop of Dallas said. You remember that during the quarantine, Louise, her son Timothy, and her nephews Oliver and Jeffrey were secretly housed in a Catholic retreat center in Oak Cliff. When everyone else was finding a way to say no, Bishop Kevin Farrell said yes. On the day the family left quarantine, the media asked him why he did it, since none of them were Catholic. He said, *We didn't do it because they are Catholic; we did it because we are Catholic.*

I love that. But the truth is, even the church that goes by the name Catholic has work to do to become truly catholic. And, certainly, we do, too.

Today is All Saints Sunday. And it's the fourth in the series of sermons I am preaching on The Once and Future Baptist Church. Christians all over the globe will share communion during worship. On this day in particular, some of them will be doing what we did earlier, that is, remembering that the church includes the saints we see and those we don't. Among those we don't see are those who are not present with us in this sanctuary but are present in some other sanctuary in the world. Others we don't see but who share communion with us are those who are absent from the body but present with the Lord. They are not somewhere far away; they are in heaven, which is the place where God is, the invisible world that is more here than there. *Heaven* and *earth* are the words we use for the full extent of created reality. And the church exists in both realms.

So, we are a communion of all saints—a church of the living and the dead. Of course, even saying it that way is not quite true to our faith. We are really only a church of the living, but the living includes those who are alive in Christ right now but who are physically dead to us. So when we talk about the catholic church (small "c," don't you know?!), we are talking about all the people of God—past, present, and future; here, there, and everywhere—who make up the body of Christ universal.

Now about the saints invisible among us—we called some of their names earlier. Some wrongly assume that Roman Catholics and others pray to saints, but actually they only ask them to pray to God with and for us. And this seems reasonable, since why should we imagine that those who are alive in Christ are doing nothing in heaven right now but waiting?

Now I know that just saying those things sounds uncomfortably Catholic to some of you. And that's because for most of our roughly four-hundred-year history, we have defined ourselves over and against Catholics rather than as catholic (even with a small "c"). Here in Texas, the closer you get to the southern border with Mexico, the more you define Baptists as whatever it means not to be Catholic. So, if Catholics have Communion every Sunday, Baptists will make sure we have it as seldom as possible in order not to look Catholic. If Catholics have crucifixes—that is, crosses with the dying Jesus on it—we will make sure our crosses are empty, and maybe we won't even have crosses at all.

When this sanctuary was built in 1966, the congregation raised the steeple and decided to put a cross on top. That was a big deal back then, and some people were a bit worried that it was too Catholic of us to have a cross on our steeple. And when we decided to name the Prayer Garden that we built some years ago in front of the James Gallery, some of us thought calling it All Saints Garden in order to pay tribute to those saints from among us who had died in the Lord and were present still in spirit would be a nice way of remembering them. But some still felt uncomfortable that such a thing sounded too Catholic and wasn't appropriate for a Baptist church.

I understand. That has been our history. We did, after all, separate from the Church of England, which had separated from the Roman Catholic Church. The Second London Confession in 1688, signed by thirty-seven Baptist ministers, did declare that the pope is *that Antichrist, that Man of Sin, that Son of perdition*. And here in America, we taught generations of Baptists that we were the true church and the Catholic church was a false church. In 2001 the president of the Southern Baptist Seminary in Louisville, Kentucky, said on *Larry King Live* that the pope holds a false office, leads a false church, and teaches a false gospel. No wonder we are squeamish about the notion of catholicity.

But isn't it time we looked deeper at this issue and saw in our Catholic sisters and brothers the presence of Christ and the signs of the church? And isn't it time that we did the same with Protestants and Pentecostals? And isn't it time that the Catholic Church and all others did the same for us? I mean, this has to go both ways if we are all going to be truly catholic.

Today a Catholic Christian was welcome at the Table of the Lord here in a Baptist church, but a Baptist Christian was not welcome at the Table of the Lord in a Catholic church. Here's the irony: Today the Catholic congregation would have recited the Nicene Creed that declares the one, holy, catholic, and apostolic church, and yet they would not have communed with other Christians, yet we who did not recite the creed because of our historical (and sometimes hysterical) allergy to creeds practiced catholicity. Go figure.

How might we begin to heal this brokenness? For one thing, we can take another look at the question of where the church is to be found. Roman Catholics claim that when Jesus said, *You are Peter and on this rock I will build my church*, Peter then and there became the first pope, the first head of the church, with many to follow. So, when someone asks where the church is, the answer is: Wherever there is a bishop of the church, there is the church. Baptists read that passage differently. (Did you know that Christians sometimes interpret the Bible differently, and even Baptists sometimes disagree with Baptists?) Baptists say that what Jesus praised was not Peter alone but Peter's confession of Jesus as the Christ. We say that the church is founded upon a confession of Christ and that the church is found wherever Christ is confessed. It's Peter's *confession*, in other words, not *Peter's* confession.

Two chapters later, Jesus promises that where two or three are gathered in his name, he is right there with them. So the church is found wherever Christ is found with members of his body. We don't need a bishop to be the church; we need only confessing Christians gathered in Jesus' name.

Now, here's the rub: I like being in fellowship with many Christians who are Catholic and Orthodox, Lutheran and Presbyterian, Episcopal and Methodist, Baptists and non-denominationalists—you get the idea—as long as they are kind of like me and especially if they kind of like me. It's harder to claim kinship with Christians who are Catholic and Orthodox, Lutheran and Presbyterian, Episcopal and Methodist, Baptists and non-denominationalists who aren't kind of like me, and especially if they kind of don't like me. This business of being the one Body of Christ in the world is easy when it's about people like us and hard when it's not. But we don't get to pick our family, and we don't get to pick our family of faith. The church is not a fraternity or a sorority or a country club or a civic club. Wherever two or three of the strangest human beings in the world gather in the name of Jesus, there is the church catholic. It's here, there, and everywhere. And if we don't like it, tough luck—we're stuck with each other. We don't get to determine for Jesus where he will be and what the church is. He gets to decide that, and we get to abide that.

So how will we, Wilshire, work toward healing the rifts that put the catholicity of the church in doubt?

First, we can refuse to let our disagreements with and our distaste for other Christians extend to the point at which we dismiss them as sisters and brothers in Christ. We need to open our hearts to one another, even when those very others have broken our hearts time and again. And that is true of radical fundamentalists and radical liberals both. Sometimes they say and do things that make me cringe. Hey, sometimes I say and do things that make them cringe. As long as we are pushing each other away, we are working against the very things we confess about the church being holy, catholic, and apostolic. But if we learn to see Christ in them, perhaps we will give them an opening to see Christ in us.

Then this: Let's continue to open our imagination to the whole catholic church, which includes those who have gone before us and live now in the presence of the

Lord. Sometimes we act as if the church is composed only of those who happen to be walking around at this time. We forget that the church is also those who have lived faithfully before us and are praying for us and with us even now. We should even account for them in our decisions. We may, for instance, ask about how they lived and handled the challenges of their times. We may draw strength from their examples. We may not do exactly what they did, because if they lived in our times they might have done something different, too. But as Chesterton said, the church that is truly catholic is the most democratic of all institutions because it even gives a vote to the dead.

The Reverend Ian Paisley died last year. He had been a Protestant fundamentalist firebrand preacher in Northern Ireland and an arch-enemy of all things Catholic. His nickname was Dr. No, because his favorite phrase was "never, never, never." By that he meant that Northern Ireland, which was ruled by Protestant Britain, would never give in to the Catholic-dominated Irish nationalism that caused the so-called "troubles" for decades. He opposed the 1998 Good Friday agreement that created the outline for a new coalition government.

But Paisley had a near-death experience during an illness in 2004 that brought a change in outlook that can only be called a conversion experience. Call it an old man coming to grips with his mortality or a desire to leave a legacy of peace and not division. Either way, Paisley eventually became the most important figure in the peace of Northern Ireland that has held ever since. Within three years he had become First Minister of the new government alongside Deputy First Minister Martin McGuinness, who had been a commander of the terror-sponsoring Irish Republican Army and then leader of the Catholic political party Sinn Féin.

Paisley and McGuinness became such close friends that people called them the "Chuckle Brothers" because of all the genuine comity they shared in public and private. Each of them had made a remarkable journey of transformation that has made peace possible.

Just imagine. If Catholics and Protestants in Northern Ireland could find their peace with one another, what is possible for the rest of us?

61

The Apostolic Church: Baptists and the Missionary Church

Fifth in the series *The Once and Future Baptist Church*

Watch and listen to "The Apostolic Church: Baptists and the Missionary Church" by following this link or scanning the QR code with your phone: youtu.be/ J9h6LkEpKrA. Sermon begins at 34:00.

November 8, 2015
Twenty-fourth Sunday after Pentecost
Isaiah 42:5-10a; Matthew 28:16-20

We've come to the final sermon in a five-part series on The Once and Future Baptist Church: A Challenge for Our Time. The truth is this has been a challenge for every time: how to conceive of what makes an authentic church of Jesus Christ.

The traditional answer is to cite the four adjectives in the Nicene Creed: *one, holy, catholic,* and *apostolic.* Baptists have no objection to that, although we have interpreted each of these in somewhat different ways from other denominations across the years. Regrettably, the net effect of difference has been distance. We have argued our way away from one another. We have been more intent on proving who's right and who's wrong than on showing that who's right and wrong is secondary to our deeper covenant of grace that binds us together in the Spirit of Jesus Christ.

This week I was at a retreat in San Antonio of about thirty pastors in the Cooperative Baptist Fellowship. We do not all see alike on everything, we are Baptists, don't you know?!, but we have managed to love each other unconditionally and work together cooperatively. Our executive coordinator Suzii Paynter reiterated one of her consistent challenges: *You can be alone or you can be a fellowship.*

I have been saying in these sermons that the time has come for us Baptists also to be in fellowship with other Christians. We don't have to compromise the essentials of faith to do so; in fact, we have to focus on those essentials. An otherwise undistinguished seventeenth-century Lutheran theologian put it well: *In essentials, unity; in non-essentials, liberty; in all things, charity.*[102] Our problems as Baptists are problems shared by all denominations: We tend to elevate nonessentials to essentials, and we neglect the command to make charity, that is, love, the overriding virtue that characterizes the Church. *Love binds all things in perfect harmony,* Paul says in Colossians. Love works to bring unity. Love works through differences to find what we have in common. Love spends itself finding out how to accept and include rather than how to reject and exclude.

We've lived long enough casting aspersions on fellow Christians inside our own Baptist churches and certainly toward other Christians. That's unbecoming of the gospel, and it undermines the affirmation of faith that says the true church is one, holy, catholic, and apostolic. So, if you want to know what my agenda is for this series of sermons, let me summarize: *While the once Baptist church spent its energies distinguishing itself FROM other Christians, the future Baptist church should spend its energies distinguishing itself AMONG other Christians. We should look to contribute our part to the larger Church rather than pulling away from the larger Church.*

The last adjective we look at today—*apostolic*—is one of our best opportunities to do just that. Baptists specialize in being apostolic. It's in our very DNA. But it's going to take some work to convince other Christians that our understanding of this concept can unite us. And it's going to take some work on our part to accept that their understanding of apostolic need not divide us.

So first let's look at how episcopal denominations view the matter. The word *episcopal* means "of or relating to a bishop." The relevant denominations include Roman Catholic, Orthodox, Lutheran, Episcopal, and Methodist, among others. These churches view the rulers of the church as the definers of what it means to be an apostolic church. Jesus gave Peter and the other apostles authority to govern the church. And when they died, that authority passed to others whom they had laid hands on and ordained to take their place. So as one Catholic writer says, *Any entity or body claiming to be the Church of Christ would have to be able to demonstrate its apostolicity by demonstrating an organic link with the original apostles on whom Christ manifestly established his Church. Nothing less than this could qualify as the "apostolic" Church which Jesus founded.*[103]

Now Baptists do assert an organic link with the original apostles, but in a different way than having clergy who exist in an unbroken chain of authority for two thousand years. Because of this view, the Catholic Church cannot consider Baptists to be formally part of the one, holy, catholic, and apostolic church since we don't recognize the binding authority of the pope and the other bishops of the church. The Catholic Church calls us *ecclesial communities,* which is a kind work-around to acknowledge that we are fellow Christians but outside the one and only true Catholic Church.

We don't have to agree with this judgment, but here's something we can do: We can see the Catholics' ordained spiritual leaders as legitimate signs of apostolicity

---

102 Often misattributed to Augustine or Philip Melanchthon, it actually seems to be Rupertus Meldenius.
103 Kenneth D. Whitehead, *The Four Marks of the Church.*

without making it the whole definition. Once granting that, we may then offer a different approach that we can all accept.

Baptists define *apostolic* by the very meaning of the word. *Apostle* means "one who is sent." It doesn't mean "one who rules." It has to do with obedience to the Great Commission more than obedience to human superiors. What we Baptists have to contribute to the larger church is a passionate acceptance of our missionary character.

We believe that what it means to be apostolic is to see ourselves standing before Jesus as the disciples did in their day and hearing him give us the selfsame commission to go and make disciples of all nations, baptizing them in the name of the Father and of the Son and of the Holy Spirit, and teaching them to observe all things that he commanded them. We are an apostolic church when we are a missionary church. Apostles are sent ones, and an apostolic church is preoccupied with going into all the world and announcing the good news of Jesus Christ.

You see, the problem with making the apostolic concept about guarding our creeds and deeds in order to keep the church in order is that we end up being a defensive church. We will always be looking for what's wrong, for who our enemies are, for the latest threat to our existence. Instead, we should be focused on people, on being a light to the nations, on sharing the good news of Jesus that God is not counting our sins against us, on being ambassadors of reconciliation, on daring to be peacemakers, on welcoming strangers, and on living winsome lives of generosity and hospitality. When we do that, then we are apostolic.

Even Baptists had to come around to this view. For nearly the first two centuries of our existence, we were more interested in defining ourselves by what we were not than by what we were. This is normal for any movement that breaks off from others at the start. But in 1792 a simple Christian cobbler named William Carey asked in a published tract *whether [the] Commission given by our Lord to his Disciples be not still binding on us*. The prevailing view of his time was that the Great Commission was fulfilled by the apostles in their generation and that *if God intends the salvation of the heathen, [God] will some way or other bring them to the gospel, or the gospel to them.*[104] Carey and other Baptists started asking whether they themselves were not the way God would do so. And so the modern missions movement began with Baptists.

Ann and Adoniram Judson answered the call and went to Burma. Their labors there seemed fruitless at first, but today we have Burmese Christians who are members of our church and are studying for the ministry. Southern Baptists were always at their best when they were focused on being a missionary people and not becoming a theologically doctrinaire denomination. When the Cooperative Baptist Fellowship started twenty-five years ago, we were not only reacting against that fundamentalism; we were fueled by a desire to reach people in the world with the gospel that no one had reached before and to do work among the twenty poorest cities in the world and the twenty poorest counties in the United States.

Wilshire has been working in the neglected Mississippi Delta. We have been working to build a middle class in the Dominican Republic by using Christian

---

104 Curtis Freeman, *Contesting Catholicity: Theology for Other Baptists* (Baylor Press, 2014), pp. 269-70.

disciplines and sound small business practices. We are working in Peru and North Africa and also here through Gateway of Grace with refugees who have come seeking safe harbor. We are helping the Gaston Christian Center to incubate new churches and ministries. I could go on and on. And we want to go on and on.

So, what else can Wilshire do to call the whole Church of Jesus Christ to a more missionary definition of what it means to be an apostolic church?

First, we can renew our missionary zeal. So much of our 20/20 Vision is focused on how to accelerate our mission work. We can't allow ourselves to become content with being a church for ourselves. If the gospel has changed us on the inside, it will move us to work for change on the outside. We want everyone to know the life-changing, world-changing grace of Christ.

We need all hands on deck to do that. And that means being an inclusive church. Not for the sake of being inclusive, but because we can't be pulling people into the church with one hand and pushing people away with the other. Immigrants and migrants and refugees are coming to us these days. We have to throw out the welcome mat of the church to anyone and everyone, whoever they are and wherever they come from. Who is to say that God is not giving us an opening for witness that is not about whether you are from this nation or that, but whether you are part of the transnational kingdom of God?

Then we have to not only open our hearts to people and open our mouths in witness but also to open our wallets in generosity to fund this missionary enterprise.

When you give to this church, what's the mental picture you have of what your gifts go to? If your imagination is focused on paying the light bill or seeing to it that I get paid, you are only halfway there. You are giving *to* the church, yes, but more than that, you are giving *through* the church.

You and I can't be everywhere at once to make the church an effective missional agent in the world. But, through our generous giving, we can support many others who are giving their lives to others in the name of Christ. The missional church can be everywhere; the one, holy, catholic, and apostolic church can be everywhere at once when we give and give and give again.

Blake Tommey grew up in our church. He heard the call to ministry here. He is the student minister now at the University of Virginia. He also writes for the Cooperative Baptist Fellowship magazine. This week he told about a fifth-grade girl named Estera in Bucharest, Romania. She attends the Ruth School, which was started by our CBF missionaries. Estera loves to read, and her favorite story in the Bible is the parable of the lost sheep. She can relate. She is from the Roma people, the Gypsies. They are hated everywhere. But when she reads that story of the shepherd who leaves the ninety-nine sheep and goes after the one lost one, she knows that God is the kind of God who goes after lost things, who looks for and after those who have been cast away or fallen through the cracks—those like Estera.[105] That's what you should think of when the plate is passed. Think of Estera and how the church is apostolic only when it is the missional church.

---

105 *Fellowship!* (October-November 2015): 17.

Not everything about who Baptists once were needs to change in the future Baptist church. But we all must change if we are to join the whole church of Jesus Christ throughout the world in pointing the way to life.

Interfaith preface by David Stern

Enlarge the size of our tent,
Extend the size of your dwelling,
Do not stint!
Lengthen the ropes, and drive the pegs firm. (Isaiah 54:2)

In the sermons that follow, Dr. George Mason challenges us to enlarge our tents of religious imagination and understanding. He affirms the blessed specific of who we are as Christians, Jews, and other people of faith, and then challenges us to see those precious particularities as part of a greater mosaic whole, the Oneness we call God.

I have had the privilege of engaging in interfaith work with George Mason for decades: in private conversation and public forums, in Dallas and in Jerusalem, in difficult questions and common cause. What emerges in these sermons is exactly what has emerged through those cherished decades of relationship: a pastor who holds his faith with both deep commitment and genuine humility; a Christian devoted to understanding his own faith by bringing it into conversation with other expressions of religious faith and community in God's world. What a gift to know a religious leader who is both committed and curious, an advocate and an explorer on the path of faith.

As congregational clergy, we easily get busy with our own shops: There are sermons to be written, children and adults to be taught, budgets to be met, the needy to be clothed and fed, worship to be designed to inspire the human spirit. And that's just with our people. So it is quite fair to ask: Why not just stay in our own religious lanes? With so much other sacred work to be done, why invest time and resource, and why take the various risks, to engage in the work of interfaith understanding and coalition? Why bother?

A couple of obvious answers suggest themselves. First, we do interfaith work because it feels like the nice, neighborly, and monotheistic thing to do. In other words, it's relatively easy to stay on the surface, comfort ourselves by homogenizing differences, and give superficial lip service to the profound idea that we all serve one God. Second, to the extent that we share practical goals in the community and broader society (feed the hungry, house the homeless, advocate for the oppressed), why not focus on these common objectives to combine forces in their pursuit?

But George is after something much deeper here. He eschews easy answers for a more discomforting climb: It is difference, not surface harmony, that lies at the heart of genuine interfaith understanding. In "Mending Walls and Moving Mountains," the brilliant sermon I was privileged to hear George deliver at Temple Emanu-El in Dallas, he reveals that the title of Robert Frost's famous poem "Mending Wall" is in fact tantalizingly ambiguous. Does the title refer to the act of mending a wall? Or does it suggest that a wall can be the source of mending—that only once we recognize what separates us can we "walk the wall together?"

For George, this task is not only relational or sociological, but also theological, the work of revelation itself. His reflections in these sermons remind me of the great teaching of the twentieth-century French philosopher and Talmudist Emmanuel Levinas as summarized by scholar Avivah Gottlieb Zornberg: "God can reveal the Divine Self to human beings only because of [the] human ability to allow the shock of otherness in the encounter with another human being." In other words, the goal in genuine relationship is not to press or suppress each other into some comfortable state of sameness. Instead, it is "the shock of otherness:" Only in seeing the "other" in you can I train myself to encounter the Ultimate Other, the revelation of God in my life. The stakes could not be higher, nor the answer to "why bother" more clear: Interfaith dialogue not only allows us to see each other, it trains us to see God.

This discomfiting recognition of otherness does something else fundamental to the spiritual life, and fundamental to George's preaching and ministry: It forces us to the other side of the stained glass, beyond the familiar comforts of our particular communities and out into a world which we can only serve by allowing it to disturb us. Because when I as a Jew become practiced in honoring the spark of God in a Christian or a Muslim, then perhaps I can begin to recognize it in the panhandler on the corner, or the immigrant in the bus station, or the genderfluid teen in my family, or the protester holding the sign declaring a view I find repulsive. Interfaith work not only thrusts us into each other's sanctuaries, it pushes us beyond them to live the very lives of empathy, faith, and compassion those sanctuaries call us to.

The Joseph story in the Book of Genesis begins with a seemingly innocuous statement about Joseph's father Jacob: "Now Jacob was settled in the land where his father had sojourned, the land of Canaan" (Gen. 37:1). But the great medieval Jewish commentator Rabbi Shlomo ben Yitzchak sees Jacob's settledness as a problem, as a mistaken sense of completion and complacency. For more than anything else, what Judaism and Christianity have in common is a sense of sacred incompletion, of being participants in the unfinished work of rediscovering and reaffirming God's redemptive light in a fractured world. In that sacred work, George Mason's ministry teaches us that the interfaith encounter with the other, the ability to both value and walk the wall, is a vital source of both revelation and repair. In his sermon at Temple Emanu-El, he called it "this sense of purposeful pilgrimage ... when we know we have come from somewhere and we know we are headed somewhere but we know we haven't arrived yet." How true of the journey we all take together, and how blessed we are to have Reverend George Mason as our teacher and guide on the pilgrim path.

David Stern is the Senior Rabbi at Temple Emanu-El in Dallas, Texas. He has served as President of the Central Conference of American Rabbis, the international rabbinic organization of the Reform movement. He serves on the Board of Governors and the President's Rabbinic Council of Hebrew Union College-Jewish Institute of Religion.

62

Peace Within the Faith and Among the Faiths

October 5, 2003
Seventeenth Sunday after Pentecost
John 17:17-23; Hebrews 7:1-4, 22-25

Steve Blow published some of Grover Gillett's jokes the other day in the paper. Like this one I like: *A family-style restaurant is one where there is an argument at every table.* Cute. Sadly, some could just as easily say that about the church that gathers 'round the Table of the Lord and calls it communion. *A church is where there is an argument at every Lord's Table.*[106]

Wouldn't it be great if that weren't true? What if the church were the one place you could go to find what family is all about? Family of spirit teaching family of blood how to live. Family that comes together by choice out of a love that has so taken us that it is no choice at all. Wouldn't that be communion?

One reason we don't know church like that is that we mistake communion for union. Most divisions in churches across time have been over forced oneness—compelled agreement in doctrine or ritual or class or race or whatever. We want everyone to be alike, to think alike, to look alike, to act alike. Stepford churches rather than Spirit churches.

I was in a car recently in East Texas with Jon Whitten and Greg White. We were passing church after church. There are a lot of them in East Texas, don't you know?! Anyway, I told them that one of my hobbies is to guess what denomination a church is by the architecture of the building. I think I could make the honor roll if you graded me on only that. But even if you blindfolded me and dropped me into a gathering of church people, I think I could tell you before long what denomination they are. Some of that is harmless; we all know that spouses start to favor each other over time, and even the dog takes on the look.

---

106 *The Dallas Morning News* (3 Oct. 2003): 1B.

More serious is when the unique personalities of people are absorbed by the conformist spirit of the church; when the diverse ways God has made us are swallowed up in a homogenizing process that is good for milk but not for church; when the Spirit of God cannot bubble up from within the congregation because there is a man or a group of men in charge that keep bursting the bubble with their controlling rule; when self-appointed infallible interpreters decide what the truth is for everyone else and say that anyone who doesn't see it that way is arguing with God not with them; when attempts to purify the church end up wringing all the joy out of it, and the hilarity of grace is muted by moral correctness. When these things take the place of genuine communion at the Lord's Table, we have left the definition of Jesus as to what makes us one, what puts us at peace, and we have substituted stifling uniformity for serendipitous unity.

We've been looking for the past five weeks at the peace that passes understanding. God is peace. Our peace with God comes through Jesus Christ. Our experience of that peace depends in part on our making peace with our betrayers and our enemies both. We complete the series today by looking at how the peace of God is revealed to the world by the peace of the church and by the church's peacemaking with other religions of the world. Peace within the faith, in other words, and peace among the faiths.

But if it is a peace that *passes* understanding, then this peace is a great mystery, a gift that invites our embrace but eludes all our attempts to manufacture it ourselves. Jesus prays that his disciples—and that would be us as much as them—would share his peace. He wants us to be one with one another as he is one with God. But it is more than an analogy of oneness—*be one as we are one*. Jesus invites us to participate mystically in God's own oneness.

God's unity is not uniformity. The Father is not the Son, nor is the Son the Father. And the Holy Spirit, too, is a unique personality in God. The divine life is a triune community of love. The Father gives himself to the Son and the Son receives his life from the Father. The Son wants nothing but to give himself back to the Father in love. And the process with the Spirit works the same. Generosity and hospitality, giving and receiving, leading and following, loving and being loved: These are uninterrupted movements in the dynamic life of God. So much so that it has been called the dance of the Trinity.

Well, what's your point, George? Real Christians dance! Even Baptists can learn how to dance like God. We are invited onto the divine dance floor; the music is playing. We are not allowed to be like a bunch of junior high boys, too cool or too shy to get out there. Grab a partner and learn the steps. [Grab partner from the chancel and dance while speaking.] The peace of the church is a relational peace. We live and move and have our being in God and with each other. Sometimes we will step on each other's toes, but grace demands that we not dishonor our partner when that happens by pointing out HER faults in public. If we share in the divine life, we will celebrate the wonder of each unique person in our midst and learn to move in beautiful rhythm together.

Wilshire, we do this better than most churches I have known. We allow for differences, and on our best days celebrate them without feeling that the unity and identity of our life together are threatened. But we must always be on guard about this because unity and mission go hand in hand. When we draw in the tent, when we stop making room for new ideas and new people and keep everything safe and neat and tidy and just so according to the taste and preferences of the pastor or a few people, we endanger our mission by closing off our open unity.

Jesus said that it was his oneness with the Father that caused the world to believe he was sent from God. It is our oneness with one another that will prove to the world we have been sent by Christ, who is sent by God. In other words, our witness to the world is at stake in our unity with one another. We need to be sanctified in the truth of this, so that we will be effective in what God wants us to do in the world.

Jesus prays that God will sanctify us in the truth just as he himself is sanctified. Now, to be sanctified is to be made holy or pure. We usually think that means to be morally perfect or hold perfectly to the absolute truths of the Bible. But to be sanctified or made pure or holy is really nothing more or less than to be fit for a task. When a soldier goes into battle, he needs to be sanctified, that is, fully prepared to offer himself to the task and not fail because of fear or lack of training. In the same way, we offer ourselves to God and to one another as partners, not just for the sake of being together but for peacemaking in the world. We hold nothing back, leave no one behind; we are brothers in arms, so to speak, laying down our lives if necessary.

Sundown tonight begins the Jewish High Holy Day Yom Kippur, or Day of Atonement, which concludes the Days of Awe that began on the New Year, Rosh Hashanah. A traditional Jewish prayer for the New Year goes this way: *Purify our hearts to serve you in truth. You, O God, are truth, and your word is truth and stands forever.*[107] To purify ourselves in truth is to be united with God in love, so that we will live out of God and for God in all things. And that means, also, that we will live for everyone God wishes to make peace with, including those of other religions that do not acknowledge Jesus as Savior of the world. If we consecrate ourselves as Christ did, we will love the world as he did, and we will not use power to claim privilege over others as a means to show them we are right and they are wrong. We will love them and engage them and befriend them and give ourselves in love to them the way Christ did for us.

In a little more than a week, Baylor University Medical Center will fulfill a founding pledge in a new and stunning way. The hospital will dedicate the Bradley Wayne Interfaith Garden of Prayer. It all started when a Jewish doctor, Bob Fine, found Muslim hospital employees praying in a stairwell because they had no place to practice their faith equally and openly. A hundred years ago, Dr. George W. Truett, a champion of religious liberty, pastor of First Baptist Church of Dallas, and founder of the sanitarium that predated the hospital, said: *Is it not now time to build a great humanitarian hospital, one to which men of all creeds and those of none may come with equal confidence?* At last Baptists will rise to that challenge in a

---

107 Cf. Raymond Brown, *The Gospel According to John*, Anchor Bible Commentary (Doubleday, 1966), p. 765.

generous and symbolic way. The garden will include a labyrinth that will serve as a prayer path for those who seek spiritual comfort in times of distress. You will also find there a bench with a plaque on it with a verse from the Psalms that reads: *Be still and know that I am God.* It was given by Wilshire Baptist Church; I am proud and disappointed both that we are the only church to have contributed to the effort. Too many are afraid an interfaith garden will bless other religions in ways that undermine the truth of Jesus Christ.

But look at how the writer to the Hebrews used the non-Israelite figure of the priest Melchizedek as a figure of Christ himself. Abraham paid tithes to this mysterious king of Salem, which means "king of peace," who knew nothing of the true God but was honored for what he did with what he knew. Christians must remember that Jesus Christ is risen from the dead and is drawing all people to himself. He is not only at work within the church; he is present everywhere in the world. And if that is so, he is not missing in action in any honest worship of people of other faiths. It is our duty as Christians to catch up to Jesus and bear witness to saving faith in him by our Christ-like relations with people of other faiths. We cannot erect walls that keep us safe within our faith, when the One who is the way, the truth, and the life, the One who was crucified outside the walls, is already outside the walls seeking all who would be saved.

In a moment we will go to the Lord's Table, and we will do well to remember that it is the Lord's Table, not ours. On this World Communion Sunday, we join Christians everywhere on the globe at the Table, celebrating our unity with Christ and each other. But it should lead us to everyday peacemaking beyond the Table, too.

The Masai tribe in Africa has a curious cultural rite that was baptized into a Christian practice after Catholic missionaries led them to faith in Christ. The passing of a tuft of grass is a gesture of peace among the Masai. If an argument becomes heated, they reach down and pass grass to each other as a sign that they will not allow the dispute to destroy their communion in Christ. It is also a promise that no violence will erupt because of the argument. When the time comes for the people to gather for Mass at the Table of the Lord, the elders of the community judge whether the grass has been honored or violated in any way that would bring sacrilege upon Christ in the Eucharist. They will not share Communion if the peace of Christ does not rule among them.[108]

My friends, let us be the kind of people who honor the peace of Christ by being at peace with one another within the faith and with those of other faiths. Then the world will know we truly belong to the God of peace.

---

108 Cited by Stanley Hauweras, *The Peaceable Kingdom* (Notre Dame Press, 1983), pp. 110-11.

63

In One Peace

Watch and listen to "In One Peace" by following this link or scanning the QR code with your phone: youtu.be/ttMx223snQQ. Sermon begins at 27:45.

July 18, 2021
Eighth Sunday after Pentecost
Ephesians 2:11-22

A salutation is the way we greet one another in a letter: *My Dearest Kim. Greetings. Ladies and Gentlemen. To Whom It May Concern.* The Apostle Paul begins this letter to the Ephesians as he does similarly to others with the salutation, *Grace to you and peace from God our Father and the Lord Jesus Christ.*

On the other end is a complimentary close, technically called a valediction. Paul closes this letter reversing the order. *Peace to the whole community,* he says. *And grace be with all.*

I often sign off a letter or email with a valedictory phrase I would like to claim but I'm sure I borrowed from someone: *In One Peace.* I mean it to spark thought. We sometimes say we are in one piece—P-I-E-C-E—in the sense of holding it all together. But *in one peace*—P-E-A-C-E—says something about our unity with God and one another. God has made us one in Christ. Christ is our peace, uniting in one peace those who were once near to God and those who were far from God.

The valediction *in one peace* is a statement and a challenge at the same time. And just that is what we have in these beautiful words of Paul in Ephesians 2.

The world in which Paul wrote was bursting with both cultural and holy hostility. The Roman Empire was obsessed with peace. *Pax Romana,* Roman Peace, was an extended period of imperial stability enforced by the empire. It was peace at any price to preserve power. The Roman historian and politician Tacitus attributed these words to Calgacus of Britain: *To plunder, butcher, steal, these things misname empire; they make a desolation and call it peace.*[109]

It's not uncommon even in our day to talk about peace this way. We send in the army or the police when there is an uprising, and when these forces quell the unrest

---

109 Noted by Verhey, Allen and Harvard, Joseph S. in *Ephesians* (WJK, 2011), p. 89.

with use of or threat of violence, we call it peace. Yet the underlying conditions of hostility still exist. This is not *Pax Christi*, the peace of Christ.

There was also holy hostility. Enmity between Jews and Gentiles was rooted in religious belief and behavior. Jews considered Gentiles dirty. They ate unclean foods, worshiped many gods, and behaved in sexually permissive ways. Jews were the people of God; Gentiles were unwashed pagans.

The religious separation between them was memorialized in the Jerusalem Temple, where a literal stone wall divided Jews and Gentiles. God-fearing Gentiles were permitted to come to the Temple but could go no further than the five-foot high wall that bore an inscription threatening death to any who tried to go beyond it. On their side, Jews were discouraged from cavorting with Gentiles. They couldn't eat with them or socialize with them lest they become unclean.

The church Paul wrote to in Asia Minor, modern day Turkey, was composed of both Jews and Gentiles. Everything had changed in Christ, Paul claimed. He had torn down the wall of division, removed the hostility between Jew and Gentile. All were one in Christ Jesus.

Two millennia before Robert Frost penned his famous poetic line, *Something there is that doesn't love a wall, that wants it down*, Paul said the same in powerful prose. Christ has *broken down the dividing wall, that is, hostility between Jew and Gentile.*[110]

But even if they knew that in their heads, they had a hard time figuring out how to live together when they had always and only understood each other as fundamentally different. Paul had to provide scriptural justification for their oneness. And how he does it is sheer spiritual brilliance.

He appeals to Jews and Gentiles both to drop the way they previously viewed each other and instead adopt a new vantage point. Christ has created a new humanity, a new social reality. An inclusive church would be a sign to the world of God's universal love for all and a peace that no earthly powers could bring.

Jesus was the Messiah of the Jews, the one to whom all the law and prophets had pointed. He was a good Jew, but he ate and drank with sinners, healed the diseases of Gentiles, and treated them as beloved children of God. When Paul says that Christ came proclaiming peace to those who were near and to those who were far off, he is citing the prophet Isaiah who proclaimed the mission of Israel to be a light to the Gentiles. They who were far off from God, who did not know the covenant of Israel or have a share in the promises of God were brought near in Christ. Jews could no longer look upon Gentiles as aliens; they were to see them as siblings in spirit, sharing one Father in the one Holy Spirit.

Jews should not expect Gentiles to become Jews in order to be part of the new community. Gentiles didn't need to be circumcised or to keep all the laws of the Jews to be part of the promised peace of God. And Gentiles should not expect Jews to stop being Jews and suddenly stop keeping kosher and observing other laws that had marked their way of life. Jews could be Jews and Gentiles Gentiles, but each had to view the other as brothers and sisters in Christ, in other words, in one peace.

---

110 From the poem *Mending Wall.*

The first big challenge for the early church was for Jews to find a place in their hearts and in the community for Gentiles. Paul's argument centers on the story and the statutes: Gentiles could share in Israel's story by being a sign of their successful witness to the one God, and Jews could continue to observe the statutes of Moses. Their identity now would be in Christ, though, not in ritual observance of laws alone.

Today, the challenge is just the opposite. When the Proud Boys marched with their tiki torches on Charlottesville in 2017, they chanted *You will not replace us*, and *Jews will not replace us*. This is rooted in the terrible idea that the true people of God are white Christians who have established a godly Western culture that is in danger of being diluted and ultimately replaced by nonwhites and Jews. Jews are always suspected of conspiring to undermine white Christian supremacy. Which is why the Ku Klux Klan was not just anti-Black but also antisemitic. And their unhooded progeny today spews the same hate.

When the church thinks of itself only in Gentile terms, even though we found our salvation in a Jewish messiah, we replace our Jewish origin with something else. For too many, whiteness has become that origin story of our blessing. White supremacy is a scourge on the soul of the church. The healing of it begins with a reclaiming of the Jewishness of Jesus and the realization that we have become part of Israel's story, not the other way 'round.

But it's one thing to get our theology right; it's another thing to get our living right. Now as then, tensions over differences in the church are real.

The church is like a demonstration plot in an agricultural project. A demonstration plot is when a section of the field is carved out for a new experiment in farming that if successful will then become the new pattern of planting and growing.

In her beautiful book *Braiding Sweetgrass*, Robin Wall Kimmerer writes about the Three Sisters approach to planting crops among Indigenous people. While the English colonists planted straight rows of single species, Native Americans from Mexico to Montana planted corn, beans, and squash in the same one square foot of soil. It turns out that this is healthier for the crops and the soil both. When you plant a single crop in a plot of land, it depletes the nutrients of the soil. But since the Three Sisters need different things from the soil and provide different benefits to the other sisters, they work together to produce more and better harvests. The corn grows up first, as the elder sister. The beans, as the middle sister, come along next, their vines wrapping around the stalk of the corn. The youngest sister, the pumpkins and squash, take their time and act independently. No surprise there, don't you know?! But that's not all bad: Squash have broad and prickly leaves, providing shade, keeping the moisture in and discouraging caterpillars from eating the other crops. Genius. Kimmerer concludes: *Being among the sisters provides a visible manifestation of what a community can become when its members understand and share their gifts. In reciprocity, we fill our spirits as well as our bellies.*[111]

When the church is homogeneous, all looking alike and thinking alike, all wanting everyone else to believe and behave as they do, they may be a comfortable and

---

111 Milkweed, 2013, p. 134.

cohesive club, but they are not the community of Christ. The church has nothing to offer a world that is divided by every kind of race, class, and political difference if all we do is mirror the culture.

What made the church the church initially and still does today is its radical vision of a new and inclusive humanity. The gospel isn't just a spiritual appeal to our hearts before God that provides inner peace; it is a communal command to be a people who practice peace with one another. Our duty is to be a demonstration plot in the field of the world, proving that living together in love, celebrating the dignity of difference, is the true direction of a genuine and lasting peace.

Let me finish by once again quoting Brian McLaren: "More than ever before in our history, we need a new kind of personal and social fuel. Not fear, but love. Not prejudice, but openness. Not supremacy, but service. Not inferiority, but equality. Not resentment, but reconciliation. Not isolation, but connection. Not the spirit of hostility, but the holy Spirit of hospitality."[112]

When we do, we will truly live *in one peace*. Amen.

---

112 *We Make the Road by Walking: A Year-Long Quest for Spiritual Formation, Reorientation, and Activation* (Jericho Books: 2014), pp. 217–218.

64

Mending Walls and Moving Mountains

February 8, 2002
Interfaith Shabbat at Temple Emanu-El
Exodus 24:12-18

Something there is that doesn't love a wall. Robert Frost began one of his most memorable and yet ambiguous poems with that familiar line. *Mending Wall*, he titled it; and on first reading or maybe even on the twenty-first, what you are apt to hear in it is something like this …

Two neighbors meet once a year in the spring to mend the stone wall that separates their homesteads. All sorts of things have happened during the year to break down the centuries-old wall. The frozen groundswell of winter, the hunters that pay no mind to the wall for the sport of having the rabbits out of hiding from behind the stones. There's no good reason for a wall there, one neighbor thinks. No danger of his apple trees bending over to eat the cones under the neighbor's pine trees and ending up with a mixed marriage of trees that dilutes the races or religions of either one. So why a wall, he wonders.

The other neighbor would rather act the part of an old Stone Age warrior, though, and do the work of rebuilding the wall to keep his defenses strong. He moves in a darkness that comes from within, the enlightened neighbor thinks. The insecure pine-wooded neighbor lives by a creed he inherited from his father: *Good fences make good neighbors.*

For a long time I would hear people quote that phrase—*good fences make good neighbors*—and think they were naïve readers, shallow dullards who never spent enough time with the text to see that that is the very thing Frost was trying to counter. He wants us to cast off all this inherited tradition we have blindly received and think for ourselves. *Before I built a wall I'd ask to know / What I was walling in or walling out / And to whom I was like to give offense,* he says. He wants us to dream of a world where we don't need good fences to make good neighbors. We should stop mending walls and start mending ourselves.

But maybe on second reading or twenty-second, another view might emerge that causes us to wonder if that is so. Is it all so clear what Frost wants us to see? Or is the very title *Mending Wall* supposed to lead us to the idea that if we didn't have that wall to go to together every spring, if we didn't have to work at it from our own sides and from our own vantage points, if we didn't have our fathers' sayings to wrestle with or our mischief notions of a world without walls and neighborliness without fences, well, would we ever meet at all? Would we really be better not to struggle over the wall between us? Would we really know one another better, respect each other more, or feel safer in the presence of the other?

I bring up this long look at Frost's *Mending Wall* because it speaks to so much about why we are here tonight and what we think is going on not only between Temple Emanu-el and Wilshire Baptist but between Jews and Christians generally nowadays. Some of us want to say, *Something there is that doesn't love a wall, that wants it down.* We are genuine and well-meaning. Christians who say that think, with Paul of Tarsus, that the Messiah has come and has broken down the wall of hostility that separates Jews and Gentiles. Why don't we all just get with it? Why don't you just get with it, is what we mean. He is our peace at last, making us one people. And to that, many Jews will say, *Good fences make good neighbors.* You are not only theologically at odds with us over Jesus; you feel that being believers in Jesus is spiritual betrayal, like having your circumcision reversed so you can compete in the Olympic games. You will point to intermarriage and tell us that what happens when the dominant culture is Christian is that Jewish identity is lost. You will remind us that Jews have been scapegoated through the centuries whenever things went wrong in Christian lands. And you will point to Israel today and tell us why good fences make better neighbors, if not good ones.

On the other hand, there are those Jews who would say to Christians, *We like Jesus and what he taught and would happily include you Gentiles in the kingdom of God as fellow persons of good will, but you have to let go of this obsession with the divine uniqueness of Jesus and the need for us to confess him as Lord.* And to that, many Christians will say, *Good fences make good neighbors.* We are only willing to acknowledge our debt to Judaism so far before we feel we are spiritually betraying the one who claimed uniquely to be the Son of God. Tolerance is a virtue and diversity is healthy, but you can't give away the church just for the sake of community.

What encourages me about this night is the chance to acknowledge the wall together, to go to it together and work it, to wonder together why we need it or if we need it, and to respect and learn from each other while we do.

You have been doing this for more than a quarter century here with this Interfaith Shabbat. We are grateful to share the time with you this year. We are Baptists, which makes it all the more remarkable that we are here. We are not the kind of Baptists that have said things like, *God Almighty does not hear the prayer of a Jew,* but those Baptists are our kin as much as the ultra-Orthodox are yours. And though we have tried to distance ourselves from them and draw closer to you in friendship, you are not fooled by the fact that we still believe Jesus is the Messiah and that he is somehow Savior of all the world, not just of us Gentiles. But you have invited us to walk that wall that stands between us and to see whether we can be at least good neighbors. By God's grace, perhaps there'll emerge enough mischief in us as we walk the wall together that God will teach us both some things we didn't know. And perhaps we will find in the end that it is not so much the wall we are mending but each other. And maybe if we go to the wall *with* each other, there will come a time when we will go to the wall *for* each other.

Allow me now to switch metaphors from mending walls to moving mountains. Ambiguity, you see, is also present in the Torah text this week, especially Exodus 24:12-18, where Moses goes up to the mountain of God, Sinai, and concludes the section of the Book of the Covenant with a fresh encounter with God's glory. The presence of God is like a cloud that falls upon the mountain. To the people at the foot of the mountain, the cloud that Moses sees is billowing smoke. *Where there's smoke there's fire*, they think. Whereas Moses had seen a bush burning that was not consumed and had learned of God that entering into God's fiery presence should evoke awe but not fear, the people see a consuming fire and relate that to a God they must fear. Moses trusts the presence of God enough to enter into it and remain there for six days, enveloped by it but without understanding. Only on the seventh day, after doing the silent work of obedience all week, God's Sabbath voice speaks the word to Moses.

So, within Israel, right at the time of covenant-cutting, there is this ambiguity in their experience and understanding. This extends also to us Christians when we read this text as if it has also to do with us. As remarkable as it may seem to some of you who think we just look at this part of the Bible as *Old* Testament or as *Hebrew* Scripture, just as you say year by year 'round the Seder table, *When WE were in Egypt* ... so when we come to a text like this, we say to ourselves, *When WE were at Sinai* ... . Some of us know you were there first, and some of you are willing to let us be there with you now. We may be on two sides of the mountain, as if on two sides of a wall, but at least we keep gathering there, both of us, to listen and to learn.

Maybe that's why we don't really know where Mount Sinai is still, except that it is probably not within the land promised to Abraham. Israel gathered there in that No Man's Land that is therefore Every Man's Land. They gathered in the presence of and on behalf of the nations. We acknowledge sadly that others of us, though— Jews and Christians both—view this mountain as their own private property, a text like this as a claim to exclusive privilege to the word of God and to being the people of God. But we come to it together as if we both somehow belong there.

The Christian lectionary has this same text on the docket for Sunday. This is the Sunday of the Transfiguration of Our Lord. We will read Exodus and then reflect on it in light also of the time in Jesus' life when he went up to a mountain with Peter, James, and John. He was transfigured there in their presence; his whole being began to shine in a way reminiscent of the Shekinah glory that came upon Moses. Moses was there on the mountain with Jesus, along with Elijah: the Law and the Prophets, the two pivotal mountain men in the history of Israel. And then the Sabbath voice from heaven spoke, saying of Jesus, *This is my beloved Son in whom I am well pleased; listen to him.*

Peter, James, and John didn't quite know what to make of all that. Peter thought of Sukkot and offered to build booths for the three holy men. Jesus quickly taught them that staying there on the mountain wasn't the point, that there was a mission down the mountain, in the valleys of everyday life, needing their attention and his. And perhaps if you would allow us to be on Mount Sinai with you, we should learn to see you on the Mount of Transfiguration with us. Moses and Elijah remind us that whatever mission we have from Jesus to the world, it is still the mission of Israel that we are joining rather than replacing.

My 18-year-old daughter asked me about this transfiguration story at dinner the other night. She couldn't quite get her mind round it. In good rabbinic fashion, I answered with a question: *What do you think it means?* That way I could maybe learn something before I told her. Anyway, we worked out a couple of things that may help us in Exodus, too.

First of all, when do these two formative mountaintop experiences occur, and where? In Exodus we have the deliverance from Egypt behind us and the settlement in the Promised Land ahead. The covenant is made and the law of God given in this transitional time in Israel's life. They are becoming a people they couldn't very well have been in captivity. But they are not all socially and economically organized in the Holy Land yet either. Similarly, this is a transitional time in Jesus' ministry. He has completed his healing and teaching work in Galilee, he has worked deliverance from sickness and ignorance, and now he is heading toward Jerusalem. He has no place to call his home, but he is headed to where God is calling him.

This sense of purposeful pilgrimage rather than senseless wilderness wandering is helpful for Jews and Christians both these days. If we were to remain tied to Egypt or Galilee in our minds, we would forever view ourselves as victims of the terrorizing powers of this world. But God has delivered us and set us on a journey through the wilderness. It is not the Promised Land yet; we have no final security here. But we travel this way of faith alongside one another, if not together.

Jews remind Christians that the world is still not redeemed, that we have a long way to go still, that we are not there yet. Christians remind Jews that our very presence on the journey should tell you that God has already done something miraculous through you that is for the whole world, that election as a people is a calling to neighborliness, not a rejection of it, to an inclusive rather than an exclusive community of God.

I would submit that we are at our best in the faith—Jews and Christians—when we adopt this pilgrim posture. When we know we have come from somewhere and we know we are headed somewhere, but we know we haven't arrived yet. This makes us open to one another rather than casting the stranger from our midst. Jews know how dangerous it feels when they are a minority in a majority of Christians all settled down in the land. American Christians are only now learning what it feels like to be out of cultural control. We're not handling it well, but you can teach us.

Second, going to these mountaintops together should lead us to a renewed experience of and reverence for God. The awesome presence of God, the fiery shining of God should inspire us to transcend our preoccupation with ourselves as the source and end of life. A deep and real existential sense of God's explosive presence in our lives is a *sine qua non* for people of faith. We must nurture that sense of awe and duty to God's fiery presence.

We are responsible to God and responsible for God to the world. Defining ourselves as a people must be done first by reference to God and not to ourselves. Many of you are preoccupied with the question, *Who is a Jew?* Many of us are preoccupied with the question, *Who is a Christian?* Perhaps we might all begin again with an awareness that we are none of us anything before God says what we are. Our worship of God is nonnegotiable, our identity a gift more than an achievement.

Finally, there is also our mission for God in the world. These texts invite us to carry out our covenant duty not only to God but also to the world. We have a witness to give about who God is and how God wants us to live. It involves justice, love, and mercy.

We have a story to tell, the basic *haggadah* of our existence. But we also have a way to live, the extensive *halacah* of God's commandments. They are present there on Mount Sinai with Moses, and they are present still on the Mount of Transfiguration with Jesus. We walk alongside one another on this salvation road. We Christians gain our bearings by following and listening to Jesus, who embodied for us the law and the prophets. But we keep one eye peeled and one ear open for you, because we know we cannot be traveling in opposite directions and be on the kingdom road. We hope and pray that you will at least keep an eye peeled and an ear open for us, too.

Our mission, though, is not simply to keep and pass on external laws, however good or godly; we are to be transfigured ourselves by the experience of God in the keeping of them. They must become internal to us, changing our very nature. The shining of Moses and the shining of Jesus are invitations to us all. We are all to be so consumed by God's presence, so in sync with God's will and way though our obedience, that we shine before the world as a sign and reminder of God.

There's a story in the ancient church that sounds almost Hasidic. A desert father called Abba Joseph was approached by a young monk who said, *As far as I can I say my prayers, I fast a little, try to live in peace and keep my thoughts pure.* What else can I do? Abba Joseph stood up and stretched out his hands toward heaven, and as he did, his fingertips were lit with flame. He said to the young monk, *If you want to, you can be totally fire.*

If you want to! May we each of us and all of us so want to embody the will and way of God that we shine as lights in this dark world.

Amen.

PART X

For Good and For Good

Peacemaking and Nonviolence

"If equal affection cannot be, let the more loving one be me."

~ W.H. Auden

"The cross symbolizes the love of God. Period. It forever stands as a powerful warning against using the name of God to do violence."

~ George A. Mason

Preface by Greg Garrett

My friend the Rev. George Mason is one of the Christian world's most accomplished preachers and pastors. A writer, teacher, activist, and media figure, during thirty-plus years as senior pastor at Wilshire Baptist Church in Dallas, Texas, he modeled a Christian love of and advocacy for the marginalized, the disdained, the set aside, that feels absolutely like the Jesus I know, love, and serve. In the process, he engaged Wilshire, Dallas, and the Christian world with his teachings about what it is God is calling us to do and be. Since I work on questions of race, justice, reconciliation, and peacemaking, it is a gift and a privilege to reflect on these powerful teachings on some of the most important issues in contemporary American life.

The Most Rev. Michael Curry, Presiding Bishop of the Episcopal Church, has a very short checklist about how we should preach, teach, and live the Christian life: "If it's not about love," he says, "it's not about God." My friend the Very Rev. Kelly Brown Douglas has a similar understanding about how we present God to the world: If we're not preaching about the liberating power of God, she argues, then we are not understanding God at all.

It is such a joy to be able to say as I look over the sermons George preached at Wilshire Baptist Church on the war in Iraq, on synagogue massacres and gun violence, on Botham Jean, murdered in his own Dallas apartment, on George Floyd, murdered in public view in Minneapolis, that his weathervane always points us toward that God. Although certain kinds of Christians command the public view, George and other faithful progressive Christians have held up an alternative vision of faith. I've always understood George's Twitter bio, where he describes himself now as "Retired Baptist pastor (not that kind)."

Yes, people continue to make assumptions about all American Christians because of white Christian Nationalists, or because some Christians decide to shoot up synagogues or to murder faithful parishioners in Charleston, South Carolina. It is painful indeed to reckon with the fact that some who claim the same Jesus we do have felt led to commit violence in his name, despite the compelling evidence that Jesus was not about "winning," but, as George puts it, about being the Anointed One of God who loved and willingly gave his life for them, about how the Cross "symbolizes the love of God. Period."

As we look at George Mason's storied career, there are a multitude of times that he stood for us in the pulpit or in other settings to say that any reading of Jesus' life, death, and resurrection that suggests a Christian nationalist reading, or a violent reaction to issues in this life, or that supports the sin of racism, is "bad Bibling." Truly, as I read and reflect on these sermons, they break and remake me, which is exactly what I imagine they were supposed to do. To hear from him that "Racism is America's original sin" (in George's June 2015 sermon on the murders at Charleston's Mother Emmanuel Church) is to hear that any theology that centers only on the privileged, or on salvation, is incomplete. The world is more complicated—and requires more grace—than those teachings.

George's most powerful preaching on God's love and on human injustice seems to me to come in his 2022 sermon on MLK weekend. In that sermon, George offers a prophetic vision of how the Church could have shaped an alternative history of America, one centered in the love and grace of Christ and in the teaching that the first will be last:

> Imagine the American story if our country at the first had a bias toward the last. By now we know that there is more than one origin story of America—one at Plymouth with the Pilgrims, the other at Jamestown with enslaved people of African descent. But it didn't have to be that way ... .
>
> What if our nation's forebears in Plymouth and Jamestown had taken up the Bible's bias toward the last? What if we hadn't needed the 1619 Project to retell the origin story of America from the view of the last?
>
> Speaking of what ifs ... What if the church in the antebellum South hadn't read the Bible to justify slavery? What if John Broadus, one of the founders of the Southern Baptist Theological Seminary, hadn't defended the Confederacy as the hope of preserving civilization, thereby setting Baptists on the side of human oppressors? ... What if our white city fathers had not made an accommodation with Black pastors to keep the Civil Rights Movement from bringing real change instead of surface peace?
>
> Well, that was then, but this is now. Happily, we have the same chance today to make things right that we have always had.

The great American writer James Baldwin has some ultimate wisdom to share, despite the American failures and disappointments he had witnessed. He spoke of the New Jerusalem and the Welcome Table—the former, a vision of a new reality where justice would flow like a mighty river, and the latter, a religious glimpse of something like the communion table, a place where all of us, the first to the last, would be seen, known, loved, and fed.

George Mason has preached and loved us into these beautiful realities, and I am so grateful for the chance to remind us of them here. This is how God is moving in the world, this is what the Church should be doing, and this is the vision of a world shaped by love, peace, and grace.

Greg Garrett is the Carole McDaniel Hanks Professor of Literature and Culture at Baylor University in Waco, Texas, and Canon Theologian at The American Cathedral in Paris, France. He has written a number of books on the intersection of literature, culture, religion, and politics, most recently the novel Bastille Day *and* A Long, Long Way: Hollywood's Unfinished Journey from Racism to Reconciliation.

65

The Third Way

March 16, 2003
Second Sunday in Lent
Mark 8:31-38

I've ridden in cars with some of you who have those newfangled navigational systems. I notice you generally don't use them. *It came with the car,* you are quick to say. *I'd never buy it as an option.* Or maybe you did, thinking you'd use it more than you do. All that GPS technology, but after the novelty wears off, you get tired of some woman's voice telling you where to go, as if you're some directionally-challenged driving imbecile. Okay, so I'm projecting. I had a rental car this week that came equipped with the Hertz *NEVERLOST* system. Well, let me tell you, you've still got to follow directions from it or you can get lost, don't you know?! You miss your turn, and you have to hear this woman come on and say, *Calculating the route.* She is kind enough not to say, *Recalculating the route,* although that's what she means. You are lost, but she knows where you are and will get you back on track.

Wouldn't it be nice to have a foolproof spiritual navigational system? You get lost and the Holy Spirit recalculates the route, based upon your current position. Well, I'm going on the assumption this morning that that is just the hope we have in Christ as we directionally-challenged disciples try to find our way. During the season of Lent we pay closer attention than usual to the way of Christ, as if we know we need a refresher course now and then, given how prone we are to wander. We are in a season of life together when we are all talking about the right way to go, what with a pending war and all.

Our text today invites us into a moment when Jesus rebukes Peter for rebuking Jesus' way with the world. Keep in mind this comes right on the heels of Peter confessing that Jesus is none other than the one and only messiah of God! Here's the comfort: Even those closest to Jesus, even those who know him best, lose their way sometimes and need to have their route recalculated.

Well, here's what I am asking you to do in the next few minutes: Try your best to take off your Republican and Democrat hats in church. (It's the polite thing to do.) Then remember that in your baptism you vowed your first loyalty to the kingdom of God, and not to any human state or leader. The issue for the church is whether we are following Jesus, not whether we are following the United Nations or the president of the United States. All powers and authorities are subject to Christ. We find our way as Christians by finding his way. And if we want to find our life truly, we will lose it in the service of Christ and his kingdom. If we are ashamed of him now, if we refuse to follow his way, we will find him ashamed of us later. And that is no prospect for peace in time or eternity, either one.

Martin Luther King Jr. said the church must never be the master of the state or the servant of the state; but it must always be the conscience of the state. Until the American and French revolutions, no one much imagined statecraft in which the church did not try to master the state or serve it. But Jesus laid the foundation for this view when he rebuked Peter for wanting him to lead a military action for Israel against Rome. He offered his way of the cross, the way of suffering love with and for others as an alternative to the two most common ways of the world—violent action or passive inaction, militarism or pacifism. Jesus' third way tackles evil vigorously and breaks the cycle of violence in the process.

Now let me begin by saying that I believe the church ought to give account to why it is not pacifist, rather than why it is not militarist. Surely we have learned by now that fighting wars in the name of God, conquering people for God's sake, crushing cultures and punishing people for believing what we don't, has proven a wrong way to carry Christ's cross in the world. When the church embarked on the Crusades in the Middle Ages, slaughtering Muslims in the name of Christ, forcing Jews to convert on pain of death or torture, we sowed seeds to the wind that we reap even now as a whirlwind of revenge a thousand years later. Make no mistake. When Muslims around the world look at the West and think they are fighting back against Christians who have done them harm, they are not talking just about our generation. They have long memories. What they believe about Christians is as much our misunderstanding and misapplication of Christianity as theirs. We have not taught the world about the Christ who loved them and gave himself for them. They picture Christ's cross upside down: a sword in the hands of oppressors. We have to rightside the cross to show them the life that really is life—a life that comes from standing up for and giving yourself up for your neighbor.

If you check the DNA of a cross-carrying Christian, you ought to find it coded for peace, not for war. Jesus insisted that his kingdom is not of this world. He did not mean by that that all he's good for is giving peace to your heart and courage to live in the world until you go to heaven and find a peaceable kingdom in daily life and politics. He means you can't identify any state with the kingdom of God on earth. God's reign holds us all accountable for how we treat one another, for whether we learn to wage war or peace in his name.

So, when Christian preachers I have read or heard these past weeks try to support the probable war with Iraq by saying that America has a spiritual duty to support

Israel against her neighbors, or that Iraqis can be equated with the Amalekites that God told Israel to wipe out entirely for their wickedness, or that we must follow Paul when he said to support those in authority that God has established no matter the matter, I would say that is bad Bibling. It doesn't seem to me consistent with the way of the one we say is the fullest and clearest expression of God among us. Jesus said to turn the other cheek when you are struck. If you're going to war, I'd say you'd more likely find Jesus on the front lines with medics and chaplains helping soldiers and civilians who are hurt than in the war room directing the bombing campaign.

But if you check the DNA of a cross-carrying Christian, you ought to find it coded for justice, too. Peace without justice is no peace at all. Jesus is not satisfied with the world as it is. He wants it to be transformed so that people may live in freedom and without fear. I have spent many years trying to figure out how to be a pacifist. Some Christian pacifists are courageous and passionate people who want to follow Christ. But it seems to me that while Jesus told Peter to put away his sword and let him get on with his redemptive work of self-sacrifice for the world, he was not laying down an absolute principle that we may never fight evil with force or take a life doing it. Some unpleasant things simply have to be faced. And sometimes, in a sinful and fallen world, we are faced with the hope that the best of evils is the greatest good to choose. Peace is not the absence of conflict. It has to be won in the trenches of life the way Christ won it on the cross. Ideas do not liberate oppressed people or protect innocent lives. Sometimes we have to put ourselves in harm's way to do that. And I shudder to think of the consequences of failing to use force in opposing the Axis powers in World War II. Jews still wonder why it took us so long to come to their aid as their families were being exterminated in concentration camps.

In *The Hours*, the movie about the life of Virginia Woolf (and so much more), Virginia is talking to her husband who has tried to shield her from the chaos of the city because of her mental instability. She objects and tells him, *You cannot find peace by avoiding life, Leonard.* I fear we cannot find peace in this matter with Iraq by avoiding it.

So, what to do? Over the last 1,600 years, Christians have worked with some kind of just war theory to accept the possibility of war, but only under the direst circumstances. I'm not sure war is ever just, but if you'd let me mince words, I'd say that sometimes it might be justifiable. So here are the rules. War must be the last resort after every reasonable peaceful means has been tried. It must be waged for restorative purposes, to right wrongs, and not to gain booty or extend a kingdom. Only authorized governments may declare war, not rogue terrorists. It must take measures to distinguish between combatants and noncombatants. And the extent of war as a remedy must be proportionate to the crime it redresses. Another consideration is whether there is a greater likelihood of peace after war than before it.

Two famous Baptists, both former Democratic presidents of the United States, have weighed in. They come to different conclusions. Jimmy Carter is convinced this war does not meet the criteria for a just war, while Bill Clinton thinks it does and that President Bush is doing the right thing. My preacher colleagues and I have talked at length over this thing, and we all agree on one thing for certain: For peace-loving and justice-seeking Christians, this is a tough call. We might begin by acknowledging that.

But if you oppose the approach of the administration, it seems to me you have a moral obligation to say how you would address the threat Saddam represents. Clarence Jordan was a radical Christian who founded Koinonia Farms in Georgia. He once said that if a mule bites you, he hopes as a human being you have more resources available to respond than to simply bite him back. Christians have a wealth of resources to use before war becomes a last resort.[113]

The most constructive proposal I know of comes from Jim Wallis of the Sojourners Christian community in Washington, D.C. His six-point plan has teeth, I think. First, remove Saddam and his Baath Party from power in Iraq by indicting him in the World Court for crimes against humanity. This puts the onus on him and Iraq to defend his actions. Eventually, it will become clear to Iraqis that they have no future in the world community as long as Saddam is in power. Second, enforce coercive disarmament. Use military personnel to insist upon compliance. Keeping a bully from hurting other people is strongly justifiable. Third, foster a democratic Iraq. Freedom from tyranny is a virtue Christians can fight for. Fourth, organize a massive humanitarian campaign before the fact instead of after. (Some of this is already happening.) Mercy and aid begin the process of turning enemies into friends. Fifth, recommit to a road map for peace in the Middle East. U.S. commitment toward a fair resolution to the Israeli-Palestinian conflict would mitigate much Arab and Muslim hatred. Finally, reinvigorate and sustain the war against terrorism. Gaining cooperation from Arab countries in this approach will likely be easier without war on Iraq, while terrorism may be inflamed with a war on Iraq.

This is an example of Jesus' third way. It seeks concrete alternative solutions to war that are aggressively pursued, and yet it does not lose focus on the end game of peace and justice both. In the meantime, we ought to pray for people on all sides of this conflict. If our allegiance is to the reign of God first and last, we do not distinguish in our concern among people made in the image of God—regardless of religion, ethnicity, or nation. Furthermore, our military men and women deserve support and respect. They do not make policy; they carry it out in an effort to bring honor to those who send them. They depend upon us to ensure that their cause is noble. And finally, commit to being a peacemaker in your everyday life, so that the church of Jesus Christ will be a living alternative to the ways of war or inaction.

If you feel lost along the way, trust that the Holy Spirit knows exactly where you are at any moment. It would be best if we would follow the Spirit's directions ahead of time, but even now, you can listen for the voice that will say, *Calculating the route.*

---

113 Thanks to Robert Parham of the Baptist Center for Ethics for recalling this story.

66

Cross-Eyed

Watch and listen to "Cross-Eyed" by following this link or scanning the QR code with your phone: youtu.be/RNPQrPWRu1E. Sermon begins at 41:55.

March 17, 2019
Second Sunday in Lent
Philippians 3:17-4:1

The Apostle Paul talks about "enemies of the cross" as if they are bad things. Shouldn't we be enemies of the cross? I mean, what is it about the cross that we should like?

Jesus hangs on the cross in humiliation, a scapegoat, as if he, the sinless Lord of all creation, were a criminal himself. Isn't that everything we should resist and fervently work against in any generation? Shouldn't we be working for a society in which devotion to God is respected, even if this means that the powers that be would rather not hear what moral prophets have to say?

After the persecution of religious minorities in seventeenth-century Europe, America decided to go a different way. We created a country of robust religious liberty in which the idea of capital punishment for civil disobedience or religious non-conformity on a cross or other means of execution would be unthinkable. We wanted a country in which the state stays out of the affairs of the church.

And yet we continue to argue over crosses that dot the American landscape. The Supreme Court has heard arguments and will rule this June on whether a 40-foot cross at an intersection in Maryland is constitutional. It was erected in 1925 as a memorial to World War I veterans and has been the site of Christian religious services for nearly a century. Those who think it should stay claim that the cross is a secular symbol that honors veterans and has no religious significance. And amazingly, Christians are making that claim. What an odd thing for Christians, given how central the cross is to our religion.

The Baptist Joint Committee in Washington, D. C., which represents us in matters of religious liberty, has come out against it. Here's what it says: *The cross matters to us as Christians. It has a powerful, specific meaning that is central to our faith. Non-Christians also recognize the specific meaning of the cross, which is why we stand with them in saying no, the cross is not a universal symbol of sacrifice. The cross symbolizes the story of the resurrection of Jesus Christ, a story not shared outside of Christianity.*[114]

It's weird that Christians like us should be considered enemies of the cross when trying to protect its spiritual meaning, while those who want to coopt it for nationalistic reasons are thought of as friends of the cross. Go figure. This is the confusion we deal with at the heart of our faith. And it's an increasingly dangerous confusion.

Paul sees enemies of the cross as those who fail to understand the real meaning of the cross. He says of them that their *end is destruction, their god is their belly, their glory is their shame, and their mind is set on earthly things.* Paul considers enemies of the cross to be those who see the cross as a symbol of victory of us against them— whoever they may be. They want a life of privilege rather than a life of humility. They want a life of worldly glory and success. They have set their minds on earthly kingdoms and their place in them. In other words, those who are enemies of the cross live by the values of the very people who put Jesus on the cross. They miss the deeper meaning of the cross that Paul says we must live by.

Our theme this Lent is *the grace of seeing.* Paul wants us to see the cross in such a way that we live through it. He even tells us that we should join him in imitating Christ, who not only died on a cross but saw it as a way of life.

There's an ophthalmic condition called strabismus, commonly called crossed eyes. People whose eyes don't work together the way they should have this condition. One eye focuses on the object directly, and the other eye appears lazy or misaligned. This condition can usually be corrected through various means, so that the two eyes are trained to work together as intended.

But Paul is calling on us to a different cross-eyedness. He wants us to see the world through the corrective lenses of the cross. Christians view the world properly when we see that the nature of reality is depicted in the cross.

Not everyone agrees. Niccolo Machiavelli was a Renaissance political philosopher from Florence, Italy. During one sabbatical years ago, I stayed in a house across the street from the St. James Episcopal Church. In the garden area behind the house was a huge grotto with grotesque sculptures from that period. Machiavelli and his friends would gather in that grotto and read things they had been writing, including drafts of what would become his most famous work, *The Prince.* Machiavelli believed that the rulers of Florence had failed because they were too soft, too humane. They had believed in a kind of moral leadership guided by virtue. This approach made them weak and vulnerable, he thought, making them ineffective at controlling their kingdom and protecting their interests.

Machiavelli became synonymous with a kind of ruthless rule that demanded loyalty at any expense. One of his biographers described his approach in a way that I want to suggest epitomizes an enemy of the cross. *"It is necessary" [he wrote] for a prince, if he wants to maintain his realm, "to learn to be able not to be good" and to use or not use this, "according to necessity." … A good prince, it has been said for centuries … should try not to instill fear in but to win the love of his subjects … .*

---

114 https://bjconline.org/crosscase/

Machiavelli argues instead that a prince ... should "know well how to use the beast and the man." ... Machiavelli [writes that] a prince should certainly hope to be considered merciful and kind but that cruelty [could be] "well-used." ... It is difficult to be loved and feared at the same time, but "it is much safer to be feared than loved if one has to lack one of the two." ... [Further] princes who have readily broken their word have, "done great things," and have triumphed over princes who have kept their word. In short, he wants a prince who knows how to win.

Now let me ask you, does Jesus hanging on a cross look like winning to you? I mean, the way too many of us think of Jesus is that he really was such a good man that if he had died in his sleep, it would have been a proper outcome of his good life. But that's the point, don't you know?!

God revealed in the cross of Christ all the folly of thinking that violence will ever work to bring peace or protect us against those we think threaten us. The cross says that God will be found identifying with those who try to separate themselves from others rather than join themselves to others. The Romans epitomized Machiavelli's way of using the cross as a license for killing. Instead, when Jesus hangs on the cross as an innocent victim, we are supposed to see every other victim of violence there. We are supposed to see God siding with the suffering and dying of the world at the hands of people who are full of fear and hatred.

When we are true friends of the cross, when we look at the world cross-eyed, we will see Jesus hanging there in love for fifty Muslims who were cruelly murdered in Christchurch, New Zealand this week. We will see Jesus hanging there in love for the Jews murdered in the Tree of Life synagogue in Pittsburgh just months ago. We will see Jesus hanging there in love for the African American Christians murdered at a prayer meeting in Mother Emanuel AME Church in Charleston, South Carolina.

The cross symbolizes the love of God. Period. It forever stands as a powerful warning against using the name of God to do violence. Every and any use of the cross as an excuse to oppress, suppress, or repress any human being is a disgrace to our religion.

It was a disgrace to our religion when Crusaders saw the Roman cross as an upside-down sword and used it to kill Muslims in the Middle Ages. It was a disgrace to our religion when Nazis saw the Jews as Christ killers and believed they were authorized in the name of the cross to murder them for their crimes against our Lord (even though it was the Romans who crucified Jesus, not the Jews). And it was a disgrace to our religion when the Ku Klux Klan burned crosses as an assertion of white supremacy and justified their lynching of Black Americans and the persecution of Jews.

Now here we are again. Another mass murder. The most dangerous terrorist group in the Western world right now is not radical Islamists but disgraceful enemies of the cross of Christ who proudly call themselves white supremacists and Christian nationalists. Let me say this as clearly as I can: White supremacy is a heresy straight from the pit of hell. It has no place in the church, and it is rotting the church's soul. And Christian nationalism is a perversion of the gospel of Jesus Christ. It makes a mockery of the church's mission to a world with no gospel borders.

We can't be silent about this anymore. We can't fail the cross of Christ by allowing it to continue.

Christianity is not a white religion; it is a universal faith. Christianity is not a national religion; it is a global faith.

When white supremacists and Christian nationalists marched in Charlottesville, Virginia, they chanted, "You will not replace us." And when the murderer in New Zealand wrote his evil manifesto, he titled it "The Great Replacement." All these ideas and events feed on one another in this internet-fueled global village. These people buy into the false view that Jews and Muslims are intent on replacing good white Christians who rightfully own the countries we rule. They believe that anyone else is an invader who wants us dead. And they take up arms to defend us against them.

Friday night we gathered at the Richardson mosque to grieve with Muslims who feel as if the shooting in New Zealand happened to them here in Dallas. That mosque has repeatedly had so-called Christians marching outside it, with semi-automatic weapons threatening the lives of our Muslim neighbors. My good friend Imam Omar Sulieman said that he didn't want Christians to think they blame us for what one lunatic did in the name of our religion. They know only too well what that feels like. But when it was my turn to speak, I reminded Christians that we have to take responsibility for how we have allowed any interpretation of our religion to be used as reason and a license to kill others rather than love them.

Every time someone picks up a gun to kill in the name of Christ, he is an enemy of the cross. Every time we stand with those who suffer and defend the vulnerable, we are friends of the cross and disciples of Christ.

One of our members was in Kroger the other day and saw a woman wearing a hijab. She went up to her and asked if her head scarf signified that she is a Muslim. She said yes, and our sister told her how sorry she was for what was happening to her people. The woman fell into her arms, hugged her, and thanked her. They wept together.

This is what it means to be a friend of the cross. This is what it means to view the world cross-eyed. Our witness to the way of Christ is powerful when the grace of seeing through the eyes of the cross yields tears of love in solidarity with those for whom Christ died, whatever their religion, wherever they come from, however they look.

67

Green Wood and the Green Mile

Watch and listen to "Green Wood and the Green Mile" by following this link or scanning the QR code with your phone: youtu.be/0rnRNzBKFm0. Sermon begins at 22:40.

April 10, 2022
Palm/Passion Sunday
Luke 23:26-31

We've traveled five days in a mere twenty-five minutes. Another case of the transport of Wilshire worship, don't you know?! Our Palm Sunday service began with Jesus' humble entry into Jerusalem. Our Passion Sunday service continues now with Jesus' humiliating exit from Jerusalem.

The first parade featured hopeful pilgrims running before him, laying their cloaks on the ground to pave his way, waving palm fronds, and singing *Hosanna! Blessed is he who comes in the name of the Lord.*

In between, the music darkens in tone. The religious establishment and the Roman authorities agree that Jesus must be sacrificed to keep the peace. This is the way of the world since the beginning of time. When people get socially anxious, they find a scapegoat to dump all their fears on. Whether guilty or innocent, the scapegoat's death relieves them of their worries—until the next time when they will do it again, and then again. It's a cycle of violence that continues unabated to this day when it is not seen for what it is. Jesus will be just one of many in their minds, but, as we shall see, his death surprisingly breaks the spell by revealing the victimizing mechanism in our systems. More on that in minute.

The second parade features wailing women following Jesus, beating their breasts in grief. Jesus has just been relieved of carrying his cross. Simon of Cyrene is enlisted to aid him. Jesus' back is bloodied from the scourging. Now he walks the last mile on the Via Dolorosa—the painful path—to his capital punishment by the Roman state. He turns to speak to the women, and we will hold that thought for now, too.

The scene reminds me of the movie *The Green Mile*, based on the 1996 book by Stephen King. Green is the color of the prison floor on which death row inmates walk their last mile to Old Sparky, where they will face electrocution at the order of the state and at the hands of death row guards. King tells the story of the lead

guard, Paul Edgecombe, played by Tom Hanks, and his experience with the innocent, wrongly convicted John Coffey. Coffey is an enormous Black man, something
of a mental simpleton. But what he lacks in intellect he more than makes up for in
empathy.

Coffey is the Christ figure of the story, and you don't have to be a preacher looking for sermon material to see it. Coffey is a healer. He feels the pain and suffering of
those around him. He has the gift for sensing the spirits of illness that afflict people
and the will to draw them into himself before expelling them harmlessly into the air.

Recalling the messianic words of Isaiah: *Surely, he has borne our infirmities and
carried our diseases.* Coffey, like Christ, is a nonviolent healer who lives in solidarity
with the hurting. He is less concerned with himself than with others around him.

And this is where we see Jesus turning to the wailing women who follow him.
This man, who knows himself to be the Son of God, has been wrongly accused and
condemned to die; and yet, instead of protesting his innocence, he feels the pain of
these women.

The religious leaders of his own tribe reject him, even though his ministry of
healing and exorcisms, along with his teaching a way of living in the world by loving
one another, should have been no threat. But they were concerned to keep peace
with Rome. Rome was always on the lookout for revolutionaries who would spawn
insurrections. Anything that caused too much attention might inspire dreams in
the common folk of overthrowing the occupying power. The religious leaders knew
opposing Rome was futile, so when Jesus is condemned to death, they are reluctantly relieved while the wailing women are inconsolably bereaved.

Jesus turns to these women, thinking less of himself than of them. *Daughters
of Jerusalem, weep not for me; weep for yourselves and your children.* He warns them
about what is coming. He doesn't so much comfort them as prepare them. While
some might think of him as a scapegoat that will relieve the pressure and send
things back to normal, Jesus sees things differently. He says: *If they do this when the
wood is green, what will happen when it is dry?*

Jesus is the green wood. He has life in him. Life comes through him.

If you have ever tried to start a fire with green wood, you know how hard it is to
kindle. Dry wood is a different story. Jesus contrasts himself as a nonviolent healer
with those who are fire-kindlers. Jesus calls for a revolution of values, an alternative
way of living that is rooted in God's justice and begins with care for the last, the
least, the little, and the lost. The dry-wood revolutionaries are driven by power more
than love, thinking the world consists only in who rules the politics. Jesus is saying
that if the empire will send the gentle to the cross to protect the status quo, imagine
what they will do to the violent.

All of this leads to the Holy Week question that has baffled Christians throughout the ages: *How does Jesus save us?* That Jesus saves is the central claim Christians
make that make Christians Christians, and yet the how has never been clear.

Among the most common answers are two: First, Jesus saves us from our sins by
doing what we cannot do for ourselves; and second, Jesus is our example of how to
live a life of love that changes us as we live like him.

The first begins with the idea that our sin separates us from God, whose righteousness demands a sacrifice to atone for sin and set things right. Jesus is sacrificed on our behalf. In this view, God offers Jesus as the innocent who stands in for the guilty; he pays the penalty for us. We then accept Jesus' gift and are made right with God.

This begs the question though as to why a merciful God who made human beings and knows our frailties would expect so much from those who are destined to fail? It doesn't speak well of God's character. And then to pour out God's wrath on the Son, even if the Son were to agree to such a thing, makes it all seem an unnecessary if not abusive act for a God of love. Besides that, it doesn't account for what will become of us afterward. How will we be different, once relieved of the burden of our guilt? How will we be changed so we don't continue to sin and need a sacrifice to be made again and again?

The second view is that Jesus is a moral example who teaches us to live like him. This has the advantage of changing our nature and making us new people. But then, Jesus is just a teacher of wisdom like any other great religious sage. It doesn't account for why dying on a cross would be needed.

We're now to the point where we can see that both things are important, even if altered. Christ had to die, and we have to be changed. So, what is really going on in this story that achieves our salvation?

In his allegorical children's book series, *The Chronicles of Narnia*, C. S. Lewis portrays this better than most. "The lion Aslan, the Christ figure, allows himself to be killed so that the evil powers will release those they hold hostage. The idea of this exchange is proposed by the evil powers. The sacrificial process is known to all from the earliest times; it is the law that an innocent one may die on behalf of others and so free them. It is called *deep magic from the dawn of time.*

"The evil powers love this arrangement and, incidentally, have no intention of keeping their side of the bargain after Aslan is dead. The resurrection comes into this story as an unexpected development, from what Aslan calls *deeper magic from before the dawn of time,* something about which the evil powers knew nothing. And when Aslan rises, the ancient stone altar on which the sacrifice was offered cracks and crumbles in pieces, never to be used again. The gospel, then, is not ultimately about the exchange of victims, but about ending the bloodshed."[115]

The point is that God is not the one who requires a sacrifice, the evil powers of the world do. When the innocent victim accepts the terms of a violent world, we see how wrong the whole thing is. The power of evil over us is broken by our seeing it for the fraud it is, and we may then live as free people. By adopting his way of sacrificial love for others and taking the suffering of others into ourselves, we share in his resurrection power and are saved.

This is where Simon of Cyrene's carrying the cross comes in. It's where we come in. We are all compelled to carry the cross on behalf of others. We are invited to be green wood, to be healers and life-givers to those who are despairing and dying.

---

115 Mark Heim, https://www.christiancentury.org/article/visible-victim.

At the end of *The Green Mile*, we see that Paul Edgcombe and the other guards see John Coffey for who he is. They know the state is killing an innocent man. But John Coffey's love for others and his desire to see them whole makes him less concerned for himself than for them. He invites Paul to hold his hand and gives him the power to see the world as it truly is. Paul is changed by this and finds that the power of life in the condemned man enters him and changes him for good and for good.

If we would know the salvation of God for ourselves, we must allow the power of Christ's life and love to enter us and change us. We must renounce our violent ways, live as green wood, and walk our own green mile. Amen.

68

Dangerous Discipleship

"Watch and listen to "Dangerous Discipleship" by following this link or scanning the QR code with your phone: youtu.be/93QJu5aj1nk. Sermon begins at 35:30.

Dangerous Discipleship" is the sermon Mason preached following the shooting on June 17, 2015 at Emanuel African Methodist Episcopal Church in Charleston, South Carolina.

June 21, 2015
Fourth Sunday after Pentecost
Acts 6:8-15, 7:54-60

Discipleship can be dangerous. Just being a faithful follower of Jesus can get you stoned to death in the street—just ask Stephen; or shot to death in a church—just ask nine Christian men and women gunned down this week in Bible study for the crime of being Black.

Welcome back from sabbatical, George. It seems never to end, this gun violence and racially charged conflict in our society. I had hoped to come back to you today all refreshed from my last month of being out of the fray and share a collective deep breath together. But, alas, evil has again taken our breath away.

My colleague Gary Simpson was staying at my house on Wednesday night when the shooting took place in the Emanuel African Methodist Episcopal Church in Charleston, South Carolina. Gary is the pastor of Concord Baptist Church of Christ in Brooklyn, New York. He was here to join me for a conversation at our Cooperative Baptist Fellowship meeting on the subject of building bridges between churches and communities. It's hard to do that when somebody like Dylann Roof burns down the bridge that you have been trying to build. This is just so painful. Gary lost his brother several years ago, and we are family to each other now. This made walking through this tragedy with my brother all the more devastating.

The act itself of murdering nine people is heinous. Murdering nine people out of racial animus makes it a hate crime. Murdering nine people and letting one live so that she could tell others about it makes it terrorism. This is exactly what acts of terror are intended to accomplish: to make others afraid, to make them cower, to make them feel unsafe even in a church. Terrorism knows no color or creed.

Racism is America's original sin. We would like to pretend that we have moved beyond it and that people like Dylann Roof do what they do only because they are medicated, mentally unstable, or simply acting as a lone wolf who uses race as an excuse for his violence. We don't want to ask about his family and how he was raised. We don't want to talk about the white culture of Confederate pride that gives cover to continuing dehumanization of Black people and is so embedded in our public policy that we can't even see it. We don't want to talk about the availability of guns—unless we talk about how if someone at the church Bible study had been packing, all this would have been avoided. We just don't want to talk about it all. It's just so unpleasant when it applies to us. But where is a better place to talk about it than church?

When Black youths are behaving badly, not obeying the police, killing each other or white people, people sometimes ask me why I don't call them out, why I don't address the Black culture, the breakdowns in family structure, the lack of moral discipline, etc. All I can say about that is that it seems arrogant to me to be throwing stones when I feel that I live in a glass house. Or to use Jesus' image, to be trying to take the splinter out of someone else's eye when I know I have a log in my own. And I have a log in my eye on the subject of racial prejudice that takes so much work that I can't afford to judge someone else. What, then, can we do? The first thing is to be brokenhearted about this incident. Then each of us should examine ourselves more than we examine others and ask what part we play that keeps us in this demonic state.

Let's look closer at our text today to find some guidance.

Stephen is standing before the council of religious leaders in Jerusalem. He's been brought up on charges—some true and some trumped up. But as he stands there, all agree that he has the face of an angel.

It's a shining moment in an otherwise dark story. It's one of those moments when beauty breaks through and earthly power has no power over it.

But how did it all come to this—Stephen getting stoned to death in the end? How do you stone an angel? I've been thinking about that this week as I heard about the hospitality of those Christians at Mother Emanuel Church. They were doing exactly what we would want. They were praying and studying the Bible. When Dylann Roof walked into their meeting, they welcomed him because that's what churches do. He sat there in Bible study for an hour listening to these good people talk about the Lord Jesus and how to follow him as disciples. They may not have been angels or had the same glow about them that Stephen had, but they were close enough that Dylann Roof felt their kindness and goodness and said he was almost deterred from his mission.

And yet he wasn't. And neither were those religious leaders who stoned Stephen. Why were they not deterred? How do you kill an angel?

If there is a way to name the underlying evil here, it may be that ideology trumps theology. This young man's Christian faith could not stand up against his racist faith. He was a nominal Christian, apparently. He was baptized in a Lutheran church where his family belongs. The pastor did not say whether the family was active, only that they were on the roll. I imagine that's his way of saying they weren't practicing disciples.

You have to work hard all the time to be a follower of Jesus because there are so many ways to get off track, so many ways that Jesus has to keep saving our souls.

An ideology is a system of ideas that allows you to organize and make sense of the world in a certain way. But it's always rigid because it starts with ideas and then fits people into them. Theology, on the other hand, is supple because it starts with God being in relationship with people. Ideas come after the fact of the relationship, not before.

Ideologies are like suckers that grow on plants. They don't belong to a plant; they are weeds that mask themselves as the plant. But over time they can so take over a plant that the plant itself is good for nothing.

Racism is a purity ideology. It masquerades as Christianity, but it distorts it to the point that it is no longer Christian. It assumes that to be white is to be pure and that to be Black is to be impure.

Let me say this plainly: There is no such thing as the Black race or the white race; there is only the human race. This is not to deny that the lived experience of people who are Black and white is different; it is a declaration that those differences are not naturally derived; they are socially constructed to favor and disfavor. At heart we are all equally human beings made in the image of God—none are superior, none are inferior.

Racism sets white cultural experience as the standard of morality that everyone else must live up to if they are to approach a holy and righteous God. But that is not, never has been and never should be Christianity.

Saying that, in so many words, got Stephen stoned. Saying that, in so many words, is dangerous for any disciple today, too.

Back again to how they killed the angel ...

Stephen appears to have been stoned because he wouldn't keep his mouth shut about what he believed God is up to in Jesus Christ. In his long speech to the religious council in chapter 7—which we didn't read because of its length (you're welcome)—Stephen stepped on their toes like any preacher does now and then. We all want our preachers to step on toes—as long as it's other people's toes.

But it's the content of what he said that put them over the edge. He was explaining to them from the story of Israel how the prophets suffered and were rejected for showing how God was always doing a new thing and stretching them beyond the rigidness of their ideas to embrace a bigger and wider grace beyond law. He ended his speech with this flourish: *You stiff-necked people, uncircumcised in heart and ears, you are forever opposing the Holy Spirit, just as your ancestors used to do. ... [N]ow you have become betrayers and murderers. ...*

Yeah, that'll get an angel killed.

But Stephen's underlying problem is not what he said but who he was. He is caught being Greek. He was a Hellenist Jew and one of the seven deacons elected to care for the church. (You learned this last week from Scott Dickison, when he wasn't taking friendly shots at his beloved mentor, don't you know?!) It's remarkable how intentionally inclusive they were about the first deacon body.

The Hellenist widows were being discriminated against in the daily distribution of food. There was food insecurity inside the church, and it was caused by social injustice. Depriving the Greek-speaking widows was a way of judging them as less godly. The Hebraic Jews were the purity cult; they kept themselves as separate from the non-Jewish world as possible because they thought of themselves as saints and others as sinners. Hellenist Jews engaged the world outside the faith by adopting its language and some of its practices. This made them impure and a threat to the whole community.

Stephen was stoned because he challenged the very basis of why and how God accepts people. In Jesus, we see that we are all sinners equally, and equally in need of God's grace. The line between good and evil runs down the center of every human heart. It is not a line drawn in the sand that separates one people from another.

But look at Stephen's death and notice how he handled this murderous injustice. He didn't whine about how Christians were being persecuted for their faith. He didn't look around at his enemies and call down God's judgment on them. He looked up to heaven and saw Jesus sitting there at the right hand of God. He alone would judge. And then when Stephen died, he echoed Jesus' words from the cross: first, *Lord Jesus, receive my spirit;* and then the kicker: *Lord, do not hold this sin against them.*

My granddaughters have been visiting this week in our home. Five-year-old Finley's favorite pastime is to sit in front of the computer and watch old videos of her mother when she was growing up. Kim has converted old VHS tapes to digital, and so Finley gets to see her mother at her age, to watch her mannerisms and listen to her voice. Finley compares herself to her mom, and I think she sees herself in her mom.

This is what Stephen was doing and what we are called to do. He found the meaning of his life at every moment in the Jesus life. He was so faithful to the way of Christ that he interpreted his own martyrdom through the lens of Jesus' death. And he looked with love and mercy upon those who killed him, asking God to forgive them.

We have seen that this week. Some of the grieving family members of those who died at the end of Dylann Roof's gun of racial hatred spoke in court at Roof's hearing. *"I will never be able to hold her again, but I forgive you,"* a daughter of Ethel Lance said. *"And have mercy on your soul. You hurt me. You hurt a lot of people, but God forgives you, and I forgive you."*

Amazing. This is what happens when Jesus gets into you so deeply that you must act out of love. Perfect love casts out fear, the Bible says. But the converse is that practiced hate casts out love. We need to decide which will win—love or hate.

69

The Quintessence of a Christian

Watch and listen to "The Quintessence of a Christian" by following this link or scanning the QR code with your phone: youtu.be/ZaVmPhfQHDg. Sermon begins at 32:20.

"The Quintessence of a Christian" is the sermon Mason preached after the killing of Botham Jean in his apartment by an off-duty police officer in Dallas, a tragic event that brought together a group of local clergy to discuss speaking out about justice in white churches.

September 16, 2018
Seventeenth Sunday after Pentecost
Mark 8:27-38

It's a beautiful place, Caesarea Philippi. It's located northeast of the Sea of Galilee in the Golan Heights at the foot of Mount Hermon. Jesus took his disciples there on retreat. He was at the peak of his popularity, after months of teaching and healing and gaining a reputation that led many to ask who he was that he could do all these things. So, he asked his disciples, "Who do people say that I am?" They reported to him, "Some say John the Baptist, others Elijah, and others one of the prophets."

Now I should stop right there and remind you that John the Baptist is already dead, having lost his head to King Herod for calling the king to account for marrying his brother's wife. Prophets used to do things like that. Go figure. Strange as it sounds to us today, some must have thought John had returned from the dead as a divine act of justice. As for Elijah, people associated him with the coming of the messiah, making way for Jewish sovereignty in the land by throwing off the yoke of Roman occupation. Jews to this day leave a seat at the table open for Elijah at the Passover Seder. Others thought Jesus was one of the other prophets returned to bring God's word and moral order to the people.

All very interesting. But then Jesus gets straight to the point, a question he not only asked of the disciples then but also is asking us as disciples now: "Who do you say that I am?" See, it doesn't matter what everyone else thinks; it matters most what those closest to Jesus believe about him if he is going to be able to depend upon us to be with him in his work.

Peter answers: "You are the Christ." You are the one we've been waiting for. You are the one God has sent to usher in the age to come and make things right.

Even today, many people think many things about Jesus. He's a great teacher. He's a man of great wisdom. He's an ethical idealist who left behind a pattern of life for us to follow. But in every human heart, and in this room today, the question demands an answer that echoes Peter's words: "You are the Christ." And that's the first thing I would say to you today. Have you come to the place in your life when you can answer Jesus for yourself, "You are the Christ"?

Settling on the identity of Jesus is crucial. If he is just another man, we can take him or leave him without consequence. But if he is the Christ, it makes all the difference for who we are and how we live our life. Confess him as the Son of God, Savior of the world and Lord of all. If you've never done so, I urge you to do so today. The question will hang over you until you do.

Now, assuming you have, I need you to see what Jesus says next about himself to see if you want to change your answer, lest you think this is only an intellectual exercise. Faith, Peter found out, is less about what you think than about what sets the direction of your life.

Jesus makes that clear when immediately he begins to tell us what being the Christ means. He must undergo great suffering, be rejected by the religious leaders, be killed, and then be raised on the third day. How Jesus knew this goes to the heart of who he is as the Christ. And I don't mean that in the sense that because Jesus was the eternal Son of God, the Second Person of the Trinity, he had special knowledge of what was to come that no other human could have known. I mean that because of his being completely grounded in the nature of God and being completely in solidarity with the world he came to save, he understood exactly how dangerous it would be to bring salvation to pass. When he says he "MUST undergo great suffering," that "must" is tied to his dynamic nature of being the link between a completely loving and self-giving God that he must reflect in all his actions and a world that is beset with self-interest and will fight for rights and privileges that don't include everyone. If it is true that Jesus is the Christ, he MUST suffer. He must because that is the quintessence of the incarnate Son of God.

Quintessence is not a word we use much unless you read the dictionary for fun. (How's that social life going?) It means the perfect or most typical example of a quality or class. It's the aspect of something regarded as the intrinsic and central constituent of a thing's character. In other words, quintessence is what makes a thing the thing it is. But that's kind of an elusive definition, isn't it? And that's by design since the word comes from physics and philosophy. The prefix quint, meaning five, comes from the idea that there must be some invisible fifth something that joins together the four elements of earth, air, fire, and water that hold everything together by being latent in all those things. We don't know what that is, but when we use the term quintessence that way, we are talking about what is really real.

Jesus is the quintessential human, joining together the true nature of God with humanity. So, if Jesus says he MUST undergo great suffering, it's because he understood that the full presence of God in him meant that he could do nothing but give himself up in love for the world and that would involve suffering.

Enter the other contestant view. Peter rebukes Jesus for saying this, and Jesus turns and rebukes him right back, saying that he's talking like Satan, the great divider—not like God, the great uniter. Peter wants to win by defeating his enemies with the sword. Jesus knows that God wants to win by defeating his enemies with love. If Peter had his way, some would be winners and others, losers. If God has God's way, everyone wins by losing.

And that's because the nature of God is, always has been, and always will be, only love. And that's because the nature of love is giving. Love binds all things together. It goes out from the self in sacrificial love to other selves. It gives up by giving everything. That's the most vulnerable thing for any of us to do, and yet it is the secret to life.

Bette Midler sang a popular song a few years ago—okay, more than a few, but I'm old, don't you know?! It was titled *The Rose*. Some of the lyrics go like this: *It's the heart afraid of breaking that never learns to dance. / It's the dream afraid of waking that never takes the chance. / It's the one who won't be taken who cannot seem to give. / And the soul afraid of dying that never learns to live.*

The soul afraid of dying that never learns to live. How many of us does that describe?

That's why Jesus next turns to the crowd and says, "If any want to become my followers, let them deny themselves and take up their cross and follow me. For those who want to save their life will lose it, and those who lose their life for my sake, and for the sake of the gospel, will save it."

If love is the true nature of God and therefore the true nature of reality itself, then that is life's quintessence. And if we are going to call ourselves Christians, followers of Christ, that is what must mark us at our core—self-sacrificing, empathetic love for others.

To have the nature of Christ then means that we will be loving people. And love is both passionate and compassionate. It is willing to be acted upon by others and suffer their rejection and scorn while loving nonetheless. It is willing to love others enough to feel what they feel, rather than to assert our own interests. This kind of love doesn't look for ways to dismiss the pain of others or play the "what-about game" to diminish the need for sympathy. Love has empathy for the plight of others. Love cares.

Frederick Buechner wrote: *Compassion is the sometimes fatal capacity for feeling what it is like to live inside somebody else's skin. It's the knowledge that there can never really be any peace and joy for me until there is peace and joy finally for you too.*

Beautiful sentiment, isn't it? Hard to live, don't you think?

It's been a hard week in Dallas. The fatal shooting of a young and impressive professional man named Botham Jean by off-duty police officer Amber Guyger is a tragedy that has rocked this city. The permutations of this crime are many: A police officer works a fifteen-hour shift and surely is exhausted when she comes to this moment; nonetheless, she shoots an unarmed citizen in his own home; the victim is Black and the officer is white, even if race didn't factor into the event initially; the preferential treatment of the officer by the criminal justice system reminds us that justice is still not blind to color, whether white, Black, or blue; and the smear campaign of the dead man's character immediately after his funeral is a long and nasty practice used against people of color to gain sympathy for defendants. Lord, have mercy.

I sat for three hours in Botham's funeral service, thinking how touched I was by the man's faith and that of his family and church, but also thinking I don't want to ever have to attend one more funeral like this as long as I live. Friday morning, I sat in a room with about a dozen Dallas pastors, including Jeff Warren from Park Cities Baptist and Todd Wagner of Watermark Church, along with Black clergy like Bryan Carter of Concord and T.D. Jakes of The Potter's House. We met with the district attorney Faith Johnson to hear how she would be handling things from here, given the pain and anger that the African American community is feeling that is boiling in outrage right now.

After the DA left the room, things got honest. One Black pastor thanked the white pastors for being there but expressed frustration with what he called the way white churches have privatized the gospel so that it keeps our congregations from understanding that the call for justice is not optional in following Jesus. He wondered why we don't speak out more. Bishop Jakes talked about how hard it is convincing Black youth that following Jesus is worth it. They are being lured by other voices who don't believe in the nonviolent love of Jesus. The main thing they hear from white preachers is defense of policies rooted in white supremacy that continue to demoralize people of color. He said, "I believe you care because you are in this room; but we need to know more than where your heart is. We need to hear you say clearly in the pulpit and in the streets that white supremacy and racism is wrong. And no more generalizations. It has to be specific. I know it will cost you something to do so, but isn't that what Jesus calls us to do, to take up our cross and follow him?"

It is. And it's not just preachers, but all Christians. What is God calling you to risk of your life for the sake of the gospel? That's what denying self means. If we want to call ourselves by the name of Jesus, we have to stop defending things he would condemn and start loving people like he did. It may cost us friends. It may even cost us our life. But after three days, give or take, there will always be a rising with Christ. Amen.

70

Beginnings

Watch and listen to "Beginnings" by following this link or scanning the QR code with your phone: youtu.be/Dd94ov5IAAM. Sermon begins at 17:07.

Mason preached "Beginnings" following the murder of George Floyd, which sparked racial justice protests nationwide.

June 7, 2020
Trinity Sunday
Genesis 1:1-5, 23-2:4a

Remember when you were a kid and you were playing a game with friends and something went wrong? Like maybe a dog ran off with the ball or a car came by and interfered with the action. Do-over, someone might say. Let's have a do-over.

Wouldn't it be great if we could have some do-overs in real life? Where we could go back to the beginning and start fresh?

If we could, I would call a do-over on COVID-19! I mean, our preparation for it. Our supply of masks and ventilators. Our coordinating of agencies and science laboratories and funding of research and development for a vaccine. Let's have a do-over.

And how about a do-over on George Floyd and the countless other African American victims of police brutality? Wouldn't we want a do-over on the police training that led to his murder? Or a do-over on how to discipline the officer who had seventeen complaints on his record but was still on the force using deadly force. Or the legacy of slavery and Jim Crow and redlining and the basic criminalization of Blackness in our society that have created one obstacle after another that makes success and prosperity among Black people something heroic instead of normal. And yes, let's have a do-over on the destruction of property and the looting of businesses that only serves to undermine the legitimate rage of protestors who feel that the only way to be heard is to take to the streets because their voices are otherwise ignored or silenced in the channels of ordinary life.

We can't change the past, but we can change the future. We can't go back, but we can go forward. And one way to do that is to return to our founding stories from our sacred texts. Genesis means beginnings.

Genesis 1 is a creation story, an account of origins. It doesn't so much tell us the what of things as the what for. It's more a sociology textbook than a science one. It's a study of power. It tells us about the nature and purpose of God's use of power with and for the world.

The temptation is to go back to Genesis 1 and lament how far we have fallen as a human race from the time of perfect tranquility. But that wasn't the reason God inspired the priestly caste of Israel to write this passage during their time of captivity in Babylon. It was instead to render an alternative view of the world in the face of the one they were experiencing under their powerful pagan rulers.

The point is not how things once were but how things should be. The writers of Genesis 1 explain who their God is and what their God expects of us. Genesis is not a longing for what is lost; it's a vision for what may yet be.

I'm going to focus today on two underlying claims of this passage: peace and parity. Peace, first.

God created the world as a free act of love. Over the welter and waste and darkness of primordial nothingness, God's breath hovered. God said, "Let there be light. And there was light." Let that sink in. God acted without a partner. God acted without self-interest. God acted by breathing upon the chaos and bringing order.

Let there be. The word choice is extraordinary. "Let" could be a command or a demand. Like when Moses went to Pharaoh and said, "Let my people go!" But it could also mean to allow or permit. When Mary hears that she is to be with child by the Holy Spirit, she replies, "Let it be with me according to your word." "I consent," in other words. There's a strong but gentle notion of power in this statement, "Let there be light." And each day of creation brings about the same result. Each day "let there be" turns into the consent, "and there was." And it was good.

The contrast is hard to overstate between this account of creation and the one the Babylonians claimed to undergird their empire and reinforce their superiority over the Hebrews. In their account, called the Enuma Elish, the god Marduk defeated the sea goddess Tiamat in a battle for who would be the high ruler of the gods. Marduk then cut the body of Tiamat in half, stretching part of it to create the canopy of the heavens and part to create the dry land of the earth. Then, from the blood of Tiamat's lover and battle commander, he made human beings. Marduk built the city of Babylon to be a home for the gods and the center of this religion. Of course, all of this would be presided over by the king and his military forces.

When creation is an act of original violence by the gods, creatures emulate them because violence is the very nature of reality. Genesis 1 is a point-by-point rebuke of the Marduk account. It claims the world was made in peace and for peace. And whatever flourishing we can expect comes not from the use of power as the shedding of blood, but from the cooperation of all things with their generous and nonviolent Creator.

Now ask yourself this: Which account of creation do empires most closely resemble when their leaders use force to dominate the streets and defeat anyone who opposes them? Which view of creation undergirds both the will to commit violence and looting by some protestors this past week and also the use of tear gas, pepper spray, and rubber bullets by law enforcement to quell the uprisings?

Imagine how different our world would be if, when our leaders held up the Bible to demonstrate their loyalty to God, they actually understood what it says about who God is and how we are to act in God's name. Violence begets violence. Peace is rooted in respect for all created beings and things. It requires a commitment to the well-being of all, not to the victory of some over others.

Next, parity. "Let us make humankind in our own image, according to our likeness ... male and female, God created them."

Once more, note that humans were not created out of the blood of the vanquished. They were created to be a reflection of the God who is so relational to begin with that the only way to reflect that is through male and female who together make up the image of God. Not male over female. Male next to female, side by side. The male is not more godlike than the female, nor the female more godlike than the male. It's both together, implying the relational character of God, which constitutes the divine image.

Now, I could follow this course today and talk more about gender equality. But I want to suggest that this text of the creation of humanity as male and female also suggests that all humans are equals. Not just the equality and mutuality of the sexes, but also the equality of all people generally. The Marduk account of creation was filled with hierarchies. And human society has always tried to organize itself that way, as if there is a caste system in which some are destined to rule and others to serve. You can't find that in Genesis 1. The vision of humanity put forward by the Hebrew priests is a radical alternative to any attempt to declare some humans superior and others inferior.

You know where I'm going with this. The image of a white police officer in Minneapolis with his knee on the neck of George Floyd is seared into our collective memory now. The words of deference from the Black man on the ground made it only more painful: "Sir," he said. Sir. That's what Black slaves and then Black men and women in the Jim Crow era were taught to call white people—Sir and Ma'am. When we white people say "Sir," it's simply a sign of respect for authority. When Black people say "Sir," it's also a survival technique. It's playing into the terrible history of white supremacy where whites needed Blacks to show them deference as their betters.

"Sir, I can't breathe." And eight minutes and forty-six seconds later, George Floyd stopped breathing for good.

The protests in the wake of this murder are about more than George Floyd. They are about the whole history of Black Americans being told to stay in their place and being systematically and legally denied equality in the eyes of their white neighbors and in the eyes of the law.

The earliest creed of the church may just be something Paul quoted in Galatians 3:28. There is no Jew or Greek, no slave or free, no male or female. All are one. No ethnic, class, or gender hierarchies. The original vision of the Jesus movement was a return to Genesis 1.

The early church understood that when you are in Christ, you are part of a do-over movement. Something called Sin, understood as domination, has interfered with the level playing field of the game. We need a new beginning, a new humanity rooted in peace and parity.

Many things will remain with me from this week. The protests, the meetings, and conversations and social media posts over how to bring lasting change. But the one imprinted on my heart is a photo of my three granddaughters with their parents in San Antonio, all clad in masks and walking through downtown with Black and Latinx neighbors. Each is carrying a homemade sign with a different message that amounts to the same thing. "Love one another," one reads. "Be kind." Finally, and fittingly: "We are all children of God."

The spirit that lives in those three little white girls is the product of your work, Wilshire. You helped shape the faith vision of both their parents, who are shaping the faith vision of their children. It's a vision of peace and parity rooted in Genesis 1 and the Gospel itself. It's a do-over vision that is changing the world from what it has been to what it will be.

Don't give up. It's happening. And you are part of it. Amen.

71

A Bias Toward the Last

Watch and listen to "A Bias Toward the Last" by following this link or scanning the QR code with your phone: youtu.be/vK3fhlwARKw. Sermon begins at 28:15.

Mason preached "A Bias Toward the Last" on Martin Luther King Jr. weekend in the last year of his ministry at Wilshire.

January 16, 2022
Second Sunday after Epiphany
Isaiah 62:1-5; John 2:1-11

On this Martin Luther King Jr. birthday weekend, I want to begin with a passage from the last chapter of the last book he wrote titled, *Where Do We Go from Here: Chaos or Community?* He recalled the Washington Irving story of Rip Van Winkle who fell asleep for twenty years on a New York mountain. What confused him most when he awoke was the sign on the front of the inn in the little town on the Hudson River. When he went up for his long nap, the sign had a picture of King George III. When he returned twenty years later, it had a picture of George Washington. King said that the most striking thing about the story is not that Rip slept twenty years, but that he slept through a revolution that would alter the course of human history. And then he said this: *Every society has its protectors of the status quo and its fraternities of the indifferent who are notorious for sleeping through revolutions.*[116]

I want you to imagine with me this morning how different history might have been if the church had not slept through one revolution after another. What if we had been awake to what God was up to in the world and cast a vision for it instead of working to protect the status quo?

To that end, our texts today from Isaiah and John call us to a spiritual vision that we must wake up to. Let me state it this way: *The God of the Bible has a bias toward the last.*

Jesus said again and again that the last shall be first. And the whole Bible is the story of the last being redeemed at last.

---

116 Wipf and Stock, 2002, p. 199.

Now, most of the time in our churches we have proclaimed this to individuals. Your sin doesn't have the last word about you, God does. Don't focus on what's lost because God sees what's left. When you have lost a job or a marriage or a reputation, don't give up. God hasn't given up on you. God holds the future and grants eternal life to all who believe.

That'll preach, don't you know?! And if that's the word you most need to hear today, let the Spirit speak. But personal salvation is not the whole story of the Bible. So, here's more, and I am so proud to be in a church that is spiritually mature enough to receive it.

There are two senses of *last* I want to hold up to you today: last, in the sense of those who have been left out, pushed down, and cast aside as if their inclusion in the Gospel story matters as little to God as they seem to the world; and last, in the sense of who gets the last word on what things will look like when God's will is finally done on earth as it is in heaven. The Bible is biased toward the last in both these senses. And if the church wants to represent God to the world, this must be our bias, too.

For that to happen, Christians need a sanctified, this-worldly, spiritual imagination. Instead of starting with what is and figuring out how to justify it as the will of God, we must start with the promises of God about what will be and work with God to bring them to pass.

The motivational speaker William Arthur Ward said: *If you can imagine it, you can achieve it. If you can dream it, you can become it.* But our faith teaches us to imagine and achieve, dream and become in the plural. We need to change those yous to y'all. We need to shift our vision to match the Bible, not to make the Bible fit our vision.

Isaiah is a visionary prophet with a God-formed imagination. Look again at his words to a people who despaired that things could ever be different for them. *You shall be a crown of beauty in the hand of the Lord, and a royal diadem in the hand of your God. You shall no more be termed Forsaken, and your land shall no more be termed Desolate; but you shall be called My Delight Is in Her, and your land Married; for the Lord delights in you, and your land shall be married.*

Israel had returned from captivity in Babylon and found the Promised Land of milk and honey to be an unpromising land of sour milk and hardened honey. But into that depressing city of Jerusalem, the prophet spoke a word of hope. God was with them. God was for them.

That was the last thing they could see with eyes of flesh. But with eyes of faith, they could see a land that would come to life again and be like a marriage of love and delight. The metaphor of a married land carries the idea of fruitfulness. God would have the last word on Israel.

And speaking of marriage, look at the story of Jesus at the wedding feast in Cana. The father of the bride was on the brink of embarrassment over the wine running out. But just then, Jesus' mother intercedes. Mary somehow knows her son has the power to make all things new. She imagines a different outcome because he is present. And when he finally acts, we are told that the guests marvel at how the wine served last is better than the wine served first.

See, history isn't inevitable. As Dr. King said: *The moral arc of the universe is long, but it bends toward justice.* Things don't have to be the way they are. But they won't be different if people of faith can't envision a better world and agitate for it the way Isaiah and Mary did.

Imagine the American story if our country at the first had a bias toward the last. By now we know that there is more than one origin story of America—one at Plymouth with the Pilgrims, the other at Jamestown with enslaved people of African descent. But it didn't have to be that way.

The Pilgrims weren't the elite of English society. You don't leave home in search of freedom and a better life if you are already at home and doing well. Those early settlers were Christians, but they weren't the landed gentry. They were working-class people on the fringes of society. But they were fueled by a vision of the New Jerusalem and a faith in the God of the last that came from texts like these.

What if our nation's forebears in Plymouth and Jamestown had taken up the Bible's bias toward the last?

What if we hadn't needed the 1619 Project to retell the origin story of America from the view of the last?

Speaking of what ifs … What if the church in the antebellum South hadn't read the Bible to justify slavery? What if John Broadus, one of the founders of the Southern Baptist Theological Seminary, hadn't defended the Confederacy as the hope of preserving civilization, thereby setting Baptists on the side of human oppressors? What if during Reconstruction after the Civil War the church had supported the "forty acres and a mule" gift of land and opportunity to freed slaves? What if in Dallas, Texas, where in the 1920s one in three of all eligible white men were members of the Ku Klux Klan, the church had stood up against white supremacy and demanded our city be a home equally for all? What if our white city fathers had not made an accommodation with Black pastors to keep the civil rights movement from bringing real change instead of surface peace?

Well, that was then, but this is now. Happily, we have the same chance today to make things right that we have always had. Today we can reclaim the vision of Isaiah and rename the desolate land in our city. Today we can intercede with Jesus to bring out the best for us at last.

As Dallas City Councilmember Casey Thomas has shown us today through the city's first real accounting by this racial equity audit, decisions were made to cut off parts of Dallas from being fruitful neighborhoods populated by Black and Latino people. Much of the land in southern and western Dallas is still unmarried, to use Isaiah's image. It is unmarried because it was cordoned off by highways built deliberately to prevent encroachment of Black neighbors into white neighborhoods. It is unmarried because of bank redlining that prevented Black renters from getting mortgages and becoming homeowners, which would have built generational wealth. It is unmarried because all the landfills and dumps and toxin-producing businesses were permitted to be located there, something we would never have allowed to happen in our North Dallas neighborhoods. It is unmarried because public transportation was not linked to schools and jobs and services, because public schools and public libraries and public parks and community centers and code enforcement, and on and on, were neglected.

Even today, demography is destiny for too many in our city. The difference in male life expectancy in a two-mile stretch between 75215 in South Dallas and 75205 in Old East Dallas is twenty-six years!

But it doesn't have to be that way. And this is the kind of thing leaders like Councilmember Thomas are working to reverse. Things are not fixed or final. Not if the spirit of Isaiah and Mary still stirs. Not if the risen Christ is loose in our midst.

Our city leaders go to church. And thank God they are seeing now what we are seeing now, which we somehow once did not see because we didn't want to see. We are reading the Bible, and we are learning to read it as it was intended, with a bias toward the last.

Just imagine the joy of God when all our neighborhoods are named My Delight Is in Her, and when together we taste the best wine last. *If WE can imagine it, WE can achieve it. If WE can dream it, WE can become it.* But it's not just a WE of you and me; it's a WE that includes the God with a bias toward the last. Amen.

PART XI

Bearing Witness

Faith in the Public Square

"The moral arc of the universe is long, but it bends toward justice."

- Martin Luther King Jr

Preface by Nancy Kasten

When I applied to rabbinical school there was one question that the admissions committee always asked. "Every rabbi has one sermon that they always give in one form or another. What's yours?" I think if George was applying to rabbinical school he might have answered, "We're all in this together, don't you know?"

Week after week, year after year, George's sermons proclaim our sacred interdependence. He compares the Bible to a spider web: "Touch it at any spot and you're caught. The Divine Webmaster moves in on you one way or the other and gathers you to the point." For George that "you" is plural because: "Spiritual discernment is never a solo act; it takes the community of faith and the guidance of the Spirit to arrive at the true meaning of the scriptures."

George urges us, in the singular and in the plural, to be our best by seeing others in their fullness and loving them. In "No Time Like the End Time" he puts it this way: "Jesus turns our attention from when the end will come to what we are going to do with our lives in the meantime. Jesus doesn't deny the end will come, but he wants us to live in the meantime in light of the end time."

So, in the meantime, while we are waiting for the end time, "our vocation as human beings is a hands-on calling to promote and protect life." George urges us to see the Spirit working everywhere, not just inside the Church, and frequently gives great examples from his own life.

In "Running Toward" he describes the "end time" moment he created during oral arguments in the Masterpiece Cakeshop case. George brought a box of Bundt cakes to his salon to let the person who cut his hair know that he loved her and her female partner. He told the Wilshire congregation assembled the next Sunday, "There was much joy in that room, I tell you. And all I could say (to the hairdresser) is how I wanted it to be in this room, too. You see, there are too many churches that seem to think they should tell everyone what to think. If you don't agree, you have to hide your thoughts or feelings about these things. That's not the kind of church we want to be. The kind of church we want to be is a kind church—the kind of church where kindness doesn't mean just politeness and niceness; it means genuine love and respect for one another amid differences. You can't have an inclusive community in which inclusion means only likeness or like-mindedness."

George is a pious person, not an ideologue. He maintains that "True religion is not about manipulating God for our purposes; it is about trusting God for God's purposes." His refutation of anti-Muslim rhetoric after 9/11 and his commitment to reclaiming Hebrew scripture by using anti-triumphalist translations and commentaries reflect his quest to experience the fullness of God's revelation to humanity and gain understanding of God's intention for us. In "Glory Be" he asserts that "it is only in our neighbor that we will find the glory of God. We cannot turn to the Lord by turning away from our neighbor. We can only turn to the Lord by turning to our neighbor."

Piety is not the same as perfection. George accepts the challenge of being human—of possessing self-conscious awareness while lacking omniscience or omnipotence. The Hasidic commentary *Degel Machaneh Ephraim* interprets the angels ascending and descending Jacob's ladder as a metaphor for human ascent and descent on the ladder of awareness. We were not created to stay "woke" all the time. But if we see our failings as opportunities for growth, we can overcome despair and deepen our faith. In "Two Ladders," George quotes the Gospel of John as a prooftext for the idea that Jesus is the ladder between God and the world. "When we only look at Jesus through eyes of flesh, we will only see him as the son of Joseph from Nazareth. We have to look deeper, to look with spiritual eyes. We have to move from sight to insight. And to do that, we need an encounter with Jesus that will open us to his true identity. Here's the principle: We have to be seen before we can see; we have to be known before we can know." Jews describe this as the spark of the Divine that resides within every human being, a spark that is both mortal and immortal. The intention of the *Degel* is the same as John's—to sustain hope for the end time through connecting heaven and earth in the meantime.

George is a cisgendered white Christian male, a scholar-athlete, a family man and a man of the world. He is the championship-winning quarterback who calls the shots, wins the game, and gets the girl. Yet he is also vulnerable and humble. He feels the pain of the orphan, the widow, and the stranger, and he wears his heart on his sleeve. George doesn't just let us know he loves us. He also lets us know that he believes in us, and that he needs us. The kind of church—and by extension, the community, the society, the city, the world—that he envisions cannot come into being without us. George has expectations of us, and he sometimes gets frustrated with us. While his rebuke is rare, when it comes it stings. But he doesn't leave us alone to suffer in our pain. Just as he identifies with the feelings of his hairdresser, and Louise Troh, and his grandson, River, he also identifies with our pain when we don't live up to our divine potential. If his gospel is interdependence, his ethos is empathy.

To me, George's one sermon is encapsulated in this passage from *Mishkan T'filah*, the Reform Jewish Prayerbook, adapted from Michael Walzer's book *Exodus and Revolution*:

> *"Standing on the parted shores of history*
> *we still believe what we were taught*
> *before ever we stood at Sinai's foot;*
>
> *that wherever we go, it is eternally Egypt*
> *that there is a better place, a promised land;*
> *that the winding road to that promise*
> *passes through the wilderness.*
>
> *That there is no way to get from here to there*
> *except by joining hands, marching*
> *together."*

As a quarterback George knew when open hands caught the passes he threw. But then he chose to become a preacher, where "Mostly I speak words into thin air and hope they fall into open ears; you don't get to see the ears do the catching."

But catch them we do.

Nancy Kasten is a Reform rabbi and the Chief Relationship Officer of Faith Commons, an interfaith organization founded by Mason. She is a community educator, volunteer, and activist, as well as a certified Jewish Mindfulness Meditation teacher.

72

Hands On, Hands Off

The following three sermons address the terrorist attacks of September 11, 2001, with increasing amounts of distance from the event. Mason preached "Hands On, Hands Off" the Sunday immediately following the attacks, "No Time Like the End Time" on the first Sunday of Advent in 2001, and "Settling Accounts" on the 10-year anniversary.

September 16, 2001
Fifteenth Sunday after Pentecost
Genesis 2:15-17

I mowed the grass Thursday. It didn't need mowing; I needed to mow it. I don't know why exactly. Maybe I needed to cut on something, take a scalp or something. (I set the mower blade real low.) Maybe Thursday I needed to do something I could look back on and see it done. Mostly I speak words into thin air and hope they fall into open ears; you don't get to see the ears do the catching.

I don't usually mow my own lawn anymore. That's why a man has sons, don't you know?! When Rhett came home from school, he was his father's son—diplomatic but on point. *Dad, did YOU cut the grass?* I wanted to say, Yeah, what's it to you? *Thanks, Dad.* He let some time pass and then came back: *Dad, uh, I really appreciate it, but ... why does it look so bad?* Well, truth is, it does look bad. About halfway through the cutting I couldn't figure why it looked like the haircuts my dad used to give me in the basement with those home barber kits. I wanted to cry the same way I did back then. I stopped and put the mower on the sidewalk. I noticed it wasn't resting on all four wheels—had a kind of catawampus look to it. I had adjusted all the wheels before I started, but it seems I made a mistake and moved the right rear wheel the opposite way from the others. So, the cut was brutally uneven. I set it straight and tried to return to normal, tried to go back over it all again, but the damage was done.

Anybody else felt like that this week? We've tried to return to normalcy, but nothing seems normal. The world stopped after Tuesday—or tried to. Baseball, football, stock market, all kinds of things closed down. In the ministry things go the other way at times like these. Peter Jennings and I were keeping similar schedules. I did two funerals on the day of the tragedy. There have been prayer services, and meetings to prepare for them. There have been statements and columns and sermons to write, news media to answer, Bible studies to lead, budgets to work on, emails to answer about the crisis, and Muslim friends to reassure. There has been marital counseling and, thank God, a wedding last night. Some of us spent Friday and Saturday in a strategic planning retreat looking toward our church's next five years. I am about out of words, so I am asking you to listen more closely than usual for the Word himself behind the words.

I wonder if beneath the radar of my consciousness I needed to mow the grass to fulfill something like the command to Adam in the Garden of Eden that he *till it and keep it.* It's hands-on work God wants of us. This is our human vocation. And thinking about our vocation—about what we are to do and not do—might be just the thing we need most today. I thought about scrapping this new sermon series I started last week called *What's the Story?* At first it didn't seem like the text fit. But it's kind of like a spiderweb, the Bible: Touch it at any one spot and you're caught. The Divine Webmaster moves in on you one way or the other and gathers you to the point.

So follow along. God created the world and called it good. God put us in a garden that would meet our needs for food and oxygen and the joy of life. But we aren't just to sit back passively and watch it work for us. It waits for us to work with it and for it. It has a prowess of life built into it, waiting upon us for its progress.

Work is not a result of sin; it is a God-given calling that comes from the goodness of creation. When we put our hands to the task, when we get our fingernails black in the dirt, when we labor in the good earth, life has a chance to be what God intends it to be. When we take shortcuts and prefer leisure to labor, when we neglect our calling to till the earth and keep it, we open the door to all kinds of evil. We are called to act in the interest of life.

Our vocation as human beings is a hands-on calling to promote and protect life. And that involves enormous PERMISSION. God gave us every tree in the garden to feed and nourish us—except one. Lots of people dumbly think religion is all about what you cannot do, what you should not touch, what freedom you have to give up to please God. But it's just the opposite. God did not put us in a garden and say, *Keep your hands off everything except that one tree you can eat from.* God gave us unbelievable freedom and latitude and choice. We can act with an amazing range of possibilities—all within our God-ordained human vocation.

But yes, there is PROHIBITION with permission. *You shall not eat of the tree of knowledge of good and evil, for as soon as you eat of it, you shall die.* Which means ... ?

It does not mean God wants us to be ignorant. It does not mean God wants us to remain in the dark about what is right and wrong, about what is good and bad. It's not a moral statement at all. Of course God wants us to know the difference between good and evil, right and wrong. *Good and evil* is a Hebrew way of saying *everything:* God does not want human beings to act as if we are omniscient, as if we know everything. God does not want us ever to forget that we are not God. The moment we think we know it all, we begin to take liberties that are not ours to take. We begin to violate creation and one another, thinking we know enough to judge, to settle scores, to do what's best for others.

There is hands-on work for us to do, and there is hands-off work, too: permission and prohibition. There is the active work of promoting and protecting life, and there is the work of refraining from acting when we cannot know enough to act in ways that will heal instead of hurt. The first principle of the Hippocratic Oath in medicine is, *Do no harm.* This is an echo of the command in the garden not to eat of the tree of the knowledge of good and evil.

But isn't that just the kind of sin we have seen this week? Instead of promoting life and protecting it—which is the true vocation of all human beings—some people thought they knew enough about justice, about how to set the world straight and even scores, that they took thousands of innocent lives in the name of God. They overreached their humanity and in doing so slithered down the chain of life to the level of beasts.

Syndicated columnist Leonard Pitts Jr. wrote an open letter to the terrorists this week.[117] I can't use all his language in the pulpit. Here's some: *Did you want us to respect your cause? You just damned your cause. Did you want to make us fear? You just steeled our resolve. Did you want to tear us apart? You just brought us together.*

Allow me to chime in. *Yes, you have some grievances against America that fueled your rage. We are not always right or righteous. It is true we have sided often with Israel against the Palestinians in ways that have not been compassionate to Arabs. It is true we have propped up puppet rulers, like the Shah of Iran, and other oppressive governments in the interest of cheap oil. We have sometimes been insensitive to the interests of the people on the ground in Third World nations, the way we pursue our business and political interests. We are also capable of repenting of our sins and living differently. But what you have done has only cut the heart out of all desire to learn. You have fueled our rage now. You have unified a nation capable of striking back with might in ways that might even take the lives of some we wished to spare. You have raised the stakes. You have declared a war we are all too eager to enter. And make no mistake, we aim to win this war by defeating you, and not likely by understanding you and seeking peace.*

This, my friends, is the way of the world when it eats from the tree of the knowledge of good and evil. In the moment we do, we are on the path of death. But we don't have to be. We can choose otherwise, as Billy Graham said at the national memorial service this week. We can choose to promote life and peace instead of being just as omniscient and dealing more death.

Many Americans have heard Christians say these things this week and made us feel un-American. We are flanked today by two flags in this sanctuary. Some of us are all draped in red, white, and blue. We do not stop being Christians to be Americans, nor do we stop being Americans to be Christians.

Someone wrote in the dust on a window near the site of the rubble in New York: *Father, forgive them for they know not what they do.* Someone else came along and struck through the word not and wrote: *Kill them all!* I heard a radio guy say, *There's a place and time for all you religious people preaching peace, but this isn't it. You people need to just back off and let the military do their duty.* So what? It's the job of religious people just to come along after all the killing and bury the dead and comfort the

117 *Seattle Times*, Sept. 13, 2001.

bereaved? Is that it? Does anyone think maybe we might have something to say ahead of time about the role of faith in restraining violence in the interest of life?

But here's the other side: That does not mean justice should be neglected. Part of our calling, part of God's command to *keep* the garden involves protecting life as well as promoting it. Stopping terrorists from killing people—sometimes maybe even by the use of force that takes life in the doing—this can be a promotion of life too. We have already bit into the fruit of that tree, and there's no way of getting the rottenness of the apple out of our systems entirely. We live on this side of the sin of Adam and Eve, and when we act we will never have the luxury of pure hearts or clean hands. That said, there is still no excuse for us to forsake our true calling to promote and protect life. We ought to exercise every bit of judgment and restraint in pursuit of justice, so that we don't just ratchet up the killing to make ourselves feel better by being avenged.

If you want to weed your garden, you don't go at it with a rototiller and a blindfold. You'll make mistakes. You can't help it. Neither do you spray Roundup on the whole thing, lest you end up killing your precious petunias, too. And if you want to get the snakes out of your garden, you don't kill the worms in the process just because they look kind of like snakes. You don't profile everything that looks suspiciously like a snake and take it out. You know what I am talking about. We must not suspect every Arab-looking person or condemn all Muslims. We must proceed with patience and care, as our president has said this week, even as we pursue with passion those who did this to innocent people.

The real models for us should be those heroes in New York and D.C. digging in the rubble night and day with bare knuckles, patiently and prayerfully looking for life and doing what they can out of love. They are determined to salvage life rather than savage it.

We must leave room for the wrath of God, Paul says in Romans, knowing there is only One who is all-knowing, and God will repay. We may try to rid the world of this evil of terrorism, but we will not rid the world of evil altogether. Even God does not seem to be moving to rid the world of evil the way we want to. Just look at Jesus on the cross and you will see God's way of suffering love. *Vengeance is mine, saith the Lord. ... Do not repay evil for evil but overcome evil with good.* (KJV)

This is a time when we want to draw together as a nation behind our president, George W. Bush, regardless of party politics. We are all Americans now, if not New Yorkers. And we are all bruised if not bereaved. We are a strong and resilient people, even if now we know how fragile and vulnerable we are, too. We want something done to answer this evil done against us. Fine and good. Let's go get them. But let's not become like them as we do. Let's be world leaders, but let's lead the world to a new wave of peace.

In our prayers for our leaders, we can ask God to give wisdom about what kind of response will promote life and not destroy it, and that we will do things that will restore freedom and chase away fear.

FDR said, *The only thing we have to fear is fear itself.* The Bible trumps that: 1 John says, *[Only] perfect love casts out fear.*[118] And the poet W.H. Auden applies the exclamation point: *We must love one another or die.*[119]

What's it going to be, America?

118 1 John 4:18.
119 W. H. Auden, *September 1, 1939*, from *Another Time* (Random House, 1940).

73

No Time Like the End Time

December 2, 2001
First Sunday of Advent
Isaiah 2:1-5; Matthew 24:36-44

It wasn't the end of the world, September 11; it was the end of our naiveté about time being on our side, about our having all the time in the world to have the time of our lives. It got us thinking about time. We hugged our children a little tighter, held on to our stuff a little lighter, opened our eyes a little wider to the world as it is instead of the world as we want it to be. We were all affected by the attacks, but those who were spiritually prepared were *shaken, not stirred.* When your outlook on life is shaped by Jesus' words, you aren't taken completely off guard by the disorienting things that come.

But was September 11 a sign of the end times? Let me answer that with a definite, resounding, unequivocal ... *I don't know.* I wish I could tell you for sure, yes or no, but if I could, and if you or I could know for sure, what would be the point of faith? Lots of people look to the Bible for all the answers, but for all the answers we get, sometimes we get questions instead. Like in our text today, Jesus turns our attention from when the end will come to what we are going to do with our lives in the meantime. Jesus doesn't deny the end will come, but he wants us to live in the meantime in light of the end time.

The images he offers are different from the catalog of wars and earthquakes and famines and what-not we usually think of in end-time thinking. Here Jesus wants us to know that things are just as likely to be downright boringly normal. As in the days of Noah before the flood, so it will be in the end time: People will be eating and drinking and falling in love and having kids and going to soccer games and burying old Beatles. You just can't wait to read the signs of the times to get your life in order. Two people will be working side by side in the World Trade Center; one will be taken and the other left behind. You board a plane like so many times before, but this time you never get off. Who saw that coming?

Now, Jesus isn't saying we ought to quit doing normal things in light of the end. He isn't saying we ought to become so preoccupied with the end time that we alter all human activities now in order to be ready for heaven. Some people live so much in the end time they fail to live meaningfully in the meantime.

David Koresh and his Waco group were guilty of this. Their imaginations were so fired with the fire of judgment to come that they holed up in a Texas compound with Bible in one hand and automatic weapons in the other, waiting for the forces of evil to attack. They were sure they knew the *when* of Christ's return, though Jesus himself says in this passage that even he doesn't know when. We see what came of them.

So quit buying all those books and listening to those TV preachers who fill you with ideas of when the end will come. The point is not *when* but *that*. That the end is coming is Jesus' one sure word. That we should be ready is our one sure work—whether it's our time that is up, or time itself.

How do you do that? There's a delightful passage in the first Harry Potter book that comes to life in the movie. Harry scoots into an unused room of the Hogwarts castle, wearing his invisible cloak to escape the notice of Professor Snape. In this room he stumbles upon a large claw-footed mirror. When he looks into it, he sees the most wondrous thing: He sees not only his own reflection but also a whole crowd of people behind him. Among the crowd he sees the moving images of his dead parents, smiling at him, reaching to touch him with pride, being right there with him. He brings his friend Ron Weasley to see his dead parents in the mirror, but instead Ron sees something else. He sees himself a little older, captain of the Quidditch team, holding the winners' cup. Harry is later made the wiser about it all by the headmaster of Hogwarts Albus Dumbledore. The mirror is called Erised—that is, *desire* spelled backward, the way a mirror might read it. The mirror shows nothing more or less than the deepest desires of the heart. Harry longed for a past he was denied, Ron for a future he doubted he could have. Professor Dumbledore explains that the happiest person is the one who can look in the Mirror of Erised and see nothing but himself. *It does no good to dwell on dreams and forget to live,* he says.[120]

Some of us dwell on dreams of the past or dreams of the future and forget to live in the present. And yet it is true that true Christian thinking is weighted more toward the future than the past. We are given reason to hope for more to come than we could ever imagine. We are told that the kingdom of heaven is where we will want to live, because in it life will be what God always intended it to be. And so, yes, we are to live with a sense of expectancy about the end time. But we don't live *for* the end time; we live in the meantime in the light of the end time. We are transformed in the present by the consciousness of what is to come.

Isn't that the way it is when you are in that stage of romance that you hope to see the one you love at any time, but you never know when? You make sure you look your best before you leave your dorm room or go to the office, just in case you meet that person. You don't want to be caught unprepared in a moment of grace.

120 J. K. Rowling, *Harry Potter and the Sorcerer's Stone* (Scholastic Press, 1997), p. 214.

You still go to class, go to work, eat, play, whatever, but your mind is never far from the one you love.

This is what Jesus is saying, I think. Be ready now, not by changing everything about your routines but by being changed yourself in your routines. Don't let yourself get so caught up in what you are doing that those things take over your soul.

The quiet Beatle George Harrison died this week. Overshadowed by Lennon and McCartney most of the time, George was always more interested in the music than the hype. Being a Beatle wore on him, made him feel like he was living in a cage. Forget Yoko. George broke up the Beatles as surely as she. He had to declare some soul freedom from all the Beatlemania. Toward the end, his guitar gently wept, don't you know?! He still wanted to make music, but he had to grow in other directions. He explored LSD and Indian religion, trying to gain some sense of what we are here for. The answers he found are not the ones Jesus offers, but the cause of the soul is the same.

We have to be alert to the ways the world comes to own us and hold us. We have to be ready to break free from those things in order to be truly ourselves without illusions and regrets, fully ready for the judgment of Christ's coming.

A woman called her pastor one day, hysterical. She could hardly get the words out amid the sobs, but he finally caught that she had been robbed. Someone had stolen all the family heirlooms; the silver, the china, everything mother had passed on to her. She was crushed. She felt her very identity had been stolen from her. Her friends worried about her future, but about six months later they saw a new person emerge. She told her pastor, *In one sense, the burglary was one of the best things that has happened to me. I had become tied down to those things. I was afraid to leave the house for what might happen to them. I would spend half my day polishing ... [which] was really stupid when you think of it. Life ought to be more. I thought I would die after the burglary. But I've come to the conclusion I might be better off without all that stuff.*[121]

There you have it. Some of you have felt the same after a divorce or after your last drink or after the death of a spouse or child. You thought you would die. You may not say you are better off without whatever it was you lost, depending on what it was, but you have learned to live in the present with a sense of the future instead of being fearful and frozen. You have learned to perform what Walter Brueggemann calls *an emotional act of civil disobedience.* You will not be bound by the expectations of yourself or others. You will live with your eyes on the end time and let it free you for the meantime.

Look at the end this way. Light travels at about 186,000 miles per second, the one constant in the universe. Because of the distance between the Sun and the Earth, the light we see comes to us about eight minutes and twenty seconds after it leaves the sun. We can never outrace the light to get to its source; we are always living in its shining.

In the same way, Christ is the Light ahead of us, always coming toward us, calling to us to walk after him, in his shining way.

He calls us out of sleep and into wakefulness.

---

121 William Willimon, in *Pulpit Resource* 29.4: 37.

He calls us out of the night and into the day.
He calls us out of bondage and into freedom.
He calls us out of fear and into faith.
He calls us out of loneliness and into love.
He calls us out of despair and into hope.

So let me ask: How ready are you for the coming of the Lord? Are you making spiritual progress, or are you getting more stuck and losing your sense of what is important? When you look into the Mirror of Erised, do you see only the you that you want Christ to see? You come to church to hear the truth about your soul's condition. Have you done anything about it lately? Today is as good as any to begin the making ready. Offer your heart anew to God. Tell someone about Christ. Let go of your money. Tell someone you love that you do. Sober up to life. Beat your swords into ploughshares. Make peace. Grant forgiveness. Do it all ... now!

The impressionist painter and sculptor Edgar Degas was fascinated with ballerinas. He did some of his most beautiful and graceful work celebrating their art. His painting *The Dance Foyer at the Opera on the rue le Peletier* hangs in Paris' Museé d'Orsay. The ballet master commands the attention of his ballerina. Other dancers are all standing 'round stretching and talking and looking on as the one ballerina takes his instructions. She is the picture of focused alertness, her right leg poised, her toes pointed, her every sinew at the ready for the music.

How is it with you? Are you standing 'round going through the motions spiritually or are you poised tiptoed, ready for the music of the kingdom of God that is breaking forth even now from the Lord of the dance?

Because there's no time like the end time, there's no time like the present time to be ready. Amen.

74

Settling Accounts

Watch and listen to "Settling Accounts" by following this link or scanning the QR code with your phone: youtu.be/AG2qG4JbFpA.

September 11, 2011
Thirteenth Sunday after Pentecost
Tenth Anniversary of 9/11 Terrorist Attacks
Matthew 18:21-35

… And forgive us our debts as we forgive our debtors. Depending upon what church you're in when you say the Lord's Prayer, you are liable to stumble over that part, since some like us say "sins," others "trespasses," and others "debts." I've noticed that Presbyterians tend to say debts, and Episcopalians trespasses. I think if you go back, you might find that Episcopalians were the landed gentry and Presbyterians the bankers who held their notes. So the one is more concerned with trespassing and the other debts. Baptists have always been just plain sinners, don't you know?! But "debts" is as good a translation as any for sins, and it goes to the point Jesus wants to make about wrongs in our text.

Peter comes to Jesus showing off his spirituality like a politician running for office. He's willing to forgive seven times someone who has sinned against him. A Jewish tradition had established three times as a fair limit for forgiveness. Which is still more than our usual bent that can be summarized in the ditty: *Hurt me once, shame on you; hurt me twice, shame on me.* So Peter's looking good here, but Jesus pushes the number beyond all reason. How many times should you forgive? Not seven times, but seventy-seven or seven times seventy—it can be translated either way. Jesus is saying that true forgiveness means you get over the hurt by getting over the counting. When you're trying to settle financial accounts, you're scrupulous about counting. But when it comes to settling relationship accounts, count Jesus out as an accountant.

He tells a parable to get his point across. A king calls in a servant to settle accounts with him. The man owes the king ten thousand talents—a ridiculous amount, because it represents about fifteen years' wages for a menial laborer. It's an inconceivable debt for a servant. But even if this man was a high-and-mighty servant of some kind, the whole notion of that kind of debt is over the top. Anyway, the man is distraught by the weight of the debt that he knows he can't repay. He begs the king to be patient with him so that he can pay. He doesn't ask to get off scot-free, but scot-free is exactly what he gets. Instead of getting what he deserves, he gets mercied up by a king who takes pity on him.

Maybe the king was a bleeding-heart liberal. Maybe, though, the king realized that he had lent the man way too much money in the first place. His own subprime lending created this problem as much as the man's irresponsible borrowing of the money. Sound familiar?

Anyway, the king doesn't just give him more time to pay; he burns his note altogether. This extravagance of grace is the true nature of forgiveness. It's over the top and undeserved. It's doesn't say that what's been done—the debt that is owed, the hurt that has been caused—doesn't matter. It says that something matters more. It says that I will not let it stand between us forever. And it knows that to do so means that I am every bit as much suffering the debt of broken relationship as you until we get past this.

The word *forgive* means literally to let go. And the image that has always helped me is that of a man walking a dog on a leash. The man thinks he's walking the dog, but that leash has two ends: As long as he holds the dog, the dog has a hold on him. He has to let go in order for both of them to be free.

Isn't that true in our experience? As long as you refuse to forgive, you carry the pain of your woundedness with you. It affects everything you do. It's like bile in your belly that poisons your body—but in this case your spirit. To forgive lets your debtor off the hook, which is a huge act of grace—no question. But it's also a huge relief for you. As long as you hold the note of your debtor, you carry that weight around with you. You're in business, but it's not the kind of business that'll make you rich; it's the kind of business that'll make you sick. The only way for you to get well is to let it go.

What Frederick Buechner says about anger describes the spirit of unforgiveness. *Of the Seven Deadly Sins, anger is possibly the most fun. To lick your wounds, to smack your lips over grievances long past, to roll over your tongue the prospect of bitter confrontations still to come, to savor to the last toothsome morsel—both the pain you were given and the pain you are giving back—in many ways it is a feast fit for a king. The chief drawback is that what you are wolfing down is yourself. The skeleton at the feast is you.*[122]

Jesus tells about a king who knows how to forgive, and we know he's really talking about God. Now, some of us would like to cite Alexander Pope at this point and say, *To err is human, to forgive divine.* But we humans are created in the image of God and therefore have the same capacity to forgive as God.

I was looking this week at my sermon from this Sunday ten years ago after the 9/11 terrorist attacks. I noted that someone had written these words with a finger in the dust from the collapsed buildings that had caked onto a storefront window: *Father, forgive them, for they know not what they do.* Someone else had come along

122 *Wishful Thinking: A Theological ABC* (Harper & Row, 1973), p. 2.

afterward and struck through the word *NOT,* then beneath it had written instead *Kill them all!*

There's no disputing that those who perpetrated that heinous crime, which took nearly three thousand lives and robbed thousands more of their loved ones, deserve to die. Not just those who killed themselves in the act, but also those who conspired with them.

The responses that followed from our nation were as varied as the extremes of those two sentiments written in the window dust. But ten years later, what we have seen more clearly is that those who have learned to forgive have found freedom and those who haven't are still bound by their pain. The most beautiful stories this week are from those who decided to rebuild their lives out of the rubble. They have honored the victims by refusing to be victimized forever by their terrorist debtors. For some that has taken the form of physically rebuilding Ground Zero. The workers on the memorial site and the new Freedom Tower are working on themselves as much as on the site. They are constructing new lives with the buildings. Others have poured themselves into helping others endure disaster and tragedy. The New York City firefighters, for instance, have gone every year at this time to places like New Orleans after Katrina to pay forward the help they received after 9/11. And countless others have reached out to people of other faiths in order to promote tolerance, understanding, and peace. Bad things can make you bitter or better. We've seen both, frankly, but those who have forgiven have proven Jesus' words truest of all.

Rais Bhuiyan is one of them. A native of Bangledesh, he had moved to Dallas from New York a few months before 9/11. Ten days after the attacks, he was working at the gas station he owned on Buckner Boulevard when a white supremacist named Mark Stroman walked in wearing sunglasses, a bandana, and a baseball cap. He pointed a double-barrel shotgun at Bhuiyan and demanded, *Where are you from?* Seconds later, Bhuiyan felt part of his face blown off from a blast. With blood pouring down on the floor like an open faucet, he fell to the ground and pretended to be dead. Stroman was caught and sentenced to death for killing another man from India. But Bhuiyan, who is blind now in one eye, spoke this week about his decade-long attempts to save the life of his attacker. His presentation at SMU was entitled "Ending the Cycles of Violence: Reflections on Compassion, Forgiveness and Healing." Bhuiyan is a Muslim, and he proves that forgiveness isn't just a Christian doctrine. *Though I lost vision in one of my eyes,* he said, *it opened the vision in my heart and I see things in a different way.* Amen.[123]

Getting to the heart is a real key. Jesus ended his parable with these sobering words: *So my heavenly Father will also do to every one of you, if you do not forgive your brother or sister from your heart.*

Many of us are prone to forgive with our heads but not our hearts. We tell someone we forgive him, but we never let go of the leash. We have no intention of seeing that forgiveness through to reconciliation. We think that as long as we say we have forgiven, we have done our part, we are right with God, we have covered the necessary demands of Jesus. But we prefer to keep the power in the relationship by

---

123 *Dallas Morning News* (Sept. 9, 2011): 10W.

never really letting go, by reminding the forgiven debtor forever that we are the ones who have forgiven. The journalist Sydney Harris captured this when he said, *There's no point in burying the hatchet if you're going to put up a marker on the site.* Or you might say that forgiveness is not burying the hatchet in the back of your offender. It's throwing away the hatchet altogether.

When the forgiven servant leaves the king and encounters a man who owes him far less, he forgets that the king has set the terms for all time on how to settle accounts. He goes back to counting and throws his debtor into prison. When the king hears about this, he is furious. His forgiveness has been trampled upon, and he won't have it. So he revokes his clemency and has the servant tortured until he can pay up.

So does our forgiveness with God depend upon our forgiving others? No, and yes. No, in the sense that God isn't waiting for us to do something to deserve being forgiven—even our repentance. God forgives because God is God, not because we are good. Forgiveness is God's way of settling accounts. If we fail to forgive others, we are saying we prefer our own rules to God's. And then God can only say, *Have it your way.* To have it our way is to be tortured by our own unforgiveness.

Corrie ten Boom was a Dutch Christian who had hidden German Jews in her home during World War II. She was caught and sent to a concentration camp, along with her sister, who died there. Two years after the war, she was in Germany talking about forgiveness. Afterward, a balding heavyset man in a gray overcoat, a brown felt hat clutched between his hands, stood before her and stuck out his hand. He explained that he had been a guard in that camp. He asked her to forgive him for the cruel things he did. She couldn't do it.

Since the end of the war she had had a home in Holland for victims of Nazi brutality. Those who were able to forgive their former enemies were able also to return to the outside world and rebuild their lives, no matter what the physical scars. Those who nursed bitterness remained invalids. It was as simple and as horrible as that.

Still, she stood there with the coldness clutching her heart. And then she prayed, *"Jesus, help me!" "And finally, woodenly, mechanically,"* she said, *"I thrust my hand into the one stretched out to me. And as I did, an incredible thing took place. The current started in my shoulder, raced down my arm, sprang into our joined hands. And then this healing warmth seemed to flood my whole being, bringing tears to my eyes. 'I forgive you, brother!' I cried. 'With all my heart!'"*[124]

Forgiveness isn't easy, or it isn't forgiveness. But it's the only path to life.

---

124 *Clippings from My Notebook* (Triangle, 1983).

75

God's Glorious Back Side

Watch and listen to "God's Glorious Back Side" by following this link or scanning the QR code with your phone: youtu.be/KeidFO9AXNI.

Mason preached "God's Glorious Back Side" in the midst of the Ebola outbreak in Dallas in the fall of 2014, which affected Wilshire directly. During this time, Mason found himself in the national spotlight, with cameras in the sanctuary and appearances on major news outlets.

Here is an excerpt from his sermon the week before this one, on October 12, 2014, that explains how Wilshire became personally connected to this crisis:

"When Ebola came to Dallas in the body of Thomas Eric Duncan, he carried it along with his dreams of a new life with the woman he loved, Louise Troh. Louise and her family had become our family. The process of caring for her began when her three nieces came to Dallas from Liberia, and the Open Bible Class took on the task, under the leadership of Max Post and with the support of teacher Craig Keith, of helping them assimilate into our country. ESL and computer training were part of that. But it all quickly became personal. Louise is the matriarch of this extended family, and she began to come among us. Before long, Louise was not content to be a guest; she wanted to be a host with us. She was baptized in June by Tiffany Wright, who leads our care ministries. And just a few months later, she was hosting me in her secluded, quarantined house, along with her son and two other young men related to her or the late Eric Duncan. (Oh, and by the way, these boys have names, too: Timothy Wayne, Oliver Smallwood, and Jeffrey Cole. I can't wait for them to get here.)"

October 19, 2014
Nineteenth Sunday after Pentecost
Exodus 33:12-23

Wherever you are in the journey of faith, you are always and only … there. I know that has a Zen-like sound to it, but truth is truth, after all. There is past, and there is future, but we can live only in the present.

One of the most common aphorisms you will hear from a eulogist at a funeral, which is intended to encourage mourners, goes like this: *The past is history. The future is a mystery. But today is a gift—that's why they call it "the present."* Clever. Not deep. But it does point us to a truth about how we are creatures caught between the times. We can't change the past, and we can't control the future, so we have to learn how to live in the present.

Our story from Exodus gives us a window into this. One commentator on this passage puts it starkly: *Exodus 33 shows Israel in a state of panic. Plain and simple, God's people were in triage management following the fiasco with the golden calf …*[125]

I think we've known something about fiascos and a state of panic in our own community this week. And we have certainly seen various strategies of triage management following the tragedy of Thomas Eric Duncan's delayed treatment, his subsequent death, and the infection of two nurses who treated him for Ebola. I believe this biblical story gives us guidance on how we might deal spiritually with these times in our lives.

First, look at how Moses dealt with God and what he wants to know. He wanted assurance that Israel's turning their back on God would not make God turn God's back on them.

The golden-calf episode amounted to a betrayal of the Israelites' relationship with God. It was an infidelity that broke the covenant. Because they substituted a god made of their own hands for the one and only living God who had gotten them out of Egypt, Moses feared, on behalf of the people, that God would withdraw from them. Moses wanted assurance that God would personally continue to go forward with Israel and not leave them on their own, even if they had tried to go their own way so disastrously.

Let's remember what the golden calf incident implied. We said last week that when the people became afraid about the future and didn't know how to live in the present, they sought certainty. They wanted a knowledge they could count on and control. They wanted, in other words, an easy kind of religion that amounted to magic.

Magical thinking promises that the future will be good for us. We will be safe. We will be prosperous. No pitcher in the World Series is likely to step on a line going to or from the mound, lest it bring him bad luck. For the same reason, players won't shave their beards. But, of course, all such "religion" is nonsense. True religion is not about manipulating God for our purposes; it is about trusting God for God's purposes.

[125] http://www.workingpreacher.org/preaching.aspx?commentary_id=2185

Moses implored God to promise God's presence with the people. At first God assured Moses that God was with him because he had found favor with God. But Moses was not the kind of leader who is interested in his own blessing without the blessing of the people. Moses understood that his life was nothing apart from God, but it was also nothing apart from God's people. No matter how they behaved, they were his people, and he was with them.

I quoted an African proverb at the prayer vigil on the night that Eric Duncan died: *I am because we are.* This is what Moses insisted on, and it is at the heart of any great leader.

In the midst of the crisis of fear and even panic, what often happens is what we have seen some of in the past few weeks here in Dallas—it's what I would call a consistent *othering* of certain people in order to make *us* feel safer and more privileged.

We know what happens when a marriage covenant is broken, don't we? In the pain of that brokenness, the tendency is to *other* the former partner, and people often then choose sides. They believe that if they can just put all of the blame on someone else, it makes them feel better that they have retained the favored status.

In this case, God initially told Moses that he had found favor with God. Moses could have left it at that, but he wouldn't; he kept pressing for the people. He wanted God to include the offending party. He essentially said that although he was God's man, he didn't want that alone. He wanted God to keep faith with the people, too.

I think that's remarkable. And I think we can learn from this. Look at what has happened in the case of this Ebola crisis. Some people are focused on how the hospital blew it, how it failed. Some focus on how the Centers for Disease Control failed to keep people safe since two others have now contracted Ebola. In too many ways they all failed. But let's remember that these are human beings who now have the benefit of hindsight in what was an unprecedented situation. It took everyone by surprise, and we now have hurting people in the healthcare world who have been vilified for not doing a better job in caring for Thomas Eric Duncan and the family. We can nurture that negative narrative, or we can advocate for them, too, the way Moses did. Even if they made mistakes that were costly in ways they can never remedy, the question is whether we want them to recover favor, or whether we are content to let them be villains and leave them to live out their lives with that scorn sticking to them forever.

Similarly, there are those who are othering Mr. Duncan for bringing the virus to this country, as if they know that he willfully and knowingly did so, even though he is not here to speak for himself. Some have political agendas about immigration and the uninsured and what the government should have done differently that would serve their interest in seeing someone else in charge in the future that they would prefer. We also hear this kind of thinking with regard to Louise and the boys, to the point that they have to be concerned about how they will regain their freedom to live among us and to be welcomed back into our community.

Let's remember that Louise is an American citizen. She is one of us. She did absolutely nothing wrong in this case. Through no fault of her own, she lost not only the love of her life and the father of her son—and a son lost a father he was hoping to know at long last—but she and the three boys also lost all their possessions. They have nothing. And yet we hear people blaming her.

I mentioned last week that we have heard some of the most beautiful things from people in the midst of this crisis. It has brought out some of the most wonderful expressions of support and generosity from individuals and government and the philanthropic community. We are truly grateful for this response, and it shows that there are people of great hearts and good will who want to be part of the solution by binding themselves to this family and not othering them. But some of the calls, emails, letters, and internet comments have been meaner and crueler than I can tell you. It disappoints and stuns me to see this type of response, and I would repeat what I have said over and over, which is that we have to ask ourselves what these responses say about us, as well. A situation like this reveals as much about who we are as who someone else is. And when we try to distance ourselves, to make ourselves the innocent party at the expense of someone else who did nothing wrong, we are tearing apart the fabric of our community.

When the second nurse became symptomatic, one of the boys turned to me in the quarantine quarters and asked, *Are they going to blame us for that?* I told him that I can't promise him how people will treat them. But we are going to do everything we can to say that we belong to each other and that we should walk this road together. We will not allow them to be othered by these circumstances if there is anything we can do about it.

But also look at how Moses kept pressing God. Not only did he ask for assurances that God would stick by the people, but he also wanted to experience God's glory, to see it, to have a window into God's ways in the world.

And here's where God gave him more and also drew a line. What God gave him is the assurance of God's presence and a revelation of God's goodness. God promised that Moses would be able to see God's presence—but only God's glorious back side. (Be sure to separate those last two words, don't you know?!)

Moses was instructed to hide himself in the cleft of a rock. And for those of us who know our gospel hymns, this sounds so familiar that we can almost break out in song. Fanny Crosby wrote: *He hideth my soul in the cleft of the rock, / That shadows a dry, thirsty land; / He hideth my life in the depths of His love, / And covers me there with His hand, / And covers me there with His hand.*

God passed by, and God shielded Moses' eyes from the powerful force of God's presence. Moses got a glimpse of God's goodness. He received insight into God's gracious and merciful nature so that he need not doubt it. He got everything he needed to go on—but only what he needed to go on.

And isn't this the nature of faith? We don't get everything we want, but we get what we need. We don't get to know the future, but we get to see where God has been in the midst of our lives. We get to see traces of God's activity among us. We get to look at life in hindsight and see the way God has left clues about the way things have turned out.

Much of the world doubts that there is anything at all going on in the world that can't be explained by the forces of nature or the acts of human beings. Even we who believe in God, like Moses, sometimes want assurances that we are not alone. God sometimes grants us what my friend David Wood calls *skylights of transcendence*. We get signs and hints and pointers. We don't get to see God face to face. We don't get to have a special knowledge that allows us to know what no one else can know. We get what we need to go on, though.

One of our residents, Erica Whitaker, commented that this has the feel of a long-exposure photograph. If you are looking at a street, say, and there is a fast-moving car on it and you keep the shutter on the camera open long enough as the car passes, what you see is not the car itself, as you would in a motion picture. What you see is the back side of the car having been there, and, in its wake, you see a glorious streak of light that follows behind it.

When God passes by, this is our experience. We get to sense that something holy and good and beautiful has come our way. But we get to know it only after the fact. We are reassured about God's presence in our lives, and we can go on with confidence that God is with us indeed.

And, really, what more do we need than that?

76

Running Toward

Watch and listen to "Running Toward" by following this link or scanning the QR code with your phone: youtu.be/hpNtn3BYa60. Sermon begins at 40:00.

"Running Toward" is the sermon Mason preached on the Sunday following the Supreme Court decision requiring all states to grant and recognize same-sex marriages.

June 28, 2015
Fifth Sunday after Pentecost
Acts 8:26-40

Where is Christ taking us next?

When Luke tells the story of the early church in the Book of Acts, that might have been the question believers were asking themselves as all sorts of new people were finding faith, being baptized, and receiving the gift of the Holy Spirit. It must have been exhilarating and exhausting at the same time. Change was in the air. Things were happening so fast they didn't know how to process it all. Sound familiar?

Change had actually been coming on for a long time before this explosion of the Spirit. It reminds me of what a character says in Hemingway's novel, *The Sun Also Rises*. The man was asked how he went bankrupt. *Two ways*, he said. *Gradually, then suddenly.*

This is how God works. Pressure building underground. Tectonic plates shifting. Heat rising. Then boom.

The volcano erupts, and we can see the result of what's been brewing out of sight for a long time.

Track this with me. When Jesus is raised from the dead, the Holy Spirit comes first upon the apostles whom Jesus had called to be his disciples. They were not part of the establishment of Israel. They held no positions among the Sadducees, who kept the Temple order, or the Pharisees, who made sure the order of Moses was kept. These two groups formed the Sanhedrin, the council that watched over the membership of the people of God.

The first leaders of the church were all Jews from the hinterlands, marginal common folk, fishermen, and tax collectors, who were hardly in a position to say who was in and who was out when it came to the power structure of Israel. But the gift of the Holy Spirit had come upon *them*.

A fresh wind blew through Jerusalem. People from all over the world had gathered there and were putting their faith in Jesus. As the story unfolded, the apostles started doing miracles: healing the sick, casting out demons, bringing people into the fold who were previously thought to be suffering from God's curse on them or their families.

Last week we learned that two Hellenist Jews, who were thought to be impure for being too cozy with Greek culture, were made leaders in the church. Stephen and Philip were elected deacons. Stephen was stoned to death for his inclusive view of the way Jesus was calling the church to welcome all kinds of people. In the first part of chapter 8, it is noted that Philip had won some Samaritans to Jesus— another group that the Jerusalem leaders deemed impure.

Now we get the story of the Ethiopian eunuch. Try to imagine this man. He was probably a proselyte to Judaism. He was certainly a bridge figure in the movement of the gospel. He functioned as a final symbol of the ingathering of all the house of Israel by the work of the risen Christ.

The Ethiopian eunuch was included in the way of Christ. He was not in Christ's way.

But, at the moment Philip was sent by the Spirit to meet him, he must have thought he was excluded. He had just come from Jerusalem. He had gone there to worship, in the way a Catholic might go to St. Peter's in Rome. It would have been a highlight of his religious life. As a eunuch in the service of a queen, he would have had the resources to travel. But when he arrived, his status in the Temple was something else. He would have been excluded from entering at all. Why? Because the Bible said so. Deuteronomy 23:1 made it clear. I'm quoting the lovely euphemism of the King James Version on account of the children in our midst (you are welcome, mothers): *He that is wounded in the stones, or hath his privy member cut off, shall not enter into the congregation of the LORD.*

Ouch. Long way for a eunuch to travel just to be turned away. At least he had the consolation that others were turned away, too. For instance, as the next verse says, anyone conceived out of wedlock couldn't enter, either—to the tenth generation! Some of you are squirming now. Didn't know that was in there, did you?

Listen, the Temple leaders were just trying to be faithful to the Bible and keep the house of God a holy place, undefiled by sinners. Guess they didn't have mirrors back then.

So the eunuch was on his way home, and he was reading aloud (as was the custom) from the prophet Isaiah in his chariot. He was wealthy enough to afford an Isaiah scroll, and he was hungry enough for God that he was reading it. The fact that it was Isaiah is significant, too, since the prophets were always chiding Israel for its scrupulous attention to purity rules while failing to observe the weightier matters of the law, like doing justice, loving mercy, and walking humbly with God. It's also the closest prophetic book to the Gospel itself.

So, what passage did the eunuch just happen to be reading? The passage about the suffering servant who was humiliated and had justice denied to him. It ended with the words that must have stuck in his throat: *For his life is taken away from the earth.*

A eunuch who could never have children of his own would have read that as the story of his life. It would all end with him. No one would keep his memory alive. The religious authorities had reinforced that judgment in Jerusalem.

And yet he wondered to Philip about whom Isaiah was speaking, hoping no doubt that it wasn't just about the prophet himself. He was hoping it included him, of course. He was hoping that all the humiliated have hope with God. But he didn't know it without help. This is why the Holy Spirit sent Philip—who represents the church—to help him interpret the Scripture in a way that included him.

Spiritual discernment is never a solo act; it takes the community of faith and the guidance of the Spirit to arrive at the true meaning of the Scriptures. And that true meaning will always point first to Christ. Philip made clear to the eunuch that Jesus is the fulfillment of Isaiah's prophecy. He is the sheep led to slaughter. He is the humiliated one to whom justice is denied. He is the one whose life was taken away from the face of the earth.

Christians read the Bible rightly when we read it through Jesus. And when we read it through Jesus, we read that all the humiliated and marginalized people of the world are included with him. Because God raised Jesus from the dead after the world took his life away, there is hope for every eunuch, too.

And so the eunuch asked if he might be baptized and join the way of Christ. Isn't this beautiful? Isn't this the good news of God's salvation though Jesus Christ?

Well, now, what do we make of all this in light of this poignant moment in which we live? I can't tell you what to make of the way the Holy Spirit works, but it was months ago that I chose these passages to preach on from the Book of Acts for last Sunday and this. Who could have imagined that last week the stoning of Stephen by religious zealots who had confused their ideology with theology would follow the massacre in a Charleston, South Carolina, church? And who would have imagined that we would be reading about the inclusion of the eunuch by the church in the wake of Friday's ruling on same-sex marriage equality? And who would have thought that these things would all take place on the only two weeks this summer that I would be with you preaching? I can't believe how lucky I am. Only the residents feel luckier than I, don't you know?!

What to make of all this? Well, first I will tell you that the Supreme Court does not dictate to churches what they should or should not do. Nor does public opinion. We are still protected by the First Amendment, and we still have the right to order our lives together according to the work of the Holy Spirit. And we will.

But that doesn't mean this ruling will have no impact upon us. The Spirit works everywhere, not just inside the church. And we must ask ourselves honest questions about the way the church treats gay people in our midst. We have been quietly doing that already, before this ruling, and we will be doing that more openly in the near future as a matter of spiritual discernment.

I know that even saying that we are going to be talking more about this makes some of you happy and some of you unhappy. Welcome to church. Welcome to our church, I should say. You see, there are too many churches that seem to think that they should tell everyone what to think. If you don't agree, you have to hide your thoughts or feelings about these things. That's not the kind of church we want to be. The kind of church we want to be is a kind church—the kind of church where kindness doesn't mean just politeness and niceness; it means genuine love and respect for one another amid differences. You can't have an inclusive community in which inclusion means only likeness or like-mindedness.

There are gay people in our church already, some who are faithfully serving the Lord among us without fanfare. Like the eunuch, they sense in themselves that some things about themselves are not changeable, no matter how hard they pray or try. Increasingly, they are comfortable with the thought that they shouldn't have to, that they have nothing to be sorry for or ashamed about in regard to how they are made. There are many more among us who have gay relatives and friends. They all deserve to hear in a time like this whether they are really welcome as they are or only if they hide their true selves.

We held a reception recently for all the people who helped our church and our sister Louise Troh during the Ebola crisis. Dallas County Sheriff Lupe Valdez was there. She is a lesbian, if you didn't know. She gave me a big hug and told me how impressed she was with our church through that crisis. She said that she and her partner had been talking about visiting. I knew you would want me to tell them what I said. *We would love to have you. You would be welcome.*

I was thinking about this on Friday when I went to get a haircut. I had called for an appointment a week ago, and the only day I could get one was Friday. The woman who cuts my hair and Kim's hair and her mom's hair owns the salon with her partner. We have talked about spiritual things over the years. I have invited her to church. She's gun-shy, though; her experience with church has been mostly about being judged.

As I was getting ready to go, I was thinking about how the Spirit sent Philip to the eunuch. The text says he *ran* to catch up to the chariot. He ran toward the one who had been judged unfit for the Temple. Did you hear that? He ran toward him, not away from him.

Kim and I talked about what the Spirit might be up to and whether this might be a divine appointment. How might we run toward our gay friends and not away from them so that they might know the good news of God's love in Jesus Christ?

While some churches are rejoicing over this marriage ruling, others are doubling down in their judging. I've asked myself what message we really want gay people to hear from the church in this time, and in what spirit they should hear it.

Since some Christians have made news recently for exercising their religious liberty by *not* making cakes for gay weddings, I decided to bring her cake. I brought a box of little Bundt cakes for the salon and told them I love them. There was much joy in that room, I tell you. And all I could say is how I wanted it to be in this room, too.

I don't have all the answers to all the questions about what the church should do or not do about this or that. I believe those will come as we consider related matters carefully and prayerfully together at some time after I return from sabbatical. As always, we will foster open conversation and go about the process through proper channels that begin with our deacons. That's the Wilshire way of finding the way of Christ.

But I do know that I want every gay person I know to know the Jesus I know. I do know that I want every gay person I know to know the church I know. And I do know that running toward and not away from these encounters is the way of Christ for me.

77

Two Ladders

Watch and listen to "Two Ladders" by following this link or scanning the QR code with your phone: youtu.be/tLSTgLPEHcc. Sermon begins at 28:50.

Mason preached "Two Ladders" following the January 6 insurrection at the nation's Capitol in 2021.

January 17, 2021
Second Sunday after Epiphany
Psalm 139:1-6, 13-18; John 1:43-51

I've been shopping for ladders. Who knew there were so many kinds? Step ladders, extension ladders, telescoping ladders. Oh, and articulating ladders. What does that even mean? A ladder you can understand when it talks to you?

Anyway, it's time for me to clean the gutters on my roof or hire someone to do it. I've put it off until all the leaves have fallen, and now they have clogged my gutters and drainpipes. It's a messy job, and I'm just the man NOT to do it. At least not without the right equipment. Which may take me some time to figure out, giving me more time not to do it, don't you know?!

A ladder connects things vertically. You can go up and down on it—one part grounded, the other elevated. Simple enough. But today I want to talk about two other kinds of ladders, both spiritual metaphors: one, a ladder that connects heaven and earth; and two, a ladder that connects the mind to what is to be known. The first describes the identity of Jesus as the Christ; the second, how we come to know that.

At the end of our Gospel text today, Jesus says something about himself that seems opaque: *Very truly, I tell you, you will see heaven opened and the angels of God ascending and descending upon the Son of Man.* What does that mean?

More than the other three Gospels, John wants us to see Jesus from the outset as the one who has always been the key to God's relationship to the world. Whereas the other Gospels lead us along, allowing us to discern his true identity gradually based on his words and deeds, John jumps right in and declares him to be the Word of God through whom the worlds were made.

Here in the first chapter, we get another image of him that combines two passages from the Hebrew Bible. The first is an allusion to the story of Jacob's ladder. You may recall the story of the patriarch Jacob sleeping on the ground with a stone for a pillow when he began to dream. He saw a great staircase or *ladder* connecting heaven and earth with angels going up and down on it. When he awoke, he declared the place where he lay holy. He named it Bethel, the house of God, because surely the Lord was in that place. Jesus says that his disciples will see the angels ascending and descending upon the Son of Man. That is, he—Jesus himself—is the Place. He is the connector of heaven and earth, wherever he is.

Then he uses the term Son of Man to describe himself. Son of Man comes from the book of Daniel and is associated with the one who comes at the End of Days to judge the world. So, if we would know Jesus for who he really is, we would understand him as the one who stands at the beginning and the end, as the agent of creation and judgment both. He is God's presence among us—the ladder between heaven and earth.

This is important in light of where we have been as a country in the past two weeks. The assault on the Capitol on January 6 was mainly by Christian nationalists who used the name of Jesus to support insurrection against our democratic government. They carried crosses and Bibles, held up signs that read *Jesus Saves* and blared Christian music as they marched on our seat of government. One man carried a Christian flag into a legislative office and others carried the Confederate battle flag through the rotunda.

Conservative Christian columnist David French has been warning the church about this defection from truth and the danger of coopting Christ to support political ends. In the wake of the deadly riot in D.C., he wrote this: *Are you still not convinced that it's fair to call this a Christian insurrection? I would bet that most of my readers would instantly label the exact same event Islamic terrorism if Islamic symbols filled the crowd, if Islamic music played in the loudspeakers, and if members of the crowd shouted "Allahu Akbar" as they charged the Capitol. If that happened, conservative Christians would erupt in volcanic anger. We'd turn to the Muslim community and cry out, "Do something about this!"* [126]

Non-Christians have a right to demand that the church say and do something about this. So, let's start with this and hope it spreads: We condemn Christian nationalism in the strongest possible terms. We repudiate the use of the name of Christ in defending violence to undermine the will of the people and to claim that somehow America is the rightful property of Christians. No more silence in the face of lies. When the heavens are opened, we will see the angels of God ascending and descending on the person of Jesus, not on the United States of America. Christ stands in judgment of every nation, including ours.

When Jacob saw that ladder in the Genesis story, he received the promise that through him *all* the nations of the earth would be blessed. To see Jesus as the ladder

126 https://frenchpress.thedispatch.com/p/only-the-church-can-truly-defeat

is not to see him replacing Israel but instead fulfilling the promise of Israel that every tribe and people on this good earth would be blessed through him.

Which is why we cannot weaponize Jesus against others. We cannot think he is on our side against others. We can only claim him rightly if we claim him as a blessing even for our enemies.

So, there's that. Now, how do we get to the place where, with Nathaniel, we can see and confess Jesus as the Son of God, the ladder that connects heaven and earth? That's the point of the second ladder.

The second ladder is the ladder of understanding. For the philosophically minded among us, ontology leads to epistemology. That is, the identity of Jesus as the Son of God leads us to the matter of how we come to know that.

The ladder of knowing is a process of climbing from earth to heaven, after heaven has climbed to earth first. Let's see how that works out in this story of Nathaniel's confession of Jesus as the Son of God.

Philip finds Nathaniel to tell him they have found the one they have waited for, the one Moses and the prophets attested to. He is Jesus, son of Joseph from Nazareth. Nathaniel wonders whether any good thing can come out of Nazareth. He is seeing Jesus purely as a human being from a town no one would logically look to for a special agent of God.

My grandson River is almost three years old. He was furious with his mother, Jillian, last week. His anger stemmed from hurt feelings. See, he was going through the trash can in their apartment and found his artwork. He pulled it out and cleaned it off, announcing to his mother that it was his favorite. Then, as if to show her what she should have done with such a marvel of coloring genius, he marched over to the refrigerator and posted it with a magnet while posing for the camera with an impish grin. The thing about being a grandparent is that you get to see karma in action.

Anyway, the point is, when we only look at Jesus through eyes of flesh, we will only see him as the son of Joseph from Nazareth. We have to look deeper, to look with spiritual eyes. We have to move from sight to insight. And to do that, we need an encounter with Jesus that will open us to his true identity. Here's the principle: We have to be seen before we can see; we have to be known before we can know.

That's what happened when Jesus tells Nathaniel that he saw him under the fig tree. Now, we don't know the exact meaning of what took place in this, but the fig tree was a symbol for Israel and a common place of Torah study and prayer. Jesus calls Nathaniel a true Israelite without deceit, so this is likely the point. In other words, Nathaniel feels seen and known by Jesus even though he has otherwise not seen or known Jesus.

And this changes Nathaniel's understanding of Jesus from sight to insight, from flesh to faith. He declares him to be the ladder, so to speak. Jesus is the Son of God, the King of Israel, Nathaniel says. That is, he is the link between heaven and earth.

Jesus then tells us that we too can see him this way. When he responds to Nathaniel's confession of faith, he says *you* will see greater things even than this. *You* will see the heavens open and the angels ascending and descending on the Son of

Man. He says you will, but the *you* is plural. *You disciples* is what he means. That is, you and me, too—any of us and all of us who answer the call to follow Jesus.

The Catholic writer on the spiritual life, Father Bruno Barnhart, says this: *As we accompany Jesus through the gospels, we are present at one dramatic meeting after another. One person after another experiences a mysterious power in Jesus that, from this moment, changes the course of his or her life. If we are fully present at the moment when we read such a narrative, we ourselves experience the liberating power of this awakening.*[127]

I pray you settle under your fig tree this morning and that you will feel seen and known so that you may awaken to the truth that Jesus is the Son of God. And once awakened, that you will join him in being nothing else but a blessing to the world. Amen.

---

127 https://cac.org/unveiling-christianity-2021-01-05/

78

Glory Be!

Watch and listen to "Glory Be!" by following this link or scanning the QR code with your phone: youtu.be/iLSsRrUyPPg. Sermon begins at 19:50.

"Glory Be!" is the sermon Mason preached on the Sunday following Russia's invasion of Ukraine in February 2022.

February 27, 2022
Transfiguration Sunday
Exodus 34:29-35; 2 Corinthians 3:12-18

There's a lot of language in our two passages today about glory and faces. Moses got to see the glory of God and his face was shining so brightly that he had to put a veil over his head so the people wouldn't be blinded. In the Gospel lesson we didn't read today about the transfiguration on the mountaintop, Jesus' entire persona, not just his face, is shining. And in the epistle reading, Paul tells us that *all of us* who look upon the Lord who is Spirit reflect the glory of the Lord and are being transformed from one degree of glory to another.

Glory be! That's a lot of glory. What's it all about?

Russia invaded Ukraine this week. After a bloody century of wars—hot wars and cold wars both—Russia seems intent on making Ukraine a client state if not annexing it altogether. Vladimir Putin, the president of Russia, has visions of restoring the glory of the Russian Empire. He's an autocrat who feels the shame and loss of Russia's greatness during the time of the Czars and the Soviet Union. He wants his people and the peoples of the world to feel the glory of Russia's renewed power. Territorial expansion is necessary in his mind for achieving that kind of glory.

Since the Russian invasion, I have been reading about how American presidents have miscalculated Putin's ambitions. George W. Bush said in 2001: *I looked the man in the eye. I found him to be very straightforward and trustworthy. We had a very good dialogue. I was able to get a sense of his soul, a man deeply committed to his country and the best interests of his country. … I wouldn't have invited him to my ranch if I didn't trust him.* Before Bush's presidency ended, Putin's forces advanced on neighboring

Georgia. Then in 2008, President Obama misjudged Putin, too, saying that *the tide of war is receding*. Six years later, Russia captured Crimea, the world community clutched its pearls and nothing much happened. President Trump met with Putin in Helsinki in 2018 and came away believing Putin over his own FBI and foreign advisors. Now Putin has invaded Ukraine, flouting democratic dreams there and seizing on hopes for renewing Russian national glory. The former president called the move "pretty smart." Go figure.

After taking Crimea in 2014, foreign correspondent Julia Ioffe wrote: *Russia, or, more accurately, Putin, sees the world according to his own logic, and the logic goes like this: it is better to be feared than loved, it is better to be overly strong than to risk appearing weak, and Russia was, is, and will be an empire with an eternal appetite for expansion.*[128]

And now that appetite is being fed again.

What is Putin's logic? Well, it's not every Sunday I quote approvingly the pastor of the First Baptist Church of Dallas. Robert Jeffress said: *Russia's invasion of Ukraine is an awful display of needless aggression by a glory-hungry dictator.*

Regardless of his propaganda about security, Putin's logic is glory. He wants to be feared more than loved. Glory is the product of greatness defined by defeating and humiliating others, not by loving and serving them.

But this is how to distinguish between the logic of Putin and all those like him, maybe even ourselves at times, and the logic of our biblical faith from Moses to Jesus to Paul. The world's understanding of glory is godless: It begins and ends with *me* and is a competition with others for it, meaning that the dignity, freedom, and prosperity of others will have to be sacrificed in the interest of my glory. The biblical notion of glory is the opposite: It begins and ends with God and is infinitely available to all. So, sacrificing myself on behalf of others doesn't diminish my share of glory; it increases it.

That's what lies underneath this passage from 2 Corinthians, but it's tricky to suss it out. On the surface, it looks like Paul is arguing that Jews who continue to read the Torah and follow the commandments given by God to Moses are blind. They follow the old covenant that has now been set aside in Christ. Only Christians see the light. God's covenant with the Jews is obsolete.

This superficial reading has led to antisemitism, persecution, and even genocide against Jews. Paul would be outraged by this. He himself was always and only a Jew, despite his belief in Jesus as the Messiah. The church must repent of this history and affirm the abiding significance of God's people, the Jews. Jesus too was a Jew and never a Christian. Our faith in Jesus is the means by which we Gentiles participate in God's redemptive work in the world, with and alongside Jews, never apart from them. We may have different roles to play in God's saving and healing work in the world, but we have not replaced Jews in God's covenantal relationship. Together we pursue the peace of God for everyone.

128 https://www.theatlantic.com/politics/archive/2014/03/
why-putin-plays-our-presidents-for-fools/461055/

So, what is Paul up to here? First, understand who he is arguing against, and it's not Jews. Paul was a missionary who preached the gospel and started churches and moved on. In Corinth, some came along after him claiming superior understanding of God and the gospel. Paul sarcastically called this group that liked to glorify themselves, "super-apostles." They had mocked Paul for seeming to be weak, and not being as eloquent as they. Hmm, some things never change, don't you know?!

Paul sees these super-apostles as threats to the new community of Christ. The coming of Christ fulfilled Jeremiah's promise to write the laws of God on every human heart. Now it wasn't just Moses who could experience glory by turning his unveiled face toward the Lord. All of us may, as each of us turns our face toward God.

This is what the word boldness means in our passage. *Since, then, we have such a hope, we act with great boldness,* Paul says. Boldness is the word *parrhesia*, which in ancient Greece had to do with the kind of free and open truth-speaking that only takes place among equals (in other words, in a democracy). Paul is calling out the super-apostles here—not Jews per se. He is using an illustration from Hebrew history, not as a theological conclusion about Jews and Christians, but as a warning to Christians. The undemocratic super-apostles think glory is always a zero-sum game of power over and against others. Get God, get glory.

In the story from Exodus, while Moses was on the mountain talking to God and getting a good shining, the people's minds were hardened as they fashioned a golden calf to worship instead of the Lord who is the Spirit. What the people didn't understand is that Moses was bringing the glory of God down from the mountain in the gift of the Ten Commandments. The commandments were democratizing laws. Moses is essentially saying that God is found in how you treat your neighbor.

We don't need to go up a mountain to find God. Paul is saying that God has come down to us all in Christ, who embodies God's law. But Christ's light was only seen through his suffering and vulnerability, as on the cross. Which means we will find God among us and experience God's glory only in each other's faces, and only in humility and vulnerability. We are being changed by our common commitment to live with and for one another, lifting each other up, not lifting ourselves up by pushing others down or away.

Where are we seeing the glory of God today on the world stage? Is it in the eyes of Vladimir Putin or Volodymyr Zelenskyy? Putin says, *Why do you think that the good must always be frail and helpless? I do not think that is true. I think good means being able to defend oneself.*[129] Actually, no, it means being able to defend your neighbor, in whose eyes, if you look long enough and deeply enough, you are able to see the glory of God reflected back at you. But that's the problem, isn't it? When we fail to look for God in our neighbors, we begin to dehumanize them and see them as obstacles to our own glory.

On the other side, Ukraine's President Zelenskyy is on the front lines with his countrymen, showing the difference between Putin's nationalism and his patriotism.

---

129 https://www.dallasnews.com/opinion/commentary/2022/02/27/
it-will-be-our-faces-you-see-not-our-backs-and-other-top-quotes-of-the-week/

As you attack, Zelenskyy said, *it will be our faces you see, not our backs.*[130] And that's the problem for Russian soldiers right now. One of them said, *We don't know who to shoot. They look just like us.* Exactly. As does every human being.

This is precisely what we are supposed to learn. No matter who the "they" is, whether Ukrainian or Russian, American or Chinese, white or Black, citizen or refugee, law abiding or incarcerated, sheltered or unsheltered, Republican or Democrat, and on and on, the only way we are going to stop this warring madness in our world, in our culture and in our politics, is by learning that it is only in our neighbor that we will find the glory of God. We cannot turn to the Lord by turning away from our neighbor. We can only turn to the Lord by turning to our neighbor.

The early church father Irenaeus said: *The glory of God is a human being fully alive.* Every person is created in the image of God, and therefore can reflect the glory of God. We do so more and more as we live in love, seeking the well-being of our neighbors. But the first step is making sure our neighbors are alive since our access to God's glory is only through them.

This is why God made *us,* not just me and not just you. We need each other to discover the glory of God. By looking endlessly in the mirrors of the pupils of one another's eyes, we see ourselves reflected. And when we refuse to look away, we are changed. We are being transfigured. We ourselves are being transformed from one degree of glory to another.

Glory be! Amen.

---

130 Ibid.

PART XII

Benediction

Final Sermons

The Lord bless you and keep you;
the Lord make his face to shine upon you and be gracious unto you;
the Lord lift up his countenance upon you and give you peace.

~ Numbers 6:24-26

Don't You Know?!

Watch and listen to "Don't You Know?!" by following this link or scanning the QR code with your phone: youtu.be/fJFSTSruALo. Sermon begins at 31:25.

April 24, 2022
Second Sunday of Easter
Penultimate Sermon
Philippians 4:1, 4-9

Don't you know?! There, I said it. Now you can check that off your list for today as you listen to my penultimate sermon. That little phrase—along with its pretentious punctuation that smashes a question mark and an exclamation point together—has appeared in every one of my sermons as your pastor. You might like to know the backstory.

When I was a fledgling pastor in Mobile, Alabama, before I wrote out my sermons word for word, I was prone to verbal tics and throwaway phrases that tend to come with extemporaneous preaching. One Sunday after the service, I was in the narthex of the church and a woman came up to me with her little boy in tow. She said, *You didn't say it today.* I asked her what she meant. She said, *You didn't say, don't you know?!* I didn't realize I had been saying it at all. She told me she had picked up on that phrase with her wiggly son and told him that he should listen to my sermon for when I said it. It was a mother's game to keep the boy's attention. I promised her to include it from then on.

I carried it with me to Wilshire. It's been a fun little thing, sort of like looking for the plastic figurine of baby Jesus hidden inside a Mardi Gras King Cake. I used this with my kids, too, and I recommended it to other parents through the years. It was also a reminder to me not to get too hifalutin in my theological language. It kept me grounded.

As today is the first of the two farewell sermons I will preach to you as your pastor, I want to use this phrase—along with its punctuation marks—to remind you of things you already know but maybe don't know you know. So, think of these words as revealing what you do and reminding you to keep doing what you do when I am not here to tell you week by week.

This is what Paul was doing with the church at Philippi. His letter to this church pulses with affection. If you ever had to choose a church from the New Testament to emulate, you should probably go with Philippi. Definitely not Corinth. So, by the time Paul gets toward the end of his letter to them, he tells them a few things to do that are probably among the things he means when he concludes: *Keep on doing the things that you have learned and received and heard and seen in me, and the God of peace will be with you.*

Now, I'm no Apostle Paul, and don't hear me trying to say to you that I have been an icon you should model yourself after. But Paul was a spiritual leader to this church, and you have allowed me to be that for you these thirty-three years. We have learned some things about how to live together as we follow Christ. And the practices we have adopted have allowed the church to remain vital amid changes in our local community and our Baptist community. So many changes.

Churches are communities of practice. We are what we do. And the more we practice the right things, the likelier it is we will strengthen the ties that bind. It's not that everything will go well if we do, because, well, *Life is like a box of chocolates,* as Forrest Gump's mama said. *You never know what you're going to get.* But regardless of what you get, good or bad, the more you stick to the things you know that develop Christian character, the more resilient you—and we—will be to face whatever comes.

The cover art on your order of worship today is Auguste Rodin's famous sculpture, *The Thinker.* Mark McKenzie told me this week that the original title of the piece was *The Poet.* It was intended to stand at the front of an exhibit titled *The Gates of Hell,* depicting the poet Dante and his *The Divine Comedy.*

This fits us, I think. We are a thinking church—something few Baptist churches are accused of, sad to say. We don't go about our business willy-nilly. We aren't driven purely by emotion, though we aren't opposed to it. We aren't tossed about by winds of culture. We try to discern the spirits and submit to the Spirit. As our mission statement puts it: *We are building a community of faith shaped by the Spirit of Jesus Christ.*

In this, we are inheritors of a faith tradition that stretches back to Philippi, back further to Israel, and forward to the seventy years of practices that have defined our congregational life together. We are not slaves of tradition; we are the products of it. A phrase we often use around here is "The Wilshire Way." It points to a pattern of life: deliberate discipleship, mindful ministry, conscious community. We are intentional about extending grace to, and a place for, Every Body. This is our living tradition.

As the church historian Jaroslav Pelikan put it: *Tradition is the living faith of the dead. Traditionalism is the dead faith of the living.*[131] We honor tradition not by doing *what* our forebears did and never deviating from it, but by doing *as* they did—seeking the mind of Christ and following in his way wherever that may lead.

131 *The Vindication of Tradition: The 1983 Jefferson Lecture in the Humanities.*

Paul tells the Philippians: *Rejoice in the Lord always, and again I say rejoice.* Joy is the major theme of the letter. But he doesn't take it for granted. He reminds them twice, as if they need to be reminded. It's an imperative: Make joy in the Lord a hallmark of your life together. Don't neglect it. Attend to it. Practice it.

My good friend Steve Brookshire is my regular golfing partner. He went for a week to Scottsdale, Arizona, a couple years ago for a course called Vision 54. The name comes from the idea that if you birdie every hole on a typical 18-hole golf course, you will shoot 54. Never been done, as far as I know. But the point is, it never will be if you can't imagine it. This wasn't a class on making the perfect swing, as if technique is what matters most. It's about thinking your way to better play. And to do that, you must clear your mind of distractions and let go of worry about the future. They had every player begin each day with a gratitude journal. You start by being thankful for the gifts of life and the joy that is already present all around you. Steve wondered why that should only be a golf strategy.

This reminds me of Chesterton's pithy words: *Thanks are the highest form of thought, and gratitude is happiness doubled by wonder.*[132] I love that. And I think it's the heart of what Paul is saying here. When we focus our mind on what we are thankful for, when we cast our worries and anxieties on God in prayer, we experience the peace of God and our joy overflows.

The next section of Paul's last words is the call to attend to virtues. *Whatever is true, whatever is honorable, whatever is just, whatever is pure, whatever is pleasing, whatever is commendable, if there is any excellence and if there is anything worthy of praise, think about these things.* Think. Think about these things.

This is not a Pollyanna Glad Game that ignores the evil and injustice of the world and just lives as though everything is fine if we just think that way. There is much work to do in challenging the things that hurt people and deface the image of God in human beings. But if we do not live as a community of virtue, we will never offer the world a vision of God's intentions for it. We will never be perfect—never shoot 54, so to speak, but we can become more of what we are meant to be by thinking about and practicing these things.

This is the secret sauce that makes Wilshire who we are. When I came to you years ago, my predecessor Bruce McIver, who had been your pastor for thirty years, told me, *George, churches are either pills or plums. Wilshire is a plum.* What he meant by that is what I have found to be true about you. Some churches find ways to make problems, some find ways to solve them. We would never have done what we have done if we had not kept this character consistently and lived into it.

I am who I am because of you. I have grown and changed and so have you. There's an African word that summarizes this: *ubuntu*. It means, *I am because we are.* The late great South African archbishop Desmond Tutu described it this way: *Ubuntu is the essence of being human. It speaks of how my humanity is caught up and bound up inextricably with yours. It says, not as Descartes did, "I think, therefore I am," but rather, "I am because I belong." I need other human beings in order to be human.*[133]

132 *A Short History of England* (New Phoenix Library, 1951), p. 59.
133 https://lookingforwisdom.com/ubuntu/

When the pastor search committee presented my nomination to you to be your next pastor, some people were concerned I was too young for the challenge. They were probably right. But after some discussion, an elderly deacon in the church rose to speak. He said, *I am not worried about whether he is up to the challenge, because I know we are. Great pastors do not make great churches; great churches make great pastors.*

He was right then, and to whatever extent I have become a good pastor to you, I owe it to you. Soon you will have a new pastor. And I am not worried, because I know you know what to do, don't you know?! You are up to the challenge if you continue to do what you have learned and received and heard and seen in our time together. Practice these things, dear church, and the God of peace will be with you … always. Amen.

Carrying On

Watch and listen to "Carrying On" by following this link or scanning the QR code with your phone: youtu.be/J-M16_691Fs. Sermon begins at 52:10.

May 1, 2022
Third Sunday of Easter
Final Sermon
Philippians 1:3-11

Looking around at this packed house, I have to ask: When did May Day become such a thing?

Thank you for being here—whether you are in the room or joining us remotely. I wish I could bottle the blessings of this day and imbibe a drop every day for the rest of my life. But God has designed us to live fully in the present and trust the goodness of God for each new day. So, here we are. Let's feel all the feels and give thanks.

Giving thanks is the way the apostle starts his letter to the Philippians. I thank my God every time I remember you, constantly praying with joy in every one of my prayers for you all, because of your sharing in the gospel from the first day until now.

Here's an example of the way Baptists read Scripture. We don't read it as if it's an historical artifact; we read it as a living word. We find ourselves in it. Time is compressed: The word then is somehow the word now, and the word now will somehow be the word to come. So, we are the church at Philippi in this moment. This [gesturing to the room] is that [pointing to the Bible]. And so, I am pleased to channel Paul as he speaks this morning to this church in the hope that you will hear these words not just as Paul's or mine but as God's word to you.

The church at Philippi was undoubtedly Paul's favorite church, just as you are mine. The mutual affection leaps off the page. The bond of love is palpable. Just look at the way he talks about the relationship: *It is right for me to think this way about all of you, because you hold me in your heart ...*

Now, this phrase, you hold me in your heart, is curious. The word for hold here can mean have, hold, or keep. Metaphorically, it can also mean marry. And that explains why we often use the phrase to have and to hold in marriage vows. It's a tie that binds.

There's another nuance to this phrase worth noting. It's unclear whether the Greek text should be translated *because you hold me in your heart* or *because I hold you in my heart*. Depending on which translation of the Bible you use, it might say one or the other. And I wonder whether that was intentional. I imagine Paul smiling at his cleverness in using a phrase that could go either way. Maybe that's just me enjoying wordplay.

But now from words to image. I chose for our cover art today the renowned painting by Gustav Klimt titled *The Kiss*. Beyond the obvious longing of the couple for each other, the thing that strikes me is the way Klimt depicts their embrace by blurring their clothes. It's hard to tell where the one leaves off and the other begins. If you look carefully, you can distinguish each of their garments, although the dominant gold color unites the two. More subtly, they are set within the backdrop of what seems to be another garment that envelopes them both. Peacock feathers can be seen in the background cloak, which symbolizes the immortality of love. In other words, while they are caught up with each other, they are together caught up in something all-embracing that transcends their individuality and even their relationship.

I take that as a hint of the love that will not let us go, the eternal spirit of love that is more than the sum of its parts. And it is that spirit, the Spirit of God to be precise, that permeates and envelopes and binds together our hearts in the church.

I hold you in my heart. You hold me in your heart. We are held together in the heart of God.

The poet e.e. cummings played with words, punctuation, and form to paint verbal pictures. In his best-known poem, cummings begins: *i carry your heart with me (i carry it in my heart)*

Nice. He ends the short poem this way:

> *here is the deepest secret nobody knows*
>
> *(here is the root of the root and the bud of the bud*
>
> *and the sky of the sky of a tree called life; which grows higher than soul can hope or mind can hide)*
>
> *and this is the wonder that's keeping the stars apart i carry your heart (i carry it in my heart)*

I think that's what Paul wanted to say to the Philippians, and I know it's what I want to say to you today, Wilshire. I carry you in my heart, and I know you carry me in yours.

In fact, you have carried my whole family in your heart. Four generations of Masons are here today to say thank you. Our psalm today has David giving thanks. The boundary lines have fallen for me in pleasant places; I have a goodly heritage.

It's been our good fortune to share life with you these thirty-three years. The blessing has grown higher than soul can hope or mind can hide. My family of blood and my family of spirit are bound together in a peacock garment of golden love. This is sadly the rarest of things in the ministry. So many pastors leave their work bruised and their family scarred. Not so with us because of your thoughtful care. You give hope to many that good church is still possible.

I realize this image of *The Kiss* and the language of love is an intimate metaphor for the relationship between a pastor and a church. I am a romantic, don't you know?! But it's surely better than some cold corporate image that is little more than a transactional relationship. This has been a calling for me more than a job; less an occupation than a preoccupation. So, if it makes you blush, so be it.

There will be room in this love for a new pastor. My predecessor Bruce McIver never made you choose between your love for him and your love for me. There was enough to go around for both of us. I am determined for that to be true again this time. But for my family and me in this moment, it is good simply to say with feeling: We carry you in our heart and we thank you for carrying us in yours.

So, there's that. Now, carrying on, listen to what Paul says about the church: *I am confident of this, that the one who began a good work among you will bring it to completion by the day of Jesus Christ.*

The one who. The church is not a social club consisting only of those visibly gathered. The invisible God is among us and at work through us. Which means we don't just carry on with one another as if church is the end itself. The love of God overflows. It can't be contained. God reaches out through us. For everyone born, a place at the table. God's love is profligate and pushes us beyond our comfort zones. It always seeks those who are other to us until they are just another to us—beloved ones to be carried in our hearts.

We have taken risks to love others and welcome them into our fellowship and our leadership. Over the past three decades, we refused to succumb to a mentality that builds walls instead of bridges. We have ordained divorced persons and women. We have honored the baptisms of all Christians. And we have fully welcomed and embraced our siblings in spirit who fall anywhere in the LGBTQ+ alphabet.

What I want to say to you today, Wilshire, is that we are not finished. We have to carry on, because God has only begun this good work in us and has promised to complete it in God's good time.

Faith always lives in the tension between the already and the not yet, the past and the future. It's a good thing for us to protect enduring values, but Christianity has a bias toward the future. The church is not finished extending grace and welcome to people until God calls time. Our work is ongoing to build a community of faith shaped by the Spirit of Jesus Christ.

And that includes our work beyond our faith community. The church ought to be good for something besides itself. Our neighbors depend upon us. Wilshire means something to people.

But engaging the world is contentious at times. People inside and outside the church sometimes prefer us to stay in our spiritual lane, as they see it. But I believe the late Congressman John Lewis was right: We sometimes need to get into "good trouble."

Notice what Paul says here about how the church shared in God's grace during his imprisonment. Too many churches today would be embarrassed to have a spiritual leader making good trouble in the community in the name of justice. They would rather we have a reputation of quietude. A church that never ruffles any feathers, respectable instead of respected.

Now, I am honored by Judge Jenkins' words today and I was honored this week also at the Dallas City Council meeting. Our councilmember Paula Blackmon is also here today, as is my county commissioner Theresa Daniel. State Senator Nathan Johnson is here, too. But these leaders know that my presence and yours in public life is not meant simply to cheer on our elected officials as if we are chaplains to the culture. We show up to remind them of their moral duty to extend the blessings of God's abundance to everybody. There is no joy without justice, and certainly no peace.

So, my friends, if some complain that we are carrying on in public, I say, carry on with the carrying on. The world needs you to stand with and for those who have been deprived of the full dignity of their created worth and denied their full participation in our democracy.

Finally, this. Keep courage as you carry on. The Brits like to say: Keep Calm and Carry On. It goes back to World War II. Very British of them. Stiff upper lip and all that. But to carry on in the power of the Spirit that will sometimes cause us to get into good trouble, we will need courage more than calm.

When people have asked me for one word to describe you, that's the word that rolls off my tongue: courage. Aristotle said it's the virtue that makes all the others possible. The English word for courage comes from the Old French meaning "having heart." To have courage is to take heart amid things that cause fear. Courage doesn't mean you will never be afraid; it means fear will not stop you from doing what is good and right.

This is what I have always loved about you—your intrepid sense of adventure. Your relentless desire to know what's next in God's purpose for you. Don't stop now. Carry on.

The poet Seamus Heaney was a personal friend of our own Jerry McElveen. Heaney was also one of my personal favorites. In the waning moments of his extraordinary life, he composed and texted his last words to his beloved wife, Marie. He chose a phrase in Latin: *Noli timere*. It's usually translated "fear not" or "be not afraid." But it's sometimes paraphrased by its remedy: "courage."

Heaney told generations of aspiring writers: "Do not be afraid" in taking up the pen. Through decades he implored Irish politicians, north and south, unionist and nationalist, "do not be afraid" in choosing the path of peace and eventually ending the Troubles by putting down the gun.[134]

134 https://www.theguardian.com/books/2013/sep/02/seamus-heaney-last-words-funeral

It's not easy to choose your final words; but, like Heaney, I think in one way or another this has been my message to you across these many years: Do not be afraid. Fear not. Take courage. God is with you, carrying you on as you carry on.

And so, then, one last time, dear church: *Noli timere.* Amen.

Afterword

After so many words, an afterword? What more is there to say?

First, I hope this book will have a long "off-the-shelf life."

Mainly, I hope it gives hope. All preaching aims to instill hope—that the wretched state of affairs in the world and in each of our lives will not stand forever. I'm reminded of the aphorism: "Everything will be okay in the end. If it's not okay, it's not the end." The gospel is good news that God and good will finally prevail.

"All shall be well, and all shall be well, and all manner of thing shall be well," Mother Julian of Norwich declared. But in the meantime, we have to live unto and lean into that hope.

God prefers to work with us rather than without us. The "arc of the moral universe is long, but it bends toward justice," Dr. King said. We are in the bending business with God, therefore, hastening the day when all shall be well. We do that through word and deed. The performative language of preaching combines the two as it brings new realities into being through speech.

The poet W. H. Auden's famous ambiguous truism, "Poetry makes nothing happen," is true of preaching, too. It may amount to nothing, but it can also make something out of nothing. In a phrase often heard in the Black church that harkens back to the exodus experience of the Israelites when facing the Red Sea, God makes "a way out of no way."

The Book of Genesis begins with God speaking into the void and saying, "Let there be light," and behold, "there was light." The Hebrew word for word, *dabar*, also means deed. God's word does things. So, when we preach the Word with our words, we are bringing into being the promised *shalom* of universal wellbeing, if only inch by inch. This is the enduring hope I pray you find word by word in this volume.

Another way I hope this work works is in teaching preachers how preaching works. Preaching books abound and there are theories of preaching aplenty. Writers say that besides the practice of writing itself, the next best thing writers can do to improve is to read good writers. If these sermons can function in that way for preaching ministers and those who aspire to the pulpit, the effort will have been worth it. Since these sermons are grouped in themes and generally rooted in the lectionary texts for the liturgical year, they may also be a resource for research and inspiration. And since the QR codes provide links to the audio and video of the original proclamations, it may be fruitful for seminary preaching classes and pastoral mentoring programs.

Finally, since the primary audience for these sermons was a living congregation, my hope is that everyone who opens this book will find them to be spiritually nourishing and theologically formative.

While times change and culture shifts under foot, the writer of Ecclesiastes was right that "there is nothing new under the sun." People are people. Old habits die hard. New heresies always come coated with a patina that betrays their age—which is why preaching ancient texts is eternally relevant and why preaching in any age is timely.

In a chapel address at Southern Baptist Theological Seminary in 1961, Dr. Martin Luther King Jr. told seminarians how he viewed his prophetic work in a time of lingering racial hatred and injustice: *Through this mountain of despair we shall dig a tunnel of hope.* He would later say that racism, militarism, and materialism were the three social sins that had to be confronted. Unfortunately, they are with us still, joined by others that mount up around us and seem impenetrable. We must keep digging then, until light at the end of the tunnel breaks through with a "hope that does not disappoint" (Romans 5:5).

About the Author

The Rev. Dr. George A. Mason is the Founder and President of Faith Commons and Senior Pastor Emeritus of Wilshire Baptist Church in Dallas, Texas. He is a nationally recognized religious leader whose legacy includes innovations in clergy apprenticeship, interfaith initiatives and community service. For many years, George has served as an op-ed contributor to *The Dallas Morning News* and has written for publications nationwide. He was instrumental in the founding of the Cooperative Baptist Fellowship and teaches at the Perkins School of Theology at Southern Methodist University.

Wilshire Baptist Church is Christian by conviction, Baptist by tradition and ecumenical in spirit—an inclusive Christian community that welcomes every body. Faith Commons is an interfaith nonprofit organization that amplifies diverse faith voices for the common good. Its programs include George's podcast *Good God*, featuring conversations about faith and public life.

George was born in New York City and has lived in Texas for many years. He and his wife Kim enjoy spending time with their children and grandchildren. More information and additional multimedia resources are at GeorgeAMason.com.

Scripture Index

Additional Resources

For additional resources, including audio and video recordings of the sermons in this book, please visit GeorgeAMason.com and WilshireBC.org.

If you enjoyed this book, consider leaving a review on the retail platform where you purchased it, or on Goodreads.com.

Read the Spirit Books

Since 2007, Read the Spirit Books has been publishing authors with a purpose: to improve our world, one story at a time. Media means connection. We often say: Good media builds good community.

We believe that our readers—men and women just like you, all around the world—are part of this larger effort to connect lives through the stories we tell. You can help by simply telling friends about this book and encouraging them to start reading. Most of our books are designed for individual reading—and also for small-group discussion. So please consider inviting friends to discuss this book with you.

The book you are holding is part of a larger collection of books by writers who encourage peacemaking, celebrate diversity, strengthen caregivers, rebuild impoverished communities, train the next generation of leaders, and inspire each of us to enjoy a better day.

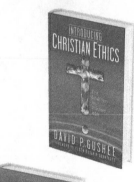

Please take a moment to look at some of the other Read the Spirit books you may enjoy reading. Your next inspiration is just a book away.

We always appreciate hearing from readers like you. Want to ask a question? Suggest an idea? Email us at ReadtheSpirit@gmail.com or info@FrontEdgePublishing.com.

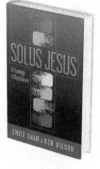

Inspiring Books

Torah Tutor
Rabbi Lenore Bohm

In *Torah Tutor*, Rabbi Lenore Bohm draws on a lifetime of teaching about the Torah, the first five books of the Hebrew Bible. Early reviewers of the book praise the timeliness of the themes lifted up in this contemporary self-guided study, which is ideal for individual seekers and group discussions.

"Reading this may become one of the most meaningful parts of your week, renewing, enriching and energizing you," writes Rabbi Sally J. Priesand, America's first woman ordained as a rabbi.

Healing the World
Daniel Buttry and Dámaris Albuquerque

In a world ravaged by crises, this inspiring biography of Nicaraguan public health pioneer and peacemaker Gustavo Parajón encourages readers to courageously reach out to the world's neediest people.

Gustavo described his mission as simply following the example of Jesus, but he did so in such a unique, tireless and effective way that his admirers included former President Jimmy Carter and U2's Bono.

Changing Our Mind
David P. Gushee

Christian denominations and churches everywhere struggle with the issue of LGBTQ inclusion. With growing scientific evidence, our wider society has taken big steps, but too many religious families and communities have not kept up. As much as ever, many people still experience deep condemnation by evangelical and other churches, getting kicked out or altogether leaving. Dr. David Gushee offers a powerful, inspiring message of hope and healing by helping Christians to return to Bible study, prayer, and reflection in a way that creates a vision for a more inclusive church.

Printed in the USA
CPSIA information can be obtained
at www.ICGtesting.com
LVHW011728141023
761116LV00037B/538

9 781641 801584